UNSUNG PATRIOTS

UNSUNG PATRIOTS

African Americans in America's Wars

Eugene DeFriest Bétit

STACKPOLE
BOOKS

Essex, Connecticut
Blue Ridge Summit, Pennsylvania

STACKPOLE BOOKS
An imprint of Globe Pequot, the trade division of
The Rowman & Littlefield Publishing Group, Inc.
4501 Forbes Blvd., Ste. 200
Lanham, MD 20706
www.rowman.com

Distributed by NATIONAL BOOK NETWORK

Copyright © 2023 by Eugene DeFriest Bétit

All rights reserved. No part of this book may be reproduced in any form or by any electronic or mechanical means, including information storage and retrieval systems, without written permission from the publisher, except by a reviewer who may quote passages in a review.

British Library Cataloguing in Publication Information available

Library of Congress Cataloging-in-Publication Data

Names: Bétit, Eugene DeFriest, 1944- author.
Title: Unsung patriots : African Americans in America's wars / Eugene DeFriest Bétit.
Other titles: How African Americans have helped fight their country's wars from the revolution to the present
Description: Essex, Connecticut : Stackpole Books, [2023] | Includes bibliographical references and index. | Summary: "Despite centuries of oppression and abuse, African Americans remained loyal to the United States, fighting for this country even as slaves even when they did not enjoy full citizenship. White supremacy has always played a major role in our history, distorting our potential as a nation. Not until recent times have Blacks experienced anything like a level playing field in the military or society, as this book graphically demonstrates"— Provided by publisher.
Identifiers: LCCN 2022027694 (print) | LCCN 2022027695 (ebook) | ISBN 9780811772341 (cloth) | ISBN 9780811772358 (ebook)
Subjects: LCSH: United States—Armed Forces—African Americans. | Discrimination—United States.
Classification: LCC E185.63 .B45 2023 (print) | LCC E185.63 (ebook) | DDC 355.0089/96073—dc23/eng/20220706
LC record available at https://lccn.loc.gov/2022027694
LC ebook record available at https://lccn.loc.gov/2022027695

♾️ The paper used in this publication meets the minimum requirements of American National Standard for Information Sciences—Permanence of Paper for Printed Library Materials, ANSI/NISO Z39.48-1992.

Dedicated to African Americans,
Freedman and slave,
Who made substantial contributions
To the freedom, growth, and wealth of America
Standing by the Union in her time of trial
Despite injustice, segregation and often, vicious hate.

In memory of Colin Powell, citizen soldier and statesman,
A graduate of the Reserve Officers Training Corps,
City College of New York in the Bronx,
Who reached the nation's highest pinnacles but remained a
Consummate officer and gentleman with the highest ideals and humility.

Now and always, we expect to insist upon it that
we are Americans, that America is our native land;
this is our home; that we are American citizens . . .
and that it is the duty of the American people to so
recognize us.

Frederick Douglass

After each war—The War of Independence and
the War of 1812, the Civil War, the Indian Wars,
Spanish American War, Philippine Insurrection—
history repeats itself in the absolute amnesia of the
gallant deeds . . . by brave black soldiers and sailors.

Sergeant Major Christian Fleetwood
Cotton States and International Exposition, 1895

CONTENTS

List of Illustrations ix

Foreword xiii

Preface xvii

CHAPTER 1: Colonial Wars, the Revolutionary War, and the War of 1812 1

CHAPTER 2: US Colored Troops in the Civil War 28

CHAPTER 3: Black Soldiers in Gray and Butternut 59

CHAPTER 4: Buffalo Soldiers 78

CHAPTER 5: African American Service in World War I 108

CHAPTER 6: African American Service in World War II 149

CHAPTER 7: Korea: 24th Infantry, the Last Buffalo Soldier Unit, Disbanded 186

CHAPTER 8: From Vietnam to the Present 213

Appendix A: African American Medal of Honor Recipients 237

Appendix B: Buffalo Soldier Regimental Histories 253

Appendix C: Black General or
  Flag-Rank Officers 283
Appendix D: Phantoms of the Alaskan
  Highway 295
Appendix E: The Highest and Purest
  Democracy 301
Notes 307
Bibliography 347
Index 363
About the Author.. 375

ILLUSTRATIONS

Crispus Attucks, Boston Massacre 5

Salem Poor at Bunker Hill 6

Washington and his body servant, William Lee 8

First Rhode Island Regiment repels Hessians at Battle
    of Rhode Island 11

James Forten, wealthy sailmaker and abolitionist 18

James Armistead Lafayette, double agent 19

New Orleans' Free Men of Color 24

John Brown, 1859 30

US Marines storm the Harpers Ferry firehouse 31

Contrabands arriving at Fort Monroe 32

Contrabands at Camp Nelson, Kentucky 34

Frederick Douglass, 1847–1852 37

Major General Lorenzo Thomas 40

Sergeant Major Lewis Douglass 43

Colonel Robert Gould Shaw 49

Illustrations

54th Massachusetts Infantry Regiment assault on
Fort Wagner 50

Crew of USS *Miami* 55

US Colored Troop casualties 56

Lieutenant General Robert E. Lee 61

Major General Patrick Cleburne 63

President Jefferson Davis 66

Major General John Brown Gordon 69

Purported Black First Sergeant 75

Mass grave of Native Americans massacred by the 7th
Cavalry Regiment at Wounded Knee 83

10th Cavalry 3rd US, and 1st Volunteer (Rough Riders)
Regiments on San Juan Hill 91

Lieutenant Henry Ossian Flipper, West Point graduate 100

Colonel Charles Young, West Point graduate 102

Buffalo Soldier statue installed at US Military Academy,
West Point, New York, August 31, 2021 104

The Birth of a Nation 110

Ku Klux Klan marching down Pennsylvania Avenue 112

Colonel William Leland Hayward, 1917 121

Sergeant Henry Johnson and Private Needham Roberts, the
AEF's first two heroes 125

369th Infantry Regiment "Harlem Hellfighters" march down
Fifth Avenue past New York Public Library 126

Sheet music for the 369th Regiment's popular band led
by Lieutenant James Reese Europe 127

Colonel Franklin A. Dennison 129

French *Croix de Guerre* 135

Black engineer and Service of Supply troops
re-inter remains 138

Illustrations

Red Summer: Willie Brown burned alive in Omaha,
Nebraska, 1919 143

Destruction of Black Wall Street in Tulsa 146

Major General Mallory Edmund "Ned" Almond 161

761st Tank Battalion in Coburg, Germany, April 1945 163

Sergeant First Class Edward Allen Baker Jr., Bastogne
volunteer and Medal of Honor Recipient 167

First Lieutenant Joseph Vernon Baker, Weapons Platoon,
C Company, 370th Infantry Regiment 169

Tuskegee Airmen of the 332nd Fighter Group, with P-51
Mustang, debriefing in Italy, August 1944 171

Colonel, then later, General Benjamin O. Davis Jr. 175

USS *Mason* (DE-529), Evarts-class destroyer escort 177

Messman Second Class Doris "Dorie" Miller 178

Port Chicago explosion 179

Sergeant Isaac Woodard 184

Korea and Japan, with approximate Pusan Perimeter
and DMZ lines annotated 188

Regimental table of organization 191

24th Infantry Regiment officer racial component,
July 1950 192

Black Units Serving in Korea, September 1950–
September 1951 194

25th Division combat losses as of August 31, 1950 198

Eighth Army artillery pieces lost to the enemy in 1950 200

24th Infantry Regiment General Courts-Martial,
July–October 1950 203

24th Infantry Regiment troops leave Kunu-Ri toward
the Ch'ŏngch'ŏn River 206

Kumch'on, North Korea, after the battle 208

A .30-caliber machine gun section after integration 209

President Kennedy briefed on current situation from
    CIA map 215

1st Battalion, 7th Cavalry, 1st Cavalry Division
    at LZ X-Ray, Ia Drang Valley 216

US Soldiers wounded during the Tet Offensive, 1968 220

Hô Chí Minh Trail 221

Operation Rolling Thunder 223

Defense Equal Opportunity Management Institute 225

Lieutenant General Calvin A. H. Waller 226

New World Order 227

General Charles Q. Jones Jr., United States Air Force
    chief of staff 233

Lloyd Austin III, secretary of defense 233

Guarding stagecoaches and Pony Express stations were
    among Black regulars' duties in the early years 255

Indian war posts and battles 256

25th Infantry Regiment soldiers in formal dress uniforms
    worn between the 1860s and 1890s. Soldier on left with
    white braids across his chest is a musician 257

10th Cavalry and 25th Infantry Regiment inspection at
    Fort Assiniboine, Montana 266

25th Infantry Regiment experimental bicycle contingent
    led by Lieutenant James Moss 277

Buffalo Soldier monument at Fort Riley, Kansas, dedicated
    by General Colin Powell 281

Map of Alaska Highway 295

Fifth Marine Division cemetery 301

FOREWORD

My interest in researching African American history began nine years ago when I audited a course in Virginia history taught by Professor Warren Hofstra at Shenandoah University. To my surprise, Dr. Hofstra emphasized racism, something I had never thought much about. His course opened my eyes—I realized that I had been blind to the world around me, or more likely, in denial. For more than two decades, I served as a Roman Catholic deacon in a parish in Arlington, Virginia, founded in 1946 by Black Catholics fed up with having to sit at the back of the church or in the choir loft. I have close friends who are African American, and I know from a lifetime of experience that skin tone plays no role in character or capabilities.

Twenty years of service in the Army taught me that racial prejudices are baseless, although they most assuredly do have great power in American society. I experienced only one tragic incident, when I was assigned to the cavalry regiment Robert E. Lee commanded many years ago. When two soldiers from the South mercilessly harassed a new Black replacement, he pulled out a knife and killed one of them. Otherwise, Black and white, Asian and Hispanic, all of us were simply soldiers. However, racism is an essential component of our history—it was the foundation on which the enslavement of an entire "race" was justified. After Emancipation, racial animosity metastasized and contaminated much of the American soul. Tragically, this animus was particularly evident in both World Wars and continues to have a half-life in some circles.

Because of my interest in the Civil War, my wife, Sheila, and I moved to the Winchester area of Virginia 12 years ago—10 major battles were fought within a 30-mile radius of the town. As I explored these and other battles as a volunteer at Belle Grove plantation, Cedar Creek Battlefield Foundation, and the National Park Service contact point for Cedar Creek National Battlefield in Middleton, I began to realize that events after the Civil War ended mattered far more than any single battle or campaign or even the outcome of the war. I could not reconcile the disenfranchisement and oppression of Blacks throughout the South by local customs and Jim Crow laws for roughly a century with the passage of the 14th and 15th Amendments. I suspected that there was a far greater story in the aftermath of the Civil War than the war itself.

I was amazed to discover how much more there is to the story as I conducted research specific for this book. At every stage of our development, African Americans have had a tremendous part in making the United States the great country it has become, although they are rarely given credit. The North was complicit and, in many ways, just as guilty of condoning the rank injustice rooted in racism and white supremacy that directly contradicts the Declaration of Independence's bold statement that we all are "created equal." What is taught in our schools often does not approach reality. More than that, some issues over which the American Civil War was fought remain unresolved today. They form a large part of the policies still disputed by the two major parties, although we seldom connect the dots.

After publishing *Collective Amnesia: American Apartheid, African Americans' 400 Years in North America, 1619–2019* in February 2019, I continued researching. While seeking a publisher for the two additional books I authored on African Americans' significant contributions to American history, I was asked if I couldn't develop a more focused topic. Choosing the subject was not difficult given my background; the chapters involving African Americans' military service engaged me most.

This book is a synthesis of more than 150 historians' work. Most of its eight chapters describe events we were not taught in elementary or high school because what really happened is tragic, profoundly embarrassing, and not in keeping with the "good guy" image we want to believe. If racism and hate are to be eradicated from the American psyche, it is important that our actual history be embraced. It is equally important that African Americans' proud accomplishments on the battlefield be recognized.

Above all, gratitude is due my wonderful wife of fifty years, Sheila, who has endured my extended hours of reading and writing to complete this study. Without her patient endurance and support, this book of would not exist.

My thanks to colleagues who commented on early drafts: Dennis J. Quinn, college classmate, retired Army colonel and strategist at the National War College; Dr. Cecile Bétit, a cousin who researches employee-owned businesses; Jim Murray, colonel USAF, retired; and Dr. Wayne Lord, a fellow graduate of Georgetown's Soviet Area Studies Program. Wayne was also Professor of International Business at Georgia State University and President of the Worlds Affairs Council of Atlanta.

As a lifelong learner, I am always grateful for comments, which can be made through my website, genebetit.com. I look forward to hearing from you. A review of this book on Amazon or elsewhere would be most welcome!

Gene Bétit
Winchester, Virginia
April 2022

PREFACE

> Won't it be wonderful when black history and
> Native American history and Jewish history and
> all of U.S. history is taught from one book.
> Just U.S. history.
>
> Maya Angelou

Despite centuries of oppression and abuse, African Americans remained loyal to the United States, fighting for this country even as slaves, when they did not enjoy full citizenship. White supremacy has always played a major role in our history, distorting our potential as a nation. Not until recent times have Blacks experienced anything like a level playing field in the military or society, as this book graphically demonstrates.

During colonial times, putting weapons in the hands of enslaved individuals was often considered a nonstarter. This was particularly true after the enslaved population of Haiti revolted and killed their French masters in 1791, eventually becoming the second independent country in the New World in 1804. The Haitian revolution also explains how the country became an international pariah. During times of necessity, as during our War for Independence from England, when whites did not enlist in sufficient numbers, Blacks were welcomed into the ranks. As a result, one-seventh of the Continental Army, state forces, and militia, perhaps

5,000–10,000 soldiers, were Blacks. In addition, two Black battalions, one commanded by a Black officer, fought with Andrew Jackson at the battle of New Orleans during the War of 1812.

Congress proscribed Black enlistment in both the Army and Navy shortly after we gained our independence, keeping African Americans out of the ranks during the Seminole wars and our war against Mexico. The crucible of the Civil War gradually changed resistance to Black servicemen after a year and a half of bloody combat. The last sentence of the Emancipation Proclamation on January 1, 1863, authorized recruitment of Blacks—they were already serving in the Navy. Ultimately, the North raised 175 US Colored Troop regiments, some 209,000 men, at a time when replacement manpower no longer existed on both sides. Black soldiers' impact was so great that the Confederacy finally authorized enrolling Black soldiers, a radical decision that contradicted the Confederacy's raison d'être, only three weeks before Lee surrendered the Army of Northern Virginia at Appomattox. By then, the South stood no chance of survival.

The record established by the US Colored Troops during the Civil War convinced Congress to authorize six Black regular Army regiments in 1866. Three years later, budget considerations reduced the total to four, two regiments of cavalry and two infantry regiments, roughly 4,000 soldiers; white regiments were reduced commensurately. These soldiers were 20 percent of the US cavalry that "won the West," fighting with distinction in the Indian Wars, where they won their nickname, "Buffalo Soldiers." The four regiments also fought with acclaim in the Spanish–American War and during the decade-long Philippine Insurrection, but widespread recognition of their valor proved to be fleeting, just as the US Colored Troops' contributions during the Civil War were erased from America's memory soon after the firing stopped.

During World War I, the four regiments provided border security and garrisoned the Philippines and Hawaii due to racial incidents involving the 24th and 25th Infantry Regiments, whose men were provoked by extreme Jim Crow harassment. Personnel from all four regiments provided trained cadre for two Black infantry divisions, the 92nd and 93rd, the last numerically of the divisions America raised for "the war to end all wars." Racism was so rampant that white troops of the AEF refused to fight alongside Black soldiers. The commander of the AEF, "Blackjack" Pershing, who got his nickname from serving twice with the 10th Cavalry

Regiment, offered the 92nd Division to the British, who declined. The 92nd Division was deployed in reserve and did not engage in combat until the final offensive of the war, when the division gave a good account of itself—it was the only one of the 2nd Army's four divisions to accomplish its mission.

The 93rd Division (Provisional) was a collection of National Guard units from multiple states. It was "provisional" because the Army did not provide requisite artillery, machine gun, engineer, transport, and other support units to make the division capable of sustained operations. Pershing detailed them to the French, who gratefully welcomed the four regiments, saw that they got realistic training, and integrated them into their divisions. Treated as men, they produced heroic results. Secretary of War Baker is said to have declared that the 369th Regiment, the "Harlem Hellfighters," was the best all-around regiment in Europe due to its superlative record.

The two combat divisions totaled perhaps 40,000 men; another 160,000 African Americans toiled in various combat service support units at French ports, unloading supplies and moving them to the front. When the war ended, many of these troops remained in Europe to clean up battlefields and exhume and re-inter American servicemen in the six American cemeteries that they built.

Despite their service, African Americans returning in uniform after World War I faced a bitter reception. At least 10 veterans were lynched simply for wearing their uniform during the "Red Summer" of 1919 because America was not willing to loosen its grasp on irrational Jim Crow laws and "folkways." Quickly forgetting the record of both infantry divisions, postwar Army studies found Blacks incapable of combat because they were "afraid of the dark" and "lacked stamina for combat." Nevertheless, when World War II came, public pressure and the need for manpower forced the War Department to reactivate both divisions. The two Buffalo Soldier cavalry regiments were assigned to the 2nd Cavalry Division, but both were disbanded and converted into stevedore and engineer construction troops upon arrival in North Africa, while white cavalry regiments were converted to armored units. The 24th Infantry Regiment deployed to the Pacific as a separate regiment, and the three regiments of the 93rd Division, including the 25th Infantry, followed soon afterward. Both units conducted mainly mopping up and logistics operations.

The 92nd Division trained in the US for nearly two years, almost twice the training time of other American divisions, before rising protests caused it to be committed to northern Italy in the fall of 1944. Its racist white commander was unhappy with the division's performance in repeated frontal assaults against well-prepared positions of the German Gothic Line in the Apennine Mountains. In February 1945, the best officers and soldiers from three Black regiments were concentrated in a fourth Black regiment to replace high losses. Those three regiments were assigned out of the division, replaced by the Japanese American 442nd Regimental Combat Team and a white regiment. Of course, when the offensive resumed in the spring of 1945, there was a big difference, as German resistance was weaker and the Nisei flanked the German positions.

After the war, the 25th Infantry was demobilized, leaving only the 24th Infantry Regiment, which became part of the 25th Infantry Division, stationed in Japan.

When North Korea invaded the South in June 1950, no American unit in Japan or Hawaii was combat ready. The 24th Infantry Regiment was more fortunate than other infantry regiments—it had three battalions, rather than two. When the 24th Regiment was finally disbanded in September 1951, its personnel were reassigned to the division's other regiments, and the integration President Truman ordered in 1948 began. The last segregated Army unit was integrated in 1954. Only the Air Force began integration in 1949, but senior officers in the other services resisted mightily.

Due to the intransigence of senior officers and noncommissioned officers (NCOs), the armed services were not truly integrated until the Vietnam War, when they began to model possibilities for the nation. The armed forces played a large role in the success of the civil rights movement. With a level playing field, talented Black officers, such as Colin Powell and Lieutenant General Calvin A. H. Waller, second-in-command of Desert Storm, began to emerge. The process has continued to evolve to the point that the current Air Force chief of staff is African American, and for the first time the secretary of defense is a retired Black four-star general. In the years since Vietnam, there have been close to 400 African American admirals and generals, most listed in Appendix 3.

It is tragic that America has gone through painful experiences rather than affirm what most of us know—America is great precisely because we are a melting pot welcoming all who come to our shores. Sadly, African

Americans and Native Americans have not been part of this inclusion. Development of the full potential of all citizens demands the elimination of racism and prejudice and is a national security imperative in today's challenging international environment.

Gene Bétit
Winchester, Virginia
April 2022

U.S. ARMY UNITS

Unit	Size	Commanded By
Field Army (Last use: Desert Storm 1991)	50K+ SOLDIERS	★★★★ GENERAL
Corps	2+ DIVISIONS (20-45K Soldiers)	★★★ LIEUTENANT GENERAL
Division	3 BRIGADES (10-15K Soldiers)	★★ MAJOR GENERAL
Brigade OR **Regiment**	3-5 BATTALIONS (2-5K Soldiers)	★ BRIGADIER GENERAL OR COLONEL
Battalion	3-5 COMPANIES (100-1K Soldiers)	LIEUTENANT COLONEL
Company OR **Battery** OR **Troop**	3-4 PLATOONS (60-200 Soldiers)	 CAPTAIN OR FIRST LIEUTENANT OR MAJOR
Platoon	3-4 SQUADS (18-50 Soldiers)	SECOND LIEUTENANT
Squad	6-10 SOLDIERS	SERGEANT

CHAPTER 1

Colonial Wars, the Revolutionary War, and the War of 1812

> The Negro has been a citizen three times in the history of the government, in 1776, 1812, and 1865; in time of trouble the Negro was a citizen and in time of peace, he was an alien.
>
> Frederick Douglass

> I would never have drawn my sword in the cause of America if I could have conceived thereby that I was founding a land of slavery.
>
> Marquise de Lafayette

In colonial times, Blacks' acceptance for military service was inconsistent. Although distrusted, they were called upon to bear arms in wartime when necessary for whites' survival. During the Revolutionary War, up to 15 percent of the Continental Army was black, although initially efforts were made to exclude African Americans. Blacks served as seamen, gunners, and Marine sharpshooters in the Continental Navy and state navies and aboard American privateers.

Despite playing a crucial a role at New Orleans during the War of 1812 and in the Navy, the Army banned Blacks' enlistment in 1820, and the Navy restricted enlistment of African Americans to 5 percent of the fleet in 1839, allowing them to serve only as cooks, mess boys, and servants, a stipulation that lasted for more than a century.

Three groups existed in an uneasy coexistence in the early British colonies—Native Americans, whites, and Africans. Although the colonists attempted to enslave Native Americans, they either ran way or got sick and died. The colonists commonly believed that Africans had hearty constitutions because they came from a "hot climate," although the African continent, the world's second largest, ranges from tropical to subarctic on its higher peaks. While the northern half, 60 percent of the continent, is mostly arid desert, its central and southern areas contain both savanna plains and dense jungles and rainforest. Numerous tribes and nations speaking a great number of languages either sold captives to Europeans or became victims of the slave trade.

BLACKS IN COLONIAL MILITIAS

British colonists feared both slave uprisings and sudden attacks by the native population. South Carolina was particularly vulnerable, surviving by driving a wedge between around 60,000 Creeks, Cherokees, and other tribes and the enslaved population of about 75,000, compared to less than 50,000 whites. As a result, as early as 1703 South Carolina authorized slaves to enlist in the militia. For a time, its militia was half European and half enslaved. The colony offered to emancipate Blacks who in time of "actual invasion," killed or captured an enemy. Masters would be compensated for any of their "property" so freed—or if their slaves were killed or disabled. In 1719, the legislation was amended so slaves could not win their freedom but rather, cash rewards.[1]

At first, the colony paid Indians to hunt down and capture runaway slaves. Over time, the colonialists began to display contempt for Native Americans; traders routinely cheated back-country tribes, and farmers kept encroaching on their land. The Indigenous peoples began to realize that they were hopelessly in debt to dishonest merchants who acquired Native American women and children to satisfy their debts. Finally, several tribes formed an alliance and attacked their oppressors on Good Friday, April 15, 1715, after Spanish agents in what is now Florida incited unrest. Virginia and North Carolina hastened to dispatch troops, and New England sent supplies. But even in this time of trouble, North Carolina authorities warned, "there must be greatest caution used lest our slaves when armed might become our masters."[2]

Fortunately for the colonists, the Cherokee Nation sided with the colonists, and normality returned, broken in September 1739 by the Stono Rebellion, when slaves, most of whom originated in the Congo or Angola, rebelled and fled toward Spanish Florida, killing some 25 colonists. Pursued by Native Americans led by whites, the uprising was suppressed. Between 35 and 50 Africans were killed; the others were sold to the West Indies. Although whites felt more comfortable with armed Native Americans, they could never fully trust the tribesmen. For this reason, within 10 years, laws to reward service by slaves returned, although officials remained reluctant to arm Blacks. When South Carolina's militia attacked Cherokees in 1759, only a handful of carefully chosen slaves were armed.

Other colonies attempted to strike a balance between the fear of Indian attacks and dread of slave uprisings. No Virginian dared arm Blacks until 1676, when Nathaniel Bacon rebelled against the colonial government then trying to protect Indian lands. Bacon and poor white farmers wanted to seize territory from Native Americans and weaken the planter class monopolizing government. The rebels offered freedom to any slave who deserted their master and supported the upheaval. After the rebellion was suppressed, slaves were excluded from militia service, although free Blacks could still serve as drummers or musicians—or in labor units.

The Massachusetts Bay Colony required both free and enslaved Blacks to complete militia training, but its Black population was too miniscule to have much effect—roughly 2.5 percent. Rhode Island, a major slave trading center, had a larger enslaved population, but for the most part enslaved individuals were transient, on their way South.

KING GEORGE'S WAR (1744–1748)

Over time, bearing arms became a white monopoly. But there were always exceptions to the rule. During King George's War (part of the War of the Austrian Succession [1740–1748], the third of four French and Indian Wars, fought mainly in New England), a militia unit from Framingham, Massachusetts, included a slave named **Nero**. He belonged to a minister of the town and served as trumpeter. Militia companies from New Hampshire, Rhode Island, and Connecticut also had a smattering of Blacks among the ranks. In addition, New England privateers preying on British commerce almost always included Black crewmen. **Toney**, a slave, cooked on several privateers. One privateer, the *Revenge*, had five Blacks in its 37-man crew.

FRENCH AND INDIAN WAR (1754–1763)

During the French and Indian War, part of Europe's Seven Year's War, the pattern of legal exclusion but de facto inclusion continued. The owner of the first Black from Massachusetts who died in military service, whose name is unknown, was paid 20 pounds for his loss. When New England colonies were unable to recruit sufficient whites to sustain the required forces, they turned to slaves, such as **Benjamin Negro** and **Cesar** from Rhode Island, or free Blacks, such as **George Gire** from Grafton, Massachusetts. Gire received a disability pension of 40 shillings, the same as other private soldiers.

AMERICAN REVOLUTION (1775–1783)

At the outbreak of the Revolution, out of a population of 2.5 million colonists, half a million were enslaved. The population of Great Britain, 7.5 million people, was three times as large, and England had the largest and most powerful Army and Navy in the world. The African American population easily could have played a far greater role winning our independence without the persistence of determined prejudice.

Crispus Attucks, a part African and Native American middle-aged whaler and rope maker from Framingham, Massachusetts, was instrumental in provoking the Boston Massacre of March 5, 1770. One witness testified that Attucks attacked a British officer and knocked a musket from the hands of a grenadier who was attempting to intervene. However, the incident was caused, when the smoke cleared, Attucks and four other young Bostonians were dead. Another died of wounds later. Attucks became a legend, hailed as a martyr to the cause of independence.

John Adams, defending the British soldiers as a lawyer for the Crown, described Attucks and the mob as "a motly rabble of saucy boys, negroes and Mollatoes, Irish teagues and outlandish jack tars." In his final remarks, Adams used a smear common to this day, describing Attucks as "a stout Molatto fellow whose very looks were enough to terrify any person.["3"] This hardly justified the soldiers' firing on unarmed individuals.

Crispus Attucks, Boston Massacre. John Bufford after William L. Champey, ca. 1856. SOURCE: NATIONAL ARCHIVES AND RECORDS ADMINISTRATION, 03-05-1770-NARA-518262.

Lexington and Concord (April 19, 1775)

Five years after the Boston Massacre, Massachusetts militia, which included Blacks, fired on British regulars at Lexington and Concord. The British party of 700 men, led by Lieutenant Colonel Francis Smith, had been dispatched by General Gage to seize key leaders and confiscate militia weapons and powder from both townships. Historian John Rees has identified the names of 35 Black men present on April 19, while John Hannigan estimates that despite incomplete records, 40 to 50 African Americans turned out with the militia that day.[4] **Peter Salem** of Framingham, a freedman, was one of several African Americas among the militia who fired "the shots heard round the world." **Prince Estabrook**, a Black slave, was wounded at Lexington, where nine militiamen were killed. A growing number of militia groups, many including Black members, kept up a steady fire during the British party's retreat to Boston, killing 73 British troops and wounding 174. In addition, 53 British soldiers were missing in action. Colonial losses were 49 militiamen killed, 39 wounded, and 5 men missing. Hard pressed by the colonials shooting at them from both sides of the road, the British force was rescued by a brigade-sized relief force of some 1,000 men armed with two cannons. The following day, New England militias consisting of some 15,000 men blockaded the narrow land accesses to Charlestown and Boston, and the siege of Boston began.

Bunker Hill (July 17, 1775)

Peter Salem and up to 150 Black patriots fought at Bunker Hill, where Salem fatally shot Royal Marine Major John Pitcairn, the leader of the British assault force. Salem later fought in the bloody battles of Saratoga and Stony Point in upstate New York. *Salem Poor*, of Captain Benjamin Ames's militia company, killed British Lieutenant Colonel Abercrombie and was commended by his regimental officers for Congressional recognition. Poor later endured the winter encampment at Valley Forge and participated in the battles of White Plains and Monmouth. He reenlisted for three years and fought with the Continental Army until March 1780, when he was discharged in Providence, Rhode Island. *Barzillai Lew*, a veteran of the French and Indian War, served in Captain John Ford's Company of the 27th Massachusetts Regiment for seven years as an infantryman, a fifer, and a drummer. *Cuff Whitamore* joined Captain Benjamin Locke's Arlington militia and made two "cuss'd Britishers bite the dust," seizing the sword of a dead British officer. Whitamore later served in the Continental Army. Blacks fought so courageously during the siege of Bos-

Salem Poor at Bunker Hill. SOURCE: LIBRARY OF CONGRESS.

ton that brigade commander Brigadier General John Thomas observed, "we have some Negros but I look upon them as equally serviceable with other men, for fatigue (labor) duties and in action," noting "many have proved themselves brave."[5]

Although Bunker Hill was fought entirely by militia units, Congress recognized the need for a regular Army and authorized the Continental Army on June 14, 1775, selecting George Washington as commander in chief. When Washington arrived in Boston on July 17, he commanded around 17,000 militiamen without a chain of command. Furthermore, the enlistments of the entire encampment expired at the end of the year. Congress authorized a strength at 23,370 men for the Continental Army, organized into 26 battalions, each with eight 100-man companies. Enlistment periods were to be three years or for the duration of the war.

After a year, Congress increased the levy and required states to provide battalions according to population. Virginia was to provide 19; Massachusetts, 15; Pennsylvania, 12; North Carolina, 9; Connecticut and Maryland, 8; South Carolina, 6; New York and New Jersey, 4; New Hampshire, 3; Rhode Island, 2; and Delaware and Georgia, 1. Less than half of the goal was achieved; at no time during the Revolution did the Continental Army field more than 30,000 soldiers. At the end of 1776, Congress authorized 2,040 artillerymen and 3,000 dragoons (cavalry).[6]

Due to the reluctance of whites to serve, an obvious solution was Blacks, roughly 25 percent of the population. However, despite the courage of numerous African Americans, objections to Blacks' service grew with the arrival of more troops from colonies whose economies depended on slavery and had large Black populations. Congress suggested that Black soldiers be consolidated into battalions commanded by white officers, with white sergeants as well, and authorized compensation of owners up to $1,000 for "each active able-bodied negro man of standard size, not exceeding thirty-five years of age." At the end of the war, each slave who served faithfully was to receive a discharge bonus of $50.[7] On May 20, 1775, the Massachusetts Provincial Committee of Safety decreed that "no slaves be admitted into this Army upon any consideration whatsoever," failing to mention free Blacks.

In General Thomas's opinion, this prejudice included a spirit of regionalism and Southern soldiers' belief they were better than New Englanders, white or Black. Pressure began to mount on Boston legislators. A growing consensus thought the War for Independence should be "a free man's fight," a recurring theme in American history. In the summer of 1775, Edward Rutledge of South Carolina suggested that the Continental Congress summarily dismiss all Blacks currently serving, slave or free. Horatio Gates, the Continental Army's adjutant general, issued a directive that forbade "Officers of the several regiments of Massachusetts Bay forces," to "enlist any stroller negro or vagabond."[8] Congress permitted those Blacks who had already enlisted to remain in the ranks.

The Continental Congress addressed the issue of accepting Blacks in September 1775, rejecting Rutledge's motion to dismiss all Blacks from service. But General George Washington and his staff unanimously agreed to dismiss all slaves and by majority, voted to reject Negroes on October 8, and Congress promptly ratified this policy. As the war dragged on, enthusiasm for enlisting waned, and it became impossible to meet Congress's manpower levies with white volunteers. Resistance to Blacks' service gradually declined, and Blacks were readily accepted as substitutes for whites. The loyalty and effectiveness of George Washington's personal servant, **William Lee**, probably had some impact on Washington's eventual willingness to accept Black soldiers. After the war, Washington emancipated Lee and left money to provide for his faithful servant in his old age.

Washington and his body servant, William Lee. SOURCE: MILWAUKEE INDEPENDENT.

Colonel Alexander Hamilton, Washington's young aide, doubtless influenced the general's change of heart. Hamilton observed, "The contempt we have been taught to entertain for Blacks makes us fancy many things founded neither in reason nor experience," insisting, "their natural faculties are probably as good as ours."[9] Hamilton hit the nail on the head: prejudice, fear, and avarice—losing valuable "property"—were at play, clearly demonstrated by Hamilton's friend Lieutenant Colonel John Laurens's experience when he sought to raise 5,000 Black soldiers in South Carolina. Laurens, like Hamilton, was an aide-de-camp to Washington and the son of the former president of the Continental Congress, a prominent politician from South Carolina. Despite Laurens's connections, South Carolina's council rejected his proposal to arm Blacks by a vote of eight to one. Laurens wrote that this decision was based on a "triple-headed monster, in which prejudice, avarice, and pusillanimity were united."[10] Hamilton had succinctly summarized the need: "I hardly see how a sufficient force can be collected in that quarter without it; and the enemy's operations are growing infinitely serious and formidable" but conceded "this project will have to combat much opposition from prejudice and self-interest."[11] A South Carolina legislator declared that the state was "much disgusted" at the proposal, and other leaders even intimated that the state might approach the British for a separate peace agreement. In March 1779, Congress recommended, but did not order, South Carolina and Georgia to "take measures immediately for raising three thousand able-bodied negroes."[12] Despite the imminent threat, nothing happened because the planters did not want to jeopardize their lifestyle. Whites in the colony were outnumbered six to four by their enslaved property.

Desperate to defend Charleston, General Benjamin Lincoln called upon the governor to enlist slaves in March 1780, but the answer was the same. The British captured the city on May 11; his successor, Horatio Gates, also failed in the theater and was replaced by Nathaniel Greene in October, who made the same unsuccessful appeal. The arrival of the French fleet and soldiers, along with the transfer of Continental troops to the south, let Greene take the offensive and eventually join Washington for the siege of General Cornwallis's Army at Yorktown despite the disaster at Charleston. Both Greene and Laurens continued to pursue recruitment of African American troops, or at least greater Black logistical support from both South Carolina and Georgia, without success. Laurens was killed in a minor engagement with a Loyalist unit at Combahee Ferry in August 1782. Washington condemned the self-interest of Southern planters in a letter to his aide that July:

> I am not at all astonished at the failure of your plan. The spirit of freedom, which, at the commencement of this contest, would gladly have sacrificed every thing to the attainment of its objective, has long since subsided, and every selfish passion has taken its place.[13]

South Carolina and Georgia used slaves as inducements for white volunteers to enlist. In April 1781, South Carolina's General Thomas Sumter offered slaves to white men volunteering for 10 months of service. New recruits were allotted one grown, healthy slave, while veterans who reenlisted received up to four Blacks. In February 1782, legislators approved a scheme for recruiters to receive a bonus of one slave for every 25 whites enlisted in a two-month period. Slaves confiscated from Loyalists provided the means to provide these bounties.[14] Georgia broadened the use of slaves as bonuses, providing slaves to soldiers for valor in combat, paying public officials with enslaved persons, even using captured slaves to pay for military provisions and supplies.[15] Despite both states' resistance, African Americans served throughout the Southern theater in Northern units and as substitutes and servants in regiments from the South.

Lord Dunmore's recruitment of slaves influenced General Washington to change his enlistment policy. On the last day of December 1775, the new commander in chief authorized recruiters to "entertain" the "Numbers of free Negroes (who) are desirous of enlisting," pointing out the eagerness of Blacks to enlist. The Continental Congress finally resolved the issue on January 16, 1776, decreeing "the free negroes who have served faithfully in the Army at Cambridge, may be enlisted therein, but no others."[16] Thus, Congress permitted only Blacks already serving to reenlist and continued to ban new Black recruits. This policy was driven in part by South Carolina's threat to defect from the revolutionary cause and align with Great Britain if its slaves were armed. Blacks vigorously protested bans on their enlistment, and fear that they would go over to the British, who were making energetic efforts to recruit them as well, influenced a cautious acceptance of Blacks.

Several colonial assemblies authorized Black units through legislative acts, such as the New Jersey Militia Act of May 1777 and New Hampshire's Act the same year. Known units include Captain David Humphrey's all-Black 2nd Company, 4th Connecticut Regiment, and the Massachusetts Bucks of America. This unit is clouded in mystery and may have been a local organization for protection against Loyalists. All that is known is that they had a Black commander, Colonel Middleton, and John Hancock presented their flag at the end of the Revolutionary War.

The Rhode Island General Assembly authorized the First Rhode Island "Regiment" in February 1778. This battalion of five companies with less than 50 men each was America's first all-Black unit, and one of the few that was uniformed. That August, the roughly 150-man unit held off battle-hardened British and Hessian troops for four hours, allowing the main body to escape a well-laid trap. After Rhode Island citizens reacted with disapproval, the Assembly repealed the slave-enlistment law in May. Slaves who volunteered received their freedom and the same bounty and salary as white soldiers.[17] The "regiment" was in the field for five years and participated in the siege at Yorktown. Its commander praised the soldiers' "unexampled fortitude and patience" throughout the "long and severe war." In 1781, the Marquis de Chastellux noted, "I met with a

First Rhode Island Regiment repels Hessians at Battle of Rhode Island. SOURCE: DAVID R. WAGNER, WWW.AMERICANVETERANSCENTER.ORG.

detachment of the Rhode Island regiment. . . . The majority of the enlisted men are Negroes or mulattoes; but they are strong, robust men, and those I have seen made a good appearance."[18] When the victorious American Army passed in review at Yorktown in July the following year, Baron von Closen observed, "three-quarters of the Rhode Island regiment consists of Negroes, and that regiment is the most neatly dressed, the best under arms, and the most precise in its maneuvers."[19]

James Madison urged Virginia's landowners to abandon their policy of confining Blacks to service as laborers and recommended Rhode Island's approach of recruiting Black troops. Madison pointed out the obvious—arming freed Blacks "would certainly be more consonant with the principles of liberty which ought never be lost sight of in a contest for liberty." He added "with white officers and a majority of white soldiers, no imaginable danger would be faced from themselves," an attitude that persisted until 1954.[20]

Blacks fought in some 50 engagements during the war.[21] By 1781, at least one in every seven soldiers in the Continental Army was Black due to the reluctance of whites to enlist. Calculating the number of Blacks who served is fraught with difficulty—estimates range from 5,000 to 10,000 Blacks who served in the Continental Army and Navy and state militias and navies, which also provides a good indication of just how small the Continental Army was.[22] These figures are a bit hazy; at one time, naval forces were part of the Army—captured British merchant shipping provided a large portion of the supplies Washington's forces relied on in the first years of the rebellion. These figures also provide a somewhat distorted picture. Historian Michael Lee Lanning points out that Blacks served an average of four and a half years, roughly eight times longer than white soldiers.[23] In July 2021, a New Jersey representative noted that on average, men of color served more than eight times as long on the battlefield as their white colleagues.[24]

Historian Thomas Fleming considers Washington's Army "more integrated than any American force except the armies that fought in the Vietnam and Gulf Wars."[25] Because most units of the Continental Line were racially integrated, Washington described the Continental Army as a "mixed multitude."[26] Many more Black soldiers likely would have served in the Continental Army of other rebel forces were it not for Southern planters' obstinate refusal to arm Blacks, either free or slave. This in large part led to the surrender of Charleston in May 1780, the war's greatest disaster for the patriot cause.

Several foreign observers provide insight into African Americans' effectiveness on the battlefield. In December 1777, a Hessian officer employed by the British wrote in his diary, "The Negro can take to the field instead of his master, and therefore there is no regiment in which to be seen in which there are not Negroes in abundance and among them are many able-bodied and strong fellows."[27] French artillery Sub-Lieutenant Count Jean-Francois-Louis de Clermont-Crevecoeur recorded:

> On July 8, General Washington reviewed the two armies. I went to the American camp, which contained approximately 4,000 men. In beholding the army I was struck, not by its smart appearance, but by its destitution: the men were without uniforms and covered with rags; most of them were barefoot. They were of all sizes, down to children who could not have been fourteen. There were many Negroes, mulattoes, etc.[28]

Another French officer, Baron Ludwig von Closen, aide-de-camp to Lieutenant General Jean Baptiste Conatien de Vimeur, Count Rochambeau, wrote later the same month:

> I had a chance to see the American Army, man for man. It was really painful to see these brave men almost naked with only some trousers and little linen jackets, most of them without stockings, but, would you believe it, very cheerful and healthy in appearance. . . . It is incredible that soldiers composed of men of every age, even children of fifteen, of whites and blacks, unpaid and rather poorly fed, can march so fast and fire so steadily.[29]

Von Closen estimated that 25 percent of Washington's troops were Negroes, "merry, confident, and sturdy."[30] This is likely far too high an estimate; there is a general consensus that about 5,000 African Americans served as soldiers during the war.

As mentioned, many Blacks served for the entire war. **Oliver Cromwell** enlisted in the 2nd New Jersey Regiment and participated in the long retreat from New York through New Jersey to Pennsylvania. He crossed the Delaware River to attack the Hessian garrison at Trenton and fought at Princeton a few days later. Cromwell participated in the battles of Brandywine, Monmouth, and Yorktown, earning the Badge of Merit for long and faithful service.[31] Cromwell's service spanned six years and nine months.

Emanuel Leutze's painting, *Washington Crossing the Delaware*, depicts **Prince Whipple**, a slave belonging to New Hampshire's General William Whipple, seated up front at the stroke oar. Whipple is also depicted in Thomas Sully's *Passage of the Delaware*. Whipple also fought at the battle of Saratoga. **Edward Hector** was a 33-year-old private in Captain Hercules Courtney's company of the 3rd Pennsylvania Artillery, positioned at Chad's Ford. When Lord Howe, the British commander, flanked and encircled Continental forces during the Battle of Brandywine, fleeing Americans discarded guns, ammunition, horses, and wagons in their haste to escape the British. Hector did not panic and left the battlefield with his horses and wagon, retrieving abandoned weapons and ammunition along the way. In his old age, the Pennsylvania legislature finally granted Hector $40, enough to bury him.[32]

In Virginia's battle at Great Bridge in December 1775, **William Flora** of Portsmouth, a volunteer in Colonel William Woodford's First Virginia Regiment, was the last man to leave the bridge, still firing. The local newspaper described him glowingly as having held his ground, firing eight times into an attacking British platoon, before he successfully escaped over the causeway into the patriots' breastwork. Virginia awarded him a hundred acres for his faithful service. It is said that Flora served as a Marine under Stephen Decatur during the War of 1812.

Agrippa Hull, an 18-year-old freeman from Northampton, Massachusetts, served six years, including more than four years as an orderly for the Army's chief engineer, Polish Count Thaddeus Kosciusko, surviving, among others, the battles of Saratoga and Eutaw Springs. Hull assisted surgeons after the Battle of Eutaw Springs and received a written discharge signed by General Washington himself in July 1883. **Lemuel Haynes**, **Primus Black**, and **Epheram Blackman** were among the volunteer force that stormed Fort Ticonderoga in May 1775 with Benedict Arnold and Ethan Allen's Green Mountain Boys to capture cannon for the siege of the British in Boston.

Lambo (Lambert) Latham, a slave, and his master, a farmer, saw British boats headed for the shore in September 1781 and ran to help defend Fort Griswold, which protected the port of New London, Connecticut. After the large British attacking force, led by turncoat Benedict Arnold, defeated the small militia force led by Lieutenant Colonel William Ledyard at Groton Heights, the colonials withdrew to the fort. The flagpole of the fort was shot down during the battle, and Lambert grabbed the American flag and held it high. As the British began scaling the fort's walls, the British officer leading the attack, Major Montgomery, was impaled and killed by **Jordan Freeman**'s pike. Freeman had been emancipated by his former owner, Colonel Ledyard. Outnumbered and out of powder, Ledyard ordered his force to surrender and offered his sword to the British commander, who ran the sword through Ledyard's body. **Lambo** killed that officer with his bayonet, then received 33 bayonet thrusts from British soldiers, who killed the entire garrison.[33] Both African Americans are memorialized on a tablet at Old Fort Griswold; their names are listed after white soldiers.

Other Blacks serving in militia units include **George Latchom**, who distinguished himself in 1781 when the British landed a small force at Henry's Point, a few miles from Yorktown, Virginia. Most of the militia dispersed in the face of a determined bayonet charge. Only the militia commander, Colonel John Cropper, and George, a slave owned by one of the colonel's neighbors, stood their ground, later withdrawing through a marsh. The colonel became immersed in soft mud, but Latchom, after killing an attacking Redcoat, pulled the colonel free and carried him to safety. Colonel Cropper bought Latchom from his neighbor, emancipated him, and they remained friends for life.

When South Carolina became the decisive theater in 1779, among the 3,600-man expedition, led by Count d'Estaing France, dispatched to rescue the colonists were 545 Blacks in a light cavalry unit recruited in Santo Domingo, the *Chasseurs-Volontaires de Saint-Domingue*, or the *Frontages Legion*. After the French expedition failed to expel the British from entrenchments around Savannah, Georgia, they were forced to withdraw due to the onset of winter. The *Chasseurs* included several men destined to play significant roles in the Haitian Revolution (1791–1804), including **Andre Rigaud**, **Louis Jacques Beauvais**, **Martial Besse**, and **Jean-Baptiste Belly-Mars**, later elected a member of the French National Convention. Serving as a rear guard at one point, the Haitian unit prevented the annihilation of allied forces at Charleston. One of the enlistees in the French force was 12-year-old **Henri Christophe**, an officer's orderly who later ruled an independent Haiti, freed by slaves who rebelled and made the country the second to win its independence in this hemisphere—and the opprobrium of the European world. France saddled the new country with a debt that predetermined its unfortunate history. The Haitian Revolution filled owners of enslaved persons with fear and hate in the colonies, South America, and the Caribbean islands.

Austin Dabney was a substitute for his owner who was drafted. Dabney served as an artilleryman in the Georgia corps commanded by Colonel Elijah Clark. He fought at Cowpens, a decisive victory for the colonists, and at the smaller battle of Kettle Creek. Georgia's governor declared, "No soldier under Clark was braver, or did better service during the Revolutionary struggle." Nevertheless, Dabney was not allowed to participate in the land lottery for veterans, and when the Georgia legislature did award him 110 acres, his neighbors protested the "indignity" of having Black men treated equally in the award of public lands.[34]

Both sides used large and small levies of slaves to build fortifications throughout the war. Even the South Carolina Committee of Safety issued a resolution directing that "able-bodied negro men be taken into public service and enrolled and employed, without arms, for the defense of the several batteries" to guard Charleston when the British threatened the city. Although South Carolina and Georgia were the most vulnerable colonies, both steadfastly refused to consider arming Blacks, with predictable and unfortunate results for the Patriot cause. Plantation owners' love of liberty did not extend to sacrificing their "property," which generated unbelievable wealth and guaranteed comfortable lifestyles.

CONTINENTAL NAVIES

The pattern of barring Blacks from enlisting but allowing them to use pickaxe and shovel did not apply at sea, where they served as ordinary seamen, pilots, gunners and sharpshooters in Marine detachments and participated in boarding parties and land assaults. Blacks also cooked, hauled sails, caulked, and participated in cleaning ships. Privateers were essential to expand the fledgling continental navies' reach since it took some time to form the US Navy and the 11 state navies. More than 1,500 letters of marque were issued during the war; a report for 1781 listed 449 privateers operating under Congressional or state authorization. Fortunately for the revolutionaries, at the outset of the rebellion, Great Britain had only 29 warships to patrol the 1,800-mile American coastline.[35] The Continental Navy commissioned about 50 warships during the Revolution, and state navies, primarily South Carolina, Virginia, and Massachusetts, had about the same number. State navies usually enlisted sailors for three- or six-month terms and patrolled within local waters. US Navy captains faced a greater challenge since they conducted longer cruises away from home ports to seek out British men-of-war and had to recruit crews for a year or longer. The US Navy Department estimates that around 1,000 Blacks served in the Continental Navy and approximately 1,500 African Americans served aboard Continental vessels or privateers, or about 10 percent of naval personnel.[36]

In 1779, Washington wrote Major Henry Lee, "I have granted a Warrant for the 1,000 Doll(ar)s promised the Negro pilots."[37] Two Blacks served on Captain John Paul Jones's *Bon Homme Richard*. Given the challenges and demands of seafaring, Blacks were a welcome resource for the Continental Navy and state navies. In March 1781, a Maryland patriot replied to the state Council that he was happy to send his schooner but with a Negro skipper and crew because "no white man would go."[38] The name of this fearless mariner is unknown, true of most Blacks who served. Three Blacks, **Peter**, **Brittain**, and **Danial Peterson**, served aboard the *Trumbull*. **Joseph Ranger**, a freeman, served in Virginia's navy for nine years—until the fleet was disbanded four years after the Revolution's successful end. Slave **Caesar Tarrant** served as a pilot on a Virginia vessel and was emancipated by the Virginia General Assembly because of his bravery. He was a well-to-do citizen of Hampton after the war.

Although the US Marine Corps did not officially accept Blacks for more than 150 years after the War for Independence, Marines served aboard ships and on land during that struggle. Thirteen veterans have been identified on Marine Corps rolls as African American—three in the Continental Navy and the others distributed in the detachments of Connecticut, Massachusetts, and Pennsylvania state navies. At least one Black Marine was killed in action aboard the brig *Reprisal* in 1777.[39]

Toward the end of the Revolution, 15-year-old **James Forten** served as powder boy on the American privateer *Royal Louis*, commanded by Stephen Decatur, Sr. Forten previously served as a drummer in the Army. Of the 200-strong ship's crew, 20 were Black. When the ship was forced to surrender to the heavily armed frigate HMS *Amphion* and two other

James Forten, wealthy sailmaker and abolitionist.
SOURCE: ATLANTA BLACK STAR.

warships, the captain's son befriended Forten and offered a life of ease in England, he refused to betray his country. He was sent to the prison ship *Jersey*, a rotting hulk anchored off Long Island, where thousands of American prisoners died. After seven months, Forten was freed and returned to Philadelphia, becoming an extremely wealthy inventor, sailmaker, and philanthropist. Forten helped found and contributed generously to the abolition movement, continually protesting slavery.

SPIES AND SCOUTS

Not all Black patriot heroes were soldiers. As during the Civil War, both sides had difficulty recognizing that slaves represented a grave threat to information security. **James Armistead**, a slave who, with his master's permission, served under Lafayette, played a crucial role as a double agent during the month-and-a-half siege of Yorktown. After the British surrendered on October 19, 1781, James surprised Lord Cornwallis, who could not believe he was a double agent. Lafayette attested to the value of the information James provided during a visit to the United States in 1784. Two years later, James petitioned Virginia's General Assembly for his freedom. That body agreed and paid his former master for his freedom. James later changed his last name to Lafayette. In 1819, the Assembly granted James an award of $100 and an annual pension of $40. James reunited with Lafayette in Richmond during the nobleman's final tour of America in 1824.[40]

Saul Matthews, a slave, helped spy on the British camp in Portsmouth, providing valuable intelligence. Colonel Josiah Parker declared that Matthews "deserved the applause of his country" for his courage and bravery. Baron von Steuben, General Peter Muhlenberg, and General Nathaniel Green all praised Matthews's service effusively. In November 1792, Matthews petitioned the Virginia General Assembly for emancipation and was granted freedom due to "many very essential services rendered to this Commonwealth during the late war."

In March 1783, a slave named **Antigua** was lauded by South Carolina's General Assembly for "procuring information of the enemy's movements and designs." The legislators noted that Antigua "always executed his missions with which he was entrusted with diligence and fidelity, and

James Armistead Lafayette, double agent. SOURCE: MANUSCRIPTS, ARCHIVES AND RARE BOOKS DIVISION, SCHOMBURG CENTER FOR RESEARCH IN BLACK CULTURE, NEW YORK PUBLIC LIBRARY.

obtained very considerable and important information, frequently at the risk of his life." It appears, however, that Antigua remained enslaved.[41]

During the occupation of Newport, Rhode Island, **Quaco Honeyman**, owned by a British colonel, fled to the Patriots' lines with such valuable information that the Rhode Island legislature set Quaco free in January 1782, declaring his "information . . . rendered great and essential service to this state and the public in general."[42] **Pompey Lamb**, a slave who delivered food to the garrison at Stony Point, is said to have helped General Anthony Wayne's troops capture that British strong point on New York's Hudson River.

These men are but a few of the thousands of Black heroes who risked their lives for the young nation, all of whom have since faded from history. Rarely are any of these heroes other than Crispus Attucks mentioned in America's classrooms.

AFRICAN AMERICANS FIGHTING FOR THE BRITISH

Use of Africans bedeviled the British as well. Shortly after hostilities began, Lieutenant General Thomas Gage sent a letter appraising the colonial secretary in London, "Things have now come to that crisis, that we must avail ourselves of every resource, even to raise the negroes, in our cause."[43] But South Carolina's Royal governor advised Gage not to "fall prey to the Negroes," and Gates took no further action. However, in November 1775, Lord Dunmore, the British governor of Virginia, issued an invitation to "all indentured servants, Negroes, or others free, that are able to bear arms," to join his limited military force. His hopes were not fully materialized because his "Ethiopian Regiment," with white officers, raised only 300 troops and was defeated in their first battle by 900 North Carolina and Virginia militiamen at Great Bridge. Ultimately, at least 800 Blacks responded to Dunmore's call, including one of George Washington's former slaves, but a smallpox epidemic ravaged the unit, leaving only 150 survivors. In June 1776, Virginia militia drove them from their base camp on Gwynn's Island at the mouth of the Rappahannock River, ending the threat of a slave rebellion in the Tidewater region of Virginia. Some 300 Black men, women, and children left with Dunmore when he abandoned Virginia in August. In March 1777, Sir William Howe, commander in chief of British forces in the colonies, directed "all Negroes, Mollattoes, and other Improper Persons who have been admitted into those Corps be immediately discharged."[44] After Howe was replaced, this directive was often ignored. Sir Henry Clinton declared in June 1779 that Blacks captured in battle would be sold as slaves unless they "deserted the rebel standard" but "any who desert the rebel cause will have their freedom secured."[45] Clinton's proclamation did not result in any widespread defection from the ranks; in general, African Americans serving with American forces had extremely low desertion rates.

The number of enslaved individuals who chose to support the Revolutionary cause is dwarfed by the tens of thousands who went over to the British or simply ran away from their owners in the chaos. Most slaves believed that Britain offered more attractive terms and had a greater likelihood of winning, at least early in the war. When Charleston, South Carolina, was captured, the British dispatched squads of African American soldiers to secure the city's cannons. In addition, a Black cavalry unit of some 100 horsemen was assigned the duty of arresting deserters.

Despite a clause in the Provisional Peace Agreement signed in Paris on November 30, 1782, which reached Congress on March 12, 1783, prohibiting "carrying away any negroes or other property of American inhabitants," a good many slaves did depart with the withdrawal of British troops. Estimates put the loss as high as 100,000; South Carolina lost 25,000 of its 110,000 slaves, almost a quarter, and Georgia lost over 75 percent, many of whom escaped to Florida, then a Spanish colony. Thomas Jefferson reported that Virginia lost 30,000 slaves.[46]

Historian Benjamin Quarles sagely observed, "it was obvious that the best way to prevent the Negro from going over to the British was to give him sufficient inducement to fight for America."[47] This was a fact that Southern plantation owners refused to grasp. African Americans served both sides in support roles—in logistics functions and engineer units, as cooks, servants, and a variety of other roles that freed up soldiers for military tasks. Since both sides to a great extent upheld the inhuman "peculiar" institution, it was not easy for African Americans to determine which side offered the better prospect for freedom. Overall, Blacks believed that England offered a clearer access to freedom, partly because of Lord Manchester's decision in the Somerset case of June 1772, which challenged the legal basis for slavery in Great Britain. Many believed that Britain would ultimately outlaw slavery, which was partially realized in the Slave Trade Act of 1807, abolishing the slave trade in the British Empire, and the Slavery Abolition Act of 1833, which abolished slavery throughout the British Empire.

The Americans did not have a monopoly on Black spies and scouts. **Quamino Dolly** insured the success of General Sir Archibald Campbell's assault against Savannah in December 1778. In his report to his superiors, Campbell acknowledged that he had intended to make a frontal attack until Dolly entered his lines and volunteered to guide British forces through a swamp so that American forces could be assaulted from the rear. Campbell dispatched light infantry with the Black guide; simultaneous attacks on front and rear resulted in a quick and decisive victory. Black guides also helped guide Colonel John Maitland's regiment from Beaufort to Savannah through a swamp, bypassing the American Army.[48]

Many African Americans served in the British Navy, making significant contributions by guiding them through the numerous channels, rivers, and waterways along the Atlantic coast.[49] Both freemen and runaways received the same pay as white sailors.

When eight and a half years of hostilities (April 1775 to September 1783) ended in England's defeat, it is estimated that British ships leaving New York, Charleston, Savannah, and other ports carried 16,000 to 20,000 Blacks to a variety of destinations. However, no reliable records were kept; many Loyalists simply shipped their slaves to other destinations, making it possible that as many as 30,000 to 50,000 African Americans accompanied the British.[50] Destinations included Nova Scotia, Jamaica, Nassau, St. Lucia, and England. Eventually, some refugees chose to go to Sierra Leone, the British colony in Africa. African Americans on some ships bound for the West Indies were sold to British or Spanish plantation owners. Some Blacks who served with Hessian units elected to go to Germany, and about 4,500 Blacks fled South Carolina and Georgia headed for East Florida.

Historian Gary Nash observed that in a real sense, the War for Independence was the first mass slave rebellion in American history.

WAR OF 1812

Service during the War for Independence suggested to many Blacks that military service represented a clear path to freedom, although this was not always the case, especially in the South. It did set the pattern, followed consistently in later wars, of grudgingly accepting Blacks during wartime crises and quickly forgetting their service afterward. Reflecting this tendency, in 1792, less than a decade after securing independence from England, Congress passed the Second Militia Act on May 8, 1792, obligating every "free able-bodied *white* male citizen" between the ages of 18 and 45 to participate in a local militia company. South Carolina and Georgia permitted Blacks to serve as musicians or laborers, but Haiti's slave uprising (1791–1804), which resulted in the slaughter of most French slaveowners, caused great anxiety and fear among American slaveowners.

Renowned historian Samuel Eliot Morison described the War of 1812 as "the most unpopular war this country has ever waged, not even excepting the Vietnam conflict."[51] The War Department was authorized to recruit 50,000 one-year volunteers, but only 10,000 men were enlisted. Although the war was extremely unpopular in New England, New York authorized two Black regiments, comprising some 2,000 Blacks, offering compensation to their masters and freedom to slaves who enlisted. However, recruitment began only in 1814, after fighting had ended in the Northeast. Pennsylvania raised a Black brigade, and Kentucky enlisted 400 Blacks.[52]

Although Congressional legislation ensured that the Army and Marine Corps became all white, due to the unattractiveness of long sea voyages, the Navy accepted all able bodies. Blacks went to sea during an undeclared naval war with France (1798–1800), and a decade later Blacks were among the crew impressed from the USS *Chesapeake* by HMS *Leopard*, which alleged that these and several white sailors were British subjects. High-handed British behavior at sea, along with the United States' desire to capture Canada, was a major cause of the War of 1812.

Up to 10 percent of American seamen were Black during the War of 1812, and they played critical roles in two major American naval victories. Commodore Oliver Hazard Perry, commander of naval forces on the Great Lakes, welcomed Blacks, who made up roughly a quarter of his complement of some 400 crewmen. They played an important role in his 1813 triumph over the British at Put-in-Bay on Lake Erie. Lieutenant Thomas McDonough's victorious flotilla on Lake Champlain also had a contingent of African Americans. In addition, numerous Blacks served aboard American privateers. Commodore Isaac Chauncey praised Blacks' performance:

> They are not surpassed by any seamen we have in the fleet and I have yet to learn that the color of a man's skin and the cut and the trimmings of the coat can affect a man's qualifications and usefulness. I have nearly fifty Blacks on board this ship, and many of them are among my best men.[53]

Despite their widely demonstrated and recognized valor, Congressional legislation passed in 1816 prohibited slaves from serving on Navy ships or working in shipyards.

In the Battle of New Orleans, fought on January 8, 1815, two weeks after the Treaty of Ghent ended the war, two Black Creole battalions comprising 500 men fought with great valor under Major General Andrew Jackson. Responding to military exigency, Jackson called upon New Orleans' Free Men of Color, a military unit with a long tradition under both Spanish and French flags, to "rally 'round the Standard of the Eagle." Although a slaveowner, Jackson acknowledged previous injustice: "Through a mistaken policy you have heretofore been deprived of participation in the glorious struggle for national rights in which our country is engaged. This no longer shall exist."[54] Both battalions, one commanded by a Black officer, fought with distinction; Jackson singled out Black Major Joseph

New Orleans' Free Men of Color. SOURCE: HUGH CHARLES MCBARRON, JR., "THE AMERICAN SOLDIER," SET 5, US ARMY CENTER OF MILITARY HISTORY.

Savory for special commendation. Jackson addressed glowing praise to the Black warriors:

> To the Men of Color: Soldiers! . . . you surpass my hopes. I have found you, united in these qualities, the noble enthusiasm which impels men to do great deeds. Soldiers! The President of the United States shall be informed of your conduct . . . and the American nation shall applaud your valor, as your General now praises your ardor.[55]

When his paymaster objected to paying Black troops, Jackson tartly wrote:

> Be pleased to keep to yourself your opinions upon the policy of making payment to particular corps. It is enough for you to receive my order for the payment of troops with the necessary muster rolls, without inquiring whether the troops are white, Black or Tea.[56]

The influence of white supremacy is borne out in Benjamin Quarles's judgment, "The typical Negro soldier was a private, consigned as if by caste, to the rank and file. Even more than other privates, he tended to lack identity. Often he bore no specific name."[57] This was affirmed in 1847, when poet John Greenleaf Whittier lamented that the service of Black men was "carefully kept out of sight." Whittier observed,

> When we see a whole nation doing honor to the memories of one class of its defenders, to the total neglect of another class, who had the misfortune to be of a darker complexion, we cannot forgo the satisfaction of inviting attention to historical facts, which, for the last half century have been quietly elbowed aside, as no more deserving of a place in patriotic recollection, than the descendants of men, to whom the facts in question relate, to have a place in a Fourth of July procession.
> Of the sufferings of the Colored Soldiers of the Revolution, no attempt has been made, to our knowledge, to preserve a record. They have no historian. With here and there an exception, they have all passed away, and

only some faint traditions linger among their descendants. Yet enough is known to show that the free men of color of the United States bore their full proportion of the sacrifices and trials of the Revolutionary War.[58]

Eight years later, Harriet Beecher Stowe, in her foreword to Black historian William Cooper Nell's book, *The Colored Patriots of the Revolution* (1855), observed:

> In considering the services of the Colored Patriots of the Revolution, we are to reflect upon them as far more magnanimous, because rendered to a nation which did not consider them as citizens and equals . . . but for a land which had enslaved them, and whose laws, even in freedom, oftener oppressed than protected. Bravery, under such circumstances, has a peculiar beauty and merit.[59]

In February 1820, the Army issued an order specifying, "No Negro or mulatto shall be received as a recruit of the army" and the following year, Army General Regulations limited military service to "free white males." Both affected the three Seminole wars in Florida (1816–1858) and the war against Mexico (1846–1848). The Free Men of Color was abolished in 1834, during Jackson's presidency, typical of the short-term gratitude America has repeatedly shown Blacks for their patriotism.

In 1839, the Navy restricted Black enlistments to 5 percent of the force. South Carolina Senator John C. Calhoun, the "Apostle of Slavery," introduced legislation in 1842 restricting Blacks to positions as cooks, mess boys, and servants. He declared, "those who have to sustain the honor and glory of the country" ought not be "degraded by being mingled and mixed up with an inferior race." Although it passed in the Senate, the House, dominated at the time by Northern states, failed to bring the measure to a vote.[60] A US Navy film, "African-Americans in the United States Navy—A Short History," notes that African Americans served aboard the USS *Treasure* and the USS *Columbus*.

CONCLUSIONS

Colonial policy regarding Black militia service was inconsistent, but in times of trouble, Blacks were invariably called upon to bear arms. During the Revolutionary War, roughly 15 percent of the soldiers in the Continental Army, one in every seven soldiers, was Black by 1781. This was mainly due to the reluctance of whites to enlist in the Continental Army, state forces, or local militia. Hundreds of Blacks also served as ordinary seamen, gunners, and Marine sharpshooters in the Continental Navy and state navies and aboard American privateers. However, many slaves judged that the British offered greater opportunities for obtaining freedom.

Few Americans appreciate that the Revolutionary War dragged on for eight and a half years, with few victories won by the Continental Army. America won its independence from England mostly by outlasting the British Empire's will to commit money and soldiers to an effort that could not be extinguished. Since Blacks served longer terms of enlistment, they had a weighted influence on final victory. Harriet Beecher Stowe was right; because they rendered their service to a nation that did not consider them citizens or equals, Blacks' loyalty was noteworthy. Frederick Douglass was also correct; history shows that African Americans are recognized as men when needed in time of war—1776, 1812, and 1863. Thus, in times of trouble, the Negro is a citizen; in times of peace, national amnesia sets in, and they became aliens or outcasts.

The Battle of New Orleans might well have ended with a far less favorable outcome had it not been for the Free Men of Color. Although Andrew Jackson recognized their contribution at the time, even acknowledging "previous injustice," his policies while in the White House were as harmful to Blacks as they were to the Native Americans he displaced westward.

CHAPTER 2

US Colored Troops in the Civil War

> Yes, the Blacks enjoy their freedom,
> And they won it dearly, too,
> For the life blood of their thousands
> Did the Southern field bedew.
>
> Paul Lawrence Dunbar
> *Lyrics of the Lowly Life*

Authorized by the Emancipation Proclamation in January 1863, US Colored Troops had a major impact on the outcome of the Civil War, providing a huge reinforcement of up to 209,000 soldiers organized into approximately 175 regiments. Their recruitment and deployment came when manpower sources were all but exhausted on both sides. This greatly enhanced the North's ability to sustain combat operations while providing rear area security for installations spread over an ever-growing distance. This was a larger force than the South had in the field in all theaters at war's end.

African American labor and auxiliary forces made major contributions to the war effort on both sides.

Only the United States and Haitian slaves fought a bitter, protracted war to end slavery. While Southern planters, the ruling class, indisputably seceded to maintain and protect their profitable "peculiar institution," the North initially fought simply to preserve the Union, not to free slaves. Only after more than a year of bloody stalemate did Lincoln begin to seriously consider emancipation. He did this in large part because recruitment of Black soldiers became a military necessity: there was no other source for replacements after months of savage bloodshed. The prevailing prejudice made Lincoln's decision to recruit and arm freemen and slaves, part of the Emancipation Proclamation, both daring and drastic, but he had no alternative. The South also faced this dilemma, but the "peculiar institution" on which the would-be country was based made arming Blacks unthinkable and was not attempted until it was too late to save the Confederacy.

Initially regarded exclusively as "a white man's fight," the war's horrendous casualties in 1861 and 1862 resulted in declining enlistment rates, which coupled with resistance to the draft enacted by the North in March 1863, caused a gradual but profound change in political and social attitudes. The South resorted to the draft in March 1862. Once it became clear that the war was not a romantic lark of brief duration, fewer men were eager to enlist, making Blacks gradually more acceptable and later necessary if sorely depleted ranks were to be filled. Desertion, a constantly growing problem, compounded the manpower problem for both sides.

Dudley Cornish, an authority on African American soldiers' service during the Civil War, put it this way: "It is hard to realize how revolutionary the experiment of permitting Negroes to bear arms was considered, how fraught with imagined dangers to the Union cause, how galling to white pride." He cited an article from the March 7, 1863, *New York Times*, only three months after the Emancipation Proclamation: "we can all recognize the prodigious revolution which the public mind everywhere is experiencing. Such developments are infallible tokens of a new epoch."[1] Cornish also emphasized the exemplary program that the Union Army and political leadership conducted educating white troops to foster acceptance of their new Black comrades, something he pointedly observed was lacking in both World War I and II.

Sectional friction over slavery began even before the United States had become a country. John Brown's attack on the federal armory at Harpers Ferry on October 16, 1859, to liberate slaves resulted in his capture by a detachment of US Marines led by Colonel Robert E. Lee, with Lieutenant J. E. B. Stuart as his assistant. Brown was tried by the state of Virginia and hung for treason. Although unsuccessful, his attack on the

John Brown, 1859. SOURCE: MARTIN M. LAWRENCE, LIBRARY OF CONGRESS.

armory to liberate slaves heightened tensions between North and South to such an extent that prominent men in the South began raising additional military units. Brown's raid struck a resounding chord in the perpetual fear of white Southerners that their large slave population would rise in rebellion, and public rage exploded in the South when it was discovered that prominent Bostonians financed Brown's attempt. Southern militias—based on slave patrols—drilled more frequently and with far greater seriousness. The Richmond *Enquirer* observed that the raid on Harpers Ferry "advanced the cause of disunion more than any other event."[2] The North also began forming its own quasi-military organizations, including the "Wide-Awakes."

Open warfare began after the Confederate attack on Fort Sumter April 12, 1861, and a gradual, snowballing process of de facto emancipation began in the chaos of war as owners began to lose their ability to capture runaway slaves. In the first few months, some Union commanders tried to return escaped slaves and discouraged Blacks from abandoning their masters. A Baltimore newspaper noted that in the first three months of the war, more escaped slaves had been remanded to their owners under Lincoln than during the whole of Buchanan's presidential term.[3] In part,

US Marines storm the Harpers Ferry firehouse. Harper's Weekly, November 1859, "The Harper's Ferry Insurrection—The U.S. Marines storming the engine house—Insurgents firing through holes in the doors."
SOURCE: HARPERS FERRY NATIONAL HISTORIC PARK.

this was because the government had no official policy and field commanders were forced to use their discretion.

In May 1861, three runaway slaves who had been building revetments for a Confederate artillery battery arrived at Fortress Monroe, Virginia, headquarters of Brigadier General Benjamin Butler, a Massachusetts politician. When their master's representative arrived to claim his "chattel" pursuant to the Fugitive Slave Act, Butler informed him that since Virginia did not consider itself part of the Union, the rebelling states could no longer rely on that legislation. Butler pronounced the men "contrabands of war" and hired the three to build a bakery for his troops. They were soon followed by thousands more, settling into an ever-growing camp at Hampton near his headquarters at Fort Monroe. Butler informed the secretary of war, and the War Department endorsed his decision.

Congress made this policy official when it passed a resolution in July 1861 declaring that it was no "part of the duties of the soldiers of the United States to capture and return fugitive slaves." This was made definitive by the Confiscation Act of August 1861, which declared that property used to support the cause of the Confederacy was to be seized. If the "property" happened to be enslaved individuals, they were forever free. Late in 1861, Secretary of War Simon Cameron declared that slaves were a "military resource" and thus should not be returned to the enemy. He declared that it was "as clearly the right of the Government to arm slaves when it may become necessary as it is to use gunpowder or guns taken from the enemy."[4] Because chaos and corruption were becoming evident in the War Department, Camron was made ambassador to Russia and replaced by Erwin M. Stanton, a lawyer whose meticulous efficiency played a large part in eventual Northern victory.

The fact that Confederate forces made extensive use of tens of thousands of slaves to build fortifications gradually changed the attitude of a growing number of Union leaders. At first, however, emancipation by field commanders could be carried too far. In August 1861, General John C. Frémont, the first Republican candidate for president in 1856, proclaimed freedom for slaves belonging to Confederate sympathizers in Missouri, an action that landed him in hot water with President Lincoln. He was directed to rescind the order and abruptly transferred to the Shenandoah Valley.

In late March 1862, Major General David Hunter, commander of the Department of the South, declared martial law and compelled escaped

Contrabands arriving at Fort Monroe. SOURCE: HARPERS WEEKLY.

slaves to "volunteer" in a military unit. This generated little enthusiasm among many of the former slaves, especially since they were not paid. Meanwhile, Hunter taunted Kentucky Congressman Charles Wickliffe, who demanded an explanation of reports that Hunter was raising a regiment of fugitive slaves. Tongue in cheek, Hunter denied that he had enlisted "fugitive slaves." Rather, he had encountered loyal slaves remaining on their plantations to "welcome us, aid us, and supply us with food, labor, and information" after their masters, "Fugitive Rebels," left their servants behind "to shift as best they can for themselves."

"In the absence of any 'Fugitive Master Law,'" Hunter deadpanned, "the deserted Slaves would be wholly without remedy, had not the crime of Treason given them the right to pursue those persons of whose protection they have been thus suddenly bereft." Hunter noted that he had been ordered to "employ all loyal persons offering their services in defense of the Union and for suppression of this Rebellion," with "no restriction as to the character or color of the persons to be employed." Pursuant to those instructions, he had "clothed, equipped and armed the only loyal regiment yet raised in South Carolina." His men were "attentive and enthusiastic"; they had "great natural capacities" and were eager to "take the field and be led into action." Hunter's letter resulted in guffaws from both sides of the aisle when it was read in Congress.

When Hunter announced "emancipation" on May 9, Lincoln rescinded the order 10 days later. Hunter's failure to obtain approval for his actions from both the War Department and President Lincoln resulted in his relief, although the federal government was moving in this direction. Authorization came just two weeks after his departure, when Secretary of War Edwin Stanton directed Brigadier General Rufus Saxton to recruit regiments of former slaves. Thomas Wentworth Higginson, one of the six men who had financed John Brown's raid on Harpers Ferry, a prominent Massachusetts abolitionist and a unitarian minister with previous service as a Union captain in a Massachusetts infantry regiment, was selected to command the 1st South Carolina Infantry (African Descent), later redesignated the 33rd US Colored Infantry. Wentworth trained the regiment rigorously, making it a highly effective military unit.

The next big step in the change of government policy, 15 months into the war, was passage of the Second Confiscation Act on July 17, 1862, seizing slaves of any Confederate military or civilian official who was in rebellion against the United States. That same day, the Militia

Act of 1862 authorized the states to draft militia units to make up volunteer shortfalls, but it also empowered the president to use freed slaves "for any purpose he may judge best for the public welfare." While this accelerated a process that had already been taking place on both sides, using Blacks as a labor force for a wide variety of tasks, the door also opened to arming Blacks, particularly in Kansas. Free men of color joined volunteer regiments in Illinois and New York and later fought in some of the most noted campaigns and battles of the war, including Antietam, Vicksburg, Gettysburg, and Sherman's Atlanta Campaign.

On September 27, 1862, the first regiment to become a US Colored Troops (USCT) regiment was officially brought into the Union Army. All the captains and lieutenants in this Louisiana regiment were men of African descent. The regiment was immediately assigned combat duties and captured Donaldsonville, Louisiana, on October 27, 1862. Before the Emancipation Proclamation was issued, two other African descent regiments from Kansas and South Carolina demonstrated their prowess in combat.

By midsummer 1862, after a year of war with far more bloodshed than either side expected and little discernable progress, Lincoln concluded

Contrabands at Camp Nelson, Kentucky. SOURCE: HARPERS WEEKLY, NATIONAL PARK SERVICE, CAMP NELSON NATIONAL PARK, KENTUCKY.

that emancipation, which would disrupt the South's great manpower reservoir, was necessary to preserve the Union. After consulting with his cabinet, especially Secretary of State William Henry Seward, Lincoln decided to wait for a convincing Union victory to announce emancipation so it would not appear that the action was taken in desperation. After Lee's defeat on the Maryland border at Antietam on September 17, 1862, Lincoln was satisfied that the opportunity had arrived. Five days after the battle, Lincoln issued a preliminary announcement warning that slaves would be freed in areas not currently occupied by Union forces unless the South returned to the Union by January 1, 1863. He also cautiously endorsed the federalization of Louisiana's Native Guards, successors to the Free Men of Color.

GROWING CONTRABAND PROBLEM

Not all commanders cared for the growing number of enslaved individuals who managed to escape from their masters. Word of Lincoln's Emancipation Proclamation spread rapidly throughout the South through the slave grapevine; as one South Carolina runaway explained, "We'se can't read, but we'se can listen." Most slaves were aware of the issuance of the Proclamation, news for which almost every enslaved individual longed. In most areas, escaped slaves suffered from lack of food, shelter, and medical care. Some speculate that as many as a quarter of runaways died, sometimes after much suffering. Due to inadequate medical facilities, one out of every four of the 1.1 million men, women, and children who managed to reach the contraband camps died, one of the worst public health disasters in US history. The number is an estimate; no one knows the actual number, and others place the number of those who fled to Union lines at between 500,000 and 700,000 formerly enslaved individuals. In any case, this caused major disruption and sowed consternation in the Confederate home front, as well as great concern for their families among those serving in the ranks.

Because the number of escaped slaves was a growing problem, Grant appointed chaplain John Eaton of the 27th Ohio Volunteer Infantry Regiment as chief of Negro Affairs for the Mississippi Valley. Eaton was tasked to provide education, food, shelter, medical care, and employment for "contrabands" in camps as far apart as Cairo, Illinois; Natchez, Mississippi; and Fort Smith, Arkansas. Eaton was later superintendent for Negro Affairs for the Department of Tennessee and was a brigadier general by war's end.

A similar process to accommodate, feed, and recruit former slaves was replicated in all areas in which Union troops operated. Freedmen's Village, just south of the District of Columbia on the grounds of the Custis and Lee estates, near the current location of Arlington National Cemetery and the Pentagon, was established in 1863 by the federal government, supported by the American Tract Society. The village included about 50 one-and-a-half story duplexes, including several schools for children; an industrial school; a 159-bed hospital; a home for the aged; and workshops for blacksmiths, wheelwrights, carpenters, and churches.[5]

Lincoln's emancipation policy faced substantial resistance, especially from Democrats. The fact that racism was at play was evidenced when a House Select Committee issued a report calling for the removal of freed slaves from the United States, declaring in part, "*the highest interests of the white race, whether Anglo-Saxon, Celt, or Scandinavian, require that the whole country should be held and occupied by those (white) races alone.*" Because of this "unbridgeable" divide, the report continued, "The home of the African must *not* be within the limits of the present territory of the Union. The Anglo-American looks upon every acre of our present domain as intended for him and not the negro." This report, advocating mass deportation of freedmen even from a committee with a Republican majority, reflected near-universal racial animosity held by most white Americans. Four days before his death, speaking to General Benjamin Butler, Lincoln reinforced his belief that deportation was the only peaceable solution to America's race problem. "I can hardly believe that the South and North can live in peace, unless we can get rid of the negroes. . . . I believe that it would be better to export them all to some fertile country."[6]

Lincoln enunciated his position on slavery in August 1862: "If I could save the Union without freeing slaves, I would do it; and if I could save it by freeing all slaves, I would do that." His next sentence is crucial to understanding this consummate politician's mind: "What I do about slavery and the colored race, I do because I believe it would help save the Union.[7]

In September, he addressed a church group in Chicago:

> I admit that slavery is the root of the rebellion, or at least its *sine qua non*. I also concede that Emancipation would help us in Europe. . . . I grant further that it would help somewhat in the North, though not so much, I fear, as you and those you represent might imagine. . . . And

then, unquestionably, it would weaken the rebels by drawing off their laborers, which is of great importance, but I am not sure we can do much with the Blacks. If we were to arm them, I fear that in a few weeks the arms would be in the arms of the rebels.[8]

Speaking to a group of abolitionists in 1864, Lincoln clarified his decision to slow-crawl the decision to abolish slavery, an institution protected by the Constitution:

> I did not consider that I had a *right* to touch the "State" institution of "Slavery" until all other measures for restoring the Union had failed. The moment came when I felt that slavery must die that the Union might live! Many of my strongest supporters urged *Emancipation* before I thought it indispensable, and, I may say, before I thought the country was ready for it. It is my conviction that, had the proclamation been issued even six months earlier than it was, public sentiment would not have sustained it.[9]

Frederick Douglass, 1847–1852. Source: Samuel J. Miller, Art Institute of Chicago, Creative Commons Zero (CC0).

Prominent ex-slave, abolitionist, publisher, and orator Frederick Douglass heavily influenced Lincoln's decision to use Black troops. From the time he ran away from his enslaver, Douglass traveled around the country as well as abroad to advance his people's cause. As early as May 1861, Douglass urged that slaves and free colored individuals be called into service to form a "liberating army." He declared, "a war undertaken and brazenly carried out for the perpetual enslavement of colored men called logically and loudly for colored men to help suppress it."[10] Lincoln expressed concern that arming Blacks at that juncture would turn "50,000 bayonets" from the loyal Border states against the Union.[11]

Douglass was extremely persistent in his call for arming Blacks, insisting,

> Never since the world began was a better chance offered for a long enslaved and oppressed people. The opportunity is given us to be men. . . . Once let the black man get upon his person the brass letter, U.S., let him get an eagle on his button, and a musket on his shoulder and bullets in his pocket, there is no power on earth or under the earth that can deny that he has earned the right to citizenship.[12]

> One black regiment alone would be . . . the full equal of two white ones. The very fact of color would be more terrible than powder and balls. The slave would learn more as to the nature of the conflict from the presence of such a regiment, than from a thousand preachers.[13]

This turned out to be an accurate prediction. Confederate troops soon came to fear assaults by fearless, determined Black soldiers.

Once the decision to enlist Black troops was made, Douglass became a dedicated recruiter. Speaking to a group in Philadelphia in July 1863, Douglass declared,

> The hour has arrived, and your place is in the Union Army. Remember that the musket—the United States musket with its bayonet of steel—is better than all mere parchment guarantees of liberty. In your hands that musket means liberty.[14]

BLACKS' ACCEPTANCE FOR COMBAT

Blacks were specifically authorized to enlist for combat in the Union Army the day the Emancipation Proclamation went into effect, on January 1, 1863. When he issued this historic Proclamation, Lincoln included the clause, "And I further declare and make known, that such persons of suitable condition, will be received into the armed service of the United States to garrison forts, positions, stations, and other places, and to man vessels of all sorts in said service."[15] Federal law guaranteed that any slave who enlisted would be emancipated.

Shortly thereafter, Army Chief of Staff Henry Halleck wrote to General Grant, "So long as the rebels retain and employ their slaves in producing grains, etc. they can employ all the whites in the field. Every slave withdrawn from the enemy is equivalent to a [Confederate] white man put *hors de combat*."[16]

One need read only a sampling of Northern soldiers' comments to appreciate the resistance Lincoln faced. Merely cynical attitudes were reflected by saying, "a black man can stop a bullet as well as a white man," but others declared, "when Uncle Abraham gets his Niggers armed and in the field, he can get along without us." One soldier insisted, "God never intended a nigger to put white people down." Another opined, "I think a drove of hogs would do better brought down here, for we could eat them and the niggers we can't."[17] A soldier from the 74th New York Infantry wrote a letter to a newspaper, declaring, "We don't want to fight side by side with the nigger. We think we are too superior a race for that."[18]

In one of the war's most fortuitous developments, Secretary of War Edwin Stanton dispatched the Army's adjutant general, Major General Lorenzo Thomas, to the Mississippi River Valley to oversee and expedite the formation of colored troops in March 1863. This veteran officer took to his assignment as if it were a religious calling and made an essential contribution to the war effort. Thomas asked each division commander to organize at least two Black regiments, organized officer selection boards to lead them, and selected recruiting officers to fill the ranks. Through his efforts, 14 USCT regiments had been trained and another 24 were in the process of formation by August 1863. By war's end, Thomas had been instrumental in organizing 70 regiments, placing over 76,000 Black troops under arms, roughly 40 percent of all Black soldiers recruited, a monumental contribution.[19] In this, he had the full support of theater commander U. S. Grant, who told Thomas, "I am anxious to get as many

Major General Lorenzo Thomas. SOURCE: MATTHEW BRADY, LIBRARY OF CONGRESS, CIVIL WAR GLASS NEGATIVE COLLECTION.

of these negro regiments as possible and to have them full and completely equipped." The large windfall of Confederate weaponry captured with Vicksburg's capitulation on July 4, roughly 60,000 muskets and 172 cannons, helped make this possible.[20]

With Grant's support, recruitment accelerated. By October 1864, 101,950 Black troops were organized into 140 regiments, including six cavalry regiments.[21] One important and unique feature of USCT regiments was that wherever they were deployed, they encouraged slaves to abandon their owners, further diminishing the South's ability to grow crops and greatly increasing chaos and anxiety on the South's home front. Black regiments recruited wherever they were located, giving them a great advantage over white units, which could not easily replenish battlefield losses.

BUREAU OF COLORED TROOPS

The Bureau of Colored Troops established by War Department General Order 143, dated May 22, 1863, under the adjutant general's office, facilitated recruitment and administration of all Black soldiers fighting in the Union Army. The Bureau at one time administered a larger force than the field armies of either Generals Meade or Sherman in their successful campaigns of 1864 and 1865, and about equal to all Confederate troops in the field in the last year of the war. The number of soldiers the USCT who served ultimately came to about 209,000 soldiers, recruited from 23 Northern states and 13 Southern states.[22]

Congress mandated that white officers would lead USCT regiments, with a preference for soldiers with combat experience. Fortunately, most regimental commanders and senior officers were committed abolitionists dedicated to assisting Blacks to integrate into society. Some less motivated company grade officers accepted commissions to be promoted from the enlisted ranks, eyeing the increased pay and better lifestyle of commissioned officers. Ultimately, some 7,100 white officers led Black soldiers. Ninety percent of the officers selected to serve with Black troops had prior combat experience.[23] Overall, the competence of the officer and noncommissioned officer (NCO) cadre of most USCT units was superior to many white outfits because every officer selected had to pass a rigid selection process to qualify. To assist in individual officer candidates' training, a Free Military School for applicants for command of colored troops was established outside of Philadelphia in late 1863 to prepare white enlisted men to lead USCT units, a forerunner of today's Officer Candidate Schools.

Aside from appointing white officers to command USCT units, the Bureau administered records and pay. The latter became an immense source of dissatisfaction for colored troops. White privates earned $10 a month, plus $3 for clothing allowance, but *all* Black soldiers, regardless of rank (including chaplains, who received $100 monthly in white regiments) received $10, from which $3 was deducted for clothing. This meant that USCT soldiers received less pay than Black laborers, who received $10 per month but were not subject to the rigors of march or combat. Addressing this disparity, *The Chicago Times* thundered, "the chief disability of the black race lies in prejudice and not in law, . . . All that was required was to take down the barriers of false pride and caste, and the black soldier would stand shoulder to shoulder on the common ground of devotion to country."[24]

Some USCT regiments refused to accept the lower pay, but despite this blatant discrimination, USCT regiments' overall combat readiness generally was not affected. An NCO in a regiment of former South Carolina slaves who encouraged soldiers of his unit to resist until pay was equal was court-martialed and shot; several other Black soldiers were executed for protesting pay disparity. Congress did not redress this disparity until

1864 and did not totally erase the injustice until late 1865. There is little doubt that the pay double standard retarded Black enlistments because there was less economic incentive for Blacks to join the Army. Many were supporting families back home.

After a hodge-podge of designations, most Black units, except a few raised directly by Northern states, were designated USCT and differentiated by branch—USCI for infantry; USCC for cavalry; and USCLA or USCHA for artillery, light or heavy. Blacks served in all combat arms, including several engineer regiments and separate battalions, as well as quartermaster, commissary, and ordnance units. In less than two years, 175 Black regiments were raised at precisely the time recruiting efforts and sources of manpower dried up on both sides. *It is difficult to exaggerate the importance of USCT to the war's outcome.* Recruited and trained at a time when the Confederate States Army was forced to consolidate many of their regiments due to the horrendous losses both sides sustained, USCT were so effective that the Confederacy was eventually forced to accept Black soldiers in the last three weeks of the war. The South resorted to this drastic action even though it violated the Confederacy's reason for existence.

Raised from March 1863 to the end of the war, Black troops were a significant augmentation of Union soldiers to the field, providing approximately the same number of soldiers as the draft, but Blacks were far more dependable and determined fighters than draftees or those who signed on simply for bounties. Blacks comprised approximately 10 to 12 percent of Union troops under arms—troop levels constantly fluctuated as white units completed their terms of service and were mustered out.

Louisiana furnished 24,000 Black troops, Kentucky supplied 23,700, and Tennessee and Mississippi each raised about 20,000. The District of Columbia furnished a regiment, the 1st US Colored Infantry. Black volunteers from Canada, South America, the Caribbean, Africa, and Hawaii also enlisted.

Massachusetts' abolitionist governor John A. Andrew issued a call for Black troops in February 1863, and within a month, around 1,000 troops, many from out of state, three-quarters of whom were freemen and half of whom were literate, answered the call. The eager recruits were organized into the 54th and 55th Massachusetts Infantry Regiments (Colored). Both of Frederick Douglass's two sons enlisted—his son Lewis rose to the highest noncommissioned rank, regimental sergeant major of the

Sergeant Major Lewis Douglass.
SOURCE: LICENSED UNDER CREATIVE COMMONS.

54th Massachusetts Infantry Regiment (of the 1989 movie *Glory* fame). The 54th experienced two years of hard combat, including the storming of Fort Wagner, on the approaches to Charleston, South Carolina; Fort Fisher, North Carolina; and the ill-fated Battle of Olustee, Florida. Later, Governor Andrew raised a third regiment, the 5th Massachusetts Cavalry Regiment (Colored), commanded by Colonel Charles Quincy Adams, Jr., into which Douglass's son Charles transferred. Governor Andrew selected quality white officers and lobbied to ensure that the regiments were used in combat and not simply detailed to fatigue duties. He also offered to have the state of Massachusetts make up the difference in pay from that of white troops, but the soldiers declined the offer and went without pay for a year and a half rather than accept the discriminatory pay offered by the government.

Other Black regiments raised by states include the 29th and 30th Connecticut Infantry (the latter was consolidated into the 31st US

Colored Infantry Regiment in May 1864), 14th Rhode Island Heavy Artillery Regiment, and the 1st and 2nd Kansas Colored Infantry Regiments. The Kansas regiments were raised in late 1862 by Senator (later Brigadier General) Jim Lane, a Jayhawker who fought with John Brown in "bloody Kansas." Lane acted after the Militia Act of 1862, operating with considerable freedom in what was then the country's frontier.

The 1st Kansas Colored Regiment was the first Black unit engaged in combat, at Island Mound, Missouri, on October 27, 1862, when its troops were still recruits. They acquitted themselves well: despite being outnumbered, they were victorious.[25] The regiment proved that this was no fluke at Cabin Creek in Indian Territory (Oklahoma) on July 1, 1863, and again on July 17 that year at Honey Springs, standing toe to toe in the open exchanging volleys for 20 minutes and driving a regiment of Texans from the field, capturing their colors.[26] Major General James G. Blunt, commander of the Union Army of the Frontier, commented, "I never saw such fighting as was done by the negro regiment. They fought like veterans, with a coolness and valor that is unsurpassed. They preserved their line perfect throughout the whole engagement and, although in the hottest of the fight, they never once faltered." Blunt summed up their performance: "The question that negroes will fight is settled; besides, they make better soldiers in every respect than any troops I have ever had under my command." An Irish Democrat serving in the 3rd Wisconsin Cavalry was more succinct: "I never believed in niggers before, but by Jasus, they are hell for fighting."[27]

Louisiana was a special case since large numbers of prosperous Blacks, some of whose ancestors lived in the area before the United States acquired the Louisiana Purchase and who fought as "Free Men of Color" alongside Andrew Jackson during the War of 1812, had joined the Louisiana Native Guard militia before the war under authority of Louisiana's governor. Most were wealthy or highly skilled property-owning Creoles or Mulattoes. Native Guard units, officered by Blacks, offered to fight for the South but were abandoned when New Orleans was captured by the Union forces in April 1862. General Benjamin Butler initially rejected Black soldiers, but his deputy, Brigadier General John W. Phelps, another West Point abolitionist in the mold of General Hunter, reorganized the Louisiana Native Guard into the *Corps d'Afrique*. Although Butler ordered him to desist, he changed his mind three months later after the War Department declared that no other troops were available. By this time, Phelps had resigned his commission. Because of Phelps's groundwork, Louisiana ultimately furnished 22 infantry regiments, one cavalry regiment, five engineer regiments, one heavy artillery regiment, and two famous marching bands. Three regiments of Louisiana's *Corps d'Afrique* originally had Black officers, including the 2nd Regiment's Major Francis E. Dumas, a multilingual slave owner who enlisted around 100 of his own slaves.

Butler's successor, General Nathaniel Banks, eliminated all Black officers in accordance with the dictates of Congress and the prevailing prejudice of the era. Banks paternalistically argued, "with a race unaccustomed to military service, much depends on the immediate influence of officers upon individual members, then those with more warlike habits and spirit acquired by centuries of contest."[28] That comment, of course, reflected prejudice coupled with ignorance of history—not the first or last time the United States suffered from racially induced shortsightedness or amnesia. Banks pragmatically observed, "The Government makes use of mules, horses, uneducated and educated white men, in the defense of its institutions. Why should not the negro contribute whatever is in his power for the cause he is as deeply interested as other men? We may properly demand of him whatever service he can render."[29]

Fourteen regimental chaplains were Black and eight USCT regiments had Black surgeons—many white professionals refused to serve in colored units. The lack of qualified medical personnel resulted in a lesser level of medical care in Black regiments. A major exception regarding officers was the 33rd USCT Regiment, first organized in April 1863 in Beaufort, South Carolina, as the 1st South Carolina Infantry (African Descent), which included Major Martin R. Delany, a Black field grade officer who was both a physician and an educator affiliated with Douglass's *North Star* newspaper. Delany obtained his commission as major and surgeon directly from President Lincoln and Secretary of War Stanton. Delany was a prominent abolitionist and the "Father of Black Nationalism" after the war.

Under General Jim Lane, Kansas had an independent artillery battery with Black officers, and Massachusetts commissioned some of its outstanding NCOs toward the end of the war. Otherwise, US white officers led Colored Troop units.

From the start, Black troops and their white officers demonstrated great determination and ability to withstand the rigors of combat because if captured in battle, there was a good chance officers would be summarily executed or in the case of Blacks, both freemen and slave, reduced to slavery. This was the official policy of the Confederate States, as enunciated by the Confederate Congress's resolution of May 1, 1863.[30] Ample eyewitness accounts make it clear that Rebel troops killed substantial numbers of Blacks and their white Yankee officers after surrender and capture, although the policy was not consistently followed.

The Confederacy's "black flag" order had unintended consequences because in response, many Black units attacked under their own Black flag. One officer of the 2nd Kansas Colored Infantry declared the Confederate order was a "godsend" since "Every officer and every soldier knew that it meant the bayonet, with no quarter whenever and wherever they met the enemy." In a sort of boomerang effect, the Southern Congress's order made some Southern units dread retaliation, fearing assaults by Black regiments. Another officer with a Black regiment declared, "The officers of the colored regiments at this time had every incentive to do the utmost within their power to make the men good soldiers. Their own personal safety was dependent on the fighting qualities of their men, more than in white regiments."[31]

COMBAT PERFORMANCE

Two *Corps d'Afrique* regiments, the 1st and 3rd, fought with distinction during the siege of Port Hudson from May 22 to July 9, 1863, as part of General Banks's 19th Corps in the campaign to eliminate one of the South's last lifelines to the west of the Mississippi River. The two Black regiments made multiple assaults, suffering nearly 200 casualties, roughly 20 percent of their strength. The Southern commander of the fort refused to extend a truce to recover and bury the dead in the Black regiments' sector, leaving their corpses decomposing in the sun for six weeks until the Confederate garrison capitulated five days after the fall of Vicksburg.

After seeing Black soldiers attack rebel defenses at Port Hudson, a white lieutenant serving in the 3rd Louisiana Native Guards admitted that he had "entertained some fears as to their pluck. But I have none now."[32] Another white officer who observed them in action wrote, "You have no idea how my prejudices . . . have been dispelled by the battle. . . . [Blacks] are far superior in discipline to the white troops and just as brave."[33] One Massachusetts soldier remarked, "A nation of serfs stepped up to the respect of the world and commenced a national existence.[34] *The New York Times* reported, "It is no longer possible to doubt the bravery and steadfastness of the colored race."[35]

Colonel Benjamin Grierson, after leading his cavalry brigade in a brilliant 17-day raid from southern Tennessee across the length of Mississippi to Baton Rouge, Louisiana, wrote to his wife, "the negro regiments fought bravely today. . . . there can be no question about the good fighting qualities of negroes hereafter—that question was settled beyond a doubt yesterday."[36] General Banks, who eliminated the Black officers in the *Corps d'Afrique*, noted in his report to Chief of Staff General Henry W. Halleck, "The severe test to which they were subjected, and the determined manner in which they encountered the enemy, leaves upon my mind no doubt of their ultimate success."[37] Grant informed Chief of Staff Henry Halleck that Black troops' discipline was superior to white troops', reporting that he had no doubt they "will prove equally good for garrison duty. All that have been tried have fought bravely."[38] Colored Troop regiments participated in the siege of Vicksburg under Grant's command, and after they had proven their valor, he transferred several USCT regiments east when he was promoted to commander in chief.

In August 1863, Lincoln wrote to General Grant that Black recruitment was "a resource, which if applied now, will soon close the contest. It works doubly, weakening the enemy and strengthening us." Grant replied:

> I have given the subject of arming the negro my hearty support. This, with the emancipation of the negro, is the heaviest blow yet to the Confederacy. By arming the negro, we have added a powerful ally. They will make good soldiers and by taking them from the enemy weakens him in the same proportion they strengthen us. I am therefore most decidedly in favor of pushing this policy to the enlistment of a force sufficient to hold all of the South falling into our hands and to aid in capturing more.[39]

Ten days after Port Hudson, Black troops distinguished themselves again at Milliken's Bend, a large Union logistics and hospital base just above Vicksburg garrisoned by about a thousand men, two understrength white companies and a Black brigade of four understrength Black regiments still being trained, equipped with antiquated Belgian muskets. Only one gunboat was initially available to provide fire support. About 1,500 Confederates from two Texas cavalry brigades attacked the outpost, but despite their rudimentary training and inferior weaponry, the garrison held out and forced the Confederates to withdraw after a vigorous bayonet counterattack. The South lost 44 killed and 131 wounded, testifying to Union resistance, although Union losses were much higher. Rear Admiral David Porter, who landed within hours after the battle ended, noted, "dead negroes lined the ditch inside of the parapet, or levee, and most were shot on the top of the head."[40] Thirty-five percent of the Black troops were killed or wounded. The 9th Louisiana Infantry (African Descent), later redesignated the 5th US Colored Heavy Artillery, suffered a 45 percent casualty rate, nearly 17 percent higher than the next higher loss suffered by a Union regiment in a single engagement, the 1st Minnesota Infantry Regiment at Gettysburg, Pennsylvania.[41]

Newspaperman Charles A. Dana, assistant secretary of war and Stanton's emissary and observer at Grant's headquarters, wrote, "The sentiment in regard to the employment of negroes has been revolutionized by the bravery of the Blacks in the recent battle of Milliken's Bend. Prominent officers, who used in private to sneer at the idea, are now heartily in favor of it."[42] Even Confederates were amazed: General Henry McCullough wrote, "This charge was resisted by the negro portion of the enemy's force with considerable obstinacy. . . . the white or pure Yankee portion ran like whipped curs almost as soon as the charge was made."[43] A Southern diarist, Kate Stone, wrote in her journal, "It is hard to believe that Southern soldiers, Texans at that, have been whipped by a mongrel crew of white and black Yankees."[44]

These actions were far removed from the Eastern power center. The event that most changed attitudes regarding Black soldiers' fighting abilities was the assault on Fort Wagner, on the outskirts of Charleston, South Carolina, on July 18, 1863, less than two weeks after Gettysburg and the fall of Vicksburg. The commander of the 54th Massachusetts Regiment, Colonel Robert Gould Shaw, volunteered the regiment's participation in the assault against the well-engineered position, which was occupied by far more defenders than anticipated. According to a *New York Herald* correspondent, division commander Brigadier Truman Seymour agreed out of bias, telling overall commander Major General Quincy Adams Gilmore, "Well, we will . . . put those damned niggers from Massachusetts in the advance; we may as well get rid of them one time as another." In his after-action report, Seymour wrote that he had selected the regiment because it was "one of the strongest and best officered."[45]

Colonel Robert Gould Shaw.
Source: Boston Athenaeum, Whipple Studio.

Despite ferocious artillery bombardment, Sergeant Major Douglass reported, "Not a man flinched. A shell would explode and clear a space of twenty feet, and our men would close up again." As Shaw and his troops charged the center, defenders blazed away from three directions. Nonetheless, Shaw and a considerable force mounted the parapet, although they were unable to overwhelm the defenders. The regiment suffered more than 40 percent casualties, and for a time, a junior captain commanded the remnant. Confederate defender Lieutenant Iredell Jones remarked, "The negroes fought gallantly, and were headed by as brave a colonel as ever lived." The *New York Tribune* proclaimed that the 54th Massachusetts' performance "made Fort Wagner such a name for the colored race as Bunker Hill has been for ninety years for the white Yankees."

Although General Gilmore attempted to have Colonel Shaw's corpse returned, a normal courtesy, the Confederates stripped his body and threw it into a mass grave with 20 of his troops. Shaw's father declared, "We hold that a soldier's most appropriate burial place is on the field where he has fallen."[46] The 54th Massachusetts's heroic effort was not the first assault, nor was it the last. All told, the Union suffered casualties exceeding 1,500 men, leading Harriett Tubman to write, "And then we saw the lightning, and that was the guns. And then we heard the rain falling, and that was the drops of blood falling; and when we came to get in the crops, it was dead men we reaped." A special effort was made to retrieve wounded Blacks out of concern for possible Southern atrocities.

That failed assault heightened the commitment of surviving troops. Two weeks later, a Black sergeant wrote to his company commander, "I still feel more Eager for the struggle than I ever yet have, for I now wish to have revenge for our gallant Curnel and the spilt blood of our Captin. We expect to Plant the Stars and Stripes on the Sity of Charleston,"[47] (original spelling), which happened two years later. Sgt. William Carney was the first African American to earn the Medal of Honor, securing the regimental banner despite being shot several times. On returning to his comrades, he assured them, the old flag never touched the ground!" These three initial combat experiences, Port Hudson, Milliken's Bend, and Fort Wagner, challenged racial stereotypes as never before, changing the minds of many Union commanders, officers, and soldiers, as well as the public at large.

The Confederate Congress's directive most likely influenced the most notorious Southern atrocity of the war, at Fort Pillow, about 40 miles north of Memphis, Tennessee, which took place on April 12, 1864. A force of about 1,500 cavalrymen under Major General Nathan Bedford

54th Massachusetts Infantry Regiment assault on Fort Wagner. SOURCE: LITHOGRAPH BY KURZ AND ALLISON, 1890.

Forrest attacked a garrison of about 550 Union troops, a little over half of whom were soldiers from the 11th US Colored Infantry Regiment. Forrest had offered $1,000 for the head of "a commander of a nigger regiment" after an action in March, when a small Union force defeated his troopers at Fort Anderson, Kentucky.[48] Two-thirds of the Black soldiers at Fort Pillow were killed, compared to 36 percent of white troops of the 13th Tennessee Cavalry (US), considered "Tennessee Tories" by Forrest.[49] Forrest and Confederate authorities denied that Southern troops committed atrocities, but a Congressional committee found that the rebel troops butchered Blacks after they surrendered, burning some alive. In his after-action report, Forrest reported that "upward of 500" of the garrison had been killed and the Mississippi was "dyed with the blood of the slaughtered for 200 yards."[50] He expressed the hope that "these facts will demonstrate to the Northern people that negro soldiers cannot cope with Southerners," a boastful comment tending to support Congress's findings.

After a Union raid on Saltville, in southwestern Virginia, in September 1864, Confederate forces killed both Black and white soldiers, at least seven of whom were patients in hospital beds, according to Union surgeons left behind to care for the wounded. Like General Forrest, many Confederates in Kentucky and Tennessee considered Southerners with Union sympathies "Tories" and gave them no quarter.[51] During the engagement, the 5th Colored Cavalry displayed such dash in their first combat experience that they impressed the troopers of the 13th Kentucky Cavalry (US), who previously had demonstrated open hatred toward Black soldiers. A captain of the Kentucky regiment declared that his men "never saw men fight like them. The rebels were firing on them with grape and canister and were mowing them down by the scores, but others kept straight on."[52] The commander of the 5th Cavalry, Colonel James S. Brisbin, reported that out of the regiment's 400 soldiers on the battlefield, 118 had been killed or wounded. He observed, "I have seen white troops fight in twenty-seven battles, and I never saw any fight better" than his troops. He noted, "On the return of the forces those who had scoffed at the colored troops on the march out were silent."[53]

ASSESSMENT
Although Black units were initially used for garrison, guard, convoy, and labor duties, colored troops began to be used in combat more frequently when many white units completed their terms of service in 1864, coupled

with horrendous battlefield losses that spring. Provided the opportunity they wanted, Black soldiers distinguished themselves. By war's end, Blacks had fought with distinction at Brice's Crossroads, Deep Bottom, Honey Springs, Franklin, Nashville, Petersburg, New Market Heights, Jenkins Ferry, and numerous smaller engagements. Grant and Lorenzo Thomas directed the transfer of USCT regiments east, so that 33 Black regiments participated in the siege of the Army of Northern Virginia at Petersburg, where African Americans were up about one in eight of Union soldiers. After two Black brigades successfully assaulted Overton Hill during the Battle of Nashville, General George Thomas, the "Rock of Chickamauga" and "Hammer of Nashville," remarked, "Gentlemen, the question is settled; the Blacks will fight."[54] Major General O. M. Mitchel, operating in northern Alabama against Confederate cavalry, testified, "The Negroes are our only friends and in two instances I owe my life to their faithfulness."[55] Colonel Thomas Wentworth Higginson, in his reminiscence of wartime experience in his classic memoire, *Army Life in a Black Regiment*, observed, "There were more than a hundred men in the ranks who had voluntarily met more dangers in their escape from slavery than any of my young captains had incurred in all their lives."[56] Major General David Hunter, commander of the Department of the South, reported to Secretary of War Stanton that Black troops were "hardy, generous, temperate, strictly obedient, possessing remarkable aptitude for military training, and deeply imbued with that religious sentiment (call it fanaticism . . .) which made soldiers of Cromwell invincible."[57]

The newly formed 25th Corps under Major General Geoffrey Weitzel, all USCT, were present at Appomattox, helping block the remnants of Lee's army, and were the first to enter Richmond, which the retreating Confederates had set aflame when they destroyed ammunition dumps and other military supplies. They efficiently extinguished the fires and established good order and discipline. On February 20, 1865, Weitzel had foretold that they were changing the way that Americans viewed Blacks. "Let history record that on the banks of the James River, 30,000 freemen not only gained their own liberty, but shattered the prejudice of the world, and gave to the land of their birth peace, union and glory." At least half of his observation was subsequently borne out.

Colonel Thomas Morgan, commander of the 14th US Colored Infantry, provided an equally emphatic if less succinct assessment of Black soldiers' performance after the Battle of Nashville:

> Colored soldiers had fought side by side with white troops. They had mingled together in the charge. They had supported each other. They had assisted each other from the field when wounded, and they lay side by side in death. The survivors rejoiced together over a hard-fought field, won by common valor. All who witnessed their conduct gave them equal praise. The day we longed to see had come and gone, and the sun went down upon a record of coolness, bravery, manliness, never to be unmade. A new chapter in the history of liberty had been written. It had been shown that marching under the flag of freedom, animated by a love of liberty, even the slave becomes a man and a hero.[58]

Overall, USCT's record shows that Blacks made excellent soldiers—18 Black soldiers earned the Congressional Medal of Honor, and eight Black sailors also earned the nation's highest award. In addition, 13 white officers serving with Black units won the award. William Harvey Carney, who rescued the 54th Massachusetts' regimental colors at Fort Wagner, was the first Black to perform an action deserving of the award, although his medal was not presented until 1900. This was common for Medals of Honor awarded during the Civil War.[59]

Black soldiers deserted at significantly lower rate than whites—4 percent for Blacks, compared to 15 percent for whites. The camps of Black soldiers were neater, and Blacks' precision in close order drill was exceptional. Most Blacks saw military service as a great opportunity. When white officers and chaplains opened literacy schools to educate them, the troops were serious and attentive. Many regimental commanders and chaplains organized schools for sergeants and corporals, who in turn shared their knowledge with the privates under their supervision. About half attained literacy before they left the service. Education had an impact on soldiers' character and behavior, instilling new confidence and expanding capabilities and horizons. This was particularly true for the roughly 16 percent of Black troops who were NCOs.

Through their bravery, discipline, and fortitude, African American soldiers made a crucial contribution to ending the war, liberating their race, and preserving the Union. This was confirmed by numerous Confederates who contributed unbiased evaluations of USCTs' effectiveness.

General Howell Cobb of Georgia reminded Secretary of War James Seddon in late September 1864 that Black soldiers had done "some very good fighting for the Yanks."[58] General Francis A. Shoup informed a Confederate senator in January 1865: "The enemy has taught us a lesson on which we ought not to shut our eyes. Lincoln induced Blacks 'to fight as well, if not better than have his white troops of the same length of service.'"[60] The Macon, Georgia, *Telegraph and Confederate* agreed: the Black Union soldier "fights willingly and fiendishly for his own freedom." The paper also published the acknowledgment of one "distinguished Tennessean" that USCT had "weakened the Confederacy very much and added manifestly to the strength of their army." The Lynchburg, Virginia, *Virginian* observed that engagements around Petersburg and Saltville, "where negro soldiers were in the van and suffered most, show that they can be disciplined to take the post of danger and fight."[61] Indeed, the Confederacy's belated attempt to recruit, arm, and train their own African American soldiers testifies to USCT effectiveness on the field of battle, as well as the equally critical role of securing lines of communication and supply facilities.

UNITED STATES NAVY

On September 25, 1861, Secretary of the Navy Gideon Welles authorized Blacks to serve in the Navy. According to a US Navy film, "African-Americans in the United States Navy - A Short History," as many as 100,000 Blacks served aboard Union Navy ships during the four years of the North's blockade of 3,500 miles of Atlantic and Gulf coastline, including 12 major ports. They enabled a near stranglehold on Confederate commerce at sea. However, Black sailors could advance no higher than "boy" and were paid $10 per month. Blacks served on gun crews, stood watch, piloted in inland waterways, and navigated aboard integrated ships, although overall, the racial attitudes of the Navy's white officers and men were probably not more liberal than the overall population. In June 1861, **William Tillman**, a Black steward and cook aboard the schooner *S.J. Waring*, singlehandedly regained control of his ship after a Confederate privateer captured it. **Robert Smalls**, a slave living near Charleston, South Carolina, seized control of the *Planter* and piloted it out of Charleston Harbor, instantly becoming a national hero. Smalls subsequently captained the ship as part of the Union blockade and served as a member of Congress after the war.

Crew of USS Miami. SOURCE: LIBRARY OF CONGRESS, NH 55510.

When Union ships sailed through coastal Georgia and the Carolinas, the number of escaped slaves they picked up defied expectations. According to historian Michael J. Bennett:

> [W]hat happened when slaves called at the railings of blockade vessels and river gunboats amazed officers and sailors alike. Union sailors looking into the faces of people they resented on sight—given their racial dispositions—did not turn them away or stage ragged protests. Instead, they helped them aboard. . . . They could have made the contraband journeys to ships difficult or nearly impossible. . . . They did not. Instead, white tars helped these fugitives aboard night after night, often at the risk of their own lives.[62]

LABOR FORCES

In addition to combat troops and sailors, up to 300,000 Blacks served the Union as cooks, officers' orderlies or servants, laborers, teamsters, carpenters, nurses, laundresses, scouts, and spies. Others were blacksmiths and leatherworkers who made harnesses, reins, saddles, and saddlebags. Blacks mined coal, salt, and saltpeter, as well as a range of minerals, including iron, gold, and lead. Others made bricks and engaged in a variety of construction roles. They served as crew members on numerous commercial ships, while others loaded or unloaded cargo.

Collectively, their efforts made a crucial contribution to the outcome of the war. Large numbers of African Americans were also employed by quartermaster, commissary, and ordnance departments at innumerable locations. Without Black laborers, the vast stores of matériel needed by the Union armies could not have been delivered to troops in the field. This pattern of widespread use of African Americans in support functions was repeated in subsequent wars.

CASUALTIES

Southern adherence to the Confederate government's official policy regarding Black prisoners is reflected in the comparatively low number of prisoners in the right-hand column of the casualty chart. Southern policy changed about a year after Black units entered combat, when Lieutenant General Grant stopped prisoner exchange because the South would not include Blacks. The exchanges were restored in early 1865 because the Confederacy was strapped for trained and combat-ready manpower.[63]

U.S. Colored Troops Service-Connected Deaths

	Non-Prisoners		Prisoners	
	Officers	Enlisted	Officers	Enlisted
Killed in action	100	1,615		
Died of wounds	4	1,102		34
Died of disease	137	29,521	1	97
Accidental deaths	14	266		1
Drowned	6	288		1
Murdered	8	98		
Killed after capture			4	21
Committed suicide	2	11		
Executed by military		52		
Executed by CSA			1	
Died from sunstroke		32		
Other causes	7	3,254	1	130
TOTAL	**317**	**36,239**	**7**	**284**

Source: Frederick H. Dyer, *A Compendium of the War of the Rebellion*.

Many of the imprisoned USCT were captured at the battle of Olustee, Florida, an ill-planned expedition to liberate slaves and obtain USCT recruits. With poor leadership and disregard of intelligence, a force of 5,500 Federals, which included seven Black regiments, one with no combat experience, was ambushed and mauled by approximately 5,000 Confederate troops in February 1864. Union Brigadier General John P. Hatch observed,

> Soon after the Battle of Olustee a list of wounded and prisoners in the hands of the enemy was forwarded to our lines by the commander of the Rebel army. The small number of colored prisoners attracted immediate attention, as it was well known that the number left wounded on the field was large. It is now known that most of the wounded colored men were murdered on the field.[64]

The lieutenant colonel of the 2nd Florida Cavalry announced that no prisoners would be taken prior to the engagement, so the 103 Black troops imprisoned at Andersonville were fortunate, although they were forced to serve as grave diggers. Food was scarce and medical care marginal, and many Union prisoners died in captivity. Life in Southern captivity was a miserable experience, causing many fatalities and disabilities that endured for the rest of many soldiers' lives. Prison life was not much better in the North, but toward the war's end, the Confederacy was hard-pressed to feed even its own troops.

One would think that the Union's success in fielding some 175 regiments, about 209,000 men, and deploying them in every theater, not to mention securing the border with Mexico with the 25th Corps after the war ended, would create a deep sense of gratitude for the freemen and newly freed slaves who risked their lives to suppress the rebellion. Nothing of the sort happened. The spirit of national reconciliation of the late 19th and early 20th centuries produced an amnesia so pervasive that *Meet General Grant*, a popular biography written in 1928 by W. E. Woodward, a Southerner born in 1874, contained the unchallenged observation:

> American negroes are the only people in the history of the world, so far as I know, that ever became free without any effort on their part. The Civil War was not their business. . . . They twanged banjos around railroad sta-

tions, sang melodious spirituals, and believed that some Yankee would soon come along and give each of them forty acres and a mule.[65]

Woodward was a popular author who published numerous "debunking" histories and biographies of America's founding leaders. *Meet General Grant* was so popular that it went through 43 editions until 1965. It would be difficult to surpass this egregious example of racism, spite, ingratitude, obtuseness, and amnesia. Unfortunately, these traits were extremely widespread.

CONCLUSIONS

The Union's overwhelming success in arming and training a massive force of highly motivated freemen and slaves dramatically hastened the end of four bitter years of fratricide—coupled, of course, with General Grant's strategic generalship and Northern industrial might. The Union's decision to arm Blacks was motivated by the fact that sources of manpower had dried up for both sides. The South was not alone in their fear of "servile insurrection," and most Americans believed that African Americans were an inferior race.

Black soldiers made an enormous impact on Union offensive operations and just as critically provided rear echelon security for installations spread over an ever-growing distance. In addition, African American labor and auxiliary forces made an essential contribution to the Northern war effort.

White prejudice and Southern revisionism after the Civil War embodied in the "Lost Cause" narrative essentially erased the considerable military contributions and exploits of Blacks, not just during the Civil War, but also the Revolutionary War and the War of 1812. Later, this would be expanded to cover the Indian Wars, the Spanish–American War, and operations in the Philippines. The harm this unwarranted bigotry did to American military strength is impossible to calculate.

CHAPTER 3

Black Soldiers in Gray and Butternut

[Our] wives and daughters and the negroes are
the only elements left for us to recruit from.

Major Thomas P. Turner
Richmond Recruiting Officer, March 1865

Arming and training Blacks negated the very reason for the South's secession—perpetuation of slavery. Furthermore, most Southerners considered Blacks inferior and incapable of being good soldiers. They also continued to fear "servile insurrection," even over survival of their incipient nation. US Colored Troops' success forced the South to reconsider because the Black soldiers in blue provided convincing evidence to the contrary and had helped put the South on the ropes.

After vociferous, extended debate, the Confederacy finally decided to enlist Blacks, the source of its wealth, three weeks before Appomattox, too late.

Neo-Confederates began to spin tales of Black soldiers fighting for the Confederacy in the 1970s to bolster Lost Cause mythology. However, the American Battlefield Trust notes that the Official Records of the War of the Rebellion, a collection of records from both sides in over 128 volumes compiled by the War Department from 1880 to 1901, mentions Black Confederate soldiers exactly seven times. Three record individual

Black men shooting at Union soldiers, one mentions capturing a handful of armed Black men, and the other three reports describe unarmed Black laborers. None of this documentation mentions an instance of Union forces encountering an organized Black Confederate battle line.[1] This is not surprising because in the main, race consciousness was high in the Confederate Army. Soldiers accused of being "mulattoes" had to prove their pure blood or be expelled from the ranks.

Flights of fancy regarding the South's use of Black troops took place even in the immediate aftermath of the South's surrender. J. D. B. De Bow, one of the most prominent journalists of the antebellum South, wrote in his *Review* in 1867, that had the war lasted longer, "three or four hundred thousand" Black troops might have been "thrown into the field," changing "the whole aspect of affairs."

Both sides used large numbers of Blacks to build fortifications and in a variety of support functions (teamsters, blacksmiths, hospital orderlies, manservants, etc.) From the outset, several individual Southern states began raising large numbers of Blacks in labor units, particularly Tennessee, where the legislature authorized the governor to enlist all free Negroes between 15 and 50 years of age. In March 1863, the Confederate Congress enacted an Impressment Act, which increased the already extensive use of slaves in a wide variety of support activities.

The Confederacy's attitude relative to arming slaves and freemen went through a series of fascinating twists and turns as hostilities progressed. Immediately after the first battle at Bull Run, General Richard Ewell, then a division commander and later a lieutenant general who commanded Stonewall Jackson's 2nd Corps, suggested to President Jefferson Davis the necessity of arming slaves to ensure Southern independence. Davis considered the proposal "stark madness that would revolt and disgust the whole South." Davis declared the proposal preposterous and asked who would command a brigade of Negroes. Ewell declared his willingness to do just that.[2]

From the start, General Lee acknowledged that the South's slave population was the chief source of information for Union commanders, an awareness all Southern commanders shared that slaves who abandoned their plantations were their enemy's best sources of information. Slaves and the few free Blacks in the South also assisted escaped Union prisoners and served as guides and scouts for Union forces. Lee initially had doubts that they could be trusted to bear arms in support of the Confederacy, but as the South's chances of obtaining independence dwindled, his opinion began to evolve.

Ten days after the Emancipation Proclamation, General Lee wrote a letter to Secretary of War James Seddon: "In view of the vast increase of the forces of the enemy, of the savage and brutal policy he has proclaimed, which leaves us no alternative but success or degradation worse than death, if we would save the honor of our families from pollution, our social system from destruction, let every means be employed, to fill and maintain the ranks of our armies."[3]

On March 11, 1864, the Confederate Congress passed "An Act to Increase the Efficiency of the Army by Employing Free Negroes and Slaves in Certain Capacities" authorizing the Bureau of Conscription to draft up to 20,000 male slaves to work on fortifications for $11 per month,

Lieutenant General Robert E. Lee. Bettmann Archive, Lee in new uniform shortly before he met Grant at Appomattox, 1865.

something individual states had been doing from the start.[4] The act directed that slaves were not to be drafted if enough free Blacks were available. Richmond's newspapers urged owners to free slaves for national defense to make sure that the Confederate government's policy could not be mistaken for abolition. The Confederate government believed that with the enrollment of slaves in large numbers, white deserters would "gladly" return to their units.[5] Virginia's governor, a former Confederate general, William "Extra Billy" Smith, noted that the issue was a "grave and important question full of difficulty." He acknowledged that Blacks represented the best means to defeat the Yankee army, noting, "the Yankees themselves boast that they have 200,000 of our slaves in arms against us."[6]

Southern attitudes changed drastically in mid-July 1863, after the resounding defeat at Gettysburg and the fall of Vicksburg a day later. In December 1863, Major General Thomas Hindman, an Alabama lawyer and commander of the Army of Tennessee's 2nd Corps, penned an anonymous letter printed in the Memphis, Tennessee, *Appeal* suggesting that slaves be organized into military units.[7] Predictably, nothing happened. But on January 2, 1864, Hindman's law partner, Major General Patrick Cleburne, an Irish immigrant who was one of the South's best division commanders, the "Stonewall of the West," presented a well thought out proposal endorsed by 13 subordinate officers at an Army of Tennessee staff meeting attended by General Joseph Johnston and his corps and division commanders. Describing the Confederacy's dire situation, Cleburne pointed out that the war to preserve slavery had effectively been lost by defeats at Gettysburg and Vicksburg in July 1863. Although Confederate President Jefferson Davis claimed to have plans to salvage victory, Cleburne dismissed this as a political smokescreen, observing, "We . . . see in the recommendations of the President only a temporary expedient, which at the best will leave us twelve months hence in the same predicament we are in now." He continued:

> Our single source of supply is that portion of our white men fit for duty and not now in the ranks. The enemy has three sources of supply: First, his own . . . population; secondly, our slaves; and thirdly, Europeans [immigrants] whose hearts are fired into a crusade against us by fictitious pictures of the atrocities of slavery, and who meet

no hindrance from their Governments in such enterprise, because these Governments are equally antagonistic to the institution.[8]

Cleburne continued, noting that slavery had originally been a major source of strength for the South, but the institution had devolved into "one of our chief sources of weakness." Moreover, slavery was also a major obstacle hindering recognition by Great Britain and France. The South's slave population was now being exploited by the North, which was rapidly arming and training a large body of Black troops. In his long and insightful proposal, Cleburne observed that arming slaves "would instantly remove all the vulnerability, embarrassment, and inherent weakness which result from slavery." Citing the experience of slaves who revolted in Haiti and defeated three empires' efforts to suppress them, the Jamaican slave revolts, as well as the effectiveness of US Colored Troops in the field in 1863, Cleburne continued:

Major General Patrick Cleburne. SOURCE: LIBRARY OF CONGRESS.

> The approach of the enemy would no longer find every household surrounded by spies. . . . There would be no recruits awaiting the enemy with open arms, no complete history of every neighborhood with ready guides, no fear of insurrection in the rear, or anxieties for the fate of loved ones when our armies moved forward. . . . It would remove forever all selfish taint from our cause and place independence above every question of property.

On the other hand, if slavery ended with Union victory, Southern whites would face "the hatred of our former slaves," who would ally themselves with the Unionists, and after the war they would "be our secret police."

Every officer present at the staff meeting, except his friend Hindman and General Johnston, who remained silent, roundly condemned the proposal. Fellow division commanders William H. T. Walker, James Patton Anderson, and Alexander P. Stewart declared that Cleburne's proposal was "incendiary," "monstrous," and "revolting to Southern sentiment, Southern pride, and Southern honor."[9] Walker went outside of the chain of command and forwarded a copy of the proposal directly to Jefferson Davis.

In the end, nothing came of Cleburne's recommendation because President Davis ordered the suppression of Cleburne's proposal, not surprising since Cleburne's proposal included a very radical sentence that suggested that the South "grant freedom within a reasonable time to every slave in the South who shall remain true to the Confederacy." Cleburne went even further and recommended that legal protection be immediately extended to slave families as well. Braxton Bragg, then serving as military advisor to Jefferson Davis, labeled the suggestion "treasonous"—Cleburne had been one of his subordinates who suggested to Davis that he be removed from command of the Army of Tennessee.[10]

Cleburne's proposal became a dead issue when Cleburne was killed in the disastrous battle of Franklin the last day of November 1864, during which Hood's Army of Tennessee lost 7,000 men, including 12 generals and half of its regimental commanders. The Army of Tennessee was decimated again two weeks later in a two-day battle launched by General George Thomas from Nashville when the Army of Tennessee lost all semblance of organization and another half of its strength. Hood's mostly barefoot remnant retreated in disorder to Tupelo, Mississippi.

Admiral Farragut's capture of Mobile Bay in August eliminated the last major Southern port, leaving only Wilmington, North Carolina, which was captured in January 1865, when a force of Army, sailors, and Marines under General Alfred E. Terry stormed Ft. Fisher, bringing most of coastal North Carolina under Yankee control. On October 19, 1864, the Army of Northern Virginia's 2nd Corps, which Lee dispatched under Jubal Early to the Shenandoah Valley in June to divert troops from Petersburg, suffered its third and final disastrous defeat in two months at the hands of three Union corps led by Phil Sheridan at Cedar Creek. Early's remnant, some 1,400 troops, was captured by Sheridan's cavalry corps under Wesley Merritt in the Upper Valley at Lynchburg in March 1865, eliminating the Shenandoah Valley "breadbasket" from supplying the South.

On October 6, 1864, the Richmond *Enquirer* urged that the Confederate government use another 10,000 Blacks for military duties and reassured readers that Virginia would "fight her Blacks to the last man." The paper also recommended that the Bureau of Conscription purchase 250,000 slaves for a "biracial army."[11] The conservative *Daily Examiner* strenuously objected on November 8, opposing both enrollment of slaves and the freeing of slave military laborers after the war. The paper noted, "While living with the white man in the relation of a slave, he is in a state superior and better for him than that of freedom,"[12] a conventional Southern position. The Charleston *Mercury* warned that should the South resort to arming and then freeing African Americans, poor whites would be "reduced to the level of a nigger, and a nigger is raised to his level. Cheek by jowl they must labor together as equals."

Lincoln's reelection in November 1864 destroyed all hope of foreign intervention and a negotiated peace. Yet another shocking blow came when General Sherman captured Savannah, Georgia, on December 22, destroying much of the South's remaining breadbasket and marching through the Carolinas. This string of disasters caused a deep sense of gloom; some Confederate congressmen suggested that Davis step down as president and that Lee replace him as dictator. Instead, Lee was appointed general in chief, and Secretary of War Seddon resigned from his post, replaced by General John C. Breckenridge. The situation had become so drastic that governors of six Confederate states—Alabama, Georgia, Mississippi, North and South Carolina, and Virginia—met in Georgia and passed a resolution advocating "changes in policy" and "increased military use of slaves."[13]

President Jefferson Davis. SOURCE: MATTHEW B. BRADY, 1861, LIBRARY OF CONGRESS.

In his last annual address to the Confederate Congress, Davis rejected the prospect of arming slaves, leaving the loophole that if the choice came down to arming slaves and defeat, "there seems to be no reason to doubt what would be our decision."[14] He noted that if the South were defeated, it would be due to its adherence to "outmoded theories of black inferiority," and the Confederacy's tombstone would read, "Died of a theory."[15]

The dismal series of Confederate setbacks finally converted Lee in the fall of 1864. On January 11, 1865, Lee responded to a letter from influential Virginia Senator and former Secretary of State Robert T. Hunter, conceding that notwithstanding his preference for white troops, Black soldiers would have to do:

> We must decide whether slavery shall be extinguished by our enemies and the slaves be used against us, or use them ourselves at the risk of effects that which may be produced upon our social institutions. My own opinion is that we should employ them without delay. I believe

that with proper regulations they can be made efficient soldiers. They possess the physical qualifications in an eminent degree. Long habits of obedience and subordination, coupled with the moral influence which in our country the white man possesses over the black, furnish an excellent foundation for that discipline which is the best guarantee of military efficiency. Our chief aim should be to secure their fidelity.[16]

Lee pointed out that enrolling Black troops would "disappoint the hopes which our enemies place on our exhaustion, deprive the North in great measure of the aid they now derive from black troops, and throw the burden of war on citizens of the North," many of whom were tired of the lengthy war. Lee also believed that adoption of a system of emancipation would "exercise a salutary influence upon our whole negro population, by rendering more secure the fidelity of those who become soldiers, and diminishing the inducements to the rest to abscond." But he still "deprecated" any "sudden change or disturbance of that relation (between master and slave) unless it be necessary to avert a greater calamity." He rationalized, "if it ends in subverting slavery, it will be accomplished by ourselves, and we can devise the means of alleviating the evil consequences to both races." Despite his reluctance to arm slaves and unwillingness to end or moderate slavery, Lee now recommended immediately adopting such a drastic measure even at risk of the South's "peculiar institution." He reminded Hunter that the Federal armies' greatest success came after Lincoln's decision to arm "280,000 black soldiers," many of whom came from Virginia.[17]

Lee also wrote a letter to Jefferson Davis imploring the government to hesitate no longer: "The services of these men (Blacks) are now necessary to enable us to oppose the enemy."[18] Lee's views were decisive. Richmond War Department clerk Robert Kean, who had opposed arming slaves the year before, noted in his diary on New Year's Day 1865 that the Confederates would now "rather accept general emancipation of Blacks than General Grant."[19]

As 1865 began, it was quite evident to informed and objective observers that the South's last days were fast approaching unless drastic measures were embraced. The British bluntly refused to recognize the Confederacy because the North was close to victory and had an extremely large and well-trained army close to Canada.[20] The head of the War Bureau lamented, "things are getting worse very rapidly. . . . Ten days ago the last meat ration was issued to (Lee's army) and not a pound remained in Richmond. . . . we are prostrated in all our resources."[21] The chief of ordnance, General Josiah Gorgas, asked in January, "Where is this to end? No money in the treasury—no food to feed Gen. Lee's army—no troops to oppose Sherman."[22] In early February, Grant obtained a poster indicating that Lee was reduced to begging local farmers to "sell or loan as much Corn Meal & Molasses as they Can spare [sic]."[23]

Confederate soldiers began to desert en masse as hopelessness soared due to lack of food, clothing, and ammunition and grossly understrength units, many lacking officers. By the time the war ended, more than 100,000 Confederate soldiers had deserted, most of them nonslaveholding yeoman farmers indispensable for the support of their families and gravely concerned about their wives' and children's welfare.[24] In what historian Ron Chernow described as a "slow-motion unraveling," the once-proud Army of Northern Virginia was thinned out by massive desertions at Petersburg equaling roughly a regiment per day.[25] Lee's Army lost 8 percent of its strength in January and a like percentage in February, making Lee's defensive line progressively more tenuous.[26] Ervin Jordon Jr. has estimated that Lee lost a third of his army to casualties or desertion in eight months while bottled up in the siege at Petersburg.[27]

The South's attitude toward arming Blacks changed out of sheer desperation. Secretary of State Judah Benjamin argued forcefully that unless Blacks were recruited and armed, Lee would be forced to abandon Richmond.[28] On February 9, Benjamin told a group of slaves, "fight for your masters and you shall have your freedom.[29] Benjamin proclaimed that there were 680,000 Black men who were potential soldiers and asserted that within 20 days, the Army of Northern Virginia could be reinforced with enough Black soldiers to resume the offensive.[30] Congressman James T. Leach of North Carolina was infuriated by Benjamin's speech, declaring it derogatory, a disgrace, and "an insult to public opinion."[31]

Lieutenant General John Brown Gordon, then commander of Lee's 2nd Corps, expressed frustration and irritation that the Confederate Congress remained reluctant to take decisive action:

> We are having many desertions—caused I think by the despondency of our ranks. It is a terrible blow—the de-

feat of the negro bill in congress—troops all in favor of it—would have greatly encouraged the army—they are much disappointed at its defeat. What mean the national legislators? We shall be compelled to have them or be defeated—with them as volunteers and fighting for their freedom we shall be successful. . . . If authority were granted to raise 200,000 of them it would greatly encourage the men and do so much to stop desertions. I can find excellent officers to take command of them.[32]

Gordon insisted that the South was "compelled to have them or be defeated." He disgustedly noted, "But I presume that we cannot hope for any assistance now from this class of our population," referring to Confederate legislators.[33]

Jefferson Davis and Secretary of War James Seddon joined General Lee in a change of attitude. Having resorted to the draft in March 1862, the South had no other options for replacement manpower and was already drafting boys as young as 14 and men as old as 60. The Confederacy

Major General John Brown Gordon. SOURCE: NATIONAL ARCHIVES AND RECORDS ADMINISTRATION.

had already scraped the bottom of the barrel; as Major Thomas P. Turner, recruiting officer in Richmond, observed, "[Our] wives and daughters and the negroes are the only elements left for us to recruit from."[34] Recruiting officers were requesting other duty because they no longer served any purpose.

Despite the Confederacy's dire straits, there was still vigorous debate over the issue of arming Blacks among the press and population of the South. The Charleston *Mercury* regarded the whole proposition absurd: "Assert the right of the Confederate Government to emancipate slaves, and it is stone dead." Not only that, but it would mean "the poor man . . . reduced to the level of a nigger." The bottom line for the *Mercury* was expressed in its editorial of January 13, 1865: "We want no Confederate Government without our institutions, and we will have none."[35] Georgia's Macon *Telegraph and Confederate* reminded its readers, "This terrible war and extreme peril of our country were "occasioned . . . more by the institution of negro slavery" than "by any other subject or quarrel."[36] The Memphis *Appeal* agreed: "For it, and its perpetuation we commenced and have kept at war." Richmond's *Examiner* went straight to the point: "Arming Blacks was opposite to all the sentiments and principles which have heretofore governed the Southern people."[37] The Richmond *Whig* reminded readers that the South's long-standing position was that "servitude is a divinely appointed condition for the highest good of the slave" and the "condition in which the negro race especially may attain the highest moral and intellectual state of which they are capable." To arm slaves, the *Whig* insisted, was a "repudiation of the opinion held by the whole South."[38] North Carolina governor Zebulon Vance declared, "Our independence . . . is chiefly desirable for the preservation of our political institutions, the principal of which is slavery." Texan Caleb Cutwell was even more emphatic, declaring, "the South without slavery would not be worth a mess of pottage." The Lynchburg *Republic* curtly observed that were slaves to be armed, the Confederacy would prove to be "not worth one drop of the precious blood which has been shed in its behalf."[39] These examples are a small sampling of the outcry raised in the press over the prospect of arming slaves.

Senator Robert T. Hunter urged the rejection of European pressure for emancipation, arguing, "What did we go to war for, if not to protect our property?" Tennessee Congressman Henry S. Foote asked rhetorically, "If this government is to destroy slavery, why fight for it?"[40] Georgia governor Joseph E. Brown, *The Richmond Whig*, and Senator Hunter all pointed out that even limited abolition of slavery violated the Confederate Constitution.[41] Hunter's opposition to this measure ran deep; he declared:

> If we are right in passing this measure we were wrong in denying to the old government the right to interfere with the institution of slavery and to emancipate slaves. Besides, if we offer slaves their freedom . . . we confess we were insincere, were hypocritical, in asserting that slavery was the best state for slaves themselves. . . . If we could make them soldiers, the condition of soldier being socially equal to any other in society, we could make them officers, perhaps to command white men.[42]

Hunter feared that a future Confederate president with dictatorial intentions could use Black troops to "seize the liberties of the country and put white men under his feet"; others were demanding that Davis do just that to save a sinking Confederacy. Hunter could not believe that the heroes of Manassas, Fredericksburg, Chancellorsville, and Cold Harbor were holding out their hands for "negroes to come out and save them."[43] Apparently, he did not appreciate that the problem was that large numbers of these very men now rested underground and the South lacked manpower reserves to replace them.

In late March, Davis wrote to Virginia's governor, "It is becoming daily more evident that to all reflecting persons that we are reduced to choosing whether the negroes shall fight for or against us, and that all arguments as to the positive advantages or disadvantages of employing them are beside the question, which is simply . . . between having their fighting elements in our ranks or those of the enemy."[44] He could point to a measure of public support, as the Richmond *Sentinel* declared any Black who volunteered would be a "brother in arms," also suggesting that whites who opposed the measure should refrain from public dissent. The paper opined that after the war, Confederate States Colored Troops veterans would wear "badges of merit" and hold "certificates of honor" as a new Black aristocracy.[45]

But before this could happen, state laws barring arming Blacks had to be repealed.[45] Not every Confederate state was so inclined—North Carolina's legislature passed resolutions that specifically prohibited undertaking this "precarious" war measure, and Texas also passed resolutions endorsing the perpetuation of slavery.[46] Ironically, the institution was crumbling along with the Confederate government. Richmond clerk John Jones recorded in his diary, "Here the price of slaves, men, is about $5,000 Confederate State notes, or $100 specie, a huge depreciation. Before the war they commanded ten times the price."[47] Edward A. Pollard, editor of the Richmond *Examiner*, wondered why, if arming slaves was such a good idea, it had not been implemented in the war's early phases when Black soldiers would have made a greater difference. He also wondered how 200,000—or any large number—Black soldiers were to be armed and fed when the Confederacy's cupboards were nearly bare of food, uniforms, and equipment.[48]

Meanwhile, rumors abounded in the North. Major General E.O.C. Ord, commanding the Army of the James, reported the presence of five Black Confederate regiments near Petersburg. A Black reporter for the Philadelphia Press wrote that 22 Black regiments were drilling at Camp Lee, west of Richmond.[49] Obviously, both were dealing with faulty intelligence. Frederick Douglass advised President Lincoln that unless the Union offered slaves who enlisted both freedom and land bounties, they would fight for the rebels.[50] Attitudes in the South could also be fanciful—a surgeon of the 57th Virginia Infantry urged that a Black corps strike a retaliatory invasion to ravage the North in the same manner Sherman's Army had visited on Georgia.[51]

Not surprisingly, even in extremis opinion continued to be strongly divided on such a drastic measure as arming slaves and freedmen. Robert Toombs, the Confederacy's first secretary of state and a brigade commander in the Army of Northern Virginia, warned "the worst calamity that could befall us would be to gain our independence by the valor of our slaves. . . . The day that the Army of Virginia allows a negro regiment to enter their lines as soldiers they will be degraded, ruined and disgraced."[52] On January 8, 1865, Georgia's General Howell Cobb, the first speaker of the Provisional Confederate Congress, wrote to Secretary of War James Seddon:

> I think that the proposition to make soldiers of our slaves is the most pernicious idea that has been suggested since the war began. It is a source of deep mortification and regret to see the name of that great and good man and soldier, General R. E. Lee, given as authority for such a

policy.... You cannot make soldiers of slaves, nor slaves of soldiers.... The day you make soldiers of [Negroes] is the beginning of the end of the revolution. If slaves will make good soldiers our whole theory of slavery is wrong—but they won't make good soldiers. As a class they are wanting in every qualification of a soldier.⁵³

Cobb's premise ignored the North's experience arming slaves over the past two years. Another Confederate observer declared this was "the last resort of a dying Confederacy; and thus the sublimest tragedy ended in the most absurd and ridiculous comedy—slaves fighting for their own thralldom; freedmen unworthy of the name; statesmen, so called, who dared not arm and meet the foe"—another jab at Confederate legislators.⁵⁴ And just a week before the city fell, a Richmond minstrel show, "Recruiting Unbleached Citizens of Virginia for the Confederate States Army," lampooned the Black Confederate soldiers and their white advocates.⁵⁵

Southern bureaucracy did not move rapidly on such a fundamental yet vital issue because of deeply ingrained opposition. After impassioned debate in secret session, the Confederate Congress finally approved a measure authorizing arming Black slaves on March 13 by a vote of 47 to 38 in the House and nine to eight in the Senate, with many abstentions.⁵⁶ Virginia's governor and legislature had to instruct the state's two senators, both of whom were strongly against the measure, to vote in the affirmative. President Davis signed the bill the same day, less than a month before Lee surrendered at Appomattox. Although Davis requested a pledge of emancipation for any slave who served, the final legislation stipulated, "nothing in this act shall be construed to authorize a change in the relation which the said slaves shall bear toward their owners except by consent of their owners and of the states in which they reside." In other words, most Black soldiers would still be slaves, as would their families.⁵⁷

Unfortunately for the Confederacy, this legislation passed at the eleventh hour and came too late. Moreover, the majority of slaveowners resisted its stipulations because they lived in a fantasyland where they imagined they would be able to hold on to their enslaved population no matter how hostilities ended. Although recruiting officers were dispatched to the states and localities, results were universally disappointing. One officer fumed, "They are willing to give their sons and brothers to the Army, saw their lives offered as a sacrifice upon the Altar of their Country." But while "there were many exceptions, the majority would I am convinced rather have placed in the Army two sons rather than one negro." Lee too regretted the reluctance of owners to have enslaved men enlisted into military service. He considered that it was almost certain that if these men did not soon wear gray uniforms, their stubborn masters would find their property wearing blue and arrayed against the waning Confederacy. Although Lee was desperate by the end of March, he could not convince Governor Smith of Virginia or President Davis to confiscate slaves from unwilling masters. Most Southerners viewed the use of Black troops as social, economic, and cultural suicide and viewed proponents of the policy of arming Blacks as guilty of racial and cultural treason. As historian William C. Oates observed, even "after slavery was practically dead, the Confederacy clung to the putrid body and expired with it."

There were other problems for the Confederacy—Black recruits had to forget that until recently they were regarded as menials if they were to display dash and initiative on the battlefield. They would also have to be persuaded that the South's promises could be trusted. Even more, their officers would be challenged to motivate them not to desert to the Yankees at the first opportunity. The *Southern Confederacy* wondered, "If a few tens of thousands of [white] deserters of our colors are too many to be arrested and forcibly carried back to their commands, where is the force to come from to arrest and put back into the ranks one or two hundred thousand of black deserters?" The chief of the Confederate War Bureau surmised that implementation of this policy would put four times as many Black soldiers into the Union Army as into Confederate service.[58]

On February 12, 1865, Dr. F. W. Hancock, chief surgeon at Richmond's Jackson Hospital, polled the hospital's hired Black slaves to see if they would be willing "to take up arms to protect their masters' families, homes, and their own from the attacking foe." Reportedly, 60 out of the 72 present volunteered to fight "to the bitter end."[59] Virginia Military Institute cadets began drilling Black recruits, both freemen and slaves, at Camp Lee, west of Richmond. On March 11, two days before the Confederate Congress authorized Black troops, up to 60 Black orderlies from Jackson Hospital organized into a local defense unit called the Jackson Battalion (three companies of white convalescent soldiers and two of Blacks) arrived at Petersburg under the command of Major Henry C. Scott, assigned to the defenses of Petersburg under General Longstreet.

The unit arrived too late but helped burn Richmond's military warehouses to keep these supplies from falling into the hands of the Union Army.[60]

Nine days later, a Black "brigade," mustered under the command of Majors James W. Pegram and Thomas P. Turner, disappointed an integrated crowd after it was announced that it would march on parade. Not surprisingly, uniforms and weapons had not arrived.[61] But at least one enlistee had deserted, taking some uniforms with him. Both Turner and one of his subordinates, Lieutenant Virginius Bossieux, managed military prisons in Richmond. On the evening of March 22, a "battalion" under Dr. Jackson Chambliss, along with a "company" commanded by Captain Grimes, paraded on Capitol Square; Charles McKnight, an ordnance clerk, informed his brother that they were "the first company of negro troops raised in Virginia."[62] A company of 35 African Americans (12 free Blacks and 23 slaves) was enrolled on March 29.[63] Blacks in Petersburg were eligible for bonuses of $100 for coming "forward to show their willingness to rescue their country."[62] At the Sycamore Street recruiting office, slaves who enlisted were promised freedom and the right to reside in the Confederacy but not voting rights.[64] On the other hand, the few Black volunteers in uniform were hooted at and pelted with mud and other objects by boys on the streets of Richmond. In toto, it appears that no more than 100–200 Blacks volunteered to become soldiers for the Confederacy.

Purported Black First Sergeant. The Coli, United States Colored Troops (USCT) Who Fought in the Civil War.

On April 2, Lee dispatched a hurried letter to Davis listing 20 men (a brigadier general, five colonels, four majors, four captains, and six enlisted men) willing to command Black units.[65] On April 4, a courier witnessed a skirmish between a Confederate supply train guarded by Black Confederate soldiers. Although they repelled the first attack by Union cavalrymen, they were overwhelmed and captured in the second assault. Two days later, refugees who observed a squad of 12 colored troops digging fortifications with their arms stacked nearby were informed that these were "the only company of colored troops in Confederate service,"[66] probably the remnant of Major Turner's command. According to many accounts, two companies of slaves and free Blacks were assembled and drilled without weapons in Richmond the week before the city fell. Many speculate they were medics.[67] In May 1865, a rebel soldier newly released from prison at Point Lookout, Maryland, described a "negro Confederate soldier," the only "dark-skinned reb," who refused to betray Dixie by taking the loyalty oath, choosing to remain behind bars, "unreconstructed and unreconstructible," ironically, the "last of the loyal."[68]

Edward A. Pollard, wartime editor of the Richmond *Examiner*, wrote in *The Lost Cause*, published in 1866, "The actual results of the legislation of Congress on the subject were ridiculously small . . . —a pretense of doing something, yet so far below the necessities of the case, as to be in the last degree puerile, absurd, and contemptible."[69] Major George Campbell Brown, Lieutenant General Richard Ewell's long-term aide-de-camp, reaffirmed Pollard's assessment: the handful of Black troops mustered in the Southern capital in March 1865 constituted "the first and only Black troops used on our side." Brown noted that Black soldiery began late and "ended with a whimper."[70] Major Brown was in a position to know; Ewell commanded forces responsible for the defense of Richmond, and he was entrusted with recruiting and training African American soldiers.

CONCLUSIONS

Historian Benjamin Quarles observed that the Confederacy was "enslaved by a system of values which stamped Blacks as inferiors." Arming and training Blacks contradicted the very foundation of the Confederacy and negated the cause of the South's secession. Most Southerners considered Blacks utterly inferior and were convinced that they could not make good soldiers—even though the North had been providing convincing evidence to the contrary since October 1862, when the 1st Kansas Colored

Infantry defeated their opponents at Island Mound despite being green recruits and outnumbered. The US Colored Troops provided a continuous string of examples after that, but the South refused to let go of slavery, its "cornerstone" and source of most of its wealth.

Had Cleburne's proposal been implemented in 1864, the Confederacy might have prolonged the war to a stalemate. The North was almost as prejudiced but realized that Blacks were the only remaining source of replacement troops. Under Grant, Union forces attacked simultaneously on all fronts augmented by 175 Black regiments, a force larger than all the forces available for the Confederacy in the last year of the war, dissecting the Confederacy and destroying its war-fighting capacity.

It is worth noting that the debate in the Southern press and among Confederate statesmen over arming African Americans provides concrete evidence that the Civil War was fought over the issue of slavery and white supremacy. The Confederate Congress' hesitation resulted in a decision that came 27 days before Appomattox, a classic case of "too little, too late." Despite fragmentary records, it is certain that less than a battalion of African American soldiers was organized to fight for the South. Even in extremis, preservation of slavery trumped military necessity, proving beyond a doubt that slavery and white supremacy were the Confederacy's twin foundations.

CHAPTER 4

Buffalo Soldiers

> Nineteenth century democracy needs no more complete vindication for its existence than the fact that it has kept for the white race the best portion of the New World's surface.
>
> Theodore Roosevelt

Congress authorized Black regular army regiments in 1866 due to the remarkable record US Colored Troops compiled during the Civil War. Two cavalry, 20 percent of the horse soldiers engaged in the Indian Wars, and two infantry regiments of "Buffalo Soldiers" distinguished themselves by professionalism and bravery at remote outposts under austere conditions. All four regiments were commanded by exceptional white regimental commanders handpicked by the Army's senior leadership.

These regiments played major roles in the Spanish–American War. Their exploits were momentarily widely applauded, then quickly forgotten. Even their widely acclaimed heroism assaulting San Juan Hill was stolen—they were literally cropped from the picture.

The last Buffalo Soldier regiment was disbanded in 1951, after 85 years of service.

Because the US Colored Troops proved their effectiveness during the Civil War, Congress authorized six Black regular army regiments in the Army Organization Act of July 16, 1866—two cavalry regiments (9th and 10th US Cavalry) and four infantry regiments (38th, 39th, 40th, and

41st US Infantry)—incorporating Black soldiers into the regular army for the first time. The army establishment at the time was 45 infantry, 10 cavalry, and 5 artillery regiments, including the six African American regiments, a total of 54,304 officers and enlisted personnel. Major General Philip H. Sheridan, commanding the Military Division of the Gulf, was authorized to raise "one regiment of colored cavalry to be designated the 9th Regiment of U.S. Cavalry on August 9, 1866." The same day, Lieutenant General William Tecumseh Sherman, commander of the Military District of the Mississippi, headquartered at Saint Louis, Missouri, directed commanders of the Departments of the Missouri, Arkansas, and Platt to recruit enlisted men from US Colored Troop regiments for these new units, serving five-year terms of service in cavalry regiments and three years in infantry regiments.[1] Veterans of the US Colored Troops provided about half of the new units' strength and most of the noncommissioned officers, but few Black veterans served long enough to retire from the Army. The remainder of the six regiments' manpower was filled out by some 2,000–3,000 newly freed slaves, who began Army life with six months of basic training. Privates received $13 per month and were provided room, board, and clothing. Sixty-four privates were allotted per company.

General Sherman wrote to his superior, U. S. Grant in 1866, "We must act with vindictive earnestness against the Sioux even to their extermination, men, women and children" after a band of Sioux wiped out an army patrol.[2] Newspapers echoed these blood-thirsty sentiments: *The Nebraska City Press* declared, "Exterminate the whole fraternity of redskins," while the *Montana Post* thundered, "Wipe them out!"[3] Unfortunately, this attitude was not novel, and the US Army enthusiastically responded to this genocidal call.

The regimental commanders of all four Black regiments were the cream of the Army.[4] One of the 10th Cavalry's first battles was near Fort Hays, Kansas, in August 1867 after a railroad work party was wiped out. Patrols from the 38th Infantry Regiment (which became part of the 24th Infantry Regiment in 1869), with a troop from the 10th Cavalry, were sent out to locate the perpetrators. In 1867 and 1868, the regiment participated in General Sherman's winter campaigns against the Cheyenne, Arapahos, and Comanches. Units from the 10th Cavalry prevented the natives from withdrawing, allowing George Armstrong Custer's 7th Cavalry to defeat them near Fort Cobb in Indian Territory.

Troops H & I of the 10th Cavalry, under the command of Captain Louis Carpenter, formerly the commander of a US Colored Troops regiment, engaged in two notable actions in September and October 1868. The first was the rescue of Lieutenant Colonel George A. Forsyth and 48 white scouts pinned down by a large hostile force on an island in Colorado. The second occurred two weeks later, when about 500 Indians attacked Carpenter's troops. After a running fight, the "hostiles" retreated. General Philip Sheridan, Commander of the Military Division of the Missouri, recommended Carpenter for the Medal of Honor for these two actions, also commending Carpenter's stalwart troopers.

On March 3, 1869, an across-the-board budget cutback of 20 regiments reduced the number of infantry regiments, consolidating the four Black infantry regiments into the 24th and 25th Infantry and reducing the white regiments proportionately. Most commissioned officers, who continued to be white, were burdened with duties noncommissioned officers performed in other units because many soldiers were former slaves unable to read or write. Stationed at remote outposts at times 600 miles distant from civilization with few comforts, boredom loomed large in the lives of officers and men. The regiments provided security for settlers entering the new frontier; guarded stagecoach routes in small posts consisting of three- to four-man detachments; built necessary infrastructure, such as telegraph lines, roads, and new forts; protected railroad and survey crews; chopped wood; and performed myriads of additional chores. Soldiers spent endless hours in drill, inspections, parades, and the care and maintenance of horses and equipment. Recreational opportunities were few, and soldiers had to be constantly on their guard for "hostiles."

Some idea of the low esteem many Army personnel had for Black troops can be inferred by the transfer of the 39th Regiment in cattle and freight cars from Goldsboro, South Carolina, to New Orleans, a trip requiring 10 days, when the 25th Infantry was formed by consolidating it with the 40th Infantry Regiment, stationed in Louisiana. When the regimental commander complained to the quartermaster general, he replied that the officer in charge was at fault for accepting substandard transportation.[5]

Sheridan directed the 10th Cavalry's Colonel Benjamin Grierson to establish Ft. Sill in Indian Territory in 1869. Grierson was the first post commander, and his troopers constructed many of the stone buildings surrounding the post quadrangle. Sheridan was impressed with the fort, calling it one of the best he had seen, an excellent facility for the "army of occupation," the regiment constituted for the reservation in Indian Territory. The Buffalo Soldiers' duties frequently included ensuring that Native American tribes returned to their reservations, a task that possibly presented a moral dilemma for some of the recently freed slaves.

Buffalo Soldiers fought in 168 of the 1,296 confrontations with Native Americans on the frontier between 1866 and 1897, nearly 13 percent.[6] Their Native American opponents dubbed them "Buffalo Soldiers." The origin of this nickname is uncertain, but it is often attributed to Native Americans' association of Black soldiers' hair with the buffalo, the animal the Indians depended on for sustenance. The earliest known use occurred in 1872, when an army wife whose husband served with the 3rd Infantry Regiment at Fort Larned, Kansas, wrote a letter that touched off a firestorm when it was published in 1902: "The officers say that the Negroes make good soldiers and fight like fiends. . . . the Indians call them 'buffalo soldiers' because their woolly heads are so much like the matted cushion that is between the horns of the buffalo. These "Buffalo Soldiers" are active, intelligent, and resolute men . . . and appear to me to be rather superior to the average white recruited in time of peace."[7] The white majority did not appreciate that observation!

The Black regulars played a decisive role in conflicts with the tribes of the Southern Plains in the early 1870s, the savage combat with Apaches from 1879–1881, and the Pine Ridge campaign of 1890–1891 in Montana. The Buffalo Soldiers constituted 20 percent of the cavalry and 8 percent of the infantry, in all 11.8 percent of the soldiers engaged in warfare with Indigenous tribes.[8] The Army faced a daunting challenge: General Sheridan reported in 1874 that his command, the Division of the Missouri, contained some 99 separate tribes, with about 192,000 Natives spread over 1 million square miles of frontier. To protect this enormous area, he had 17,819 officers and men.[9] By 1875, the US Army's authorized strength was down to about 25,000 men, with Civil War veterans still forming its core. In 1878, Sheridan noted that he had to garrison 73 posts with only 13,468 men.[10] This left few troops for deployment in the South, much less to military establishments in the North.

The service records of the roughly 4,000 Buffalo Soldiers were exemplary. They deserted less and reenlisted more often than their white counterparts, even though deployed to the most remote and undesirable outposts. Fewer Blacks committed court-martial offenses. Between 1866 and 1885, only 2 out of 1,000 Black soldiers reported on sick call for drunkenness, as opposed to 54 out of 1,000 white soldiers.[11] Ten Blacks earned 18 of the 416 Medals of Honor awarded during the Indian Wars

(1866–1891).[12] Six white officers assigned to Buffalo Soldier regiments and four Black Seminole scouts also received the nation's highest award.

In 1875, the 9th Cavalry Regiment was transferred to the New Mexico Military District, which included parts of what is now New Mexico, Colorado, and Texas, to operate against Apaches. A small element led by Sergeant George Jordan participated in the battle of Fort Tularosa, New Mexico, in May 1880, saving the settlement's inhabitants and defeating Victorio's Chiricahua Apaches, for which Jordan received the Medal of Honor. The regiment also surveyed; constructed roads; and strung telegraph lines in this vast, uncharted territory while policing the Mexican border. The other regiments performed similar duties in their sectors.

In April 1875, the 10th Cavalry was transferred to Fort Concho, Texas, to protect mail and travel routes, control Indian movement, police Mexican revolutionaries and outlaws, and gain knowledge of the area. The regiment scouted 34,420 miles of uncharted terrain, built more than 300 miles of new roads, and laid over 200 miles of telegraph lines in harsh terrain, producing excellent maps detailing scarce water holes, mountain passes, and grazing areas that later facilitated combat action and settlement. In December 1877, Colonel William Shafer, then commanding the 24th Infantry Regiment operating on the southwest Texas border with a detachment of the 10th Cavalry Regiment, drafted a glowing report of the detachment's activities:

> Officers and men were exposed to very severe weather and having only pack animals were necessarily restricted to the small allowance carried on the saddle. The country scouted in was exceedingly difficult, more so than any part of Texas, the officers and men deserving great credit for the patience, fortitude, and energy they exhibited on this scout, and they are to be complimented on its successful issue.[13]

The 10th Cavalry played an important role in the 1879–1880 campaign against Victorio's Mescalero band, who struck terror in the hearts of ranchers and settlers in Chihuahua, Mexico; New Mexico; and West Texas for 11 months after they left their reservation near Ruidoso, New Mexico, in August 1879. Colonel Grierson decided that the best way to intercept Victorio was to control the water holes. The regiment engaged in two significant confrontations, Tinaja de las Palmas and Rattlesnake Springs, blocking Victorio, denying him water, and forcing the exhausted Apaches to retreat to Mexico, where they were annihilated by Mexican troops in October 1880. Grierson's tactics were a model of counter-guerrilla operations, beating Victorio at his own game.

Elements of the 25th Infantry joined the 7th and 9th Cavalry in the last major Indian campaign against starving and destitute Lakota near Pine Ridge, South Dakota, at Wounded Knee Creek in December 1890. More than 300 Indians, nearly half of whom were women, children, and old men, were killed by the 7th Cavalry under Colonel George A. Forsythe even though most of the band was disarmed. Colonel Philip Harvey, the 25th Infantry's commander, noted, "there can be little doubt that the condition of destitution . . . brought about by reduced rations and the dishonesty and mismanagement of minor government officials had a far-reaching effect."[14] The government consistently reneged on promises to honor its treaties with Native Americans, in particular, feeding and caring for the tribes. A large part of the problem was rampant corruption among Indian agents tasked with assisting the tribes.

Mass grave of Native Americans massacred by the 7th Cavalry Regiment at Wounded Knee. SOURCE: ORIGINAL PHOTO, 1891, BY NORTHWESTERN PHOTO COMPANY, CHADRON, NEBRASKA; SIOUXLAND PUBLIC MEDIA.

During this campaign, 9th Cavalry elements twice rescued 7th Cavalry units attacked by Indians. Corporal William O. Wilson won a Medal of Honor for carrying a dispatch from an encircled wagon train through country occupied by hostile Sioux, the eighth trooper from the regiment to be so honored.[15] The 9th Cavalry was the last unit to leave the area, spending the winter of 1890–1891 on the reservation in tents in near-arctic temperatures. A Black private, W. H. Prather, wrote a poem in which he observed, "The 9th were the first to come, will be the last to leave, and we poor devils and the Sioux are left to freeze."[16]

Officers assigned to the four regiments either retained preexisting prejudices or learned to appreciate the sterling qualities of the troops they led. One example of racial bias was provided by the 25th Infantry's Lieutenant G. P. Ahern, who wrote a local newspaper while bivouacking with the regiment near Fort Keough, Montana, during the Pine Ridge campaign:

> Our "cullud" battalion here is under canvas and in fine shape for a winter campaign, and when Jack Frost freezes the mercury out of sight the gay and festive coon will be found ready to dance the "Virginia essence" and be ready to sing as joyfully as ever.[17]

A detachment of 10th Cavalry fought one of the last battles of the Apache Wars along the Salt River in March 1890, the same year that Colonel Grierson was finally rewarded for his 23 years of service with the 10th Cavalry by promotion to brigadier general. Grierson retired three months later. No doubt, Grierson's promotion was substantially delayed due to his enthusiastic support for his Black soldiers and his lack of militant hostility toward Native Americans.

After more than 20 years of service on posts in the Southwest and despite the widespread assumption that Blacks could not function well in cold environments, the regiment was transferred to the Department of Dakota in 1891, serving at posts in Montana and the Dakotas until 1898.

In 1894, elements of the 10th Cavalry protected railroad property from striking workers, while several companies of the 25th Infantry were deployed to break a railroad strike.

In 1896, Lieutenant John J. Pershing, commanding the 10th Cavalry's D Troop, led an expedition that deported a large number of Cree Indians under Little Bear from Montana back to their reservations in Canada.

EDUCATION AND EXPERIMENTATION

Normally, chaplains were assigned to posts, but Congress expressly created the position of regimental chaplain for each of the four regiments to facilitate the education of former slaves. The results were significant, sometimes spectacular: two Black chaplains made lasting contributions to the entire army education program. Chaplain George G. Mullins assumed duty with the 25th Infantry Regiment at Fort Davis, Texas, in 1875 and pioneered today's system of army education by organizing a cadre of assistants who helped recruit and train illiterate soldiers. Mullins noted the correlation between education and good discipline, attracting the attention of department commander General Edward O. C. Ord. In July 1886, Mullins was dispatched to serve as assistant to the Army's chief of education, where he devised a system for organizing post schools, establishing reading rooms and libraries. The fruits of his efforts led to Mullins's appointment as Army chief of education, where he lobbied Congress, an unheard-of position for a Black man.

Chaplain Allen Allensworth reported for duty with the 24th Infantry in April 1881. He built on Mullins's program by training promising enlisted men as teachers. Due to Mullins's efforts, the Army made education compulsory for all soldiers. Because chaplains were also responsible for educating children of post personnel, Allensworth established a curriculum for both children and enlistees. He published a booklet detailing his graded programs, separated into components for each type of student. As a result, he was invited to deliver a paper at the National Education Association's meeting in 1891.

The Army's adjutant general's 1882 report recognized the efforts of both chaplains:

> The importance of the question of education in the army cannot be overestimated, whether we consider the immediate benefits in raising the standard of intelligence in the ranks, or its ulterior advantages to the country at large whenever the soldier re-enters civilian life. After a term of salutary discipline and education, every man leaving the service becomes a factor of importance (under our system of government) in the civilization and well being of the State.[18]

Black chaplains made a significant contribution to the elimination of illiteracy and significantly enhanced the effectiveness of their units.

In the mid-1890s, the War Department decided to explore the possibility of using bicycles instead of horses. In 1896, seven soldiers from the 25th Infantry took a 700-mile round trip from Fort Missoula, Montana, to Yellowstone National Park. The following year, 20 soldiers from the regiment rode 1,900 miles from the fort to Saint Louis, Missouri. When hostilities in Cuba ended, a 100-man-strong bicycle company from the 25th Infantry performed riot duty in Havana.

SPANISH–AMERICAN WAR

War fever was building well before the USS *Maine* exploded and sank in Havana harbor in February 1898, killing 266 seamen, including 22 African Americans. National Guard or militia units from the states were called to national service since the US standing army had only 28,000 troops. Secretary of War Russell Alger requested that at least half a dozen "special regiments" of "yellow fever immunes" be recruited for service in Cuba, responding to the widely held but erroneous view that persons exposed to yellow fever developed immunity to the disease. Congress authorized recruitment of 10,000 men in 10 "immune" regiments, four of which were Black, with mostly white officers, the 7th through 10th US Volunteer Infantry Regiments. The 8th Volunteer Infantry assembled at Fort Thomas, Kentucky, with three officers' messes: one for field and staff officers, one for captains (all white), and one for lieutenants (all Black). Two Black staff officers, the chaplain and assistant surgeon, ate with the lieutenants.[19] Benjamin O. Davis Sr., who became the first Black general officer in 1940, was an 18-year-old lieutenant in the regiment. When the regiment moved to Chickamauga Park, Georgia, racial hostility was so intense that someone planted dynamite on the base. Davis's cool conduct so impressed his commander, a former Confederate officer who had served under Nathan Bedford Forrest, that he made Davis battalion adjutant.

The 9th Immunes arrived in Cuba in March 1899, tasked to neutralize bandits operating in the province of Santiago. Although the bandits were dealt with in less than a month, the regiment was blamed for a lynching in Georgia! The *New Orleans Times-Democrat* opined in an editorial:

> Governor Allan D. Chandler of Georgia . . . rightly places the responsibility for the crime upon those who

organized negro troops and placed weapons in their hands.... Mr. McKinley... was warned again and again that the arming of negroes meant race war.

These regiments have been enjoying social equality in the island, where a large proportion of the population is negro or of mixed blood, and where the race line which the Anglo-Saxon insists on does not exist. Every one of these men will come back filled with the idea he can play the social equality racket here.[20]

All four Buffalo Soldier regiments arrived in Florida in the spring of 1898, assigned to V Corps, commanded by Major General William R. Shafter, former commander of the 24th Infantry Regiment, who had earned the nickname "Pecos Bill" during the Indian Wars. At the time, Shafter was commander of the Department of California and was an unlikely candidate for command since he was then 63 years old, weighed 300 pounds, and was incapacitated by gout.

On June 30, 1898, an American force of 26 regiments, 15,000–17,000 troops, disembarked. The 9th and 10th Cavalry served as dismounted cavalry in the division of ex–Confederate Major General "Fighting Joe" Joseph Wheeler, of Civil War cavalry fame. The Spanish garrison surrendered on July 17. The "splendid little war" lasting only 113 days, cost 285 American soldiers killed in battle and 1,662 wounded, but disease caused 2,565 deaths. Spanish casualties were 800 killed and about the same number wounded, but about 15,000 Spanish soldiers died of disease and 40,000 were captured.

After the war, the 9th Cavalry served as Roosevelt's honor guard in San Francisco. In 1899, 1904, and again in 1905, the 9th Cavalry patrolled Yosemite National Park, joining other cavalry and infantry units as the first park "rangers." Our National Park rangers' "Smokey the Bear" hat is modeled after the troopers' distinctive "Montana Pinch" campaign hat.

The chaplain of the 9th Cavalry, George W. Prioleau, asked,

Talk about fighting and freeing poor Cuba and of Spain's brutality.... Is America any better than Spain? Has she not subjects in her very midst who are murdered daily without a trial of judge or jury? Has she not subjects in her own borders who are half-fed and half-clothed, because their father's skin is black. . . . Yet the Negro is loyal to his country's flag.[21]

This was demonstrated by the bonding of white and Black soldiers, which began with the landing at Daiquiri, when a Rough Rider captain and several sailors rescued 10th Cavalry soldiers whose boat had capsized. At Tayacoba, four 10th Cavalry members in a rescue party were awarded the Medal of Honor for braving the surf to rescue stranded members of a reconnaissance force. At the Battle of Las Guasimas on June 24, 1898, the 10th Cavalry, using Indian-fighting tactics, assisted Rough Riders in a battle involving about 1,000 Americans against 1,500 Spanish. The *Washington Post*'s war correspondent wrote:

> If it had not been for the negro Cavalry, the Rough Riders would have been exterminated.
>
> I am not a Negro lover. My father fought with Mosby's Rangers and I was born in the South, but the Negroes saved that fight and the day will come when General Shafter will give them credit for their bravery.[22]

Theophilus Gould Steward, a Black chaplain with the 25th Infantry, wrote, "All the army made history during the short Cuban war; but the colored regulars practically revolutionized the sentiment of the country with regard to colored soldiers."[23] L. B. Channing's poem, "The Negro Soldier," also suggested America's change of heart: "We used to think the Negro didn't count for very much . . . but we've got to reconstruct our views of color, more or less, now we know about the 10th at Las Guasimas!"[24]

Spanish forces held the Americans at bay for almost 12 hours at the battle of El Caney ("Hell Caney") on July 1, 1898. The 24th Infantry Regiment offered to take the lead after the 71st New York Volunteers "fled like sheep in the presence of wolves." The 13th US Infantry stood aside as the 24th Regiment assaulted the summit and captured the Spanish flag, supported by the 25th Infantry. Men from the 25th were among the first to reach the summit, where a private from the regiment seized the Spanish flag. An officer of the 12th Infantry Regiment demanded the banner and claimed credit for the victory.[25]

Later that afternoon, during the battle for the main objective, San Juan Heights, the 9th and 10th Cavalry Regiments participated in taking the two main objectives, Kettle Hill and San Juan Hill, as part of the 2nd Brigade, which included the 1st Volunteer Cavalry "Rough Riders," the 1st US Cavalry, and Cuban General Calixto Garcia Iniguez's 5,000 insurgents. The 10th Cavalry moved into position and took fire from San Juan Heights. The incoming Spanish fire began to take a toll on men and morale, so a staff officer rushed to the front of the 1st Brigade, urging them to support the regiment's charge. Other units, seeing the 10th Cavalry's assault, began to attack, and General Wheeler ordered the whole division forward. The regiment's color sergeant carried the colors of the white 3rd Cavalry along with the 10th's banner to the summit when its bearer was struck down during the assault.

Regimental adjutant 1st Lieutenant John J. Pershing took command when Troop A reached the summit, supported by elements of the 24th and 25th Infantry on the left flank. American losses were 144 killed, 1,024 wounded, and 72 missing in action storming the San Juan Heights, while the Spanish, in defensive positions, lost 114 dead, 366 wounded, and 41 captured. Major General Joseph Wheeler expressed appreciation for the 10th Cavalry's actions: "You forded the San Juan River and gallantly swept over San Juan Hill, driving the enemy from its crest. Without a moment's halt, you bravely charged and carried the formidable entrenchments of Fort San Juan."[26] Their gallantry came at a price: the 10th Cavalry lost 20 percent of its men and half of its officers assaulting San Juan Hill.

In many ways, the Spanish–American War was the most integrated American war since the Revolution, a time of well-publicized Black heroism and general interracial comradeship. Spanish soldiers were impressed by the Buffalo Soldiers' bravery and called them "smoked Yankees." Several Black soldiers received battlefield commissions. Black chaplain W. Hilary Coston recalled:

> A black corporal of the 24th Infantry walked wearily up to the "water hole." He was muddy and bedraggled and stretched himself out over the stepping stones in the stream, sipping up the water and mud together out of the shallow pool. A white Cavalryman ran up to him shouting, "Hold on, bunkie, here's my cup!" The negro looked dazed a moment, and not a few of the spectators showed

amazement, for such a thing had rarely, if ever, happened in the army before. "Thank you," said the black corporal. "Well, we are all fighting under the same flag now." And he drank out of the white man's cup.[27]

In August 1889, the *New York World* published a lengthy poem-reflection, titled "The Rough Rider 'Remarks'":

> You bet your sweet life them darkies is white!
> The cowboys always pay their debts;
> Them darkies saved us a El Caney;
> When we go back on the colored vets,
> Count Texas Bill out of the play.[28]

War correspondent Richard Harding Davis reported that "Negro soldiers established themselves as fighting men," while the *New York Sun* emphasized the role the Buffalo Soldiers played in the charge.[29] The *New York Mail and Express* exulted:

> Firing as they marched, their aim was splendid, their coolness superb, and their courage aroused the admiration of their comrades. Their advance was greeted with wild cheers from the white regiments, and with answering shouts they pressed onward over the trenches they had taken close in pursuit of the retreating enemy. The war has not shown greater heroism. The men whose own freedom was baptized in blood have proven themselves capable of giving up their lives that others might be free.[30]

The commander of the Cuban Army addressed the Buffalo Soldiers, "If you will be as brave in the future to your country as you have proved yourselves today it will not be very long before you will have generals in the Army of the United States."[31] After the battle, Rough Rider Frank Knox said, "I joined a troop of the 10th Cavalry, and for a time I fought with them shoulder to shoulder and in justice to the colored race I must say that I never saw braver men anywhere."[32] Although he declared that these Buffalo Soldiers would "live in his memory forever," as secretary of the Navy during World War II, Knox refused to accept Black sailors in any capacity other than as messman.

Theodore Roosevelt commented, "We went up absolutely intermingled, so that no one could tell whether it was the Rough Riders or the men of the 9th who came forward with the greater courage to offer their lives in the service of their country. . . . I don't think any Rough Rider will forget the tie that binds us to the 9th and 10th Cavalry."[33]

Both Knox and Roosevelt later succumbed to the pervading spirit of white supremacy, in line with most of their countrymen. Despite initial praise, in the interest of political expediency, Roosevelt later wrote in his book, *The Rough Riders*, "Negro troops were shirkers in their duties and would only go as far as they were led by white officers."[34] It worked; Roosevelt became New York's governor in 1899, vice president in 1900, and president in 1901 when McKinley was assassinated.

Lieutenant John J. Pershing seconded both Knox's and Roosevelt's original observations: "White regiments, black regiments, regulars and Rough Riders, representing the young manhood of the North and South fought shoulder to shoulder, unmindful of race or color, unmindful whether commanded by an ex-Confederate or not." Pershing gushed, "We officers of the 10th Cavalry could have taken our black heroes in our arms."[35] The commander of the 10th Cavalry troop that led the charge

10th Cavalry 3rd US, and 1st Volunteer (Rough Riders) Regiments on San Juan Hill, often cropped to show only Teddy Roosevelt and the Rough Riders.
SOURCE: HARPER'S WEEKLY, LIBRARY OF CONGRESS PRINTS AND PHOTOGRAPHS DIVISION.

agreed, "Their conduct made me prouder than ever of being an officer in the American Army and of wearing the insignia of the 10th US Cavalry."[36] These sentiments were seconded by the last commanding general of the US Army, Lieutenant General Nelson A. Miles: "The white race was accompanied by the gallantry of the black as they swept over intrenched lines and later volunteered to succor the sick, nurse the dying and bury the dead in the hospitals and Cuban camps,"[37] a reference to the members of the 24th Infantry who volunteered to nurse yellow fever patients. About half of them succumbed to illness, yet some sick or wounded Black soldiers were refused care in Southern hospitals. The euphoria of appreciation went only so far.

At a speech made at Abraham Lincoln's home in Springfield, Illinois, in October 1898, President William McKinley noted,

> If any vindication of that act or of that prophecy [Lincoln's Emancipation Proclamation] were needed, it was found when these brave black men ascended the hill of San Juan, Cuba, and charged the enemy at El Caney. They vindicated their own title to liberty on that field, and with other brave soldiers gave the priceless gift of liberty to another suffering race.[38]

PHILIPPINE INSURRECTION (1899–1913)

The First Philippine Republic's struggle for independence from Spain began in 1896. When the United States refused to acknowledge the Philippine's declaration of independence in 1898, fighting erupted against forces of the United States after the Treaty of Paris ended the war and the United States annexed the islands. In June 1899, the First Philippine Republic officially declared war against the United States; Philippine President Emilio Aguinaldo was captured on March 23, 1901. Hostilities were officially declared over by the US government on July 2, 1902, but several Philippine groups, some led by veterans of the Philippine revolutionary society, which began the revolution against Spain, continued to battle US forces. Other groups, including Muslim Moro peoples in the south and various Catholic religious movements, continued to resist in remote areas. Guerrilla actions in the Moro-dominated provinces, called the Moro Rebellion by Americans, ended with their defeat on June 15, 1913. The United States ceded sovereignty to the Philippines in 1946.

When the rebellion was three months old, Major General Shafter, commander of the Department of California, declared:

> It may be necessary to kill half the Filipinos in order that the remaining half of the population may be advanced to a higher plane of life than their present semi-barbarous state affords.[39]

He reiterated his opinion in January 1900:

> My plan would be to disarm the natives of the Philippine Islands, even if I have to kill half of them to do it. Then I would treat the rest of them with perfect justice.[40]

Reacting to this major rebellion, President McKinley asked the states, territories, and the District of Columbia to provide militia units to suppress the insurrection of about 40,000 guerrillas led by Aguinaldo against American colonial rule. African Americans expected the hundreds of Black officers in 22 states and the District of Columbia's segregated militia units would be accepted into the volunteer army. When this was not the case, the outspoken editor of the *Richmond Planet* declared, "No officers, no fight!"[41] Ohio's governor offered command of his state's Black regiment, a battalion with only four companies, to First Lieutenant Charles Young, a West Point graduate and the single Black line officer in the regular army qualified to lead soldiers in combat. Young's acceptance earned him a temporary promotion to major of volunteers, although the 8th Ohio saw duty in Virginia, Pennsylvania, and South Carolina.[42] Officers of most Black militia units were Black, except for the 3rd Alabama and the commander and assistant surgeon in the 6th Virginia, but Black militia units would not last much longer in the South.

Another 25 volunteer regiments were authorized for service in the Philippines in September 1899. Two of these regiments, the 48th and 49th US Volunteer Infantry, had Black enlisted men and company grade officers (lieutenants and captains). The 24th and 25th Infantry were already part of the garrison of 12,000 US troops on the island. Ultimately, 70,000 American troops commanded by General Wesley Merritt, including both the 9th and 10th Cavalry Regiments, finally quelled the Philippine independence movement in 1911. Resistance in the Moro-dominated provinces in the south continued two additional years.

The Black *Washington Bee* disapproved of American expansionism in the strongest terms:

> Particularly while she is busy, on a hair brained attempt to go into the organizing business against its own Declaration of Independence and while she is making such frantic clamor of some kind of independence which she has up her sleeve for Cuba and the Philippines, would it be extremely wise for the American negro to show up to the entire civilized world the class of liberty they enjoy here.[43]

Support of operations in the Philippines was controversial in the African American community. Bishop Henry M. Turner of the African Methodist Episcopal Church, former chaplain of the 1st US Colored Infantry Regiment during the Civil War and later a member of the Freedmen's Bureau, described US operations in the Philippines as "an unholy war of conquest."[44] Booker T. Washington remonstrated, "Until our nation has settled the Indian and Negro problems, I do not think we have a right to assume more social problems." The chaplain of the 9th Cavalry asked, "Is America any better than Spain? Has she not subjects in her midst who are murdered daily without trial?"[45]

The Philippines was a difficult environment for Blacks because white Americans called Filipinos "niggers." In a letter home, the 24th Infantry's Sergeant Major John W. Galloway wrote, "The whites have begun to establish their diabolical race hatred in all its home rancor in Manila, even endeavoring to propagate the phobia among the Spaniards and Filipinos so as to be sure of the foundation of their supremacy."[46] Soldiers of the regiment wrote a letter to Secretary of War Lindley M. Garrison complaining that white officers treated them worse than the Philippine prisoners they guarded.[47] In spite of this, Black soldiers did their duty, serving honorably and admirably. Commissary Sergeant Middleton W. Sadler of the 25th Infantry observed, "We are now arrayed to meet a common foe, men of our hue and color. Whether it is right to reduce these people to submission is not a question for soldiers to decide. Our oaths of allegiance know neither race, color, nor nation."[48] Another Buffalo Soldier wrote, "We're only regulars and black ones at that, and I expect that when the

Philippines question is settled they'll detail us to garrison the islands. Most of us will find our graves there."[49]

Despite the moral dilemma presented by white supremacy, only six Buffalo Soldiers deserted. The protracted conflict in the Philippines provided an opportunity for several senior noncommissioned officers to serve as commissioned officers, including Medal of Honor winner Edward Baker, who served as a captain in the Philippine Scouts. The Buffalo Soldiers' initial service was short-lived, however, because the first American governor general (1901–1904), future President William Howard Taft, who coined the term "little brown brother" to describe Filipinos, sent the four regiments home. Nonetheless, the 25th Infantry fought Moro tribesmen in the Philippines as late as 1907 and 1908. The 9th Cavalry was stationed in the Philippines during World War I.

MEXICAN PUNITIVE EXPEDITION

The 10th Cavalry Regiment was posted to Fort Ethan Allen, at Burlington, Vermont, in 1909. There they enjoyed greater comfort and civilization and displayed their horsemanship to appreciative civilians, members of Congress, foreign dignitaries, and President Woodrow Wilson. During the fourth Mexican revolution since 1910, Francisco "Pancho" Villa's paramilitary force attacked Columbus, New Mexico, killing 15 American citizens, including seven soldiers, in March 1916. In response, the regiment was posted to Fort Huachuca, Arizona, to become part of Brigadier General John J. "Black Jack" Pershing's expedition of more than 10,000 US troops, almost half the standing army, which also included the 24th Infantry. Pershing had served with the 10th Cavalry during the Spanish–American War. The expedition penetrated 400 miles into Mexico, engaging in dozens of minor skirmishes with small bands of insurgents, failing to catch Villa's main force. Two of Pershing's three lead columns were squadrons of the 10th Cavalry led by Major Charles Young, the third Black West Point graduate. In April, the 10th Cavalry Regiment rescued the 13th Cavalry at Santa Cruz de Villegas, leading the commander of the 13th to exclaim, "By God, Young, I could kiss every Black face out there."[50]

This and other exploits again made the 10th Cavalry national heroes again. But on June 21, 1916, two troops totaling 92 troopers attacked Mexican federal army troops at Carrizal, Chihuahua. Although a Mexican general and 45 Federales were killed, twelve 10th Cavalry troopers, including two officers, were killed and 23 troopers were taken prisoner. The engagement nearly precipitated war with the Mexican government, but negotiations and a prisoner exchange resulted in the expedition's withdrawal from Mexico in February 1917 as war with Germany loomed.

RACIAL INCIDENTS, BROWNSVILLE, TEXAS, 1906

When a battalion of the 25th Infantry Regiment was sent to Brownsville in the summer of 1906 to train with Texas National Guard units, the Army's commanding general in Texas warned, "The Citizens of Brownsville entertain race hatred to an extreme degree." The regiment's chaplain, Theophilus G. Steward, wrote, "Texas, I fear, means a quasi-battleground for the 25th."[51] Gunfire erupted in Brownsville in August 1906, killing a white bartender and wounding two others, including a Hispanic police officer. The local grand jury thought that the Army's case was so flimsy that they refused to return any indictments against the soldiers. However, soldiers of the 25th were *suspected* and without evidence, a hearing, or trial, President Theodore Roosevelt issued dishonorable discharges to 167 soldiers from three companies on no other basis than they *might* be guilty—including three soldiers who were on leave when the incident occurred. Some were veteran soldiers who charged up San Juan Hill alongside Roosevelt and the Rough Riders. All were denied pensions or benefits.

RIOTS IN TEXAS, 1917

In late May and early July 1917, outbreaks of race-related labor violence by white Americans in East St. Louis, Illinois, left roughly 40 whites and 250 African Americans dead and another 6,000 Blacks homeless. The large-scale burning and vandalism cost approximately $400,000 in property damages ($8 million in 2021).

In late July, two battalions of the 24th Infantry rioted at two locations in Texas. Soldiers of the 1st Battalion guarding construction at Camp McArthur in Waco, Texas, ignored the town's Jim Crow laws and, when threatened with arrest, engaged in a shootout on city streets. Seven soldiers were court-martialed, sentenced to five years imprisonment and given dishonorable discharges.

That same month, 645 men of the 3rd Battalion were sent from Minnesota to guard airfield construction at Camp Logan in Houston, Texas, where racial animosity was intense, with the white populace and the

Houston Police Department harassing local Blacks as well as the newly arrived Black soldiers. In August 1917, a white policeman beat and arrested a Black private who attempted to intervene in the arrest of a Black woman. Both were jailed. A military police corporal sent to inquire after the private was pistol-whipped and shot at before being arrested. Rumors of the corporal's murder spread, causing about 150 soldiers to draw weapons and march toward Houston. Confronted by local policemen and a mob of armed Houston residents, soldiers killed 15 armed whites, including four policemen and an Illinois National Guard officer mistaken for a local policeman. Twenty-four other whites were seriously wounded, and four Black soldiers were killed.

The battalion was recalled to regimental headquarters in Columbus, New Mexico, while the Army hastily convened a court-martial at Fort Sam Houston, San Antonio, Texas. Sixteen servicemen were hung without their sentences being reviewed as required by regulation. A subsequent court condemned three more soldiers to death by hanging and sentenced 47 others to life imprisonment.

WORLD WAR I

Both incidents convinced the War Department to revise its plans and avoid large concentrations of Black troops in the South. Some officials and many of the public became concerned about Blacks' loyalty.[52] Congress considered disbanding all four regiments, and even though this was not done, regimental strengths diminished to about half of authorized level, partly so the Army could increase the size of its aviation component. As a result of the riots, the 25th Infantry Regiment performed garrison duty at Schofield Barracks, Hawaii, during World War I, and the 9th Cavalry Regiment was transferred to the Philippines. The 24th Infantry served along the border during World War I, crossing the border to engage rebels and Mexican troops at Juárez, opposite El Paso, Texas, in 1919. The 10th Cavalry regiment also patrolled the Mexican border and in January 1918, was involved in a firefight with Yaqui Indians just west of Nogales, Arizona. In August 1918, the regiment and elements of the 35th Infantry Regiment fought a border skirmish, the "battle of Ambos Nogales," involving German military advisors. This was the only battle fought against Germans soldiers in North America.

Noncommissioned officer cadres from the regiments were used to train other Black units formed during the war.

AFRICAN AMERICANS AT WEST POINT

West Point was an extremely hostile environment for Blacks after the Civil War and into the late 1940s. Despite Reconstruction and the 14th and 15th Amendments of the Constitution, the Military Academy, a bastion of Army tradition, was unwilling to accept Blacks as "officers and gentlemen." Between 1870 and 1898, 23 Blacks were appointed to West Point. Only 12 reported to the Academy, six lasted longer than one semester, and only three graduated. Those who reported as cadets were ostracized or "silenced"—no one spoke to them outside the drill field or classroom. It took years for entrenched racism to dissipate, but in 1991, West Point graduated its 1,000th Black, along with its 1,000th female.

The attitude at West Point was amply documented in the remarks of Major General John D. Schofield, superintendent from 1876 to 1881:

> To send to West Point for four years' competition a young man who has born in slavery is to assume that half a generation is sufficient to raise the colored man to the social, moral, and intellectual level which the average white man has reached in several hundred years. As well might the common farm horse be entered in a four mile race against the best blood from a long line of racers.[53]

In July 1870, Grant's son Frederick Dent Grant, Class of 1871, swore to his father that "no damned nigger will ever graduate from West Point."[54] This was all but guaranteed by a war of terror, silencing, and unmerciful hazing. A comment by an 1876 graduate bound for the 10th Cavalry was typical: "I would much rather to get into a white regiment but my class is crazy for the Cavalry. . . . as to their being mokes [Blacks], I won't have near as much to do with them personally as you would with a black cook."[55]

Henry Ossian Flipper, born a slave in Thomasville, Georgia, was the seventh Black at West Point in 1873 and the first African American to graduate from the Military Academy. He was "silenced" during his entire career at the Point. Although Flipper's portrait was in his class yearbook, he was omitted from the class picture. However, when he received his diploma in June 1877, General Sherman led the applause. Liberia offered Flipper command of its army, but Flipper chose an assignment to the 10th Cavalry at Fort Sill in Indian Territory. Flipper served at Forts Elliott,

Concho, Quitman, and Davis in Texas and was twice engaged in battle against Apache Indians during the Victorio campaign of 1880–1881 near Eagle Springs, Texas, serving as scout and messenger for regimental commander Colonel Benjamin Grierson. Throughout his years of service, Flipper displayed great competency and an exceptional talent for engineering. A complex of drainage trenches he designed at Fort Sill to mitigate the danger of malaria is still known as "Flipper's Ditch" and was designated a Black Military Heritage Site in 1977.

Flipper was transferred to Fort Davis, Texas, late in 1880 as quartermaster and acting commissary officer under the post commander, Colonel William R. Shafter, who disliked Blacks. In July 1881, Flipper discovered that over $2,000 (roughly $52,986 in 2019) was missing from the commissary safe. When word spread about the missing money, many felt it was a setup. Colonel Grierson wrote a long letter of commendation in Flipper's behalf, and soldiers and community members contributed to replace the missing funds. Shafter still convened a court-martial, which found Flipper innocent of embezzlement. A new charge of "conduct unbecoming an officer" was concocted based on Flipper's friendship with a white woman, a gross breach of "etiquette" at the time. He was convicted of making a false statement and writing a check on a nonexistent bank account. The judge advocate general recommended punishment other than dismissal, but President Chester A. Arthur accepted the court's decision. Flipper was dismissed from the service in June 1882, while two white officers convicted of embezzlement remained in the service.

Flipper had a successful mining and surveying career in the Southwest and Mexico, authored several books, and edited a white newspaper, the *Nogales Sunday Herald*. He petitioned Congress nine times to clear his name, and his offer of service during the Spanish–American War was rejected. Following his death in 1940, Flipper's descendants continued advocating to have his dishonorable discharge overturned, and in 1976, after his mistreatment was acknowledged, he was granted an honorable discharge by the Department of the Army. President Bill Clinton pardoned Lieutenant Flipper posthumously in February 1999, 117 years after his conviction. A bust of Flipper was unveiled at West Point that year, and the military academy presents an annual award in his honor to a cadet who exhibits "leadership, self-discipline, and perseverance in the face of unusual difficulties" at an annual Henry Flipper Dinner.

Lieutenant Henry Ossian Flipper, West Point graduate.
SOURCE: NATIONAL ARCHIVES AND RECORDS ADMINISTRATION.

Flipper was fortunate compared to his roommate Johnson Chestnut Whittaker, who entered West Point in 1876, the only Black cadet after Flipper graduated. He had no friends or social life; his only solace was the Bible. Just as Flipper experienced, no one spoke to him outside the classroom or field training. On April 4, 1880, two months before graduation, he found a note warning, "You will be fixed. Better keep awake."[56] Three masked assailants entered his room that night, and Whittaker was found tied to his bed, unconscious, bleeding, and bruised. The Academy's administrators did not believe him but apparently had second thoughts. Schofield was replaced as commandant by Oliver Otis Howard, founder of Howard University and former head of the Freedmen's Bureau. Because Whittaker failed his philosophy course, he was dismissed just before graduating. He endured two courts-martial. Both found him guilty, although the second court recommended leniency. The Army judge advocate general overturned the decision, and in March 1882, Secretary of War Robert Todd Lincoln (Abraham Lincoln's son) declared the court-martial invalid. This was ratified by President Chester A. Arthur. But Lincoln ordered Whittaker dismissed from the Academy because he failed an examination in June 1880. Although officially innocent and the victim of a brutal, inexcusable attack, Whittaker never became an Army officer. President Bill Clinton awarded a commission to Whittaker's heirs in 1995.

John Hanks Alexander, born in January 1864 in Helena, Arkansas, to formerly enslaved parents, graduated 10 years after Flipper. He was 32nd out of 64 classmates and was assigned to the 9th Cavalry in 1886. In 1894, he became professor of military science at Wilberforce University in Ohio, a Black institution, but he died later that year of a ruptured aorta at age 30.

West Point's third Black graduate, Charles Young, born enslaved in Lick, Kentucky, in 1864, entered West Point in 1884 and graduated in 1889 after repeating a year because of a failed math course. Although he had low engineering grades, he was coached by his instructor, Lieutenant George Washington Goethals, builder of the Panama Canal. After graduating, Young joined the 9th Cavalry at Fort Robinson, Nebraska, and accompanied the unit to Fort Duchesne, Utah, the following year, serving there until 1894. When Alexander died, Young was assigned as professor of military science to Wilberforce University, where he began a lifelong friendship with Black scholar W.E.B. Du Bois. Young also became an early supporter of the National Association for the Advancement of Colored People (NAACP), serving on its board from 1917. During the Spanish–American War, Young was promoted to the temporary rank of major as commander of the 8th Ohio Volunteer Infantry Regiment. When the war ended, Young reverted to lieutenant but was promoted to captain in February 1901. Young proved to be an exceptional leader, commanding troops in the Philippine jungles for 18 months, earning the nickname "Follow Me!"

In 1903, Young served as captain commanding the 10th Cavalry's I Troop at the Presidio of San Francisco. He was appointed acting superintendent of Sequoia and General Grant National Parks, the first Black superintendent of a national park. This was a short-term, summer assignment due to limited funding, making it difficult to accomplish significant goals. However, Young had a major impact on the park, supervising road construction and developing the park to make it accessible to more visitors. Young's men accomplished more in one summer than in the previous three years. A wagon road to the Giant Forest in Sequoia National Park, home of the world's largest trees, and another road to the base of the famous Moro Rock made it possible for visitors to enter the mountaintop forest. Young established fire watches to guard against wildfires and evicted sheep herders grazing their flocks on meadows at the foot of Mount Whitney.

In 1904, Young became one of America's first military attachés when he posted to Port-au-Prince, Haiti, for three years. In 1908, Young was sent to the Philippines to command a squadron of two troops of the 9th Cavalry Regiment, his second tour there. After his return to the United States, he served for two years at Fort David A. Russell in Wyoming. In 1912, Young served for three years as military attaché to Liberia, the first African American to hold that post. For his accomplishments, the NAACP awarded Young the Spingarn Medal in 1916, the second year of the prestigious award's existence.

In 1912 Young published *The Military Morale of Nations and Races*, an insightful study of the cultural sources of military power. He argued against prevailing racial stereotypes, using history and social science to demonstrate that supposedly servile or unmilitary races, including Negroes and Jews, displayed courage when fighting for democratic principles. Young noted that the key to raising an effective army from diverse peoples was to link patriotic service with the democratic ideals of equal rights and fair play.

Young led the 10th Cavalry Regiment during the Mexican Punitive Expedition in 1916 as a regular Army major, commanding two of Persh-

Colonel Charles Young, West Point graduate. SOURCE: LIBRARY OF CONGRESS.

ing's three lead columns. While leading a pistol charge against Pancho Villa's forces at Agua Caliente on April 1, 1916, he routed the opposing forces without losing a single man and led his troopers to the rescue of the 13th Cavalry at Santa Cruz de Villegas.

Because of his exceptional leadership in Mexico, Young was promoted to lieutenant colonel in September 1916. He commanded Fort Huachuca, Arizona, headquarters of the 10th Cavalry, until June 1917, when he was abruptly medically retired against his wishes. Blacks were held in such contempt that no chance was taken that Young might command white troops. He returned to Wilberforce University as professor of military science through most of 1918, but that November, he traveled by horseback from Ohio to Washington, D.C., to prove his physical fitness. Secretary of War Baker refused to rescind the order forcibly retiring him—President Wilson was adamant that no Black officer could command white troops. A white lieutenant had already complained about serving under Young. In 1919, Young was again assigned as military attaché to Liberia. He was on a reconnaissance mission in Nigeria in late 1921 when he suddenly became ill and died of a kidney infection in January 1922. He was buried with honors in Arlington National Cemetery, and today, his home in Wilberforce, Ohio, is a national park. Young was posthumously promoted to brigadier general in the Kentucky National Guard in February 2020, and two years later Secretary of the Army Christine E. Wormuth announced his promotion to permanent regular Army brigadier general, effective November 1, 2021.

WORLD WAR II

As World War II approached, Black regiments were understrength, often used for post maintenance and ancillary duties, with less emphasis placed on marksmanship and combat training. A detached troop from the 9th Cavalry taught riding instruction, mounted drill, and cavalry tactics at West Point from 1905 to 1947, commemorated in August 2021 with the unveiling of a statue on the West Point plain of a Buffalo Soldier sergeant mounted on his steed.

The 9th and 10th Cavalry Regiments joined the skeletal 2nd Cavalry Division in February 1941. After being brought up to strength and conducting field training, the division deployed to North Africa in January 1944 but was inactivated in Oran, Algeria, in March 1944. 9th Cavalry personnel were assigned to labor and service units, many serving

Buffalo Soldier statue installed at US Military Academy, West Point, New York, August 31, 2021. Source: Good Black News.

as stevedores unloading supply ships. The 10th Cavalry was reorganized into the 1334th Engineer Construction Battalion (Colored), assisting in constructing airfield facilities for the Tuskegee Airmen. Soldiers from both regiments later volunteered to serve with elements of the 92nd Infantry Division, which took heavy losses assaulting the Germans' well-engineered Gothic Line in the Apennine Mountain range of northern Italy.

When World War II broke out, elements of the 24th Infantry were serving as school troops at the Fort Benning, Georgia, Infantry School. After participating in the fall maneuvers in Louisiana in 1941, the 24th Infantry Regiment deployed as an independent regiment to New Hebrides, now the country of Vanuatu, on April 4, 1942. Their duties mainly included road building, off-loading ships, and installation maintenance. The regiment moved to Guadalcanal in August 1943 to conduct mop-up operations after US forces had seized the island. The regiment arrived on Saipan and Tinian in the Marianas in December 1944 for garrison duty and elimination of residual Japanese forces, where their superior conduct in combat operations merited the commendation of a War Department survey group. The regiment deployed to the Kerama Islands off Okinawa in July 1945, accepting the surrender of Japanese forces on the island of Aka-shima, the first surrender of a Japanese Imperial Army garrison. After

World War II, the 24th pulled occupation duty in Okinawa, relocating to Gifu, Japan, in February 1947, assigned to the 25th Infantry Division.

The 25th Infantry Regiment became a component of the 93rd Infantry Division, activated in California in May 1942, with advance elements deploying to Guadalcanal in the Pacific in January 1944. With the Division's 368th and 369th Infantry Regiments, the 25th Infantry campaigned in New Guinea, Northern Solomons (Bougainville), and the Bismarck Archipelago (Admiralty Islands), mostly conducting mop-up operations, unloading ships, and clearing battlefield damage. In the main, the division was used as a rear echelon force, reflected in its combat losses: 12 men killed and 121 wounded. Once the war ended, the regiment was demobilized at Camp Stoneman, California, in February 1946 with the rest of the 93rd division, leaving the 24th Infantry as the sole Buffalo Soldier regiment on active duty.

KOREAN WAR

Despite Truman's Executive Order 9981 signed on July 26, 1948, directing desegregation of the US armed forces, the 24th Infantry was still all-Black, except for senior officers, when the Korean War began. A Black lieutenant colonel commanded one of the three battalions, but he elected to remain in charge of the home base in Gifu when the unit deployed to Korea in late June 1950 to assist in what was initially termed a "minor police action." He did not believe the regiment was ready for combat. As it turned out, none of the US forces sent to the peninsula were ready or equipped for the intense combat they encountered, first from the North Korean Communist Army and later, by swarms of the Chinese Communist Peoples' Army. The regiment fought in temperature extremes ranging from over 100 degrees to −20, participating in six campaigns for 17 months. Two of the regiment's soldiers were awarded the Medal of Honor, and numerous other members of the regiment won an array of awards for valor. When the regiment was disbanded in North Korea in October 1951, midway through the war, its soldiers were integrated into other units. The 24th Infantry Regiment completed 85 years of continuous and distinguished service. Its experience in Korea is described in Chapter Seven.

THE PRESENT

Under the Army's Combat Arms Regimental System, the Army reactivated the 24th Infantry Regiment's 1st Battalion at Fort Lewis, Washington, in

August 1995 as a component of the 25th Infantry Division. Awarded an Army Superior Unit Award in 1996, in the spring of 2002, the battalion was reorganized and equipped as a Stryker (8 x 8-wheeled armored fighting vehicles) battalion. In October 2004, the battalion deployed with the 1st Stryker Brigade, 25th Infantry Division to Mosul, Iraq, where the unit received a Valorous Unit Award. Deactivated in June 2006, it was reactivated at Fort Wainwright, Fairbanks, Alaska, in December. Battalion elements served at Forward Observation Base Lagman, Zabul Province, Afghanistan, in 2011 and 2012. The 24th Infantry remains at Fort Wainwright today, evolving into part of a brigade combat team of the 11th Airborne Division of the Alaskan Command during the summer of 2022.

CONCLUSIONS

All four regular army Buffalo Soldier regiments compiled remarkable records from 1866 to 1951, one spanning 85 years of service. Constituting 20 percent of the cavalry troops who fought the Indian Wars, Black regulars distinguished themselves by professionalism and bravery at remote outposts under austere conditions, led by distinguished white regimental commanders and a few Black officers. All four regiments played major roles in the Spanish–American War, where their exploits were widely applauded but quickly forgotten. Even the memory of the glory and the heroism of their assault of San Juan Hill was stolen from them—they were literally cropped from the picture of the victors.

Both infantry regiments were involved in racial incidents in the years before World War I. Three companies of the 25th Infantry were involved at Brownsville, Texas, in August 1906 in an incident resulting in the death of a white bartender and wounding of a police officer. Without evidence, President Theodore Roosevelt dishonorably discharged 167 soldiers, who were exonerated by President Nixon in 1972. Facing the same virulent racism, two battalions of the 24th Infantry were involved in separate incidents in Texas during the summer of 1917. In Houston, 15 whites were killed, and 12 others were seriously wounded. A court-martial indicted 118 enlisted men and found 110 guilty. Nineteen soldiers were summarily hanged and 63 received life sentences. All three incidents demonstrate the consequences of bigotry and white supremacy and are a sad commentary on American justice.

Three out of the four regiments participated in the Punitive campaign against Pancho Villa in 1916, but because of the incidents in Texas, none of the four Buffalo Soldier regiments saw service in Europe during World War I due to racial incidents involving both infantry regiments. The 9th Cavalry was stationed in the Philippines, and the 25th Infantry spent the war in Hawaii, both American protectorates, while the 10th Cavalry and 24th Infantry Regiments patrolled the Mexican border. During World War II, both cavalry regiments were disbanded upon arrival in North Africa and used as service troops, engineers, or replacements. The 25th Infantry Regiment deployed to the Pacific in January 1944 as part of the 93rd Infantry Division, campaigning in New Guinea, Northern Solomons, and the Bismarck Archipelago, mostly conducting mop-up operations, unloading ships, and clearing battlefield damage. The unit was demobilized along with the rest of the division when the war ended.

The last of the Buffalo Soldiers, the 24th Infantry, was among the first American forces deployed to the Pacific in April 1942 as an independent unit, used mostly for logistical and mop-up operations. The regiment ended the war in Okinawa and was subsequently integrated into the 25th Infantry Division and stationed in Japan. When North Korean Communist forces attacked South Korea in late June 1950, the 24th was among the first American units to deploy, establishing a mixed record. Although there was much individual heroism—two Medal of Honor winners and many other awards for valor—racism corroded unit cohesion and mutual trust. The regiment was disbanded in September 1951, three years after President Truman's 1948 integration order.

For more than three-quarters of a century, the Buffalo Soldiers established a record of faithful service under challenging conditions, earning a reputation as fierce and disciplined fighters despite ostracism and rabid racism. Briefly appreciated for their exploits during the Spanish–American War, in the Philippines, and during the Mexican Punitive Expedition, their exploits were forgotten soon afterward, as had the US Colored Troops' illustrious Civil War record. President Wilson and his administration were so biased against Blacks that the distinguished senior African American officer, Charles Young, was forcefully retired because his potential promotion to brigadier general meant he might command white soldiers.

Throughout their service, the Buffalo Soldiers displayed a deep inner strength that overcame the disdain of most white officers and fellow white soldiers, enduring adversities that would have daunted and broken lesser men.

CHAPTER 5

African American Service in World War I

> In these days of conservation, when every rag and bone and tin can is saved, human beings cannot be wasted. These colored men have to be inducted into the service by draft in their turn . . . which . . . will release men available for other service.
>
> Colonel E. D. Anderson
> Chief, Operations Branch,
> War Plans Division, May 6, 1918

Two Black infantry divisions, the 92nd and 93rd, provide excellent case studies of the corrosive effects of American bigotry. The French army, bled dry in combat since 1914, eagerly received the men of the 93rd Infantry Division's four regiments, trained them well, and integrated them into their divisions. Treated like men, each performed exceptionally, and all four were awarded the Croix de Guerre. Numerous soldiers and officers won individual American and French awards.

The 92nd Division, rejected by the British, was held in reserve under the American Expeditionary Forces (AEF) and treated as second-class citizens. They rose to the occasion in the final offensive and were the only division of the four in the 2nd Army to take its objectives. That did not stop a dishonest high command from maligning their valor.

The roughly 200,000 Black soldiers who served in Europe were stereotyped, oppressed, and constantly accused of rape. Most—160,000—served as service or support troops.

PREWAR ERA

A month before Woodrow Wilson was elected president in 1913, Josephus Daniels, Wilson's campaign manager and later secretary of the Navy, published an editorial in his North Carolina newspaper declaring that the South would never feel secure until the North and West adopted the Southern policy of political proscription and racial segregation of the Negro.[1] This was perhaps a pale reflection of the South's attitude that had precipitated secession and the Civil War, a conviction that the region should dominate national politics.

The nationwide spread of the virus of white supremacy was facilitated by emerging motion picture technology as well as the rebirth of the Ku Klux Klan, which spread the "Southern way." Thomas F. Dixon Jr. (1864–1946), Baptist minister, lawyer, politician, and prolific author, was responsible more than any other individual for perpetuating the South's racist fervor. His first novel, *The Leopard's Spots: A Romance of the White Man's Burden, 1865-1900* (1902), distilled stories of the Lost Cause and white supremacy recounted from his youth. Dixon intended to counter *Uncle Tom's Cabin*, purposely importing Simon Legree, Uncle Tom's fictional overseer, and converting him into an equally villainous Southern Republican scalawag and emphasizing the supposed exploitation of Blacks by Republicans during Reconstruction.

Dixon portrayed Southern white Democrats as the Blacks' "true friends" in what eventually became a trilogy, including *The Clansman: A Historical Romance of the Ku Klux Klan* (1905) and *The Traitor: The Story of the Fall of the Invisible Empire* (1907). All three works were overtly racist. The trilogy's core purpose was to demonstrate the superiority of the white race, coupled with an obsessive fear and hatred of "inferior" races.[2] The title of *The Leopard's Spots* is based on a line that reads, "The Ethiopian cannot change his skin, or the leopard his spots. . . . The Negro is the human donkey! You can train him, but you can't make him a horse. . . . What is called our race prejudice is simply God's first law of nature—the instinct of self-preservation."[3]

Because much of the powerful influence *Uncle Tom's Cabin* had on ending slavery came from traveling theatrical performances, which made

Beecher's novel an integral part of American culture, Dixon wrote a stage version for *The Clansman*. The motion picture industry was just beginning at the time, so Dixon contacted film director David Wark Griffith, the son of a Confederate Army colonel from Kentucky, to produce *The Birth of a Nation*, one of the first cinema blockbusters released in 1915.

Dixon and Griffith made extensive use of Woodrow Wilson's scholarly five-volume *History of the American People* for their source material. Dixon and Wilson were roommates at Johns Hopkins University, and Dixon persuaded President Wilson, the first Southern-born president since the Civil War, to host a screening of the film in the White House. The movie's second showing was attended and endorsed by Chief Justice Edward Douglas White, a former slave owner and Confederate soldier who had also been a member of the white militia that fought in New Orleans against state and federal forces commanded by Louisiana Adjutant Gen-

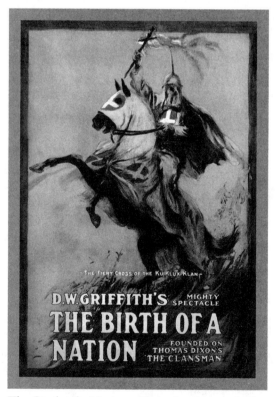

The Birth of a Nation. *Poster for America's first blockbuster movie, 1915.*

eral James Longstreet.⁴ Wilson and Edwards's implied endorsement represented two of the three branches of government, enabling the movie's long, prosperous, and influential commercial life, even though much of it was sheer fantasy and racist in the extreme. The movie featured Southern forces defeating federal troops President Grant sent to stop the terrorism rampant in the South.⁵

However, Wilson had his private secretary release a statement:

> It is true that "The Birth of a Nation" was produced before the President and his family at the White House, but the President was entirely unaware of the character of the play before it was presented and has at no time expressed his approbation of it. Its exhibition at the White House was a courtesy extended to an old acquaintance.⁶

In 1918, Wilson told his secretary that he thought *The Birth of a Nation* was "a very unfortunate production," which he hoped would not be shown "in communities where there are so many colored people." In 1937, 22 years after the screening and 13 years after Wilson's death, a magazine article said that the president had reacted to *The Birth of a Nation*'s depiction of the Civil War and Reconstruction period by saying, "It is like writing history with lightning. And my only regret is that it is all so terribly true." Sadly, the "history written with lightning" quote, although never true, stuck firmly in the popular consciousness.⁷

The original Ku Klux Klan, a purely terrorist organization, the "Invisible Empire of the South," gradually disappeared once "Redemption" was achieved in each of the Southern states. But the night before Thanksgiving 1915, "Colonel" William J. Simmons, a preacher and professional promoter of fraternal organizations, held a service at Stone Mountain, near Atlanta, Georgia, on almost the same day *The Birth of a Nation* was released. With President Wilson's viewing of the film in the White House and Chief Justice White's admission that he had been a former member of the Klan, many nativist-minded Americans reassessed the organization in a more acceptable and romantic light.

Denigration of Blacks became a national obsession, as thousands hastened to join the ranks of the Klan, which set huge crosses aflame during initiation rites, tokens of "glorifying the light of Jesus Christ." This resurrection of the Ku Klux Klan was aimed not only against Blacks, but its flag-waving xenophobia also attacked Jews, Roman Catholics, and immigrants. Reframed with a broad program to unite "native-born white Christians for concerted action in the preservation of American institutions and the supremacy of the white race," the organization flourished nationally, claimed 100,000 members, and was still growing by 1920.

At least five US senators acknowledged membership in the Klan, as did thousands of pastors.[8] This incarnation of the Klan included tens of thousands of respectable community members, including up to half a million women. By the mid-1920s, the Klan claimed to have 4 million members, with some estimates ranging up to 9 million. By 1925, Michigan claimed more members than any other state, an impressive 875,000, followed by New Jersey. This time the Klan's popularity expanded beyond the South. The Klan enjoyed considerable political power in Georgia, Texas, Oklahoma, Oregon, and Maine. For a time, the Klan ranked ahead of the Boy and Girl Scouts as the most popular organization in America.[9] In the 1920s and 1930s, the Klan flirted with fascist-flavored political power, and some members were elected to political

Ku Klux Klan marching down Pennsylvania Avenue, 1928. SOURCE: NATIONAL ARCHIVES AND RECORDS ADMINISTRATION.

office, especially in Indiana, the Klan's national headquarters. The Klan paraded down Pennsylvania Avenue in mass parades in the late 1920s.

William Gibbs McAdoo, Woodrow Wilson's son-in-law and secretary of the treasury, ordered the segregation of all federal bathrooms, affecting around 5,000 Blacks in the District of Columbia and another 10,000 across the country.[10] Jerold M. Packard, author of *American Nightmare: The History of Jim Crow*, asserts that Wilson wasn't a particularly vicious racist, although as a Southerner and a Virginian, he was imbued with a conviction of white supremacy to his core.[11] Unfortunately, Wilson and most of his cabinet, and probably most white Americans at the time, were racists as well. This was true of the War Department, Army, Navy, and Marines, even though Black troops had fought heroically during the Civil War, in the Indian Wars, Cuba, Puerto Rico, and the Philippines. Jim Crow followed the American flag; the fact that the 9th and 10th Cavalry Regiments and the two Black regular army infantry regiments had attacked enemy forces on San Juan Hill alongside Teddy Roosevelt's Rough Riders and established exemplary records of heroism in Cuba simply did not matter. After brief acclaim, their achievements were almost instantly forgotten.

The "Southern way" metastasized into the "American way." The migration of Blacks into what became the residential slums of larger Northern cities to fill jobs in war industries increased racial tensions. Blacks were excluded from labor unions because Northern labor feared and resented Black competition. During the war, whites reacted violently to Blacks taking jobs in war industries. One of the most egregious reactions was the multiday race riot in East St. Louis, Illinois, in July 1917. In response, the National Association for the Advancement of Colored People (NAACP) organized a silent parade down Fifth Avenue in New York City, protesting continuing acts of violence toward Black Americans. German propaganda magnified racial incidents in an unsuccessful attempt to arouse antiwar sentiment in the American Black community. Although President Woodrow Wilson ultimately publicly denounced mob violence and lynching, lawlessness continued—54 lynchings occurred in 1916 and 38 in 1917.

"THE WAR TO END ALL WARS"
Overall, about a half million Blacks were drafted and served either in the United States or abroad before the war ended. When the United States finally declared war, General John "Black Jack" Pershing, who derived his

distinctive nickname from his service with the 10th Cavalry Buffalo Soldiers, was named commander of the AEF.[12] At the time, Blacks were held in such contempt that Colonel Charles Young, the third Black West Point graduate, who commanded the 10th Cavalry with great distinction during the Punitive Expedition in Mexico in 1916, was medically retired in June 1917 against his wishes. This was done rather than risk the possibility that he might command white troops should he be promoted to brigadier general and command more white troops—a white lieutenant serving in his regiment already complained. Furthermore, the all-pervading racism of the time and distrust of Blacks due to three incidents involving both Black infantry regiments in Texas in 1906 and 1917 ensured that none of the four regular army Black regiments saw duty in Europe. Instead, they were deployed to the Philippines, Hawaii, and along the Mexican border, although soldiers from all four units provided a cadre of officers and noncommissioned officers for the two Black infantry divisions, which, after much lobbying by Blacks and others, saw overseas service. In addition, about 5,300 Blacks served in the US Navy.

Mississippi Senator James K. Vardaman warned that Black military service threatened the South's status quo in a declaration providing an indication of the racism prevalent at the time:

> Impress the negro with the fact that he is defending the flag, inflate his untutored soul with military airs, teach him that it is his duty to keep the emblem of the nation flying triumphantly in the air—it is but a short step to the conclusion that his political rights must be respected, even though it is necessary for him to give his life in defense of those rights and you at once create a problem far-reaching and momentous in its character.[13]

When running for governor of Mississippi in 1903, Vardaman exclaimed, "The only effect of Negro education is to spoil a good field hand and make an insolent cook."[14] Having made it all but impossible for most Blacks to get a decent education, the South, the Army, and the nation had the nerve to blame *Blacks* for their ignorance.

Whereas during the Spanish–American War, 20 to 40 percent of ships' crews were Black, according to a US Navy film, "African-Americans in The United States Navy - A Short History," by World War I, thanks to Wilson's administration and prevailing Jim Crow racial antagonism, Blacks were almost excluded from the Navy, constituting a mere 1 percent, confined to oil and coal rooms, cooks, or stewards. Official policy completely excluded African Americans from 1922 through 1932.

A total of 6,451,856 men were enrolled in the first draft; 342,247 Blacks (31.74 percent) and 1,416,750 whites (26.84 percent) were called up for service.[15] Selection boards, particularly in the South, were biased (most had no Blacks): 51.65 percent of Blacks and only 32.53 percent of whites were placed in Class I.[16] Ultimately, a half million Blacks were drafted or enlisted. Around 200,000 African Americans served overseas, most of whom—160,000—served in service and support functions. However, roughly 40,000 Blacks served in two combat divisions that the War Department grudgingly organized, the 92nd and the 93rd Infantry, perhaps not by accident the last numerically of the divisions America raised for World War I. Overall, Black enlisted men made up 13 percent of the total active-duty force, but only .07 percent of the officer corps, reflecting the pronounced white bias that Blacks were incapable of leading troops in combat.[17]

The government's official propaganda depicting the war as a crusade for democracy naturally raised expectations that this might happen at home as well as worldwide. Once again, Blacks hoped that their wartime service would facilitate their achievement of justice and equality.

After Joel Spingarn, the white president of the NAACP, contacted General Leonard Wood, former Army chief of staff, a training camp for Black officer candidates was organized at Fort Des Moines, Iowa, which ultimately trained 1,200 Black officers, some of whom were former Buffalo Soldier noncommissioned officers. The first class of 639 men—captains and first or second lieutenants—graduated July 22, 1917. It contained four recent Harvard graduates and two graduates of Harvard Law School. A later class trained doctors and dentists. Emmett J. Scott, former assistant to Booker T. Washington, appointed by Secretary of War Newton Baker to serve as special advisor on Black affairs, helped establish Reserve Officer Training Corps (ROTC) programs at more than 20 Black colleges and universities. The ROTC and Officer Candidate School (OCS) together yielded far more Black officers than in any of America's previous wars. However, promotion restrictions ensured that most Blacks advanced no higher than captain. The War Department was loath to promote Blacks to field grade rank out of fear that they would command white troops; delusions of white superiority played a heavy role in their phobia.

92ND INFANTRY DIVISION

The first Black combat division, the 92nd Division, nicknamed the Buffalo Division, was authorized in October 1917, after considerable political debate and pressure from prominent Black and white citizens. In addition to its four infantry regiments, the 92nd division had a field artillery brigade; two machine gun battalions; and engineer, signal, and other support units making it capable of independent operations—a typical table of organization and equipment of the time totaling 27,000 men. The 92nd was composed entirely of Black draftees, including the 365th Infantry Regiment, raised predominantly from Texas and Oklahoma; the 366th, from Alabama; the 367th, from New York; and the 368th from Tennessee, Pennsylvania, and Maryland.

The War Department selected a white officer, Major General Charles Ballou, to command the division based on his five years of service with the 24th Infantry Regiment and recent command of the Fort Des Moines, Iowa, officer training camp for Black officers. The division's officers included graduates from Des Moines, but most ranking officers were whites who had served in Black regular army regiments. This was emphatically a Jim Crow division; General Ballou's Bulletin 35 in part declared: "The Division Commander repeats that the success of this division . . . is dependent upon the good will of the public. The public is nine-tenths white. White men made the division, and they can break it just as easily if it becomes a trouble maker."[18] On the other hand, Ballou wrote to the assistant Commandant of the General Staff College, "It was my misfortune to be handicapped by many white officers who were rabidly hostile to the idea of colored soldiers, and who continually conveyed misinformation to the staffs of superior units, and generally caused much trouble and discontent. Such men will never give the negro the square deal that is his just due."[19]

The division's four infantry regiments and support units trained briefly at seven widely dispersed camps in the South, having no interaction with each other until they landed in France in June 1918. Upon arrival in Europe, Pershing tried to foist the 92nd Division off on the British. But the British, equally racist, declined, so the division languished in reserve with all its training deficiencies, inexperience in trench warfare, and racial hostility with white officers who expected little from Black troops.[20] The division was assigned a sector in Saint-Dié in the Vosges Mountains in the northwest salient of France. Training was problematic; the chief of the AEF's G-5 (training) section inspected the division on June 27 and discovered startling deficiencies: no transportation, no heavy machine guns or automatic rifles, no pistols for officers and noncommissioned officers, no mortars, no artillery pieces, no grenades, and only 10 rounds of rifle ammunition on hand per soldier.

The 92nd Division was finally committed to attack over unfamiliar ground during the 47 days of the Meuse–Argonne offensive, which opened September 26, 1918, involving 1.3 million Americans who suffered some 1,000,000 casualties, including 26,000 killed in action. Colonel Greer, the 93rd Division's chief of staff, believed that the 368th Regiment was the best regiment of the division.[21] Much would be made of the regiment's "failure"; although two battalions failed in their first attempts, the 1st Battalion, led by a soldier of fortune, Major John N. Merrill, succeeded and captured its objective, Binarville, 20 minutes after French elements entered the hamlet.[22] Despite the failure of white field grade officers, intense criticism was focused on Black junior officers. General Ballou labeled them "worthless," "inefficient," "untrustworthy," and "cowardly," although an inept white battalion commander of the 368th Regiment was perhaps the biggest problem. The lack of maps and an adequate supply of wire cutters, rifle grenades, and signal flares reflected poor staff planning by senior white officers. But as historian Chad Williams notes, the 368th's "misfortune" pales in comparison to the disaster endured by the all-white 35th Infantry Division from Missouri and Kansas.

Thirty Black officers were relieved of command. One battalion commander court-martialed five Black officers for cowardice in the face of the enemy; four were convicted and sentenced to death by firing squad, while the fifth received a sentence of life imprisonment.[23] The commander of the 2nd Army, Lieutenant General Robert Lee Bullard, recommended clemency because "these Negroes should not be held as responsible as white men." Born in Alabama, Bullard apparently was a "thoroughgoing Negro hater" who believed that all Black officers were incompetent simply because of their skin color.[24]

After the war, an Army investigation into the 368th Regiment's operations concluded that the regiment failed not only due to not enough heavy wire cutters but also inadequate maps and lack of artillery support. The soldiers, who had yet to experience combat, had just completed a long march from the rear in the rain and had not eaten for two days. Normally, troops served in a defensive sector before conducting an assault, but this was their first battalion- and regimental-scale frontal attack aside from conducting small reconnaissance raids. The 368th's misfortune was replicated by the experience of more than one entire white division, but white soldiers' poor performance was attributed to lack of training and experience. No one implied that their failure had anything to do with their race.[25]

General Bullard, who regularly used the racial slur "nigah," apparently had absolutely no respect for Blacks and had a personality conflict with the 92nd Infantry Division's commanding officer, Major General Charles C. Ballou, so deep that he fired Ballou a week after the Armistice. On November 19, Ballou was replaced by Major General Charles H. Martin, whose mission was to remind the African American soldiers in the 92nd Division that they were not to construe their wartime service as creating any kind of equality with whites. Martin insisted that "the negro is of very little importance . . . not by any means equal to the average white man" in 1920, when the Army's authority to maintain Jim Crow regulations came under criticism.

The 92nd Division's 167th Artillery Brigade, commanded by Brigadier General John H. Sherburne, a reserve officer who in professional life was an engineer from Boston, was an outstanding outfit by any measure. It consisted of the 149th and 150th Regiments, armed with 24 French 75s, and the 151st Regiment, equipped with a like number of 155mm cannon. Unfortunately, this equipment was not available in the United States, but Sherburne trained the unit in France in an abbreviated time to an exceptional standard. To defeat doubts that Blacks could be adequate artillerists, special canvasses of Tuskegee Institute and other institutions of higher education were made. Sherburne later wrote, "The enlisted men . . . worked with a zeal I have never seen equaled, and while slow to learn, appeared to be fully as accurate in their final work as were white artillery personnel. Their rate of fire was unequaled." In handling trucks and tractors for the heavy artillery, he judged the men of his brigade "fully as good if not better than their white opposites." A French artillery officer concurred; he remarked that one barrage laid by one of the light regiments was the fastest and most accurate he had ever seen.[26]

The 317th Engineer Regiment, commanded by white officers, was another phenomenal success. The regimental commander was a railroad engineer who managed to keep both light and standard gauge railroads operating so they could deliver the massive tonnage of ammunition required for the final offensive as well as other supplies needed for units in the field. The regimental deputy commander was a regular army engineer who kept the roads and railroads in the division's sector operative, no mean feat given the constant disruption of German artillery. The regiment had only four trucks and had difficulty finding adequate paving material. They solved another important problem—ensuring that ammunition and troop replacement convoys did not block critical arteries, constantly pulling overturned trucks out of ditches. He recognized the utility of Caterpillar tractors and directed his men to "borrow" them at night from French heavy gun crews.

Despite proof that Blacks did as well or better than white divisions in their ability to withstand gas attacks, senior officers constantly formed rationalizations that confirmed their biases to the contrary. Rexmond C. Cochrane, the leading historian of World War I chemical warfare, conducted extensive studies in the 1950s and concluded that Blacks' chemical defense was among the best in the AEF. Aside from the division gas officer, all the 92nd Infantry Division's gas officers were Black.[27]

As if the hostility of their white officers was not enough, white regular army units camped near the division spread rumors that Blacks were subhuman creatures with an insatiable lust for white women, a standard Jim Crow tactic used to dehumanize and demonize Blacks. 2nd Army commander General Bullard's assessment after only three weeks of "observation" was harsh: "The negro division seems to be in a fair way a failure. It is in a quiet sector, yet can hardly take care of itself while to take any offensive action seems wholly beyond its powers. . . . They are really inferior soldiers; there is no denying it."[28] Nevertheless, the 92nd Division surprised its detractors when finally given a chance in the last big offensive before the Armistice in 1918. In fact, the only division of the four assigned to Bullard's newly formed 2nd Army that accomplished its mission on the last push of November 10–11 was the 92nd Infantry Division. All three of its assigned regiments achieved their objectives, while the 2nd Army's three white divisions failed.[29]

Despite Bullard's blanket condemnation, General Pershing's assessment was far more complimentary when he reviewed the division for the last time at Le Mans on January 28, 1919. As recorded by Emmett Scott, the War Department's observer, "Black Jack" informed the troops that the division "stands second to none" and had "acquitted yourselves with credit" ever since the division had taken over its first sector. He particularly noted that they had not simply performed well in the field but also in their individual conduct. That last statement was significant given the widespread slander spread by senior officers that this was a division of rapists—without a scintilla of evidence.[30] Apparently, concrete evidence was not important relative to the absolute need to confirm delusions of white superiority, even at the cost of combat readiness, much less justice. To say that this was a phenomenon of the times does not excuse this fatal flaw of the American vision of democracy and equality, which significantly detracted from combat readiness.

93RD INFANTRY DIVISION (PROVISIONAL)

The other Black division, the 93rd Infantry Division (Provisional), formed mostly from Black National Guard units, was commanded by General Roy Hoffman and was organized at Camp Stuart, Newport News, Virginia, in December 1917. This division was "provisional" because the Army did not bother to organize the normal support units needed for a division to conduct independent operations, such as machine gun, engineer, artillery, and logistical units. As a result, its strength was around 14,000 men, and it was incapable of independent operations. Its four regiments were the 369th (15th New York National Guard); the 370th (8th Illinois National Guard, with all Black officers and combat experience in Cuba and along the Mexican border in 1916); the 371st (draftees from the cotton fields of the Carolinas, Georgia, Florida, and Alabama); and the 372nd (an amalgamation of National Guard units from the District of Columbia, Connecticut, Massachusetts, Maryland, Ohio, and Tennessee, rounded out with a leaven of 250 draftees from Michigan and Wisconsin).

When America entered the war, roughly 5,000 Blacks served in National Guard units, mostly concentrated in the North and Midwest—the South was, to say the least, wary of Black men under arms. After minimal training due to racial incidents in and around training bases in the South, all four regiments were hastily transported to Europe, where the 93rd Division's regiments were assigned to French divisions. The French were desperate to replace the hemorrhage of thousands of soldiers from its ranks after years of bitter trench warfare and the previous year's widespread strikes. They had little bias against Black soldiers because troops from Algeria, Morocco, and Senegal served in the French Army.

369TH INFANTRY REGIMENT

Colonel William Hayward, the son of a Republican senator from Nebraska and a prominent white New York lawyer active in the Union League

Colonel William Leland Hayward, 1917. SOURCE: UNDERWOOD ARCHIVES.

(sponsor of the Civil War's 20th and 26th US Colored Infantry Regiments), commanded the 15th New York National Guard Regiment from its organization in 1916 through the duration of the war. When the regiment mustered into service in May 1917 and went to Camp Whitman near Peekskill in upper New York state, the entire unit had only 250 rifles and lacked uniforms as well as individual equipment, such as mess kits. The regiment was rejected from inclusion in the newly formed 42nd "Rainbow" National Guard Division because "black is not a color of the rainbow."

The regiment received only two weeks of training due to severe racial tension around their base at Spartanburg, South Carolina, although the standard length of training was half a year. The town's mayor had taken it upon himself to admonish the War Department, New Yorkers, and members of the regiment in a piece published in the *New York Times*:

> I am sorry to hear that the Fifteenth Regiment has been ordered here, for, with their northern ideas about racial equality, they will probably expect to be treated like white men. I can say right here that they will not be treated as anything except Negroes. . . . This thing

is like waving a red flag in the face of a bull, something that can't be done without trouble. We have asked . . . the War Department not to send the soldiers here. You remember the trouble a couple weeks ago at Houston.[31]

A Chamber of Commerce representative observed, "We wouldn't mind if the Government sent us a regiment of Southern Negroes, for we understand them and they understand us." He observed, "We don't allow Negroes to use the same glass that a white man may later drink out of." The War Department made it clear that "The Race segregation system will be carefully observed."[32]

After two weeks of training, a provocative incident convinced Colonel Hayward to travel to Washington to seek early orders for Europe. The 369th Infantry was the first American military unit deployed to Europe, arriving on December 27, 1917, after a challenging Atlantic crossing. The regiment became a labor force for nearly two months while the AEF headquarters decided how to employ them—white units did not want to serve with Black soldiers. Pershing cabled Washington that he intended to initially use all four of the 93rd Division's regiments as Services of Supply troops or convert them to pioneer infantry. He changed his mind because the provisional Black division fulfilled his promise of four combat regiments for the French.

On March 10, 1918, the 369th was transferred to the French, given three weeks of instruction in trench warfare and use of French weapons, and sent to the front. The transfer was done with such alacrity that Colonel Hayward wrote to a friend, "Our great American general put the Black orphan in a basket, set it on the doorstep of the French, pulled the bell, and went away." Hayward affectionately called his men *"les enfants perdus"*—lost children.[33] The French, desperate for replacements because of their heavy losses, were delighted to welcome this "leetle black bébé" and readily accepted the Black soldiers as their own. Only when he encountered a French liaison officer did Hayward learn that the War Department had re-designated the regiment the 369th Infantry. This did not sit well with the regiment's soldiers because the 300-series applied to draftee units. They were volunteers and preferred either the 15th New York or the "Rattlers" until their record and fame after the war made the 369th acceptable.

The French welcomed the regiment with open arms and provided realistic and effective training. The fact that France had Black colonial troops doubtless was a factor, but the same was true for Great Britain. The regiment was issued French weapons, helmets, equipment, and ammunition and reorganized on the French table of organization with additional machine gun units. Fortunately, the regiment developed a cohesiveness and esprit de corps among themselves and their French compatriots enabling them to compile a combat record equaled by few if any units in the AEF. By war's end, the unit won acclaim and military honors as the "Harlem Hellfighters," an appellation bestowed by their German opponents due to their toughness under fire. They continued to call themselves "Rattlers," while the French called them the "Men of Bronze."

Five Black officers accompanied the regiment to Europe, including Charles Fillmore, who lobbied for years for the regiment and hoped to become regimental colonel. He accepted an appointment as captain, led his company courageously, and won a Distinguished Service Cross. Then, AEF headquarters decided that Black regiments had to have either all Black or all white officers, so all five Black officers were transferred to the 92nd Division, including Harvard-educated Captain Napoleon Bonaparte Marshall, who was the regimental judge advocate and gas officer. Even Lieutenant Jim Europe, assigned to a machine gun company, fell under this directive until he was granted a reprieve due to his unique talents as band leader.

The 369th Regiment went into combat in mid-April 1918, assigned by the French to a 4.5-mile sector. At that time, the regiment comprised less than 1 percent of American troops in Europe, yet it held 20 percent of the territory defended by American forces. Two soldiers of the 369th, Sergeant Henry Lincoln Johnson, a railroad porter from Albany, New York, and Private Needham Roberts, achieved national fame for their actions while serving in a listening post attacked by a German platoon on the night of May 13, 1918. Throwing grenades and shooting as many of the enemy as possible until his gun jammed, Johnson used his rifle as a club and took on the others with his bolo knife. Having had enough, the German raiding party began to withdraw, as Johnson continued to hurl grenades until he collapsed from his wounds. The two managed to kill four Germans and seriously wounded about a dozen more. The incident became known as "The Battle of Henry Johnson," and the press had a field day, using stereotype and caricatures to invoke images of African savagery. The French Amy recognized their bravery with the *Croix de Guerre*, the first awarded to Americans of any race. Although this was widely recognized as a heroic action, including by General Pershing and Teddy Roosevelt, Johnson and Roberts were not awarded the Medal of Honor, Distinguished Service Cross, or any other American award until seven decades had passed due to the virulent bigotry of the time.[34] Fittingly, one of the recommendations of the Base Naming Commission is to name Fort Polk in Louisiana Fort Johnson.

The 369th Regiment had another significant hero, Sergeant Bill Butler, who disrupted a German raiding party that had captured five privates and a lieutenant during the night of August 12, 1918. Butler was alone but attacked the Germans with his French light machine gun, killing 10 and capturing a German lieutenant. Like Roberts and Johnson, Butler later died alone and in poverty. Surely, a grateful nation would have done better but for race. Although recommended for the Medal of Honor, Butler's recommendation was "lost." Butler died in obscurity, hanging himself in his Washington home in 1947. Efforts continue to ensure that he receives the Medal of Honor he deserves.[35]

The 369th set a record for 191 consecutive days in combat, longer than any other regiment in the AEF—after the shortest training period. The regiment continually received drafts of mostly illiterate, untrained replacements, often not accompanied by an officer, something about which Hayward complained regularly and vociferously to Pershing. However, the bulk of conscripts, white and Black, were mostly illiterate and rarely well trained. The regiment had its baptism of fire in the Argonne Woods and "went over the top" at Chateau-Thierry and Belleau Wood. It could also boast that it never lost a foot of ground nor had a man been taken prisoner, although men were captured on two occasions and later recovered. The 369th was the lead regiment for the French 161st Infantry Division in the final offensive. The regiment, accidentally assisted by a detachment of the 272nd Regiment, captured the strategic railroad junction of Séchault, netting 125 prisoners, six 77mm guns, 25 machine guns, and a huge quantity of military stores. The regiment's record of valor came at a cost: the regiment experienced roughly 1,500 casualties, among the highest of any American regiment in Europe for the war.

The regiment was the first Allied unit to reach the Rhine, where the men were finally paid after several months. The French loved the regiment because many of its personnel made the effort to learn French. The commander of the 161st French Division affectionately called the regiment his "Black Watch." Secretary of War Baker reportedly declared the

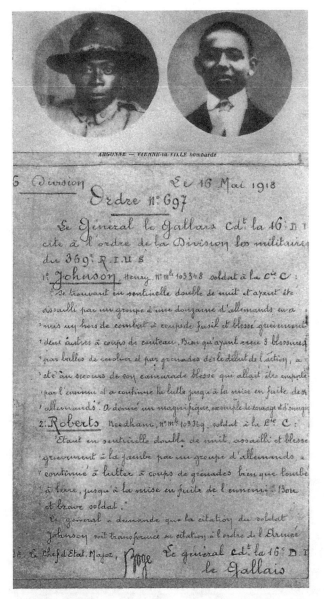

Sergeant Henry Johnson and Private Needham Roberts, the AEF's first two heroes. Frontispiece of From Harlem to the Rhine *by Arthur W. Little.*

regiment "the all-round most serviceable regiment sent to France."³⁶ The regiment spent about a month in Germany before it was recalled, after the Weimar Republic adopted the South's favorite propaganda in a movie, *Die Schwarze Schande am Rhein* (*The Black Scandal on the Rhine*), using fabricated scenes to depict Black soldiers as bestial rapists.

Determined to avoid racial conflict with white American soldiers and minimize their exposure to French civilians, especially women, who generally accepted them as men, the War Department ensured that Black units were the first units returned stateside. However, this did not happen without three weeks of abuse from white military police while waiting at the port of embarkation. The MP's behavior was not accidental: it was designed to teach Black soldiers to accept submissiveness to white superiority and the Jim Crow system. The MPs even disrespected the regiment's white officers. Robert Russa Moton of the Tuskegee Institute was dispatched to lecture Black troops on the necessity of assuming "modest and unassuming" attitudes required to accommodate white Americans.³⁷

369th Infantry Regiment "Harlem Hellfighters" march down Fifth Avenue past New York Public Library. SOURCE: WAR DEPARTMENT; US NATIONAL ARCHIVES AND RECORDS ADMINISTRATION, COLLEGE PARK, MD.

Once they returned stateside, Colonel Hayward used his connections to ensure that New York welcomed his men home properly. On February 17, 1919, the 369th Infantry Regiment paraded down Fifth Avenue from Washington Square to its armory in Harlem in the impressive solid French phalanx formation, 15 men abreast, as Harlem's heroes were welcomed home by crowds estimated to have been as large as a million people. During the victory parade in New York City, 23 men were awarded the French *Croix de Guerre* and the American Distinguished Service Cross, according to the *New York Tribune*. For the extraordinary and memorable occasion, the popular regimental band, directed by First Lieutenant James Reese Europe, played French and American martial airs. Lieutenant Europe was a well-known prewar musician and band leader who attracted many prominent musicians and a dazzling drum major. The 369th's band was a significant goodwill ambassador, instilling a tremendous sense of pride in members of the regiment. Lt. Europe's band brought jazz and ragtime music to Lt. Europe for the first time, played at hospitals, recuperation centers, and many civil and martial events. The band went on a 10-week stateside tour, visiting 18 major cities, including Boston, St. Louis, Pittsburgh, and Philadelphia.

Sheet music for the 369th Regiment's popular band led by Lieutenant James Reese Europe. M. Witmark & Sons, New York, 1919. SOURCE: LIBRARY OF CONGRESS, AMERICAN MEMORY COLLECTION, DIGITAL ID: RPBAASM 1148.

This parade was replicated in the 1920s and 1930s when the regiment marched through Harlem from their armory to catch the train to annual summer camp, returning two weeks later. Despite its stellar record, the Army converted the regiment to a variety of other roles; it deployed to Hawaii during World War II as an air defense regiment. Today's 369th Sustainment Brigade, directly descended from this proud World War I unit, deployed to Camp Arifjan, Kuwait, in late 2016 and assumed command and control of support operations in 17 Middle Eastern countries under the United States Central Command.

370TH INFANTRY REGIMENT

The 8th Illinois National Guard Regiment, from Chicago and other Illinois cities, was redesignated the 370th Infantry Regiment when it arrived in Europe. The regiment was unique in having a full complement of Black officers, including Colonel Franklin A. Dennison, who evoked tremendous racial pride through his military bearing and experience. The regiment also benefited from field experience in Cuba and along the Mexican border in 1916, but it arrived in France with minimal training in modern trench warfare due to racial tensions at its stateside training areas. The 370th Infantry and the division's other two regiments arrived in Europe in April 1918. Colonel Dennison was removed from command in July 1918, purportedly for "health" reasons, and replaced by Colonel T. A. Roberts, who signed his letters to friends as "the White Hope in a Black Regiment." The regiment's Black chaplain described Roberts as the "arch enemy, vilifier and traducer of the Negro soldier."[38] Lieutenant Colonel Otis Duncan, a Black battalion commander, was the Army's senior Black at war's end. When the Armistice came, the regiment had only three white officers; its Black leadership survived due to the AEF's ludicrous "either/or" policy.

Corporal Isaac Valley of Company M received the Distinguished Service Cross for absorbing a grenade blast to protect his comrades. Corporal Clarence Van Allen won the *Croix de Guerre* with palm, the *Médaille militaire*, and the Distinguished Service Cross for single-handedly cleaning out a German machine gun nest and later capturing a trench mortar battery and its crew. Sergeant Matthew Jenkins led a platoon of 32 men from Company F in an assault on the "Hindenburg Cave," a massive command center capable of holding up to a regiment. They seized this section of enemy works from 275 Germans and held it two days, without food or water, using captured machine guns and ammunition. Jenkins was

Colonel Franklin A. Dennison. NAACP's Crisis Magazine.

awarded both the *Croix de Guerre* and Distinguished Service Cross—but not the Medal of Honor. On November 9, Company C was decorated with the *Croix de Guerre* for capturing a German position, including three 77mm cannons and several machine guns.

The Germans called the men of the regiment "Black Devils" because they were ferocious and unwavering in combat, while their French comrades admiringly called them "Partridges" due to their proud military bearing. Twenty percent of the regiment were casualties, but the regiment lost only one prisoner to the Germans. The 370th Infantry were the first American troops to enter the French fortress of Laon and fought the last battle of the war, capturing a train of 50 wagons a half hour after the Armistice went into effect. According to Emmett Scott, special advisor to the secretary of war, the 370th Regiment was decorated with the *Croix de Guerre*.[39]

371ST INFANTRY REGIMENT

Because insufficient National Guard units were available, the 371st Regiment was composed of draftees from the cotton fields of the Carolinas, Georgia, Florida, and Alabama. Two white regular Army officers successively commanded the regiment. Although the soldiers complained that three-quarters of their officers had typical Southern racist attitudes, and even though most Black draftees arrived illiterate, frightened, and underfed, they rapidly adapted to military life, excelled in marching and close order drill, took great pride in their uniforms and weapons, and soon developed a remarkable esprit de corps. After two weeks of drill and training with the French, General Pershing inspected the regiment and left impressed.[40]

Under an effective leader, the 371st earned considerable glory. It was the first regiment made up entirely of draftees to depart for Europe and the first to assume a sector in the trenches. In the final great Allied offensive of September and October 1918, the regiment experienced the heaviest action in the Meuse Argonne offensive under the French 4th Army, attacking in a sector near Verdun and capturing a vital communications center as part of the 157th "Red Hand" Division. Private Junius Diggs of Columbia, South Carolina, earned a *Médaille militaire*, *Croix de Guerre* with palm, and a Distinguished Service Cross. Another soldier, Corporal Freddie Stowers, a 22-year-old squad leader and farm laborer from Sandy Springs, South Carolina, assumed command of an attack on Hill 188 when nearly half of his company was killed or wounded after the Germans pretended to surrender but then unleashed devastating machine fire on the exposed soldiers. Stowers eliminated a machine gun nest and continued to lead despite mortal wounds. He received the Medal of Honor more than 70 years later, after a review of the discrimination that prevailed in the AEF.

372ND INFANTRY REGIMENT

The 93rd Division's 4th Regiment, the 372nd, was an amalgamation of National Guard units from the District of Columbia, Connecticut, Massachusetts, Maryland, Ohio, and Tennessee, rounded out with a leaven of about 250 draftees from Michigan and Wisconsin. Both Black and white officers commanded it. The regiment arrived in Europe on April 13, 1918, and took over a sector in the trenches on May 31. Like the 371st, the 372nd Regiment was brigaded with the 157th French "Red Hand" Division. Reflecting the bias typical of the times, the regimental commander declared, "I wouldn't make a god-damned one of these black sons-of-a-bitch an officer if I didn't have to."[41] He conducted an ongoing campaign to rid the regiment of Black officers. A military court composed of white officers from the 371st and 372nd reviewed the competence of Black officers in the 372nd. When only one out of the 21 officers reviewed was judged acceptable, morale in the regiment sank to a dangerous low.[42] The regimental commander requested that no additional Black officers be sent to his regiment.[43] The French liaison officer declared that he could not understand why Americans could "treat each other so harshly and cruelly when it was momentarily expected that the division could be plunged into battle."[44] The 372nd still had eight Black line officers in November, but they were subsequently transferred to the 92nd Division.[45]

On October 5, the regiment repulsed a major attack with heavy hand-to-hand fighting, taking prisoners from 12 different German regiments. On October 8, the French demonstrated their appreciation of the martial ability of the regiment, noting they "Gave proof, during its first engagement, of the finest qualities of bravery and daring" and commending their "superb gallantry and admirable scorn of danger," taking a position despite exceptionally violent machine gun and artillery fire and taking severe losses. General Goybert, commander of the 157th Division, noted in a communique dated December 15, that the 372nd had been one of two American "crack regiments" assigned to his command that "overcame every obstacle with a most complete contempt for danger."[46] Despite the hostility of their white regimental and battalion commanders and the turbulence created by the elimination of the Black officers, the men of the regiment performed their duty in an exemplary manner. As Goybert noted, they advanced eight kilometers; captured nearly 600 prisoners; seized 15 artillery pieces, 20 mortars, close to 150 machine guns, and an important supply base with engineer and artillery ammunition; and brought down three enemy aircraft by small arms fire.

RACIAL BIAS

The American Army's racial prejudice was documented on August 7, 1918, when Colonel Louis Albert Linard, the French liaison officer on the staff of the 92nd Division, issued a memo to French officers serving with the division. Linard emphasized that reports of cordial relations between Blacks and French officers, especially with French females, irritated

Americans. On behalf of the American high command, his confidential memo, "On the Subject of Black American Troops," declared that the "Negro question" was no longer open for debate. "American opinion is unanimous," he warned. French "indulgence and familiarity" with Blacks grievously concerned Americans "because although a citizen of the United States, *the black man was regarded by the white American as an inferior being*" (emphasis added). His "vices" made him a "constant menace to the white American who had to repress them sternly." Linard went on to assert, repeating what he had been told by ranking American officers, "For instance, the black American troops in Europe in France have, by themselves, given rise to as many complaints for attempted rape as all the rest of the army." Linard stated, "We must prevent the rise of any pronounced degree of intimacy between French officers and black officers," emphasizing that this goal especially applied to Black soldiers and French civilians. He concluded, "It is all right to recognize their good qualities and their services, but only in moderate terms, strictly in keeping with the truth."[47]

In July 1919, Linard's document was read in the French National Assembly and roundly condemned. The member who presented the document appended documentation of mistreatment of Black troops by white American soldiers and MPs, including cases of Black soldiers decorated for bravery by the French who were subsequently abused, beaten, or murdered by white American soldiers. He suggested that the French government pay reparations for the men killed. The French Chamber of Deputies then passed a resolution, which cited the Rights of Man and condemned prejudice based on religion, class, or race.[48]

Major General Ballou, the 92nd Division commander, issued a severely restrictive memo on August 21, 1918, in which he announced, "On account of the increasing frequency of the crime of rape, or attempted rape, in this division, drastic preventative measures have become necessary." He informed his soldiers that "all resulting hardship has been brought on themselves by their failure to observe and report suspicious characters." The document called for periodic one-hour checks between reveille and 11:00 p.m., as well as a strictly regulated pass system granted only to "men of known reliability," within a one-mile limit from camp. General Ballou warned that if conditions failed to improve, offenders' units would be placed under armed guard.[49] The next day, he issued another memo to white brigade commanders under which the four regiments served, which contained an ominous threat, quoting General Pershing who allegedly declared that if measures to address "the crime of rape" were not taken seriously, the AEF commander would "send the 92nd Division back to the United States, or break it up into labor battalions, as unfit to bear arms in France."[50] These drastic threats were no doubt due to the fact that the 92nd had unjustifiably been labeled "the rapist division." No concrete instances were cited to justify this slander, but that did not hinder the spread of innuendo.

Southern lynch law was transported to Europe despite the Uniform Code of Military Justice. Eight of 11 soldiers tried by military courts-martial and executed in France were African American. All the cases involved charges of rape, and three included the additional charge of murder. In addition, rumors were rife both during and after the war of extralegal hanging of white soldiers enforcing vigilante justice. In mid-August 1918, a battalion commander in the 370th Infantry gathered his troops and pointed out that a Black soldier from a labor battalion had been court-martialed and hung in the very village square where they stood. His body was left hanging for 24 hours to warn other soldiers of the consequences of their actions. The interplay of French acceptance and white Americans' intolerance made France a volatile environment for Blacks.[51]

Most egregiously, the 92nd Division's chief of staff, Colonel Allen T. Greer, in a letter dated December 6, 1918, to Tennessee Senator Kenneth McKellar, implied that men of the division had committed 30 rapes in France. Division records indicate that 10 men assigned to the division were tried for rape or assault but only one soldier was convicted. Greer also viciously maligned Black officers, alleging, "The undoubted truth is that Colored officers neither control nor care to control their men. They themselves have been engaged very largely in the pursuit of French women, it being the first opportunity to meet white women who did not treat them as servants." Even this racist slander was not enough. Greer went on to assert, "During the entire time we have been operating there has never been a single operation conducted by a colored officer, where his report did not have to be investigated by some field officer to find out what the real facts were. Accuracy and ability to describe facts is lacking in all and most of them are just plain liars in addition." Stepping outside the bounds of military propriety, Greer suggested to the senator that Blacks were not fit for duty in the combat arms, asserting that the 92nd Division had consistently failed in all its missions because Black officers and men were cowards.[52] Similar racial and sexual rumors enveloped the

93rd Division and the roughly 160,000 troops laboring in the ports as stevedores and laborers.

American bias was typified by the regimental intelligence officer of the 371st Regiment, who requested that civil authorities in the regiment's sector take steps to prevent "harmful relationships" with the Black soldiers because "The question is of great importance . . . to the American towns, the population of which will be affected later when the troops return to the United States." He urged that "undue social mixing" of the races "be circumspectly prevented."[53]

A determined effort was made to make all of Europe off limits to Black troops. Black officers were routinely replaced, with rumors spread of their "incompetence," although Black officers' performance was, in fact, simply the equal of comparably inexperienced white officers. On November 7, a War Department official advised Newton Baker to "get colored troops out of France as soon as you can." Shortly after the Armistice, white officers in the 92nd Division told a State Department official that "Negro troops at Chateau-Thierry, in drunken excess, terrorized villagers, murdering some and attempting to rape women."[54] Southern politicians warned Baker that there could be no question of extending rights to Black soldiers and suggested that the Army prevent soldiers from returning home in uniform or in groups, cooperating with states to transform Black troops into submissive civilians.[55]

The Army refused to accept Black nurses until November 1918, when the epidemic of "Spanish flu" that originated in Fort Riley, Kansas, overwhelmed existing resources. In the face of such an emergency, authorities decided that Black nurses could even treat white soldiers and assigned 18 Black nurses to two integrated camps in the United States. The Red Cross accepted a total of 1,800 Black women as nurses. The YMCA's attitude was like the Army's: only three Black volunteers served in France. They ministered to stevedores, pioneers, and various labor units where the men faced stern discipline, cruel discrimination, and long hours of toil with little appreciation while exposed to death from accidents, cold, and exposure.[56]

AWARDS

Ironically, neither Henry Johnson nor Needham Roberts received a single American award until decades later. The entire 369th Regiment was cited 11 times for bravery and awarded the *Croix de Guerre* for their assault as part of the French 161st Division the morning of September 26, gain-ing about seven kilometers and securing the vital transportation hub of Séchault. One hundred seventy-one officers and men also received this highest French award. A few were awarded the French Legion of Honor for exceptional gallantry in action. One white officer, Lieutenant George S. Robb, won the Medal of Honor; others, enlisted and officers, were awarded the American Silver Star and Distinguished Service Cross.[57] Surgeon Willis H. Keenan was awarded a Distinguished Service Cross for Valor for operating a hospital at the front lines, treating gravely wounded soldiers under constant shelling by German artillery.

The 370th also received a unit *Croix de Guerre*; 71 of the unit's members received the award, 4 soldiers were awarded the *Médaille Militaire*, and another 21 received the US Army's Distinguished Service Cross. Company C received the *Croix de Guerre* for an act of conspicuous bravery, capturing three 77mm cannon and several machine guns.

French Croix de Guerre. SOURCE: WIKIPEDIA.

The entire 371st Regiment, with its white officers and Black draftees, received the *Croix de Guerre* with palm, and 60 officers and 124 men were awarded the Distinguished Service Cross. Three officers were awarded the French Legion of Honor. Fourteen officers and 12 enlisted men won the US Distinguished Service Cross. When they departed, French General Mariano Goybert, commander of the 157th "Red Hand" Division, under whom the regiment served, declared, "They have scattered their dead without counting and the view of the battlefield is more eloquent than any report."[58]

The 372nd likewise earned a unit *Croix de Guerre*, presented in Brest by Vice Admiral Moreau just before the men embarked to return home. The accompanying citation praised the unit's "superb spirit and an admirable scorn of danger."[59] In addition, 41 officers, 14 noncommissioned officers, and 97 privates received an individual *Croix the Guerre*, while two officers and one enlisted man were awarded Distinguished Service Crosses.[60]

Not bad for a "provisional, orphaned" division. French acceptance of the troops from the 93rd Division made a huge difference. But the price the 93rd division's four regiments paid for their courage and gallantry was heavy—584 men killed and 2,582 wounded, representing 32 percent of the division's assigned strength.[61]

Unfortunately, the 92nd Division "Buffaloes" were not so fortunate, languishing mostly in reserve under the AEF and commanded by rabidly racist Southern officers. Despite this, the entire 1st Battalion of the 367th Infantry Regiment was cited for bravery and received the *Croix de Guerre* for their drive to Metz in the last engagement of the war. Three of the division's regiments participated in the last big assault of the war and were the only units of the newly formed 2nd Army's four divisions to achieve their objectives. Fourteen African American officers and 43 enlisted men were cited for bravery in action and awarded the Distinguished Service Cross, and numerous soldiers and officers were cited for "meritorious conduct in action." The 92nd Division suffered 1,748 casualties; 255 killed in action; and 1,527 wounded, of whom 715 were gassed, plus 28 missing in action, proof that this division was heavily engaged, albeit mostly in the last push, which began in September 1918.[62]

Not all senior officers were blind racists; Brigadier General Malvern Hill Barnum, commander of the 183rd Brigade, which included the 365th and 366th Infantry Regiments and the 350th Machine Gun Battalion, wrote fondly that his "association of over a year" with these troops had been "one of the pleasantest recollections" of his Army career. Barnum observed that the officers and enlisted men of the Brigade could be "justly proud of the record made and I believe history will accord them no little credit." How wrong he was!

The disparate experiences of the two divisions make the effects of American racism apparent. The French ensured that the soldiers of the 93rd Division were adequately trained, but most important, treated them as men and recognized their exploits, whereas the 92nd Division bore the burden of American racism and white supremacy, capped by the criminalization of Black manhood. In retrospect, the behavior of white leadership and many white enlisted men was criminal in view of the need for capable fighting men. Succumbing to American bigotry resulted in a tremendous misuse of resources, damaging to members of both Black divisions who were subject to unconscionable treatment, not to mention the abuse showered on the troops who labored in the Services of Supply.

Due to the animosity of their white compatriots over racial stereotypes of Blacks as rapists, both combat divisions shipped out of the European theater soon after the war ended, the first American combat troops home. Black soldiers were abused by American MPs who had instructions to "reacclimatize" these confident combat soldiers to life stateside. One soldier had his head cracked open for using a latrine, and the MP captain explained, "The Niggers were feeling their oats a bit," and as instructed, his men "took it out of them quickly, just as soon as they arrived, so as not to have any trouble later on."[63] A group of Black veterans loaded baggage on a ship and received the captain's compliments for their efficiency, only to have him refuse to transport Blacks on his vessel. The pay of the 92nd Division for January was withheld for "disciplinary reasons" although no incident was cited. Pay for the 93rd Division's 369th Infantry mysteriously stopped in May 1918, and they were excluded from special holiday rations issued to all other American soldiers for Thanksgiving and Christmas.[64] No African American units marched in the final victory parade in Paris, although Black contingents marched with both the British and French. Fortunately, their reception in their Black communities back home was often far more positive.

SERVICES OF SUPPLY TROOPS

From June 1917 until the end of the war, Black stevedores labored under all weather conditions, sometimes in 24-hour shifts unloading the supplies vital for combat. Blacks made up about one-third of the Services of Supply troops, organized into stevedore regiments, engineer service battalions, labor battalions, pioneer infantry battalions, and cook and butchery companies. Roughly 160,000 African Americans in about 115 service units served at the ports of St. Nazaire, Brest, Le Havre, Bordeaux, Marseilles, Antwerp, Rotterdam, and elsewhere, where they performed menial tasks essential to the logistics effort. They also maintained roads, transported supplies to the front, and maintained forward supply dumps.

Many labor troops were not as fortunate as the men in the two infantry divisions: when the war ended, their work was far from over. They salvaged equipment and matériel from the battlefields, cleared away mountains of barbed wire, filled in miles of trenches, and removed unexploded shells. Worst of all, in fields copiously fertilized by human blood, they exhumed bodies and body parts and reburied them. Four Black pioneer infantry regiments and numerous Black labor service battalions assisted in grave registration, while three pioneer infantry regiments created six major cemeteries where 23,000 American servicemen were laid to rest.[65] Because of unremitting racial discrimination and insults, not to mention the "gruesome, repulsive and unhealthful" task they were assigned, some became sullen and hostile, even talking of mutiny. Nonetheless, they performed their racially stigmatized tasks.

Black engineer and Service of Supply troops re-inter remains. SOURCE: US NATIONAL ARCHIVES AND RECORDS ADMINISTRATION, COLLEGE PARK, MD, RG 111-SC, 153215.

POSTWAR UNREST

After the Armistice, racism reared its head almost immediately. As mentioned, Black combat units were hurried out of Europe and demobilized as rapidly as possible. Once they were home, Blacks were extremely conscious of the irony and hypocrisy of Wilson's famous pledge to make the world "safe for democracy." Indeed, Wilson's clarion call rang totally false to Black Americans, as any semblance of democracy remained a very distant ideal for most of the 10 million Black citizens of the United States. The *Baltimore Afro-American* declared, "It does seem that we ought first set at liberty our own slaves before recommending liberty for the slaves of other countries. Let us have a real democracy for the United States and then we can advise a house cleaning over on the other side of the water."[66] Before the war, W.E.B. Du Bois, editor of the NAACP's *The Crisis*, wrote an editorial that urged Blacks to "close ranks" with their fellow white citizens and the Allied nations fighting for democracy. A. Phillip Randolph, head of the Railroad Porters' Union, and Chandler Owen, both editors of the more radical *Messenger*, took a pacifist stance throughout the war, insisting that there was little in America any Black should die for. They argued, "Let Du Bois, Kelly, Miller, Pickens, Grimke, etc. volunteer to go to France to make the world safe for democracy. We would rather make Georgia safe for the Negro."[67]

If the World War I and the rhetoric that followed bred any hope for Blacks, it was quickly dashed by postwar violence, which was unprecedented in scope. Blacks were pushed out of the more desirable industrial jobs they had obtained during the war, particularly government employment. The *New York World* asked its readers:

> Who is foolish enough to assume that with 239,000 colored men in uniform from the southern states alone, as against 370,000 white men, the Blacks whose manhood and patriotism were thus recognized and tested are forever to be flogged, lynched, burned at the stake or chased into concealment whenever Caucasian desperadoes are moved to engage in this infamous past time?[68]

In 1909, W.E.B. Du Bois, Ida B. Wells, and several influential whites cofounded the NAACP, whose charter was to "Promote equality of rights and eradicate caste or race prejudice among citizens of the United States;

to advance the interest of colored citizens; to secure for them impartial suffrage; and to increase their opportunities for securing justice in the courts, education for their children, employment according to their ability, and complete equality before the law."

From 1910 to 1934 Du Bois was one of the few Black members of the NAACP's majority white board, as well as editor of its influential magazine, *The Crisis*. Initially against Black participation in the war, Du Bois changed his mind and embarked on a three-month fact-finding tour in Europe to see firsthand the treatment of African American soldiers. He returned thoroughly enraged, having collected documents that illuminated the American chain of command's virulent racial bias. Du Bois had the foresight to obtain statements from 21 French mayors affirming that no Black soldier had been guilty of a single rape in their jurisdiction. Du Bois was rightly disgusted with what he had discovered in Europe and returned determined that changes would be made. He penned a poem article, titled "Returning Soldiers," printed in *The Crisis* for May 1919, which began with a proclamation:

> We are returning from war! *The Crisis* and tens of thousands of Black men were drafted into a great struggle. For bleeding France and what she means and has meant and will mean to us and humanity and against the threat of German race arrogance, we fought gladly and to the last drop of blood; for America and her highest ideals, we fought in far off hope; for the dominant southern oligarchy entrenched in Washington, we fought in bitter resignation. For the America that represents and gloats in lynching, disfranchisement, caste, brutality and devilish insult—for this, in the hateful upturning and mixing of things, we were forced by vindictive fate to fight, also. Having risked and given their lives for a nation characterized by lynching, disenfranchisement, the denial of educational and economic opportunities, and racial insult, Black servicemen returned singing: "This country of ours, despite all its better souls have done and dreamed, is yet a shameful land."[69]

In his indictment of white America, Du Bois included, "*It lynches. It disenfranchises its own citizens. It encourages ignorance. It steals from us. It insults us.*" Reminding Blacks that this was their country, too, Du Bois sternly warned that African Americans were determined to make America live up to its democratic ideals:

> But by the God of heaven, we are cowards and jackasses if now that the war is over, we do not marshal every ounce of our brain and brawn to fight a sterner, longer, more unbending battle against the forces of hell in our own land.
>
> We return
> We return from fighting.
> We return fighting!
> Make way for democracy! We saved it in France, and by the Great Jehovah, we will save it in the United States or know the reason why.[70]

As the violent reception of Black veterans heated up, Du Bois penned a trenchant trumpet call to former soldiers and other members of their downtrodden race published in the August issue of *The Crisis*:

> Behold the day, O Fellow Black Men! They cheat us and mock us; they kill and slay us, they deride our misery. When we plead for the naked protection of the law, there where a million of our fellows dwell, they tell us to "GO TO HELL!" TO YOUR TENTS, O ISRAEL! And FIGHT, FIGHT, FIGHT for FREEDOM.[71]

Predictably, white America responded with anger and violence at any suggestion of change in the status quo. James Weldon Johnson, the first Black executive secretary of the NAACP, labeled the bloody demobilization months "Red Summer" as race riots broke out in at least 26 American cities in the last six months of 1919. Huge mobs of whites took over cities for days at a time, flogging, burning, shooting, and torturing any Black they encountered at will. When Blacks resisted, the violence increased. There was also a noticeable uptick in lynchings, from 64 in 1918 to 83 in 1919. Seventy-seven of the victims were Black, 10 of them veterans. Many riots took place in the South—Charleston, South Carolina; Elaine, Arkansas; Norfolk, Virginia; Longview, Texas; Knoxville, Tennessee; and Omaha, Nebraska, but the worst took place in Chicago. Townspeople and the police of Bisbee, Arizona, even attacked 10th Cavalry troops. Southerners found a Black man wearing his country's uniform extremely offensive—mobs also accosted Blacks in uniform at train stations and forced them to undress. Fourteen Blacks were burned publicly; 11 were burned alive. In the 10 months after the war ended, members of the Ku Klux Klan made over 200 public appearances in 27 states.

With close to a half million Blacks in uniform, Southerners were anxious about their ability to perpetuate the "Southern Way" even before the war ended, demonstrated by the case of Sergeant Edgar C. Caldwell. A veteran of the 24th Infantry Regiment, Caldwell was drafted and served in the 157th Depot Brigade, part of the 200,000-plus African American force that labored stateside to move American supplies and equipment to Europe. Stationed at Camp McClelland, near Anniston, Alabama, the sergeant boarded a streetcar headed for the Black enclave of Hobson City one Sunday in December 1918 and sat in the "white" section. The conductor decided to make sure Caldwell "knew his place" and aided by the driver, threw him off the streetcar, claiming that he had not purchased a ticket. Caldwell insisted that he had. When the conductor began kicking Caldwell in the stomach, the sergeant drew his pistol and put a bullet through his head, also wounding the driver with a shot through the neck.

Even though he was arrested by military police and placed in the stockade, civil authorities demanded custody, and the Army, contrary to military justice statutes, surrendered him. Three days later, a grand jury indicted him for murder. When the case came to trial nearly a year later, his defense pointed out that Caldwell was still a serving soldier and should be tried by a military court, not civil authority. The case went through a series of jurisdictions, ending up before the Supreme Court, where former slaveholder, Confederate veteran, and Ku Klux Klan member Chief Justice Edward Douglass White affirmed Alabama's right to convict Caldwell for murder in a nine-page decision.[72]

Sergeant Caldwell's last words are worth contemplating:

> I am being sacrificed today on the altar of passion and racial hatred that appears to be the bulwark of American

civilization. If it would alleviate the pain and sufferings of my race, I would count myself fortunate in dying, but I am but one of the many victims among my people who are paying the price of America's mockery of the law and dishonesty in her profession of world democracy.[73]

Once troops returned home, white planters were distraught that few discharged Black ex-servicemen returned to Southern farms—an estimated 100,000 demobilized Black veterans relocated to Northern cities. Small wonder, since Army pay was significantly more than the pittance earned as sharecroppers. One obvious remedy to the extremely low pay of farmworkers was the formation of unions or granges, but with the threat of "Bolshevism" in the air, this action was viewed as subversive in an atmosphere not unlike the McCarthyism that plagued the United States in the 1950s.

Red Summer: Willie Brown burned alive in Omaha, Nebraska, 1919. SOURCE: LIBRARY OF CONGRESS.

One of the more egregious reactions to this "threat" took place in Phillips County, Arkansas, in September 1919, when local white vigilantes surrounded a grange meeting in a small church in Hoop Spur. After a shootout that resulted in the death of a white man, white gangs, some from Tennessee and Mississippi, combed the countryside, hunting down Blacks and killing them at will. The governor called out white National Guardsmen, who assisted in the pogrom, ending in the slaughtering of uncounted hundreds of Blacks. The murder of Leroy Johnson, a bugler in the 369th Infantry who bore scars from Chateau-Thierry, the youngest son of a prominent Black middle-class family in eastern Arkansas, was a particularly heinous part of this racial massacre. The son of a presbyterian minister and a schoolteacher, Leroy went squirrel hunting with his brothers, a doctor and a dentist. Advised to return to Helena by train, they were ambushed by a body of whites who boarded the train, forced them off, and shot them repeatedly, leaving their bodies on the roadside, mutilated beyond recognition.[74]

The violence extended to nearly every corner of the South. When one elderly white minister was asked if he had experienced any racial tension in his community following the war, he declared, "No, we had to kill a few of them, but we didn't have any trouble."[75] A New Orleans city official told a group of returning Black veterans, "You niggers were wondering how you are going to be treated after the war. . . . you are going to be treated just like you were before the war: this is a white man's country and we expect to rule it."[76]

After the *Washington Post* ran a series of inflammatory front-page articles alleging attacks by Blacks on white women, four days of rioting took place in Washington, D.C. In July 1919, mobs of white civilians, veterans, soldiers, sailors, and Marines spilled out of nearby Camp Meade, Maryland, to exact revenge for a rumored attack on a white woman. Blacks began to defend themselves, and the riot ended only after Congress ordered over a thousand troops to the capital. With the help of a summer downpour, they were able to restore order, but only after six people had been killed and hundreds wounded.

The Chicago Black community's newspaper, the *Defender*, editorialized on February 17, 1919, after the 8th Illinois/370th Infantry Regiment's triumphant parade, "we shall look forward to a new tomorrow, not of subservience, not of meek and humble obeisance to any class, but with a determination to demand what is our due." The paper concluded, "the nation that cannot furnish its citizens with such a guarantee has no right to demand service in time of war." Four months later, Chicago exploded when a Black youth swam into a white beach. The sweltering heat exacerbated tempers of both races, and gangs of white "athletic club" members were met by sniper fire as they invaded Black enclaves. Seventeen people died on July 28 alone, and the riot raged for nearly two weeks. When it was over, the nation was stunned: 38 were dead, 23 Blacks and 15 whites; more than 500 seriously injured (193 whites and 365 Blacks); and 229 arrested (75 whites and 254 Blacks). More than 1,000 families, mostly Black, were left homeless. Because white America refused to accept Blacks as equals, violence flared up spasmodically. Police focused principally on arresting Blacks, often with assistance from Klan members or other white vigilantes. After the riot, the *Defender* warned, "A Race that has furnished hundreds of thousands of the best soldiers that the world has ever seen is no longer content to turn the left cheek when smitten upon the right."[77]

When Oklahoma became a state in November 1907, many former Southern slave owners settled there, using violence to intimidate Blacks and achieve white supremacy. In 13 years of statehood, there had been 31 lynchings, mostly of Blacks, in the state. Jealousy and racial hatred smoldered, and postwar unrest climaxed in Tulsa, Oklahoma, on May 31 and June 1, 1921, in one of the largest and most violent race riots and massacres this country has ever seen. A young Black shoeshine boy was accused of raping a young white woman after an innocuous encounter in an elevator. Newspapers sensationalized the supposed incident, and a lynch mob gathered. Black residents, including former servicemen, hurried downtown to protect him, which enraged part of the white populace. Fanned by the lurid journalism, thousands of whites rampaged through Greenwood, a Black section so prosperous that it was known as "The Black Wall Street." The alleged "perpetrator" was never indicted and quietly left the state after the "victim" refused to press charges.

A white mob leveled a 35-block area of Tulsa, destroying 191 businesses, a junior high school, hotels, restaurants, theaters, and several churches, assisted by incendiary devices dropped from aircraft. The fire department made no effort to extinguish the flames, and Blacks insisted that police assisted the rioters. Tulsa's Real Estate Exchange estimated property loss at $1.5 million worth of real estate and $750,000 in personal property, more than $30 million in current values. Loss of life was calamitous: at least 300 deaths, with at least 800 admitted to local hospitals. The number

Destruction of Black Wall Street in Tulsa. 1921 postcard in the Melanin Project collection.

of killed and injured was probably much higher because the single Black hospital was destroyed and Blacks were not admitted to white hospitals. Officially, the Oklahoma Office of Vital Statistics counted only 39 deaths. Over 6,000 Blacks were detained in open-air holding pens, some for more than a week.

Not only did the city leaders fail to assist Greenwood's victims, but they declined offers of assistance from across America. The Tulsa Real Estate Exchange unsuccessfully attempted to exploit the Blacks' disastrous situation by displacing the community outside the city and building a new transportation and industrial center on Greenwood's ashes.[78] Both city and state attempted to cover up the riot, and the event was not mentioned in Oklahoma or Tulsa schools until 2002. Not until June 2020 did archeologists begin excavating mass graves to determine the true extent of this atrocity. The mayor has now acknowledged the horror that took place, and a suitable memorial is being considered. The horrific event finally received national attention in 2021.

Reacting to mob violence, the *Pittsburgh Courier* editorialized sharply in October 1919:

> As long as the Negro submits to lynchings, burnings, and oppressions—and says nothing he is a loyal American

citizen. But when he decides that lynching and burnings shall cease even at the cost of some bloodshed in America—then he is a Bolshevik."[79]

The more militant *Crusader* echoed and amplified the *Courier*'s position. Denouncing white mob violence, murder, and riots against Blacks in America, the paper declared, "If to fight for one's rights is to be Bolshevists, then we are Bolsheviks and let them make the most of it."[80] Deeply influenced by both war experiences and their homecoming reception, many veterans became mentors to younger African Americans in the growing struggle for civil rights that continued through World War II—and to this day.

CONCLUSIONS

The experiences of the two segregated World War I infantry divisions provide an excellent case study of the corrosive effects of bigotry. The French Army, bled dry since 1914, were delighted when reinforced by the four 93rd Infantry Division regiments. Treated like men, all four regiments received the *Croix de Guerre*, and numerous other French and American individual awards. All four performed valiantly, whereas the 92nd Infantry Division's four regiments remained in reserve in the AEF until the final offensive in the fall of 1918, treated as second-class citizens. When finally given the opportunity to engage in combat, they rose to the occasion but not without undeserved criticism from contumacious white officers. The roughly 200,000 Black soldiers in Europe were constantly stereotyped and accused of rape yet performed their duties as loyal Americans.

America's racist reality made President Wilson's talk of "making the world safe for democracy" laughable and hypocritical as far as Blacks were concerned. W.E.B. Du Bois, editor of the NAACP's magazine, spent three months gathering material in Europe. Among other documents, he obtained memos from 21 French mayors attesting that there had been NO rapes by Black soldiers in their towns. Only one Black was convicted of rape in the entire AEF. Constant rumors and lies fabricated by white soldiers and abetted by the American high command were accepted as truth and used to denigrate and oppress Black soldiers. Du Bois's documentation definitively refuted white soldiers' slander and that of the military leadership.

Blacks' service during the war laid a firm foundation for an ongoing struggle for self-respect, acceptance as full American citizens, and equality as promised by the Constitution, a struggle still not fully realized. Self-confident New Negroes were not dissuaded by any amount of persecution, disparagement, or discrimination, although equality was a century-long struggle that remains elusive even today due to the determined proponents of white supremacy.

CHAPTER 6

African American Service in World War II

> [Black] soldiers were fighting the world's worst racist, Adolph Hitler, in the world's most segregated army.
>
> Stephen Ambrose
> *The Longest Day*

Although more than one million African Americans served during World War II, only 15 percent were assigned to combat units. The 92nd and 93rd Divisions were reactivated, and numerous independent black infantry, tank, engineer, artillery, antitank, and anti-aircraft regiments and battalions also deployed. Under duress, the Marine Corps accepted Black troops for the first time since the Revolutionary War. The Tuskegee Airmen shattered stereotypes, and the Navy deployed two ships manned by African Americans.

Most Blacks continued to serve in labor and service units critical to the war effort. Three-quarters of the "Red Ball Express," which transported supplies, ammunition, and food from French ports to the dynamic American spearheads moving across Europe, were Black soldiers, as were 20 percent of the engineer units clearing roads and building bridges in the European Theater. One third of the troops who built the Alaskan Highway and two-thirds of the troops who built the

Ledo Road and transported supplies from Burma into China were African American.

Most Black units were activated and trained at bases in the South, where serious racial incidents were constant, marring fighting cohesion. Racism also created problems overseas.

INTERWAR YEARS

After "the war to end all wars," military leaders argued that African American troops were competent only for combat support and service roles. However, an Army study released in 1922 warned, "To follow the policy of exempting the Negro population of this country from combat means that the white population, upon which the future of the country depends, would suffer the brunt of loss, the Negro population none."[1]

In 1939, Howard University professor of history Rayford W. Logan, along with others, formed the Committee for the Participation of Negroes in National Defense. Logan left the Army during World War I disturbed by the offensive and constant discrimination he encountered. The National Association for the Advancement of Colored People (NAACP) and the *Pittsburgh Courier*, the most widely read African American newspaper at the time, joined the committee in calling for a drastic increase of Black military personnel and their employment in combat units. Although powerful members of Congress supported a broader role for Blacks, the military establishment circumvented their suggested amendments to the Selective Service and Training bill.[2] After Franklin Roosevelt signed the Selective Service and Training Act on September 14, 1940, Blacks who flocked to recruitment centers were turned away because the phrase "until adequate provision shall be made for shelter, sanitary facilities, medical care, and hospital accommodations" was universally interpreted as "segregated facilities."

Although Section 4(a) of the Selective Service Act declared, "There shall be no discrimination against any person on account of race or color," racial discrimination in the armed forces continued unchanged because the military hierarchy doggedly ignored legislation. Military officials, from Army Chief of Staff General George C. Marshall on down, insisted that it was not the military's place to "solve vexing social issues." In January 1942, the commandant of the Marine Corps, General Thomas Holcomb, bluntly declared, "The Negro race has every opportunity now to satisfy its aspirations for combat in the army . . . and their desire to enter the naval service is, I think, to break into a club that doesn't want them."[3]

President Roosevelt promoted Benjamin O. Davis, an old Buffalo Soldier, to brigadier general in November 1940 to court the Black vote, a move the Black press readily recognized. In June 1940, less than 5,000 Blacks were on active duty, most serving in the four regiments authorized after the Civil War. They constituted only about 1.5 percent of the peacetime regular army of 230,000 soldiers. Even this paltry percentage of Black soldiers was being drawn down to build up the Army Air Forces. Moreover, soldiers in the four Buffalo Soldier regiments were frequently used in installation housekeeping and miscellaneous details, infrequently receiving tactical training. Only five African American officers served on active duty, although Blacks were about 10 percent of the population.[4]

After mobilization, the United States armed services remained as segregated, possibly more than they had been during "the war to end all wars" barely 20 years earlier. German and Italian prisoners of war (POWs) were treated better than Black soldiers. Enemy POWs were allowed access to officers' and noncommissioned officers' clubs and post exchanges, whereas Blacks were confined to "separate but equal" accommodations. At Fort Lawton in Washington state, Italian POWs could patronize local bars that refused to admit African Americans.

Resentment built into a full-scale riot in August 1944, when Black soldiers stoned the Italian prisoners' barracks. One prisoner was killed and 24 injured; a court-martial found 23 Black servicemen guilty. This was no isolated phenomenon: race riots were a regular feature of the American landscape throughout the war in training centers and cities across the United States, such as the three days of rioting that broke out on Detroit's Belle Isle in June 1943, the riot in Harlem that began the next month after a white policeman shot a Black serviceman, and riots in Mobile, Alabama, and Los Angeles. Many disturbances broke out between white Military Police and Black GIs, as in Fayetteville, North Carolina, or Camp van Dorn, Mississippi. In addition, countless white civilians and service members directed Black soldiers and sailors to the back of the bus—the court-martial of Lieutenant Jackie Robinson is a tangible reflection of thousands of other unrecorded incidents.

American soldiers even exported racial prejudice. The "Battle of Bamber Bridge," occurred days after the Detroit race riot of 1943 when white Military Police (MPs) attempted to arrest African American soldiers of the 1511th Quartermaster Truck Regiment, 8th Air Force, at an English public house in Lancashire. When MP reinforcements arrived armed with machine guns, Black soldiers armed themselves with rifles. Both sides exchanged fire through the night. One Black soldier was killed, and several MPs and soldiers injured. Although a court-martial convicted 32 African American soldiers of mutiny and related crimes, the commander of the 8th Air Force blamed white officers' poor leadership, racist attitudes, and racial slurs used by the MPs as the underlying causes. One tangible result was that MP patrols were integrated. When US commanders requested a bar for African Americans, all three pubs of the town posted "Black Troops Only" signs.[5]

In September 1943, African American soldiers wounded two MPs in Cornwall; in October 1943, Black troops faced a court-martial for mutiny and attempted murder of white GIs at Paignton, Devon; in February 1944, there was serious fighting between Black and white troops at Leicester; and in October 1944, a British citizen was killed in crossfire between Black and white troops near Newbury, Berkshire. The high command made a concerted effort to bury such incidents. However, the high command decided that in addition to Black ombudsman Brigadier General Davis, the Services of Supply and 8th Air Forces needed a "special officer" to monitor racial issues, appointing Brigadier General George M. Alexander, a Virginian and Virginia Military Institute graduate. The most Alexander accomplished was assigning additional officers to supervise Black units and integrating MP patrols. NAACP Secretary Walter F. White set about to ascertain the situation for the Black GIs serving in Europe. In February 1944, White presented a 20-page report with a dozen specific and detailed ways race relations could be improved to Generals C. H. Lee, commander of the Services of Supply, and General Eisenhower, Supreme Allied Commander. His recommendations were dismissed contemptuously by an Inspector General report prepared less than six days later.

Two months after the Japanese attack on Pearl Harbor launched the United States into World War II, the *Pittsburgh Courier* proposed a campaign to mobilize Blacks and at the same time challenging the country to live up to its democratic ideals in a "Double V" campaign. The *Courier* urged Blacks to give their all for the war effort, at the same time challenging the government to make a sincere effort to make the rhetoric of the Declaration of Independence and the equal rights amendments of the Constitution true for every citizen, regardless of race. The *Courier's* campaign came about after James G. Thompson, a cafeteria worker at an aircraft factory, wrote, "surely those who perpetuate these ugly prejudices here are seeking to destroy our democratic form of government just as surely as the Axis forces."[6]

Walter White, the executive secretary of the NAACP, sent a letter to General Marshall proposing the formation of a volunteer division "open to all Americans irrespective of race, creed, color, or national origin" in order to "set a new and successful pattern of democracy." White's proposal was inspired by a recent Yale graduate, Roger Starr, who asked his draft board to allow him to serve as an enlistee with Black troops. After Starr's letter was published, the NAACP received many letters from young white men wanting to follow his example, but nothing came of the proposal.[7]

The editor of the NAACP's *The Crisis*, Roy Wilkins, observed, "Negroes did not need us at the NAACP to tell them that it sounded pretty foolish to be against park benches marked JUDEN in Berlin but to be *for* park benches marked COLORED ONLY in Tallahassee, Florida. . . . Negroes were not being sent to any concentration camps, of course, but what a thing to be thankful for."[8] The Army's policies were influenced by a racist report on the use of Black troops completed in 1920 and a 1925 Army War College study that found Blacks "physically unqualified for combat duty," allegedly because Black brains weighed 10 ounces less than whites'. The Army War College study's conclusions would be ludicrous if they did not have profound impact:

> An opinion held in common by practically all officers is the negro is a rank coward in the dark. His fear of the unknown and unseen will prevent him from ever operating as individual scout with success. His lack of veracity causes unsatisfactory reports to be rendered, particularly on patrol duty. World War I experience implies that the negro may not stand grilling combat with heavy losses.[9]

The Army brass believed that statistics backed this up: Only 20 percent of Black registrants for the draft, compared to 74 percent of whites, scored in the upper three IQ categories. Eighty percent of Blacks, versus 26 percent of whites, fell into the lowest two ranks. But 75 percent of Black registrants were from the South, where 80 percent of Blacks had not completed even the fourth grade—due to "separate but markedly unequal" schools. Rural Blacks in the South had only three months of schooling each year due to the need to work in the fields to support their families—and to provide cheap labor to harvest crops. Policy makers blamed Blacks without considering their limited education and economic opportunities over which they had absolutely no control. Educational arrangements were orchestrated by the white power structure. War Secretary Stimson noted, "The Army had adopted rigid requirements for literacy mainly to keep down the number of colored troops."[10] In any case, this is clear proof that deficient education is a national security issue, particularly with the high levels of technology in armed forces today.

Commander in Chief Franklin D. Roosevelt was a master of sleight of hand in juggling policies that appeased conservative Southern congressional leaders. Even Social Security, his landmark legislation, deliberately excluded domestic and farmworkers, predominant occupations of Southern Blacks. Wage supports were adjusted so white employers could continue to underpay Black workers in the South. When attempts were made to enforce the minimum wage, Black workers were simply fired. However, his wife, Eleanor, a member of the NAACP board, spoke out freely. In general, Roosevelt agreed with his wife's liberal positions and found it useful when she advanced various causes that Southern politicians opposed. Eleanor famously declared, "The nation cannot expect the colored people to feel that the U.S. is worth defending if they continue to be treated as they are treated now." Mrs. Roosevelt also declared shortly after Pearl Harbor, "The race question is agitated because people will not act justly and fairly toward each other as human beings."[11]

Southern senators continued to use the filibuster to ensure that no progress was made on making lynching a federal crime or in desegregating the military, which in many respects was more segregated during World War II than it had been in "the Great War." Racist leaders like New Yorker Secretary of War Henry L. Stimson and Massachusetts-born Secretary of the Navy Frank Knox, who were bound by their versions of racist tradition, ensured that no progress toward integration was made. Stimson, formerly President Hoover's secretary of state, reacted to a proposal to integrate Black officers and enlisted men throughout the armed forces with position and rank based solely on ability:

> I saw the same thing happen twenty-three years ago when Woodrow Wilson yielded to the same sort of de-

mand and appointed colored officers to several of the Divisions [sic] that went over to France, and the poor fellows made perfect fools of themselves and at least one division behaved badly. The others were turned into labor battalions.[12]

Stimson concluded that "segregation has proven satisfactory over a long period of years and to make changes would produce situations destructive to morale and detrimental to the preparations for national defense."

Their intransigence did not dissuade Mrs. Roosevelt. She received a letter from Sergeant Henry Jones of the California-based 349th Aviation Squadron, who wrote, "The fact that we want to do our best for our country and be valiant soldiers, seems to mean nothing to the Commanding Officer of our Post as indicated that 'Jim Crowism' is practiced on the very grounds of our camp." He reported that although the base theater seated 1,000 soldiers, Blacks were allocated 20 seats in the last row. Although they could purchase food and refreshments at the post exchange, they could not consume them there like other soldiers. Furthermore, Blacks had to sit in the back rows on base buses, forcing most Black soldiers to walk to and from camp. One hundred twenty-one fellow soldiers signed Sergeant Jones's letter.[13]

When Eleanor received no reply from Secretary of War Stimson, she bombarded General Marshall with a continuous volume of inquiries, forwarding letters she received from Black servicemen during the war, forcing him to assign two staff members to respond to the volume. Although progress was grudging, modest headway was made. In March 1943, the War Department officially banned segregation in all services' recreational facilities. "Colored Only" and "White" signs were forbidden. In July 1944, the War Department decreed that all buses, trucks, or other transportation owned or operated either by the government or by a "government instrumentality" henceforth had to be available to *all* military personnel "regardless of local custom."

This set off a firestorm in the South: Blacks were beaten, shot, and killed. Lieutenant Nora Green, a Black nurse stationed at Tuskegee Army Airfield, near Montgomery, Alabama, was beaten and thrown into jail for refusing to move out of a "white" seat. When the NAACP protested to the War Department and Department of Justice, Lieutenant Green was ordered not to talk about the incident, and the War Department attempted to bury the case, but racism remained a serious morale problem throughout the entire war. Black GIs were forced to sit behind Axis POWs, could not use restaurants German and Italian prisoners were permitted to use, and were continually made to feel like second-class citizens.[14] Jackie Robinson, an officer in a tank battalion, was court-martialed for a similar "infraction." Had he been convicted, he would not have had a career in Major League baseball.

In addition to the president's wife, African Americans had another well-positioned ally in Attorney General Francis Biddle, who told the *New York Times* in 1941, "I intend to see that the civil liberties in this country are protected so that we do not fall into the disgraceful hysteria of witch hunts, strike breakings and minority persecution which were such a dark chapter in our record of the last World War."[15] Leaders in the Black community exerted enough pressure on Roosevelt that he signed Executive Order 8802, the *Fair Employment Practices Act*, on June 25, 1941, which declared that segregation was unacceptable in a democratic society. Although this sounded nice, the order lacked any enforcement provisions. This was evident in the fact that air raid shelters in Washington, DC, were planned to be segregated and the Red Cross declared that it would no longer accept blood from Blacks. That was especially ironic since a Black doctor, Dr. Charles Drew, discovered the technique of extracting plasma from whole blood. Drew promptly resigned from his position as head of the Red Cross blood bank when the armed forces ruled that the blood of African Americans was required to be stored separately from that of whites, a policy the Red Cross maintained until 1950.[16]

The 9th and 10th Cavalry Regiments joined the skeletal 2nd Cavalry Division in February 1941. After buildup and training, the division deployed to North Africa in January 1944 but was inactivated in Oran, Algeria, in March 1944. Personnel of the 9th Cavalry were assigned to labor and service units, many serving as stevedores unloading supply ships. The 10th Cavalry was reorganized into the 6486th Engineer Construction Battalion, Provisional (Colored) on March 20, 1944, and redesignated the 1334th Engineer Construction Battalion (Colored) nine days later, assisting in constructing airfield facilities for the Tuskegee Airmen. Such treatment contrasted with two of the division's white cavalry regiments—the 2nd and 14th Cavalry Regiments, both reorganized as mechanized armored groups. Some soldiers from the two Buffalo Soldier regiments later volunteered to fight with the 92nd Infantry Division in Northern Italy.

By the end of December 1942, the number of Black service members in the Army grew to nearly half a million men. About 5 percent were in combat units, 21 percent were in service organizations, and a little over 8 percent were assigned to Army Air Forces support units. By the end of the war, half a million African Americans had served in North Africa, Europe, or the Pacific. The Army had the largest Black enlistment at 701,678, but the Army Air Forces were a close second at 677,966 enlisted men and 1,050 officers. The Navy had about 65,000 and the Marine Corps, 17,000. In addition, 4,000 African Americans served in the Coast Guard and female components of the Army and Navy combined.[17] During World War II, only about 15 percent of about 1.2 million Blacks who served were assigned to combat units; the remainder served in labor and service units. Twenty percent of the engineer units in Europe were African American, clearing roads, rebuilding bridges, and performing myriads of other functions. A third of the troops who built the Alaskan Highway; two-thirds of the troops who built the Ledo Road from Burma (Myanmar) into China; and three-quarters of the "Red Ball Express," moving supplies, ammunition, and food from French ports to the dynamic spearhead of American forces moving across Europe, were Black soldiers.[18]

More than 4,000 African American service and support units were organized during the war, a reflection of white arrogance that most Blacks were not suited for combat. Although most African Americans served in support functions, they were critical to the war effort—the 1,000-man 490th Port Battalion landed on Utah Beach on D-Day, earning the *Croix de Guerre* with bronze arrowhead for their service to the assault troops, while roughly 700 men in the 320th Very Low Altitude Barrage Balloon Battalion landed on Utah and Omaha beaches at Normandy on D-Day to provide protection from strafing German aircraft. One of the battalion's many heroes was a young medic, Waverly B. Woodson, who for thirty hours treated more than two hundred men from multiple units while under intense German fire, which also wounded him severely. He refused to be evacuated and rescued four soldiers from drowning. Often, these units engaged in combat. For example, the 57th Ordnance Ammunition Company was attacked by German forces in Péronne, France, with no other support. The company killed 50 and captured 15 Germans. Four men were cited for bravery: two soldiers received the *Croix de Guerre*, one was awarded a Silver Star, and another got a Bronze Star.

The 92nd and 93rd Divisions of World War I were reactivated with the new triangular table of organization of three regiments, numerically different from the previous war. They trained at Fort Huachuca, Arizona, the only large, isolated base with sufficient segregated housing. Smaller independent Black combat units were organized and trained, mostly at bases in the South, where racial incidents were constant. There were serious riots at Camp Lee, Virginia; Camp Davis, North Carolina; Fort Dix, New Jersey; Fort Bragg, North Carolina; and Camp Robinson, Arkansas. Smaller racial incidents were regular features at most service posts, including civilian areas outside of cantonments, fostered by the Army's racist policies and Jim Crow laws and customs that permeated American society. Indeed, the United States exported Jim Crow wherever US troops were stationed and expected citizens of other countries to embrace our prejudices. After an inspection tour of camps around the United States, Brigadier General Benjamin O. Davis Sr. noted sadly, "the army, by its directions and actions of commanding officers, has introduced Jim Crow practices in areas, both at home and abroad, where they have not hitherto been practiced."

When World War II began, the 24th Infantry was serving as school troops for the Infantry School at Fort Benning, Georgia. After participating in the Carolina Maneuvers the fall of 1941, the 24th Infantry was the first Black unit to deploy as a separate unit to the Pacific, arriving in the New Hebrides Islands in May 1942. The regiment moved to Guadalcanal in August 1943 and was assigned to the US XIV Corps, where they promptly became stevedores and assisted Seabees in building piers. The 1st Battalion deployed to Bougainville, attached to the 37th Infantry Division, from March to May 1944 for perimeter defense duty. The regiment left Guadalcanal in December 1944, bound to Saipan and Tinian and garrison duty, mopping up the remaining Japanese forces. The regiment shipped out to the Kerama Islands, Okinawa, in July 1945, taking the surrender of forces on the island of Aka-shima, the first formal surrender of a Japanese Imperial Army garrison. The regiment remained on Okinawa until integrated into the 25th Infantry Division and transferred to Japan in February 1947. The African American 159th Field Artillery Battalion and the 77th Engineer Combat were assigned at that time and formed a regimental combat team.

93RD DIVISION

The 93rd Division activated in California on May 15, 1942, consisting of the veteran 25th and the 368th and 369th Infantry Regiments, four field artillery battalions, and support units. As with most regiments raised during World War II, they were composed of 60 percent draftees, 26 percent volunteers, and 14 percent veteran soldiers. The original 8th Illinois/ 368th Regiment had first been converted into two artillery battalions, and in January 1944, it became two engineer combat battalions, while the 369th became an anti-aircraft regiment stationed in Hawaii, destroying the two regiments' proud heritage. Two entirely new regiments were formed for the 93rd. The division transferred to Fort Huachuca, Arizona, where training dragged on for 19 months, nine months more than the standard preparation time for US divisions. A large part of the problem for both Black divisions was the high percentage of poorly educated products of segregated education, hardly the result of innate Negro ability but a manifestation of white superiority in the poor education allowed in "separate but equal" Black schools. According to historian Stephen D. Lutz, a full 45 percent of the division's enlisted men tested at the Army's lowest classification; the corresponding percentage for a white division was less than 9 percent. Once more, education impinged on national security.

Hamilton Fish, an officer in the 369th Infantry Regiment during World War I, and now a congressman, observed on the floor of Congress, "it is astonishing that after 26 months of World War No. 2 virtually no Negro units have been engaged in combat except for the 99th Pursuit Squadron and a few antiaircraft units."[19] This generated national attention and produced results.

An advanced party of the 25th Infantry Regiment arrived on Guadalcanal in January 1944, and the rest of the division landed in early February and March. One regiment disembarked on the Russell Islands in February. The division's regiments moved separately to New Guinea, Northern Solomons (Bougainville), and the Bismarck Archipelago (Admiralty Islands), training, conducting mop-up operations, unloading ships, clearing battlefield damage, and performing security duties. Frequently, individual battalions were attached to regiments of the Americal Division. On August 2, 1945, two weeks before Japan's surrender, the highest-ranking Japanese officer captured during the war in the Pacific surrendered to elements of the 93rd Division on the island of Morotai, part of Dutch New Guinea, now eastern Indonesia. When Black troops landed, open warfare with soldiers from the 31st "Dixie" Division nearly broke out: a Black sailor on a landing craft observed that they were "the Goddamnest set of Ku Kluxers ever seen . . . gonna lynch any nigger that looked cross-eyed" at an Army nurse. Fortunately, the 31st soon departed to invade the Philippines.

The division went through four commanders in its four years of existence. Elements of the 93rd Division were frequently used as rear echelon and support troops in scattered detachments, which are reflected by the division's losses—12 men killed, 121 wounded. But decorations paint another story: One soldier won the Distinguished Service Cross. Other decorations included a Distinguished Service Medal, 5 Silver Stars, 5 Legions of Merit, 5 Soldier's Medals, 686 Bronze Star Medals, and 27 Air Medals. There was a good deal of heroism in the division, although no member received the Medal of Honor, even after the Shaw review in the 1990s.

It is apparent that General MacArthur preferred not to use Blacks in combat because he distrusted their fighting abilities. The fact that 18 out of 21 soldiers executed in the Pacific theater, all with General MacArthur's approval, were Black is doubtless another reflection of the general's racial bias.[20]

When the division deactivated at Camp Stoneman, California, in February 1946, one vet said, "I got through fighting in the PTO [Pacific Theater of Operations] and now I've got to fight in the STO [US Southern Theater of Operations]."

92ND DIVISION

The 92nd Division, activated in October 1942 at four widely dispersed posts in Alabama, Arkansas, Kentucky, and Indiana due to lack of facilities for another Black division, consisted of the 365th, 370th, and 371st Infantry Regiments. Major General Edward Mallory Almond, a Virginia Military Institute graduate and protégé and in-law of General Marshall, who shared the same racial bias, commanded the division. After the 93rd Division deployed to the Pacific, the division relocated to Fort Huachuca. After nearly two years of training, twice that of other divisions, complaints from Black leaders and the need to replace combat losses in the European Theater finally motivated the division's deployment to Italy.

The 370th Regimental Combat Team landed near Naples, Italy, on July 30, 1944, attached to the 1st Armored Division. By September, the entire division was engaged in Northern Italy, including the attached 758th Tank Battalion (Colored) and 679th Tank Destroyer Battalion (Colored). Almond was disappointed that his three regiments could not break through strong positions occupying high ground of the German Gothic Line in the Apennine Mountains, conducting a series of repetitive, costly frontal attacks. Once more the Army made no plans to provide Black reinforcements, although the division suffered more than 3,000 casualties in extremely heavy combat.

Major General Mallory Edmund "Ned" Almond. US Army photo. SOURCE: NATIONAL ARCHIVES & RECORDS ADMINISTRATION, COLLEGE PARK, MD.

To provide replacements for high combat losses, the 366th Infantry Regiment, which had all Black officers and provided air base security at scattered sites in Italy for more than half a year, was attached to the division in November 1944. Its commander requested a refresher course in infantry tactics, but Almond parceled out the regiment to the division's three regiments with little training, leaving no role for the African American regimental commander and staff. In February 1945, Almond transferred the best officers; noncommissioned officers; and troops from the 365th, 366th, and 371st Regiments into the 370th. Two regiments moved to a quiet sector under the US 5th Army, while the 366th Infantry Regiment became two general service engineer regiments. The all-Japanese-American (Nisei) 442nd Regimental Combat Team, one of the most decorated US military units, which had suffered some of the heaviest casualties of the war, was attached, along with the 473rd Infantry, a white regiment consisting of several retrained anti-aircraft battalions, making the 92nd a "rainbow" division.

Despite General Almond's belief that Black troops were malingerers and cowards, two officers of the 366th and 370th Regiments won Medals of Honor (awarded in 1997, 52 years later, by President Clinton). In addition, members of the division were awarded two Distinguished Service Crosses, an Army Distinguished Service Medal, 208 Silver Stars, 16 Legion of Merits, 6 Soldier's Medals, 1,166 Bronze Star Medals, and 1,891 Purple Hearts, in addition to Italian and Brazilian awards. The division suffered 548 killed in action, 2,187 wounded in action, 206 missing in action, and 56 prisoners of war, a total of nearly 3,000 casualties. None of these facts is consistent with General Almond's allegations of cowardice.

OTHER BLACK COMBAT UNITS

At least 24 other Black combat units fought in Europe, including the 3334 Field Artillery Group, nine heavy field artillery battalions, an anti-aircraft battalion, three tank battalions, two tank destroyer battalions, and eight combat engineer battalions. Among the most successful Black combat units that fought in Europe during World War II was the 761st Tank Battalion, consisting of 6 white and 30 African American officers, plus 676 Black enlisted men.

After arriving on Omaha Beach in early October 1944, Patton addressed the battalion on November 3 after its assignment to the 3rd Army:

> Men, you're the first Negro tankers to ever fight in the American Army. I would never have asked for you if you weren't good. I have nothing but the best in my Army. I don't care what color you are, so long as you go up there and kill those Kraut sonsabitches. Everyone has their eyes on you and is expecting great things from you. Most of all, your race is looking forward to you. Don't let them down.[21]

Once he returned to his headquarters, Patton declared, "They gave a good first impression, but I have no faith in the inherent fighting capabilities of the race."[22] The tankers of the 761st proved Patton wrong, spearheading five 3rd Army divisions and four other divisions in 7th and 9th Armies in the drive through France, Belgium, Holland, Luxembourg,

Germany, and Austria while participating in 30 major engagements in 183 continuous days of combat. The 761st spearheaded the 3rd Army's relief of Bastogne and was the first American unit to meet the Russians on the Enns River near Regensburg, Bavaria. Between March 31 and May 6, 1945, the battalion faced at least 14 German divisions; captured 106,926 prisoners, including 20 German generals; and liberated a concentration camp. Members of the battalion were awarded 1 Medal of Honor, 11 Silver Stars, 69 Bronze Stars, and about 300 Purple Hearts. Fourteen German tanks were destroyed, and 113 men were killed or wounded in their first month of combat. But they persevered with uncanny accuracy and determination. In their first month of deployment, the battalion suffered 24 men killed in action, 81 men wounded, plus 44 nonbattle-related casualties. The battalion received no replacements until December, and they were untrained.

Despite this amazing record, a young white company commander observed, "These guys were better than heroes because they weren't supposed

761st Tank Battalion in Coburg, Germany, April 1945. SOURCE: US ARMY PHOTO, NATIONAL ARCHIVES & RECORDS ADMINISTRATION, COLLEGE PARK, MD.

to be able to fight, and they were treated worse than lepers. . . . I used to ask myself, why the hell should these guys fight?"[23] Despite six nominations for the Presidential Unit Citation by four major generals and the undersecretary of war, the European chain of command pigeonholed the recommendation—General Eisenhower, the theater commander, would not sign off on it. President Jimmy Carter finally presented the award in 1978.[24] This memorable unit was inactivated in Germany on June 1, 1946.

After the war, Patton declared, "Individually they were good soldiers, but I expressed my belief at the time, and have never found the necessity of changing it, that a colored soldier cannot think fast enough to fight in armor."[25] In other words, he let race prejudice override what he had seen men of the 761st do repeatedly—think fast, survive, and excel in armored warfare.

The 6888th Central Postal Directory Battalion, 855 women strong, was the sole Black female unit deployed to Europe. Their herculean efforts—working seven days a week in three eight-hour shifts—accomplished wonders for the morale of nearly 7 million soldiers deployed to the European Theater of Operations (ETO) as they sorted mountains of letters and packages destined for servicemen throughout Europe. They began in Birmingham, England, where they tackled a huge backlog, sorting an average of 65,000 pieces of mail each day in poorly lit warehouses without heat. After three months, they deployed to Rouen, France, and cleared a two-year backlog. By war's end, the SixTripleEight had cleared over 17 million pieces of backlogged mail, ensuring the troops stayed in touch with their loved ones back home. The unit was disbanded at Fort Dix, New Jersey, in March 1946 with no expression of appreciation for their service. A monument honoring the battalion was erected at Fort Leavenworth, Kansas, in 2018, 72 years later. The Army awarded a Meritorious Unit Commendation to the SixTripleEight the following year, and Congress unanimously voted to award the battalion a Congressional Gold Medal, signed by President Biden on March 14, 2022. In the summer of 2022, a base Naming Committee recommended that Fort Lee, Virginia, be renamed Fort Gregg-Adams, in part after Lieutenant Colonel Charity Adams, the battalion commander.

The 555th Airborne Infantry Battalion had all Black officers but was diverted from action in Europe or against Japan to fight forest fires in Washington and Oregon. To his credit, Virginian Major General James Gavin, commander of the 82nd Airborne Division, invited the battalion to join the 82nd in their postwar parade down New York's Fifth Avenue. He also welcomed the "Triple Nickel" to Fort Bragg, North Carolina, after the war; the battalion was officially assimilated into the 82nd Airborne Division on December 9, 1947.[26] Other all-Black units that excelled included the 614th Tank Destroyer Battalion, which heroically stopped German armor attacks near Climbach, France, and the 452nd Anti-Aircraft Artillery Battalion. Doubtless, there were other Black combat units in Europe, but even these units that have been mentioned have faded into obscurity and service and supply units were rarely recognized.

BATTLE OF THE BULGE: HITLER'S LAST OFFENSIVE IN THE WEST

At dawn on December 16, 1944, three German armies with 410,000 men, about 1,400 tanks and tank destroyers, 2,600 artillery pieces, 1,600 anti-tank guns, and more than 1,000 aircraft attacked in a weakly defended 50-mile front through Belgium's Ardennes Forest in their last assault in the West. The German offensive caught Allied headquarters by surprise, and understrength and un-battle tested frontline divisions thinly deployed across the sector resulted in close to 90,000 American casualties in a few weeks. Understrength and unexperienced frontline units were overrun and thrown into confusion. The commander of the understrength, untested 106th Infantry Division requested that the Black 333rd Artillery Battalion leave a battery forward to support the withdrawal of his hard-pressed men and the 14th Cavalry Regiment. Two of the division's three regiments were surrounded and forced to surrender, but the division's fate could have been even worse. Most of the men of Headquarters Company and C Battery of the 333rd Artillery Battalion were taken prisoner—the unit lost 6 officers, 222 men, 9 artillery pieces, and 12 weapons carriers, sustaining the second-highest losses of any unit during the war.

In the confusion, 11 men escaped and found shelter in Wereth, a small Belgian hamlet. Betrayed by a German sympathizer in the hamlet, they were captured and tortured, beaten, and executed on the second day of the offensive by elements of Task Force Keitel, a spearhead of the elite SS (Schutzstaffel) Leibstandarte (bodyguard) Hitler Panzer Division. Some had their faces bashed in, and others were bayonetted or had fingers cut off, legs broken, or bodies run over by tracked vehicles. Six weeks later, a patrol from the 99th Division discovered the site.[27]

Two batteries of the 333rd Field Artillery Battalion joined the 969th Field Artillery Battalion at Bastogne to help suppress the German advance. The 969th earned a Distinguished Unit Citation for superior performance during the defense of Bastogne.

The American Army endured a catastrophe with few reserves to stop the German onslaught. A significant number of the frontline artillery and reserves available were African American. The situation was so desperate that the Allied logistics chief suggested the formation of rifle platoons from volunteers among Black service troops. When the news reached Washington that Negro and white Americans would be battling the German Army in mixed companies, all hell broke loose on Capitol Hill. The War Department brusquely cabled Supreme Allied Headquarters demanding an "explanation" of this "violation of American racial policy." That month, future Senator Robert Byrd of West Virginia sent a letter to Mississippi's notoriously racist Senator Theodore G. Bilbo divulging the depth of white supremacy. In a letter for which he later apologized, Byrd wrote:

> I am a typical white American, a southerner, and 27 years of age, and never in this world will I be convinced that race mixing in any field is good. All the social "do-gooders," the philanthropic "greats" of this day, the reds and the pinks . . . the disciples of Eleanor . . . the pleas by Sinatra . . . can never alter my convictions on this question. I am loyal to my country and know but reverence to her flag. BUT I shall never submit to fight beneath that banner with a negro by my side. Rather I should die a thousand times, and see old Glory trampled in the dirt never to rise again, than to see this beloved land of ours become degraded by race mongrels, a throwback to the blackest specimen from the wilds.
>
> Integration of the Negro into White regiments is the very thing for which the Negro intelligentsia is striving and such a move would only serve to lower the efficiency of the fighting units and the morale of the average white serviceman as well.[28]

Such racism notwithstanding, Black platoons served in eight infantry and two armored divisions. Brigadier General Benjamin O. Davis Sr.

recognized the initiative's significance, writing, "The decision from the High Command is the greatest since the enactment of the Constitutional amendments following the emancipation."[29] By March 1945, around 5,000 men had volunteered; many took reductions in rank. Over 2,500 volunteers received infantry training and formed into 37 rifle platoons under white officers, augmenting the 1st and 7th Armies. Despite the heroics of the 761st Tank Battalion, General George Patton refused to accept any of these volunteers in his 3rd Army. Patton believed that Blacks did not possess the reflexes or intelligence, although the 761st should have opened his eyes.[30] The commander of the 104th Infantry Division filed a glowing report: "Morale: excellent. Manner of performance: superior. The men are eager to close with the enemy and to destroy him. Strict attention to duty, aggressiveness, common sense and judgement under fire has won the admiration of all the men."[31]

Sergeant First Class Edward Allen Baker Jr., Bastogne volunteer and Medal of Honor Recipient. SOURCE: US ARMY PHOTOGRAPH, NATIONAL ARCHIVES AND RECORDS ADMINISTRATION.

A War Department study concluded that the Black volunteers "established themselves as fighting men no less courageous than their white comrades." The Army Research Branch established that before the Battle of the Bulge, only 33 percent of whites responded favorably to including Blacks in their companies; after the experiment, 77 percent approved.[32] White acceptance had made perceptible progress, but despite their effectiveness as soon as the war ended in Europe, the Army returned the men to their support units or discharged them.

The most significant conclusion one draws from African Americans' service during World War II is that although they were treated as second-class citizens by most of their countrymen, Blacks did not let that deter them from responding as full, red-blooded Americans. It is difficult to appreciate how deeply the evil of American racism permeated our society and the armed forces at that time, to the extent that Black soldiers were constantly denigrated and their heroics most often went unrecognized. Most Black GIs were forced to fight fascism on two fronts, waging a genuine "Double V" struggle. Many African American servicemen brought bitter memories back home, only reinforced when their government did not extend to them the same generous Veterans Administration benefits in education and housing provided to whites.

BELATED RECOGNITION

By war's end, 7,768 Blacks had been commissioned officers, less than 1 percent of Blacks in the Army. The corresponding figure for white officers was 10 percent. A single Black, Benjamin O. Davis Jr., was promoted to general, and out of 5,220 officers promoted to full colonel, only seven were Black.[33] Over a million Black men served in the armed forces during World War II, but only nine received the Army's second-highest honor, the Distinguished Service Cross. No Black soldier received the Medal of Honor; it took 52 years before this injustice was rectified.

Blacks encountered discrimination after the war as well. African Americans were disproportionally issued "blue" discharges, an administrative discharge neither honorable nor dishonorable. Out of 48,603 blue discharges the Army issued between December 1, 1941, and June 30, 1945, African Americans received almost one quarter when they were only 6.5 percent of the Army. The *Pittsburgh Courier* rebuked the Army in October 1945 for "allowing prejudiced officers to use it as a means of punishing Negro soldiers who do not like unbearable conditions."[34]

The May 1996 edition of *U.S. News & World Report* featured an article, "Military Injustice: No Black soldier received the Congressional Medal of Honor, America's highest award for valor, during WW II. The reason was racism."[35] Prodded by a Shaw University study initiated in 1992 due to requests and complaints from veterans of both races, the Department of the Army conducted a three-year study into the reasons why no Black received the Medal of Honor. The Department of Defense concluded, "Segregated units by race complicated and slowed training, exacerbated relations between officers and EM [enlisted men] and between commanders and their units and undermined the morale of those units in both subtle and obvious ways."[36]

First Lieutenant Joseph Vernon Baker, Weapons Platoon, C Company, 370th Infantry Regiment. SOURCE: US ARMY, NATIONAL ARCHIVES AND RECORDS ADMINISTRATION.

In January 1997, President Bill Clinton presented the Medal of Honor to seven Black servicemen. Only one, First Lieutenant Joseph Vernon Baker, of St. Maries, Idaho, a veteran of the 92nd Division's 370th Infantry Regiment, was still living. He led his platoon against heavily fortified German positions at Castle Aghinolfi, destroying six machine guns and killing 28 enemy. Only six men from his platoon survived. Others belatedly awarded the Medal of Honor include First Lieutenant John R. Fox of Ohio, Canon Company, 366th Infantry Regiment, who called in artillery fire on his own position, destroying a large enemy force threatening his regiment; First Lieutenant Charles L. Thomas, 614th Tank Destroyer Battalion, of Detroit, Michigan; Staff Sergeant Edward A. Carter Jr., 56th Armored Infantry Battalion, 12th Armored Division, of Los Angeles (a "Bastogne Volunteer"); Staff Sergeant Ruben Rivers, 761st Tank Battalion; Private First Class Willy James Jr., 413th Infantry Regiment, 104th Infantry Division, of Kansas City, Missouri (another "Bastogne Volunteer"); and Private George Watson of the 29th Quartermaster Regiment, from Birmingham, Alabama. Watson lost his life in Portlock Harbor, New Guinea, saving crewmates after the Japanese bombed their ship before he was pulled down by the boat's suction.[37]

THE ARMY AIR FORCES—TUSKEGEE AIRMEN

The struggle Blacks went through to serve in the newly formed Army Air Corps, today's Air Force, is a fascinating saga. Four months before the 1940 Selective Service Act, General Henry H. "Hap" Arnold declared that if forced to accept Blacks, they would be used "in labor battalions or labor companies to perform the duties of post fatigue and as waiters at our messes." Arnold also stated, "Negro pilots cannot be used in our present air corps units since this would result in having Negro officers serving over white enlisted men. This would create an impossible social problem."[38] However, prodded by a lawsuit filed by a Howard University student, the War Department announced the formation of the 99th Pursuit Squadron in January 1941, to be trained at Tuskegee, Alabama. The pilots began training in August 1941. Among the first five March 1942 graduates was Captain Benjamin O. Davis Jr., son of the Army's first Black general officer and the fourth Black graduate of the US Military Academy (Class of 1936), appointed commander of the 99th Pursuit Squadron.

Tuskegee Airmen of the 332nd Fighter Group, with P-51 Mustang, debriefing in Italy, August 1944. SOURCE: US ARMY AIR FORCE PHOTO NATIONAL ARCHIVES & RECORDS ADMINISTRATION, COLLEGE PARK, MD.

Eventually, 600 pilots qualified at Tuskegee. When the 99th Pursuit Squadron deployed to French Morocco in April 1943, its members experienced intense racial harassment. In September 1943, the commander of the XII Air Support Command wrote, "the Negro type has not the proper reflexes to make a first-class pilot." Other commanders wrote that Black pilots lacked aggressiveness. That same month, General Arnold wrote a memo to Lieutenant General Carl Spaatz, senior air commander in North Africa, encouraging more adverse reports about the 99th to justify reduction of the number of Black pilots trained.[39]

But time and rapid acquisition of combat experience were running against blind prejudice. Pilots of the squadron scored their first kill in July and in January 1944, achieved the highest number of confirmed kills of any squadron in support of the Anzio invasion. Even General Arnold had a conversion, officially commending the squadron. *Time* magazine reported in their February 14, 1944, edition, "Any outfit would have been proud of this record. These victories stamped the final seal of combat excellence on one of the most controversial outfits in the army."[40]

As a result of the squadron's success, the Black 332nd Fighter Group was activated in October 1943, consisting of the 100th, 301st, and 302nd Fighter Squadrons, and deployed to Europe in February 1944. Pilots of the 302nd painted their planes' tails red, prompting the bomber crews they escorted to call them "Red Tails." They flew 179 bomber escort missions, losing very few of the bombers they escorted. Overall, Black airmen flew 1,578 missions, comprising 15,533 combat sorties, during which they destroyed 262 enemy aircraft and damaged another 148. Tuskegee Airmen also destroyed 950 railroad cars, trucks, and other motor vehicles, as well as 40 boats and barges. Two pilots, Captain Wendell "Hot Rock" Pruitt and his wingman Lieutenant Gwynne Pierson, sank a German destroyer in Trieste harbor, a feat unique for the Army Air Forces. Wing cameras provided hard evidence to a skeptical 15th Air Force.[41]

The norm for bomber crews was 25–50 missions; most fighter pilots flew 50–75, but Black pilots flew at least 100 combat sorties because their squadrons had fewer pilots (only 26, compared to 30 to 35 in white squadrons.) The 332nd Fighter Group earned a Distinguished Unit Citation for a bomber escort mission to Berlin on March 24, 1945, during which three German advanced Me-262 jet fighters were shot down. The 99th Fighter Squadron earned three, two for actions over Sicily and one over northern Italy. Tuskegee Airmen earned 1 Silver Star, 95 Distinguished Flying Crosses, 14 Bronze Stars, and 744 Air Medals; their overall record changed minds. A 2012 movie, *Red Tails*, publicized the valor of these Black World War II Tuskegee Airmen just as *Glory* did for the 54th Massachusetts Infantry Regiment (Colored) and US Colored Troops of the Civil War in general. Both films conveyed a new awareness to most white Americans, a reflection of African Americans' ability to rise above the racism and amnesia endemic to our education system and society.

However, the 477th Bombardment Group (Medium) (Colored), made up of the 616th, 317th, 318th, and 619th Bombardment Squadrons, did not experience the same extraordinary record of combat achievement attained by the 99th Fighter Squadron and 332nd Fighter Group. Its men distinguished themselves quite differently. When confronted with illegal segregation, they protested and risked imprisonment to challenge the exceptional bigotry of their commanders. The 477th was activated on January 15, 1944, at Selfridge Army Airfield, Michigan, about 40 miles from Detroit. Because the Army Air Forces had no schools to train Blacks as navigators and bombardiers until well into the war, the unit lacked officers in these critical specialties. Pilots for the 477th were in great supply, either from recently graduated Tuskegee aviators or veterans from the Mediterranean Theater—many pilots of the 477th with previous combat tours as fighter pilots volunteered to become proficient in B-25s.

Born under an extraordinarily racist cloud, Army Air Forces commanding General Henry H. (Hap) Arnold tried to abort the unit before it was authorized and then assigned the unit to the 1st Air Force, commanded by an ardent segregationist, Major General Frank O. Hunter. Moreover, the 477th never entered combat because its commander, Colonel Robert E. "Jesus Bob" Selway, was so prejudiced that he drove more than 100 Black officers of this unit to mutiny. He ran the unit as a promotion mill for white aviators, would not associate socially with the Blacks in his unit, and encouraged other white officers to act the same. He reserved command of all four squadrons for whites, even though many of the Black veterans of combat in Europe had more flying time and combat experience and outranked the whites.

Selway, concerned about race tensions and the riots in Detroit June 20–22, 1943, which did not affect his group, moved the unit to Godman Army Airfield near Fort Knox, Kentucky, despite the pressures of preparing a unit for combat. The base was inadequate because it could not house the entire group and had inadequate apron and hanger space. It was a bad move done for racial reasons, seriously delaying the 477th's training program and damaging morale. The aircrews constantly repeated routine proficiency missions without combat crew training, thus lowering morale, although the unit maintained an exceptional safety record. By mid-January 1945, even though the 477th was not fully manned, combat crew training began. But winter weather arrived, and flyable hours were reduced by 60 percent. Despite the poor flying weather, in its first year, the unit accumulated 17,875 flying hours with two minor accidents, neither due to crew error.

When the unit transferred to Freeman Army Airfield near Seymour, Indiana, in March 1945, a high proportion of the town was hostile to Black airmen. Some grocery stores refused to sell food to spouses of the aviators, and restaurant owners refused to serve Blacks. Much more crippling to the progress of the 477th than the unit move or local hostility was the mutiny that occurred in April 1945. Morale in the unit completely collapsed, resulting in five fatal flying accidents beginning in mid-April. The group returned to Godman Army Airfield.

Under orders from the 1st Air Force commander, the group commander established separate officers' clubs on the subterfuge that one was for white supervisors and one for Black trainees. However, there were whites on the post who were trainees, and about 20 Black officers were supervisors. When Selway and Hunter telephoned each other or the Pentagon to talk about the club issue, both called the supervisors' club the "white officers' club," although Army regulations required that officers' clubs be open to all officers. The racist tone set by the commander so lowered morale that segregated officers' clubs ended up being only the match that enflamed the tinder. On April 5, 1945, Black officers began to enter the white club despite written orders. By April 7, over 100 officers and men were under house arrest in an organization that was needed for imminent combat.

The Black press publicized the situation, sympathetic members of Congress called for an investigation, and the NAACP championed the cause. As was common in such matters involving Black troops in the Army, Assistant Secretary of War John J. McCloy, who led the Committee on Special Troop Policies, became involved. On May 18, the Committee published its report, finding that Selway's actions violated Army regulations. McCloy sent a letter to the secretary of war directing the commanding general of the Army Air Forces to take "appropriate action" regarding Selway's noncompliance with Army regulations and War Department policies.

General Arnold replaced every white officer of the 477th Group with African Americans and made Colonel Benjamin O. Davis Jr. group commander in late May 1945. Davis and his team quickly improved the unit's morale and fighting fitness, confirmed by a 1st Air Force inspection. That summer, the unit received orders to the Pacific to fight in the war against Japan, but the war ended before the 477th could deploy. While the group never met a foreign enemy, it engaged the domestic foes of racism and bigotry and won.[42] The history of the 477th Bombardment Group is a further demonstration that racists and bigots have ignored patriotism and disdained military assets needed to win America's wars simply to satisfy their prejudice and delusions of white supremacy.

US NAVY

Meanwhile, the Navy and Marine Corps resisted integration with might and main. In response to Executive Order 8802, the *Fair Employment Prac-*

Colonel, then later, General Benjamin O. Davis Jr. SOURCE: US ARMY AIR FORCE PHOTO, NATIONAL ARCHIVES & RECORDS ADMINISTRATION, COLLEGE PARK, MD.

tices Act, in April 1942, the secretary of the Navy approved a plan opening a wide range of ratings to Black seamen, including gunners, clerks, radio operators, and signalmen, at Camp Robert Smalls (named after the heroic Black Civil War captain and Congressman) in an isolated area of the Great Lakes Naval Training Center near Chicago. Unfortunately, the Navy assigned Blacks who completed specialized training to shore duty, ammunition units, or construction battalions.[43] Fifteen newly enlisted messmen wrote a letter published in the *Pittsburgh Courier*:

> We sincerely hope to discourage any other colored boys who might have planned to join the Navy and make the same mistake we did. All they would become is seagoing bellhops, chambermaids, and dishwashers. We take it upon ourselves to write this letter regardless of any action the Naval authorities may take. We know that it could not possibly surpass the mental cruelty inflicted upon us on this ship.[44]

Naval authorities attributed Blacks' low enlistment rate to "relative unfamiliarity with the sea" and "consequent fear of water," revealing their ignorance of the history of Blacks serving in the US Navy. Despite Roosevelt's directives, only 150,000 African Americans, about 5 percent of the total force, served in the US Navy during World War II, mostly as mess stewards. Out of 78,000 Black enlistees inducted into the Navy in 1943, 38,000 were mess attendants.[45]

Assistant Secretary of the Navy Adlai Stevenson, in a September 1944 memo to Secretary Knox, suggested that the Navy initiate an accelerated commissioning program for "10 or 12 Negroes selected from top-notch civilians just as we procure white officers." The result was the graduation of the "Golden Thirteen" at Great Lakes Naval Training Station in Illinois in March 1944 after a 10-week course. However, the Navy would not permit them to use officers' clubs. By the time that the war ended, the Navy had commissioned about 60 Black officers.[46]

The treatment of Blacks at the US Military Academy at West Point is reviewed in Chapter Four. The situation was much worse at the US Naval Academy in Annapolis, Maryland, which found myriad ways to eliminate five Black midshipmen in the 1870s and did not admit a single Black midshipmen until 1945.[47] Wesley A. Brown was the first Black graduate, commissioned in 1949.

The Navy commissioned two ships, a destroyer escort and a submarine chaser, with Black crews and a white command structure in March 1944. The petty officers on the two ships were initially white until later that year, but in the fall of 1944, the Navy announced that 500 African American seamen were serving on 25 auxiliary vessels, serving primarily in the Pacific. These experiments proved that Black seamen could perform every shipboard task. In addition, 12,500 Black Seabees constructed naval facilities and airfields.

Close to 1,000 Blacks served in the Coast Guard in the Atlantic, Pacific, and Alaskan waters. Another 24,000 African Americans served in the vital Merchant Marine. Four Liberty ships had Black captains, 14 Liberty ships were named for prominent African Americans, and 4 more were named for Black merchant seamen who lost their lives at sea.

A Black steward serving aboard the USS *West Virginia*, Ship's Cook Third Class Doris "Dorie" Miller, received the Navy Cross for his heroic actions at Pearl Harbor on December 7, 1941. After removing the ship's captain, who was mortally wounded by shrapnel from the burning bridge,

USS Mason (DE-529), Evarts-class destroyer escort. Source: US Navy photo, National Archives & Records Administration, College Park, MD.

Miller manned an anti-aircraft gun, achieving two confirmed kills and two more "possibles." Although he was the war's first legitimate hero, Miller's actions went unrecognized for almost five months until the NAACP and the Black press forced the Navy and War Department to acknowledge Miller's heroism and Admiral Nimitz awarded him the Navy Cross in May 1942. Dorie died almost two years later when his ship, an escort carrier, was sunk by a Japanese submarine. Three other Black seamen received the Navy Cross during World War II: Steward's Mate Second Class Eli Benjamin, Messman Leonard Harmon, and Cook William Pinckney.

James Forrestal replaced Frank Knox as secretary of the Navy when Knox died in April 1944. Forrestal was a longtime member of the National Urban League. That summer, he met with Chief of Naval Operations Admiral Ernest King to discuss integrating the Navy. King observed, "You know, we say we're a democracy, and a democracy ought to have a democratic Navy."[48] The Navy began by integrating auxiliary ships, tankers, and troop transports and found that this experiment was successful, an important incremental step.

In July 1944, Forrestal recommended that Black women be accepted into the Navy. African American WAVES (Women Accepted for Volunteer Emergency Services) were trained in integrated classes and assigned "wherever needed within the continental limits of the United States,

Messman Second Class Doris "Dorie" Miller. SOURCE: US NAVY PHOTO, NATIONAL ARCHIVES & RECORDS ADMINISTRATION, COLLEGE PARK, MD.

preferably to stations where there are already Negro men."[49] Thomas Dewey, the 1944 Republican candidate for the presidency, helped accelerate integration of the armed services by urging the end of segregation in his campaign speeches. In October 1944, a directive was issued authorizing the enlistment of Black females in the Navy, Coast Guard, and Marines. The Coast Guard accepted few Black female enlistees, but the Marine Corps Women's Reserve did not enroll Blacks until 1949. In January 1945, Phyllis Mae Daly became the first Black member of the Navy Nurse Corps, and six more Black nurses received commissions before the war ended.[50]

In July 1944, two military cargo ships loaded with ammunition exploded at Port Chicago, California, killing 320 sailors and civilians, including 202 Black enlisted ammunition handlers. The worst domestic disaster of the war, this incident was more than 15 percent of all naval casualties during the war. Although initially $5,000 was proposed to compensate the families of each victim, but Congressman John Rankin of Mississippi objected because most victims were Black, and the figure was reduced to $3,000.[51] About a month later, 258 of the surviving Black sea-

Port Chicago explosion. SOURCE: US NAVY PHOTO, NATIONAL ARCHIVES & RECORDS ADMINISTRATION, COLLEGE PARK, MD.

men, denied the 30-day leave granted to white survivors, refused to load ammunition under the same unsafe conditions. The Navy arrested and court-martialed 50 of them, all of whom were convicted of mutiny and sentenced to 15 years of prison at hard labor and dishonorable discharges. NAACP lawyer Thurgood Marshall defended the sailors, noting, "This is not fifty men on trial for mutiny; this is the Navy on trial for its whole vicious policy toward Negroes." Marshall observed, "Negroes in the Navy don't mind loading ammunition. They just want to know why they are the only ones doing the loading."[52] Thanks in part to the efforts of this future Supreme Court justice, 47 of the 50 were released in January 1946. The remaining three served additional months in prison. It was not until June 2019 that the 116th Congress exonerated all 50 men court-martialed by the Navy.[53]

MARINE CORPS

Despite the remarks of Major General Thomas Holcomb, commandant of the Corps, "Blacks were not needed in a 'club' that didn't want them," the Marine Corps was integrated in May 1942 after Secretary of the Navy Frank Knox ordered the Marines to accept 900 Blacks per month. General Ray Robinson complained, "Eleanor says we got to take in Negroes, and we are just scared to death; we've never had any; we don't know how to handle them; we are afraid of them."[54]

The new recruits trained in segregated facilities at Montford Point, Camp Lejeune, North Carolina. The recruits in the first Black platoon were probably as "scared to death" as the general. They were supervised by a drill instructor named Sergeant Germany whose "welcoming" speech went something like:

> I did not come here to make friends. I came to undertake the impossible assignment of making Marines out of you goddam people. When the first load of y'all got here it made me want to puke, then go get drunk. . . . The Marine Corps is not for cooks and janitors. Which is about all you son a bitchin' people are qualified to do as far as I can see. . . . If I have to kill you to do it then you are dead. . . . My name is Sergeant Germany. I'm a redneck peckerwood and I hate a goddam nigger.[55]

Graduates of the first course were assigned to the 51st Defense Battalion, which had both artillery and air defense components. These men excelled in gunnery—the 51st was known as a "hot shot" outfit. Their first shot off Onslow Beach was a direct hit on a moving target—the beach was otherwise off limits to Blacks. When they left for the Pacific in January 1944, a sheriff refused to allow them to get off the train in Atlanta, Georgia, even though German POWS were dining at the station. Some wanted to get off the train and tear the station apart, while others wept. San Diego was nearly as bad: they were informed that they had to sit at the rear of the open-air theater. Although they feared that the Marines would trick them and reassign them to other duties, they left in February for Funafuti, Ellice Islands, a backwater three miles long, at most three-quarters of a mile wide, and 12 feet above sea level. Six months later, the battalion deployed to Eniwetok Atoll, where all the vegetation was blasted away. Through it all, the men drilled and according to records, were the best gunners in the Corps, although they never saw combat. Follow-on graduates were assigned to the 52nd Defense Battalion, which sailed for the Marshall Islands in October 1944—they also never saw combat.

Black Marines also served in fifty-two 110- to 165-man depot companies and 12 ammunition companies with 255 Marines each. Ironically, these logistical units were the only units that experienced combat. After delivering their loads, the companies carried wounded Marines back to the beach for medical care. Members of the 3rd Marine Ammunition Company and 18th and 20th Depot Companies hit the beach on D-Day on Saipan. The 3rd Ammo Company helped repulse a night counterattack. The three units, along with the 19th Depot Company, received the Presidential Unit Citation. Marines of the 2nd and 4th Ammunition Companies were heavily engaged in the capture of Saipan and earned a Navy Unit Citation. And two companies took part in the bloody struggle for Peleliu in September 1944, where the 11th Depot Company had the highest casualties of any Black Marine unit—9 Marines killed and 78 wounded. In December, Private First Class Luther Woodward earned a Silver Star for tracking fresh footprints near an ammunition dump he was guarding. He crawled through the brush, killed one man, and wounded another, then returned to the ammunition dump and encouraged five other Marines to join him in killing two more Japanese.[56]

The most intense action any of these units experienced was on Iwo Jima in February 1945, on D-Day plus 25, when a company of Japanese made a night attack on the ammunition dump guarded by the 8th Ammunition Company. After a harrowing all-night encounter, morning revealed piles of bodies. Black Seabees were tasked to provide medical care for two wounded members of the 36th Depot Company because white Navy corpsmen would not touch Black Marines.[57] The Marines' performance led the newly appointed Marine commandant, General Alexander A. Vandergrift, to declare, "The Negro Marines are no longer on trial. They are Marines."[58]

Despite their dedication and heroism, fewer than 20,000 Marines, or less than 5 percent of the Corps, served during World War II. More than 65 percent of them served overseas, but few saw combat.[59] The first Black Marine officer, Lieutenant Frederick C. Branch of Hamlet, North Carolina, did not pin his bars on until November 1945. Soon afterward, the Corps disbanded both composite artillery defense battalions and the commandant received a report declaring, "So long as social conditions make segregation desirable, it is believed that Negro Marines would be more advantageously employed in almost any other type of unit."[60] It did not matter that both were first-rate artillerymen; their skin color disqualified them.

THE HOME FRONT

World War II precipitated an even greater migration of African Americans from the South. Over the war years, about 1.5 million African

Americans, 15 percent of the population, migrated out of the South, a phenomenon that continued after the war ended. The consequences of this mass movement are difficult to fully appreciate. By the 1970s, nearly half of American Blacks, 47 percent, lived in the North. Before this migration began, only 10 percent of the country's Black population lived above the Mason Dixon Line.[61] What started as a little-noticed trickle of the impatient became a flood of discontented masses during World War II, as Blacks chose the option to "vote with their feet." The greatest increase occurred in Southern California; Los Angeles grew from a small Black population to more than 340,000. Over the course of six decades, 6 to 7 million Southern Blacks left the land of their ancestors and migrated to every state of the union outside the South.[62]

With so many men in the armed services, 600,000 Black women found opportunities in industrial jobs. As many as 400,000 of them previously were domestic servants. As one female aircraft worker expressed it, "Hitler got us out of the white folks' kitchen." Those who continued in domestic work found their wages increased due to reduced availability of such workers.

Thanks to training programs offered by Roosevelt's National Youth Administration (NYA), a part of the Works Progress Administration (WPA), which included a Division of Negro Affairs headed by Mary McLeod Bethune, who worked at the agency from 1936 to 1943, thousands of Blacks were prepared for work in industry once the war began. The NYA provided work and education for Americans between the ages of 16 and 25, operating from June 26, 1935, to 1939. Overall, the NYA helped over 4.5 million American youth find jobs, receive vocational training, or afford higher standards of education. This number was augmented by the US Office of Education, Vocational Training for War Production Workers, and the Engineering, Science, and Management War Training Program. By the summer of 1943, 65 historically Black colleges or universities were participating in the latter program, in which 50,000 African American students enrolled.

African Americans participated in Civilian Defense activities at all levels and were essential in efforts to conserve food and other essential commodities. Blacks served in the Red Cross as Gray Ladies, nurses' aides, and drivers. They worked in camps, clubs, and hospitals in training areas, as well as overseas. By 1943, more than 180 of 1,326 United Services Organization (USO) operations were designated for African Americans. By war's end, this grew to more than 300 USO clubs; only about a dozen had interracial staffs.

POSTWAR

On October 1, 1945, senior Army officers convened in Washington at the direction of Secretary of War Robert P. Patterson to review Black participation in the war and develop future policies. In April 1946, they produced the Gillem Report, which built on the success of the Battle of the Bulge. There would no longer be all-Black divisions, but companies would have Black platoons, battalions would have Black companies, and regiments would have Black battalions, although each subunit was still segregated. This was only an incremental improvement, as dining and living facilities remained segregated.[63]

Secretary of the Navy James Forrestal abolished separated training facilities in June 1945 and integrated all Navy schools. In February 1946, he directed "all restrictions governing types of assignments for which Negro naval personnel are eligible are hereby lifted." The Marine Corps responded by reducing the number of Black Marines they had grudgingly accepted during the war, dropping to 2,580 Blacks out of their postwar 100,000 strength. In early 1947, the Corps declared that Black Marines could only be mess stewards. The Marine Corps chose to retrench after the war ended. When Forrestal became the first secretary of defense in September 1947, Blacks constituted 3 percent of the Marine Corps, less than 5 percent of the Navy, 6 percent of the Air Force, and less than 9 percent of the Army. On many Army posts, Black soldiers picked up trash, cut lawns, and performed other manual labor duties as they had prewar.[64]

For discharged veterans, little changed after the war. The American Legion, Veterans of Foreign Wars, and the Disabled American Veterans had segregated chapters, although all veterans fought a common enemy. Mississippi's Senator Theodore Bilbo urged "red-blooded Anglo-Saxons" to stop Blacks from voting "by any means." He added, "If you don't know what that means, you are not up on your persuasive measures."[65] Blacks in uniform were once again beaten, and in 1946, six Black veterans were lynched, as they had been after World War I. In July 1946, a sign was nailed on a Black church reading, "The first nigger to vote will never vote again." Macio Sipes, a war veteran and the only Black in Taylor County, Georgia, who voted, was dragged from his home and shot to death. In Monroe, Georgia, two Black veterans and their wives were removed from their car and shot; their bodies were riddled with some 60 bullets.[66]

Sergeant Isaac Woodard. SOURCE: US ARMY PHOTO, NATIONAL ARCHIVES & RECORDS ADMINISTRATION, COLLEGE PARK, MD.

The most egregious case was that of recently discharged Sergeant Isaac Woodard, who was on his way home to North Carolina after being outprocessed at Fort Gordon, Georgia. The bus driver cursed Woodard for taking so long to use the COLORED ONLY restroom and summoned the local sheriff at the next stop in Batesville, South Carolina. Charged with drinking, even though he had not touched a drop, Woodard was beaten with a blackjack and had the end of a nightstick poked into his eye on February 12, 1946. He was locked up overnight and fined $50. When he arrived at the military hospital in Spartanburg, South Carolina, doctors found that his cornea was so severely damaged that he was permanently blind.[67]

When he ran for reelection as president in 1948, Truman was already under tremendous political pressure—two previous Republican presidential candidates had publicly endorsed integration. When informed of the mayhem and murder ongoing in the South, President Truman exclaimed, "My God! I had no idea it was as terrible as that! We've got to do something."[68] Myriad other incidents began to convince white Americans that Jim Crow violated the spirit of democracy and equality, especially after Nazi war criminals were publicly tried during the Nuremberg trials for acting out racial hatred. As it turns out, this World War I artillery officer and haberdasher from Missouri took decisive and courageous action soon after reelection by issuing an executive order directing integration of the military.

CONCLUSIONS

Despite racial persecution, about 1.2 million Blacks served their country with great dignity and bravery during World War II. They demonstrated that their capacities equaled whites' and managed to overcome considerable societal handicaps and oppression to make major contributions to the war effort, although handicapped by the inferior education they received. Many illiterates or near-illiterates proved to be exemplary soldiers.

The image of America seen through Nazi eyes revealed uncomfortable aspects of our legal, cultural, and moral structure. The Nazis saw the United States as the world's leading racist country, although they recognized that our Jim Crow laws and mores coexisted with the Constitution's democratic insistence that "all men are created equal." It is no wonder that Nazi Germany considered the United States extremely hypocritical. It is chilling to examine the Nazis' fascination with our dark side, realizing that the National Socialists saw the germ of the Holocaust in our treatment of both Native and African Americans. The ultimate horror is that the Nazis judged that some of our practices—lynching—were simply "too harsh" to adopt.

Throughout American history, bigotry has blinded us to the extent that we have been willing to foreclose the potential of roughly one-tenth of our population. Our racism and meanness, even in the armed forces during wartime, spawned a range of societal problems that shouldn't exist in a democracy. Fortunately, President Truman's executive order and the impetus provided by the Korean War sparked the beginning of a revolution in race relations in the military, although we are still far from achieving true equality. Almost 250 years after becoming a nation, there is much work remaining before we realize the Declaration of Independence's bold proclamation that "all men are created equal." In today's challenging world, it is in our national interest to make it so!

CHAPTER 7

Korea: 24th Infantry, the Last Buffalo Soldier Unit, Disbanded

> The Army and the nation must be aware of the corrosive effects of segregation and racial prejudices that accompany it. The consequences of that system crippled the trust and mutual confidence so necessary among the soldiers and leaders of combat units and weakened the bonds that held the 24th together, producing profound effects on the battlefield.
>
> Brigadier General John W. Mountcastle
> Chief, US Army Office of Military History

The last Buffalo Soldier Regiment, the 24th Infantry, fought as a segregated unit in Korea. Organic to the 25th Infantry Division, it was among the first American units committed from Japan. Like other US Army units, it was poorly equipped and trained, with the additional burden of racism. Facing overwhelming assaults, the regiment went through leadership turbulence at all levels, but racial issues created an unhealthy additional dynamic. The regiment was disbanded midwar, three years after President Truman issued his 1948 executive order directing integration.

The services did not achieve full integration until 1954, six years after Truman's directive was issued.

At the Yalta Conference in the Crimea on the Black Sea in February 1945, Churchill, Stalin, and Roosevelt agreed to divide Korea into two zones of occupation at the 38th parallel, with the Soviet Union controlling the northern half and the United States administering the south. Japan annexed Korea in 1910, and Roosevelt wanted Soviet troops to invade Korea to save American lives and hasten the end of the war with Japan. Kim Il-Sung became the totalitarian leader of a Communist country in the north, while Syngman Rhee ruled an authoritarian capitalist state in the south. Neither side regarded the border as permanent. In the fall of 1949, two Chinese Peoples' Liberation Army (PLA) divisions, composed mainly of ethnic Korean troops, entered North Korea, accompanied by smaller supporting units. Veterans of Mao's three-year civil war with Chang Kai-Shek's Chinese Nationalists, these battle-toughened warriors brought with them not only intensive training and combat experience but also heavy weapons and equipment. They simply changed uniforms. This reinforcement of the Korean Peoples' Army (KPA) with PLA veterans continued into 1950, when another division and other units of the former Chinese 4th Field Army arrived with their equipment in February. By mid-1950, between 50,000 and 70,000 former PLA troops had entered North Korea, forming a significant part of the KPA's strength on the eve of the war.[1]

STATUS OF THE US MILITARY

A US Army board, directed to review racial policies, recommended early in 1950 that the secretary of the Army maintain the racial quota set by a 1946 study because the peacetime army needed to form a cadre to "provide leadership and skills which an emergency may require." The new board expressed the opinion that Blacks were "well below 10 percent of the leadership and skills of the nation as a whole" and believed that it was incumbent on the "white man" to "supply that deficiency."[2] Later, the 8th Army Inspector General recommended using the normal course of troop rotation and incoming replacements to distribute Blacks so that they constituted about 15 percent of each unit's strength. He believed that this would avoid concentrating men with low aptitude test scores in one unit

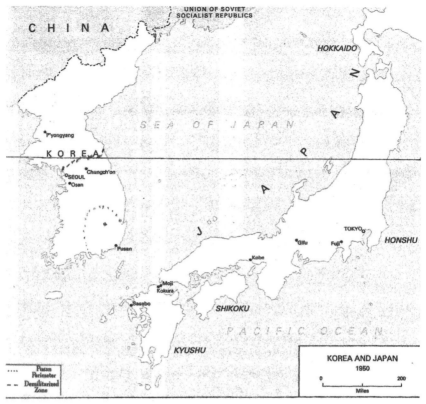

Korea and Japan, with approximate Pusan Perimeter and DMZ lines annotated. The horizontal line is the 38th parallel. William T. Bowers, William T. Hammond, and George L. MacGarrigle, Black Soldier, White Army: The 24th Infantry Regiment in Korea. SOURCE: UNITED STATES ARMY CENTER OF MILITARY HISTORY, WASHINGTON, DC, 1996.

and avoid the problems the 92nd Division experienced in Italy during World War II.[3] His recommendations were ignored.

At the start of the Korean War, the US military had roughly 100,000 Black service members, about 8 percent of its manpower. More than 600,000 Black service members would serve during the three-year-long war. In his forward to *Black Soldier, White Army* (1996), the Army's detailed study providing a second look of what went wrong with the last Buffalo Soldier regiment; General Mountcastle, the Army's chief of military history, stressed,

In the early weeks of the Korean War, most American military units experienced problems as the US Army attempted to transform understrength, ill-equipped, and inadequately trained forces into an effective combat team while at the same time holding back the fierce attacks of an aggressive and well-prepared opponent.[4]

Despite Truman's Executive Order 9981, signed on July 26, 1948, directing integration of US armed forces, the United States was still vexed by the same historic racial problems during the early years of the Cold War. The heavily segregated double standard of American citizenship provided ample fuel for Communist propaganda and had success in less-developed countries. The secretary of the Army initially resisted Truman's directive but was quickly replaced. In the spring of 1950, the Army's training centers began to be integrated, and by year's end, all 10 basic training centers had eliminated segregation. The commander of the first integrated training center observed:

> I would see recruits, Negro and white, walking down the street, all buddying together; the attitude of the southern soldiers was that this was the army way; they accepted this the same way they accepted getting booted out of bed at five-thirty in the morning.[5]

When World War II ended, the 24th Infantry Regiment was stationed in Okinawa. In February 1947, the regiment was redeployed to Gifu, in the middle of Japan, at which time it was integrated into the 25th Infantry Division, along with two white regiments. Except for some white officers, the 24th Infantry Regiment remained an all-Black outfit. In 1948, the regiment was tasked with port security at Kobe, a major port, where venereal disease, black marketing, and drugs had become a growing problem for troops of all races.

After the regiment was alerted for deployment but before the regiment left Japan, a Black chaplain mentioned in a sermon that it was inappropriate for the unit to fight other men of color on behalf of whites. A very competent Black lieutenant colonel commanded the 1st Battalion, but he declined to accompany the regiment to Korea because he believed that the regiment was nowhere near combat ready. He elected to remain in Gifu to command the installation and support activities there, but unfortunately, the reason for his decision was not shared. Black enlisted and noncommissioned officer personnel thought that he had been sidelined so that he would not command white officers. In addition, a rumor circulated that the white regimental executive officer feigned a heart attack to avoid going into combat with the all-Black outfit. The rumor mill was in overdrive; the regiment suffered from lack of an effective internal communication means to quash false stories.[6]

Although the 24th was the only all-Black infantry regiment in the Korean "police action," there were numerous separate African American combat battalions and Black support units. In all, nearly 100 Black units served in the combat zone.[7] The 77th Combat Engineer Company and 159th Field Artillery Battalion were permanently attached to the regiment, performing with distinction, but never received press attention for their exemplary service.

Unwritten but firmly held assignment policies still ensured that Black officers, irrespective of competence, rarely commanded whites. Throughout the years prior to the Korean War, except for the one lieutenant colonel who commanded a battalion, all the senior commanders of the 24th Infantry were white. Aside from the lieutenant colonel, only the chaplain and a few majors in less important assignments were Black. The issue of whether Blacks could command whites remained unresolved army-wide. In addition to racial tension, competition among officers for regular Army commissions under the Competitive Tour Program produced a constant churning within Army units. Officers arrived, spent three months in a position, and departed for a new assignment. In addition, officers were transferred abruptly to ensure that Black officers did not command whites, although this changed in combat. This resulted in mistrust from both parties, remaining hidden behind a screen of military convention and good manners in peacetime. Once in combat, these tensions were fully exposed, working in combination with other wartime stressors such as high casualties and continuous onslaught of the enemy. Then, the most competent officer available was selected for command.

All four of the Army's divisions in Japan were understrength and nowhere close to being combat ready. Due to drawdowns and personnel turbulence, most regiments in Japan had only two battalions, making it tactically awkward to deploy them in combat since they lacked a reserve.

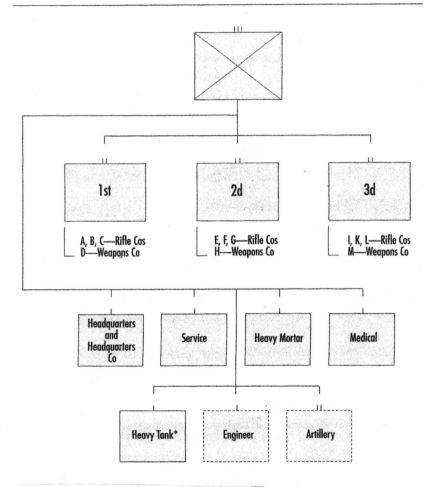

Regimental table of organization. SOURCE: BLACK SOLDIER, WHITE ARMY: THE 24TH INFANTRY REGIMENT IN KOREA, 271.

In this regard, the 24th Infantry Regiment enjoyed an advantage because it had three battalions and a strength approaching 4,000 men.

Training was lax, the soldiers were not physically conditioned, and essential equipment and clothing were lacking. This was a peacetime army, and the troops in Japan were far from mentally prepared for the rigors of combat. There was a limited amount of drug use in Japan, and American soldiers and officers led an extremely comfortable life. Many white officers held racially prejudiced attitudes, manifested in condescension and paternalism, which was obvious to most Black soldiers. Many of the soldiers in the 24th Regiment were the products of the demonstrably inferior Southern "separate but equal" education system. Because young people were needed to plant, tend, and harvest crops and help feed their families, some Southern Blacks received only three months of education each year. Few graduated from high school, accounting for the high percentage of Blacks who scored in the low end of the Army's aptitude tests.

THE KOREAN WAR

North Korea invaded South Korea at 4:00 a.m. on June 25, 1950, in a massive attack across the 38th parallel with matériel support from Communist China and the Soviet Union. South Korea's 154,000-man army of nine divisions, with no heavy weapons and supported by less than 500 US

Unit	Race	Comment	Capt	1st Lt	2d Lt
1st Bn, A	Black		1	4	2
B	White		1	3	2
C	White		1	5	1
D	Black	Weapons Co.	1	1	3
2d Bn, E	Mixed	(1 Black 2d Lt)	1	3	3
F	Black		0	2	5
G	White		1	2	2
H	Mixed	Weapons Co. (1 Black 1st Lt)	1	2	2
3d Bn, I	Black		1	1	4
K	White		0	2	3
L	Black		1	4	2
M	White	Weapons Co.	0	5	1
Totals	5 White 5 Black 2 Mixed		9	34	30

24th Infantry Regiment officer racial component, July 1950. SOURCE: BLACK SOLDIER, WHITE ARMY: THE 24TH INFANTRY REGIMENT IN KOREA, 72.

advisors, faced an onslaught of 135,000 well-trained North Korean troops, including battle-hardened veterans, supported by 1,400 artillery pieces and 150 Soviet T-34 tanks. Both the Soviet Union and China supported North Korea with equipment, and the Chinese provided advisors to the North Korean Army.

The United Nations Security Council denounced the North Korean invasion in Resolution 82 the same day, authorizing the formation of a United Nations Command and calling on member states to dispatch forces to Korea to repel the attack. The UN Security Council resolution passed unanimously because the Soviet Union was boycotting Council meetings because the UN refused to replace Taiwan on the Security Council with the recently victorious People's Republic of China. Twenty-one countries of the United Nations eventually contributed forces, with the United States providing around 90 percent of the military personnel and a large percentage of the logistical and air support.

The United Nations Command controlled the Republic of Korea's eight surviving divisions, seven US divisions, and a British Commonwealth division made up of troops from the United Kingdom, Canada, Australia, and New Zealand. Turkey furnished a brigade, and Belgium, Columbia, Greece, the Netherlands, and the Philippines sent battalions. Other countries sent medical and support personnel. The first units deployed to the Korean Peninsula saw extended, unrelieved service from July 1950 to October 1951 in temperatures ranging from 100-plus degrees to 20 below zero, often in biting wind and without appropriate clothing or protective gear.

Because he arrived in Korea in July 1950 with two understrength white battalions and a Black battalion that was 10 percent overstrength, the commander of the 2nd Infantry Division's 9th Infantry Regiment decided to integrate his unit without permission from headquarters. After casualties and insufficient replacements attrited the number of white soldiers in the first month of fighting, the regimental commander transferred Black troops into the white units. Noting that the mixed units worked well, he insisted that he never had any doubt that they would get along because "misery loves company."[8]

Integration was not supported by General Douglas MacArthur, who refrained from using Black troops in heavy combat in the Pacific during World War II. Observers noted that not a single Black enlisted man or officer served on MacArthur's staff in Tokyo. Moreover, his chief of staff,

Black Units Serving in the Korean War
September 1950–September 1951

2d Ranger Infantry Company
2d Rocket Field Artillery Battery
24th Infantry regiment
25th Chemical Decontamination Company
28th Transportation Truck Company
42d Transportation Truck Company
46th Transportation Truck Company
47th Transportation Heavy Truck Company
48th Transportation Heavy Truck Company
49th Transportation Truck Company
51st Military Police Criminal Investigation Detachment
54th Transportation Heavy Truck Company
55th Engineer Treadway Bridge Company
55th Ordnance Ammunition Company
56th Army Band
57th Ordnance Recovery Company
58th Armored Field Artillery Battalion
58th Quartermaster Salvage Company
60th Transportation Truck Company
64th Tank Battalion
65th Ordnance Ammunition Company
69th Ordnance Ammunition Company
69th Transportation Truck Battalion
70th Transportation Truck Battalion
71st Chemical Smoke Generator Company
73d Engineer Combat Battalion
73d Transportation Truck Company
74th Engineer Combat Battalion
74th Transportation Truck Company
76th Antiaircraft Artillery Automatic Weapons Battalion
76th Engineer Dump Truck Company
77th Engineer Combat Company
78th Antiaircraft Artillery Automatic Weapons Battalion
78th Antiaircraft Artillery Gun Battalion
91st Ordnance Medium Automotive Maintenance Company
93d Engineer Construction Battalion
95th Transportation Car Company
96th Field Artillery Battalion
112th Army Postal Unit
130th Quartermaster Bakery Company
159th Field Artillery Battalion
167th Transportation Truck Battalion
212th Military Police Company
231st Transportation Truck Battalion
250th Quartermaster Laundry Detachment
375th Chemical Smoke Generator Company
376th Engineer Construction Battalion
396th Transportation Truck Company
402d Engineer Panel Bridge Company
403d Signal Construction Company
503d Field Artillery Battalion
505th Quartermaster Reclamation and Maintenance Company
506th Quartermaster Petroleum Supply Company
512th Engineer Dump Truck Company
512th Military Police Company
513th Transportation Truck Company
514th Transportation Truck Company
515th Transportation Truck Company
529th Quartermaster Petroleum Supply Company
539th Transportation Truck Company
540th Transportation Truck Company
541st Transportation Truck Company
546th Engineer Fire Fighting Company
548th Engineer Service Battalion
549th Quartermaster Laundry Company
551st Transportation Truck Company
553d Transportation Heavy Truck Company
556th Transportation Heavy Truck Company
558th Medical Collecting Separate Company
558th Transportation Amphibious Truck Company
559th Medical Ambulance Company
560th Medical Ambulance Company

563d Military Police Service Company
567th Medical Ambulance Company
568th Medical Ambulance Company
570th Engineer Water Supply Company
571st Engineer Dump Truck Company
573d Engineer Pontoon Bridge Company
584th Transportation Truck Company
595th Engineer Dump Truck Company
619th Ordnance Ammunition Company
630th Ordnance Ammunition Company
636th Ordnance Ammunition Company
665th Transportation Truck Company
696th Ordnance Ammunition Company
715th Transportation Truck Company
726th Transportation Truck Company
811th Engineer Aviation Battalion
821st Quartermaster Bath Company
822d Engineer Aviation Battalion
839th Engineer Aviation Battalion
849th Quartermaster Petroleum Supply Company
863d Transportation Port Company
866th Transportation Port Company
933d Antiaircraft Artillery Automatic Weapons Battalion, Battery A
945th Quartermaster Service Company
999th Armored Field Artillery Battalion

Source: Army Directory and Station List, published bimonthly during the Korean War. In this directory, black units were designated by an asterisk ("*") before the unit name through September 1951. After that date black units are not separately designated, so it is impossible to state which black units served in Korea from November 1951 through the end of the conflict.

Summary:

3rd Battalion, 9th Infantry Regiment was all-black
14 Combat Units
14 Engineer and Military Police Units
9 Ordnance Units
9 Quartermaster (supply)
3 Chemical Units
4 Medical Units
2 Miscellaneous Units

SOURCE: BLACK SOLDIER, WHITE ARMY: THE 24TH INFANTRY REGIMENT IN KOREA, 272–73.

Lieutenant General Edward Almond, had commanded the all-Black 92nd Infantry Division in Italy during World War II. Dissatisfied with the results of repeated frontal attacks against well-entrenched German positions in mountainous terrain, Almond reassigned three Black regiments out of the division and acquired the renowned 442nd Nisei Regiment, forming a third white infantry regiment by combining and retraining anti-aircraft units for the final 1945 spring offensive. Probably because of their racist views, MacArthur and Almond used poorly trained South Koreans (KATUSAs) to replace horrendous casualties in frontline units rather than permit integration of Black Americans into white units. With only 10 days of training, the KATUSAs created serious language barriers and also faced racism from white troops.[9]

On paper, the 24th Infantry Regiment appeared more prepared for combat than the other regiments of the 25th Division. Although its equipment was old and worn and its men nervous and inexperienced, it had conducted field maneuvers at the regimental level, and as stated, it had three full battalions. The 24th Infantry Regiment deployed to Korea on July 11 and 12 on a variety of small seagoing vessels. The regiment, accompanied by its three attached Black units (159th Field Artillery Battalion, 77th Combat Engineer Company, and 512 Military Police Company), was among the first American units on the Korean peninsula—after an odyssey involving 20 hours on trains in Japan, 17 hours aboard ship, and 12 more hours on Korean trains. With little sleep, food, or water along the way, the men of the regiment ate their first regular meal at 11:00 p.m., seven hours after they arrived.[10]

Their mission was to defend Kumch'on, a vital crossroads on the Naktong River between Seoul and the southern port of Pusan, where UN forces prepared a final defensive perimeter. Things did not go well for most US Army units in the early days of the war. US planners arrogantly erred in their belief that a US display of resolve would deter North Korea. The first significant US engagement of the Korean War, the Battle of Osan (about 30 miles southwest of Seoul) involved a 540-man task force, half of the 1st Battalion, 21st Infantry Regiment of the 24th Infantry Division, flown in from Japan on June 30. On July 5, 1950, the task force encountered Korean Peoples' Army elements at Osan without weapons capable of destroying KPA tanks. The North Korean assault, involving one tank and two infantry regiments totaling about 5,000 men, resulted in 180 American dead, wounded, or taken prisoner. The North Koreans continued southward, pushing back US forces at Pyongtaek, Chonan, and Chochiwon and forcing the 24th Division to retreat to Daejeon, 100 miles south of Seoul and 130 miles northwest of Inchon. In one week, the 24th Division's strength went from 15,965 to 11,440 men, with 1,500 missing in action, 3,602 dead and wounded, and 2,962 captured, including its division commander, Major General William F. Dean at Daejeon.[11]

On July 14, the 24th Infantry Regiment's 3rd Battalion was dispatched with an artillery battery and one platoon of the 77th Combat Engineer Company to establish a blocking position at a city on the Naktong River named Yech'on, halfway between Seoul and Pusan, a position critical to stop the North Korean Army's rapid advance. The first contact with North Korean forces was not positive: a platoon on a reconnaissance patrol abandoned some of its equipment after receiving light mortar fire.

On July 20, the 24th Regiment and supporting units' objective was again the capture of Yech'on. The 3rd Battalion, supported by elements of the 159th Field Artillery Battalion and 77th Engineer Combat Company, captured the town, the first US "victory" of the war. An Associated

Press reporter called it "the first sizeable American ground victory in the Korean War," and the exploit was entered in the *Congressional Record*.[12] Captain Charles M. Bussey, a World War II Tuskegee pilot and commander of the 77th Combat Engineer Company, buried 258 enemy dead in a mass grave.[13] But in the emerging pattern of victory and defeat, the action soon faded from memory. The official Army history of the first six months of the war, *South to the Naktong, North to the Yalu*, ignored the fact that a battle took place there at all. In the opinion of many Black GIs, the Army did not want the first Korean War heroes to be Black, or possibly any Black heroes at all.

On July 21, numerous soldiers from the regiment's 2nd Battalion abandoned their positions in the face of an enemy ambush, leaving those still engaged vulnerable and vastly outnumbered. Four men accompanied a single wounded man to the rear, and jeeps grossly overloaded with personnel raced from their positions, leaving elements of one artillery battery still firing from an advanced position because one of its guns was in a ditch. This was repeated on July 24, when as many as 200 men moved to the rear after taking incoming artillery fire. Positions were so poorly defended that one company had only four men left to defend an entire hill. The only action the regimental commander took was to ensure that abandoned weapons and equipment were replaced, when disciplinary action should have been taken to discourage "bugging out." The battalion supply officer reported that all 17 light and heavy machine guns were abandoned.[14]

"Bugouts" reached pandemic proportions by the end of July, as the regiment was engaged in progressively heavier fighting. Military Police units deployed on roads behind the regiment to arrest deserters. On August 5, 1950, one battalion with an attached South Korean company was ordered to Sobuk-San, a large hill five miles south of the village of Haman. The main body of the unit halted on a small plateau on an approach just south of the village to await the return of patrols that had been dispatched to reconnoiter the enemy. The battalion commander fell asleep without ordering preparation of defensive positions. Just after dark, when a patrol was returning, a small group of about 30 North Koreans infiltrated to small arms range and opened fire. Both South Koreans and battalion members ran down the hill, overturning two jeeps and abandoning a radio, numerous rifles and carbines, and the unit's heavy weapons.

Unit	Strength on Arrival in Korea	Battle Casualties	Nonbattle Casualties	Percent Loss	Strength on 31 August	Authorized Strength	Weeks in Combat
24th Infantry....3157		883	352	39.1	3024	3793	6
27th Infantry....2370		535	255	39.0*	2557*	3793	6
3d Battalion, 29th Infantry (attached to 27th on 7 Aug 51).......922		437	58				
35th Infantry....1979		318	350	37.4*	2810*	3793	6
1st Battalion, 29th Infantry (attached to 35th on 6 Aug 50).....922		284	133				
5th RCT......3497		724	403	32.2	3221	4653	4

*Includes totals for attached battalions

25th Division combat losses as of August 31, 1950. SOURCE: BLACK SOLDIER, WHITE ARMY: THE 24TH INFANTRY REGIMENT IN KOREA.

On August 6, at Masan, a town 20 miles south of Yech'on, Private First Class William H. Thompson remained behind while his company withdrew, laying down covering fire with his machine gun until his unit was evacuated. He was mortally wounded by small arms fire and grenade fragments and died two weeks later of his wounds. Thompson was the first American soldier to receive the Medal of Honor in Korea, although he was not officially recommended for this award until January 1951, five months after his death. The fact that a Black soldier won the first victory and that a Black soldier was the first to receive the medal in Korea was a source of immense pride in the 24th Infantry Regiment and other Black units on the peninsula.

The 24th Infantry held the center of the line in the 25th Division's 20-mile vital sector in the southern tip of the Pusan Perimeter featuring rugged mountain ridges and peaks. Neither Hill 665, Battle Mountain (also called "Bloody Peak)," or Hill 743 at Pil-bong had roads or trails leading to their summits. North Koreans forced the 24th Infantry Regiment to withdraw from Battle Mountain on the night of August 31. Loss of the hill, or any position on the perimeter, threatened to push UN forces into the sea in a Dunkirk-like situation. Some members of the unit were seized by mass hysteria even before the North Koreans opened fire, ignoring their superiors' orders to maintain their positions. Desertion, abandoning weapons and equipment, and self-inflicted wounds were common. The

Army's first history of the initial stage of the war declared, "Two battalions evaporated in the face of the enemy, and a large part of them repeated this performance four nights later."[15]

The only problem with that assessment is that the regiment retook the hill 19 times, never backing down from the Communist onslaught.[16] Had that first assessment been true, UN forces would have been pushed back into the sea. North Korean forces attacked in swarms at night, and the most well-prepared positions of all UN units were threatened. But the 24th continued to hold the vital and contested real estate.

On September 1, the regiment's 2nd Battalion collapsed during an onslaught of several thousand North Koreans. Poorly trained South Korean troops on both flanks gave way, and between one-third and one-half of the battalion's soldiers stampeded, abandoning both weapons and equipment, leaving too few troops to deal with the attack. The regimental reserve was insufficient to contain the North Korean surge. For a time, the 2nd Battalion ceased to exist until it was reformed. This inspired a derisive Army song, "When them Chinese mortars begins to thud, the Old Deuce-Four begins to bug." The regiment became known as the "Bugout Brigade" and the "Runnin' 24th" by other units and the press.[17] This and disparaging other ditties were sung in the presence of members of the regiment. Racial prejudice manifested itself in general disdain for all troops of the regiment, resulting in frequent racial insults and slurs, unlikely to enhance the regiment's esprit de corps. In one incident, when the regiment moved up a road to relieve a white regiment at Kumhwa, the white regiment "hurled terrible insults and racial slurs" without interference from their officers. A white officer with the regiment described it as "ten hours of crap" and questioned how any soldier could summon up the resolve to fight for a country that permitted such abuse.[18]

Soldiers and officers on the ground contested stories of cowardice. Fox Company commander Captain Roger Walden, formerly a member of the all-Black 555th Airborne Battalion "Triple Nickels," insisted in a 1989 article in the *Los Angeles Times* that his company did not "disappear" but was "up there all-night fighting." Lieutenant David Carlisle, a Black West Point graduate who commanded a platoon of the 77th Combat Engineer Company, insisted that the 24th Regiment fought "magnificently" despite poor leadership, sweltering heat, and lack of water. He observed, "On this night, the regimental commander bugged out and if the Black soldiers withdrew, they were withdrawing to catch up with their regimental commander, who was panic stricken and running away from the action himself." Captain Charles M. Bussey, commander of the 77th Engineer Combat Company agreed: "The regimental commander led them out. His battalion commanders were all with him. It was not a matter of the troops breaking and running. They went out under leadership. And they went back and retook it the next day."[19]

The commander of the 77th Combat Engineer Company, Captain Bussey, cited convincing evidence that all US forces were equally unprepared to face the onslaught of the battle-hardened Chinese Communist/ North Korean Army. During all of World War II, the US Army lost only 53 guns from abandonment or being overrun or forced to surrender, but the record in Korea was far worse.[20]

1st Cavalry Division	November 1950	21
2nd Infantry Division	November 1950	62
7th Infantry Division	December 1950	12
24th Infantry Division	July 1950	36
25th Infantry Division	August 1950	11
8th Army Total		142*
ROK Army		95

Total: One 8-inch howitzer, 27 155mm howitzers, and 114 105mm howitzers.

8th Army artillery pieces lost to the enemy in 1950. SOURCE: CHARLES M. BUSSEY, FIRE-FIGHT AT YECHON: COURAGE AND RACISM IN THE KOREAN WAR, BRASSEY'S, WASHINGTON, DC, 1991, 107.

Furthermore, personnel turbulence at all levels was a major cause of the regiment's woes—the regiment had three commanders during 15 months of combat. Bussey also notes that there were 16 different battalion commanders in the first three months of combat—two were killed and two were promoted, but many of the other battalion commanders were relieved or transferred out of the unit to find less demanding duty.[21] Casualties among junior officers reached critical levels; some companies went through five commanders in less than a month, and enlisted replacements were often inexperienced and untrained in infantry skills—some were even unable to load and fire their rifles without being trained. They also needed instruction in the necessity to frequently field strip and clean their weapons.

The situation was little better among noncommissioned officers. In addition, the relationship between white and Black officers was often strained, further damaging bonds of trust between officers and men. During July, the 24th received 24 new officers but only 94 enlisted men to replace 408 casualties. By the end of August, there was still a shortage of enlisted men, although 841 enlisted replacements, 53 officers, and 4 warrant officers had arrived. These men did not keep up with the regiment's losses. And finally, at least one company commander believed that the original members of the regiment had been far more determined fighters.[22]

Although the regiment received the Republic of Korea Presidential Unit Citation for its heroism in the initial defense of the Pusan Perimeter and participated in six UN campaigns on the peninsula, the 25th Division commander, Major General William B. Kean, recommended that the regiment be disbanded as early as September 9, 1950. He strongly believed that the regiment was "untrustworthy and incapable of carrying out missions expected of an infantry regiment," endangering the rest of his division as well as the entire United Nations command.[23] There was a basis for concern: between August 15 and September 15, at least 460 troops abandoned their positions. Kean recommended that the unit's soldiers be integrated into the division's white units at a 1 to 10 ratio, but the 8th Army did not implement this request, in part, because there were insufficient resources to form another white regiment.[24]

Many unprepared, understrength, and outnumbered US Army units experienced similar dismal performances in the first few months of the Korean War fighting for survival against the numerically superior and aggressive North Korean Army, with superior weaponry and attacking in swarms. Nonetheless, every member of the 24th Infantry Regiment was branded as inferior because of their race, whereas poor or even disastrous performances of individual white units were not ascribed to race. Much of the damage was caused by one experienced regimental commander, a veteran of both World Wars I and II, who made public remarks about the inferior performance of Black troops from experience serving on the staff of the 92nd Infantry Division during World War II. The regiment's soldiers absorbed slights and abuse from all directions, making unit and individual pride a challenge—it was difficult to make a first-class soldier out of men considered and treated like second-class citizens.

American and Republic of Korea troops in the Pusan Perimeter began a counteroffensive after the successful Army and Marine Corps landing at Inchon September 15–19, 1950, which involved 75,000 troops and 261 naval vessels. Although American forces achieved a strategic surprise in the Inchon landing, they frittered away their advantage by a slow 11-day advance on Seoul, which was only 20 miles away. Nevertheless, the daring landing severed the Korean People's Army lines of supply and led to the rapid collapse of the KPA as UN forces broke out of the Pusan Perimeter at the same time, killing or capturing from 36,000 to 41,000 of the 70,000 KPA troops facing them. Within a month of the Inchon landing, UN forces had taken 135,000 Korean and Chinese troops prisoner. MacArthur ordered UN troops to continue attacking north, and they moved rapidly toward the Yalu River, China's border—against President Truman's clear directive.

During the attack north that followed the US landing at Inchon and the breakout from Pusan, the regiment's troops gained time to train which restored their confidence. The test came during the offensive into North Korea following the recapture of Seoul, when United Nations forces crossed the Ch'ŏngch'ŏn River and neared North Korea's border with China. Chinese forces of the People's Volunteer Army (PVA) crossed the Yalu and entered the war on October 19, 1950. Although there had been many indications of impending Chinese intervention, which MacArthur chose to ignore, masses of well-trained and -equipped Chinese Peoples' Army units took UN forces by surprise and triggered a precipitous retreat, during which some UN units were utterly annihilated.

Mid-November brought a cold snap; there were 85 cases of frostbite in the regiment due to insufficient cold weather clothing. By Thanksgiving 1951, the 25th Division opposed two Chinese divisions and part of a North Korean division, plus reserves, for a combined force of about 34,000 men. Advancing in late November through rugged terrain north of the town of Kunu-ri while flanking units moved on either side along valley floors, the 24th Infantry Regiment played a minor defensive role when the Chinese first counterattacked, but the regiment incurred heavy damage in the following prolonged retrograde action. Chinese forces pushed the UN command back into South Korea by late December and recaptured Seoul, which changed hands four times. Ultimately, Communist forces were pushed back to positions around the 38th parallel, close to where the war started. After this, the front stabilized, and a war of attrition began, lasting two more years. The air war was never a stalemate: North Korea was subject to a massive US bombing campaign, as jet fighters confronted each other in air-to-air combat for the first time. Chinese and Soviet pilots flew covertly in support of their Korean allies.

When the regimental commander and battalion commanders began to court-martial those who "bugged out," the tendency to abandon their positions began to change. Enhanced discipline meant that deserters or stragglers faced serious sentences for dereliction of duty. Adding to the regiment's shame, First Lieutenant Leon A. Gilbert received a death sentence in September 1950 for refusing an order to lead an attack. An outpouring of public sentiment persuaded President Truman to commute Gilbert's sentence to 20 years; he served five years. In all, 55 men went before military courts, and 32 were convicted. Black officers initiated 28 of these charges. There were only four acquittals, and 19 cases were withdrawn.[25]

In late 1950, those convicted and other soldiers of the regiment contacted the NAACP. As a result, Thurgood Marshall spent five weeks in Korea investigating the convictions of Black soldiers, finding that one case was resolved in 42 minutes, another in 44, and two were resolved in 50 minutes.[26] Marshall noted the negative effect this had on morale and remarked, "Even in Mississippi a Negro will get a trial longer than forty-two minutes if he is fortunate enough to be brought to trial."[27] Overall, twice as many Blacks were court-martialed as whites, even though Blacks were only about 15 percent of the troops in theater.[28] Marshall wrote a

Commander	Number Charged	Charges Preferred by Blacks	Number Convicted	Number Acquitted	Number Withdrawn
White	4	3	3		1
Champeny	38	16	17	3	18
Corley	13	9	12	1	
Total	55	28	32	4	19

24th Infantry Regiment General Courts-Martial, July–October 1950. William T. Bowers, William T. Hammond, and George L. McGarrigle. SOURCE: BLACK SOLDIER, WHITE ARMY: THE 24TH INFANTRY REGIMENT IN KOREA, UNITED STATES ARMY CENTER OF MILITARY HISTORY, WASHINGTON, DC, 1996.

memorandum to General MacArthur on February 15, 1951, in which he observed:

> Several of the white officers . . . would have preferred not to be commanding Negro troops. There is considerable lack of understanding and mutual respect in many of the companies. If the 24th had been completely integrated, I am not sure that there would have been this disproportionate number of charges and convictions of Negro troops under the 75th Article of War. . . . Although the morale is better now . . . I am convinced that . . . [the unit)] will never reach its highest efficiency as long as . . . it remains a segregated outfit.[29]

In a May 1951 edition of the NAACP's magazine, *The Crisis*, Marshall noted that the Inspector General's Office and the Office of the Judge Advocate General were all white until each staff received a single Black officer just days before his arrival.[30]

By November 1950, the continuous, overwhelming assaults by North Korean troops forced the US 8th Army to retreat southward. On November 29, the Chinese 40th Army flanked the regiment's defensive line in North Korea, forcing a neighboring regiment to withdraw. With the help of air support, the 24th Infantry Regiment's 3rd Battalion extricated itself, losing 1 soldier killed, 30 wounded, and 109 missing. Overall, the regiment lost one-fifth of its officers and one-third of its enlisted men while withdrawing across a river. The regimental commander fired the white battalion commander for this disarray.

The 8th Army continued retreating below the 39th parallel, and in early March 1951, it counterattacked. On March 7, 25th Division elements crossed the Han River with heavy artillery and air support. The 3rd Battalion initially performed well, advancing through rough country against well-dug-in Chinese troops while separated from the 1st Battalion. While assaulting up steep terrain, the battalion withdrew in disorder under Chinese attack. This further degraded the regiment's reputation. Assaulting across the Hant'an River in April 1951, the regiment added to its poor image in the eyes of white higher commanders. In that operation, the 1st Battalion performed well, securing a crossing, and then advanced through difficult terrain against a strongly emplaced enemy. The

3rd Battalion crossed the river, but a last-minute change of plans put the unit well downstream from the 1st Battalion in difficult terrain heavily defended by a strong enemy force. The unit made the crossing and attacked up a steep mountainside but collapsed under enemy fire and fell back in disorder. Commanding officers on the scene passed information to division headquarters depicting a far more favorable situation than the prevailing chaos. When the situation became known to the division commander, all confidence in the regiment was finally lost.

During this period, a courageous and resourceful cadre of enlisted men, noncommissioned officers, and officers held the regiment's subordinate units together and performed deeds of great valor. In July 1950, 2nd Lieutenant William D. Ware earned the Distinguished Service Cross for ordering his men to withdraw from a position attacked from three sides by a superior force, covering their withdrawal. During the counterattack by US and UN forces against the Chinese juggernaut in Operation Piledriver during the summer of 1951, Sergeant Cornelius H. Charlton assumed command of a platoon attacking Hill 542 near Chipo-ri on June 2, 1951, after his platoon leader was killed. Advancing at the head of the unit, leading three assaults against heavily entrenched enemy positions, Charlton killed six enemy soldiers and destroyed two Chinese positions to take the objective. Charlton became the second African American in the regiment to earn the Medal of Honor posthumously. Other soldiers, noncommissioned officers, and officers of the regiment received awards for their bravery.

When the regiment's last commander, Colonel Thomas D. Gillis, took charge in August 1951, the 25th Division commander warned him that the 24th Regiment was the weakest link in the 8th Army. Gillis decided his superiors were mistaken, concluding that the problem was leadership, so he relieved several officers. His efforts were justified on September 15, when Fox Company of the 2nd Battalion conducted a successful, heroic bayonet and grenade assault that took their objective in the first assault. That accomplishment, however, like much of the service the 24th Regiment rendered, received little notice, remembered only by Colonel Gillis and veterans of the regiment.

The 24th Infantry Regiment's record was affected by a complex range of factors, including high officer and noncommissioned officer turnover and casualty rates (some companies went through five commanders in a month), weak leadership, race problems, and inadequately trained replacements. Overall, the regiment endured a nearly 40 percent casualty rate, suffering 741 killed in action; 3,195 wounded in action; 258 prisoners of war, of whom 126 died in captivity; and 141 missing in action, for a total of 4,335 casualties, more than the division's other two regiments. Its record in Korea demonstrated both poor and extremely heroic leadership at all levels, with a lack of unit cohesion due to racism. Segregation and the racial prejudice that produced it hindered the emergence of effective leadership, cohesion, and esprit, mired in a system of beliefs that regarded Blacks as inferior. Soldiers of the regiment were aware of the insults and sneers of fellow soldiers, which did not inspire them to performs acts of heroism in the face of an aggressive enemy. Despite this, individuals and units often did respond heroically, offset by the tendency of some of the regiment's soldiers to "melt away," leaving their weapons and equipment. This improved over time, with experience and military discipline, but high combat losses and turbulent leadership always presented a challenge.

It is important to remember that the 24th Infantry Regiment was not alone in its difficulties. A significant number of white regiments responded poorly to the rigors of combat, but their setbacks were not ascribed to race, whereas the 24th Regiment's poor performances reinforced racial prejudice manifesting itself in near universal disdain for Black troops. When the regiment's soldiers performed poorly, it was attributed to their race; their achievements were frequently ignored. The regiment had been on the line more than 120 days without relief, from July 1950 through the

24th Infantry Regiment troops leave Kunu-Ri toward the Ch'ŏngch'ŏn River.
SOURCE: US ARMY PHOTO, NATIONAL ARCHIVES & RECORDS ADMINISTRATION, COLLEGE PARK, MD.

dead of winter, often without proper clothing and equipment, when the 24th Regiment disbanded on October 1, 1951. The last of the Buffalo Soldier regiments was integrated into the 37th Infantry Regiment and the division's two other regiments, ending 85 years of mostly distinguished service to the nation.[31] The other two elements of the 24th Regimental Combat Team, the 159th Field Artillery Battalion and the 77th Engineer Combat Company, were integrated and remained active, serving in all 10 campaigns of the Korean War. The 77th Engineers continued to serve with the Tropic Lightning division and was inactivated after the Armistice in July 1953. The 159th Field Artillery Battalion received a Navy Presidential Unit Citation for its support of the 1st Marine Division near Wonju in April 1951 while assigned to the 25th Infantry Division. In November 1951, the battalion was assigned to the 8th Army and remained in Korea until 1955.

OTHER DEVELOPMENTS
MacArthur continued to publicly feud with President Truman over the employment of Taiwanese ground forces and the use of nuclear weapons, inadvisably using the word "appeasement" in his public argument with his commander in chief. MacArthur had the indiscretion to send a letter to the Republican Speaker of the House on March 20, 1951, urging the employment of Taiwanese forces. President Truman relieved MacArthur on April 11, 1951, due to his insubordination.[32]

Truman appointed 8th Army Commander Matthew B. Ridgeway as commander of US and UN forces. The new commander deeply believed that segregation was immoral as well as inefficient—desperately needed Black infantrymen remained in Japan because white units would not accept them. Ridgeway obtained permission from Washington to implement Truman's executive order three years after it was issued because he believed that he needed Washington's permission to integrate California's 40th and Oklahoma's 45th Infantry Divisions.

When the Korean War began, the 74,000-man-strong Marine Corps included only 1,075 Blacks, mostly stewards. The Corps grew rapidly in response to requirements for Korea. At first, most African Americans were assigned as ammunition handlers, clerks, and cooks, but infantry and artillery units required so many replacements that eventually Blacks were assigned to frontline units. General Oliver P. Smith, who led the 1st Marine Division to safety from the Chosin Reservoir despite bitter cold and overwhelming Chinese forces in November and December 1950, noted that Negro troops "did a good job because they were integrated, and they were with good people. . . . Two of the Negroes got the Navy Cross . . . and there were plenty of Silver and Bronze Stars."[33] By June 1953, as the armistice approached, there were nearly 15,000 African American Marines—the Corps expanded to about a quarter of a million men. This was about 6 percent of the Corps, nearly six times the proportion at the start of the war. When the war ended, all units, specialties, and facilities were integrated.[34] The first Black Marine aviator, Frank E. Peterson, flew 64 combat missions in Korea and went on to become a general officer.[35]

Black officers did not constitute even 1 percent of the officer corps in any of the services, but they made their presence felt. First Lieutenant Dayton Raglan, a Black Air Force pilot who would later achieve the rank of colonel and be shot down over North Vietnam, destroyed the first North Korean MIG of the war. The first Black naval aviator, Ensign Jesse L. Brown, was shot down near the frozen Chosin Reservoir in December 1950. His white wing mate, Lieutenant Junior Grade Thomas J. Hudner, made a belly landing nearby to rescue Brown. Although Brown died, Hudner received the Medal of Honor for his attempted rescue. Major Daniel "Chappie" James Jr., a Tuskegee Airman, became the first Black commander of an integrated squadron, switching from P-51 Mustangs to jets

Kumch'on, North Korea, after the battle. SOURCE: US ARMY PHOTOGRAPH, NATIONAL ARCHIVES & RECORDS ADMINISTRATION, COLLEGE PARK, MD.

midwar. He became an ace and later the Air Force's first Black four-star general in 1975.

Roscoe Robinson, West Point Class of 1951, became the Army's first four-star general in 1982. Between 1950 and 1955, fewer than four Black cadets graduated from the US Military Academy each year; Annapolis commissioned only one officer each year from 1952–1955. Still, in its February 22, 1954, edition, *Time* magazine opined that the military was the nation's most integrated institution.[36]

The Navy professed acceptance of integration and equal opportunity but did not implement either policy. As the Navy expanded, the number of Black sailors rose from 15,000 to 25,000, but their overall percentage fell below 4 percent of the fleet. At the start of the war, 65 percent of the Navy's Black sailors were messmen, and fully a half of enlistees were assigned as servants. The Air Force disbanded its last Black unit by late 1952 and adopted a policy of assigning Black airmen to all units in any specialty for which they qualified, the first of the services to comply with Truman's executive order.

In late fall 1951, the Army commissioned a study, Project Clear, conducted by the Operations Research Office of Baltimore's Johns Hopkins

A .30-caliber machine gun section after integration. SOURCE: US ARMY PHOTO, NATIONAL ARCHIVES & RECORDS ADMINISTRATION, COLLEGE PARK, MD.

University, to review the effect of troop integration in combat and in stateside training centers. Over 85 percent of officers interviewed responded that Black soldiers performed as well as white soldiers, and the same percentage judged that Black officers were as effective as whites. When the study was released in November 1951, its findings stated conclusively that integration increased the effectiveness of the army. When the Korean War ended, there were nearly 220,000 Black enlistees, making up 12.8 percent of Army strength worldwide.[37]

The last holdout was US Army Europe Commander General Thomas C. Handy, a Virginian who refused to believe reports from Korea that integration enhanced combat effectiveness. Army Chief of Staff J. Lawton Collins paid Handy a visit to encourage integration. The Army's strength in Europe nearly tripled during the Korean War, reaching a total of 234,000 officers and men due to a concern that Korea was a feint for possible Soviet aggression to seize the rest of Europe. The buildup increased Black strength from 9,000 to more than 27,000 while integration continued, increasing the proportion of Black strength to 16 percent by July 1963, which Handy's successor, General Alfred M. Guenther, completed. The Army's last segregated unit, a Black engineer battalion, was integrated in April 1954.[38]

Dwight David Eisenhower became president in 1953 with a mandate to end the Korean War. His secretary of state, John Foster Dulles, using "brinksmanship" as a tactic, threatened to involve the Republic of China (Taiwan) and employ nuclear weapons. However, the situation changed after Stalin's death on March 5. Five days later, Georgy Malenkov, his successor, proposed an exchange of prisoners of war. Hostilities ended on July 27, 1953, when the Korean Armistice Agreement was signed, creating a Korean Demilitarized Zone (DMZ) separating North and South Korea. No peace treaty was signed—the two Koreas remain technically at war, although 7,245 American prisoners were repatriated. Over 2,800 American service members died in captivity. In April 2018, the leaders of North and South Korea met at the DMZ and agreed to work toward a treaty to formally end the Korean War, a process that remains incomplete, despite President Trump's visit to Kim Il Sung in 2017.

The Korean War was among the most destructive conflicts of the modern era, with approximately 3 million fatalities and a larger proportional civilian death toll than World War II or the Vietnam War. It resulted in the destruction of virtually all of Korea's major cities, widespread massacres by both sides, mass killings of tens of thousands of suspected Communists by the South Korean government, and torture and starvation of prisoners of war by the North Koreans. North Korea was among the most heavily bombed countries in history. US casualties included 36,574 killed, 103,284 wounded, and 4,714 missing, most prisoners of war. The South Korean Army suffered nearly 138,000 killed. Total UN casualties came to 170,927 dead, more than half a million men wounded, and 32,585 missing. North Korean and Chinese Peoples' Army losses were 398,000–926,000 dead, 686,500 wounded, and over 145,000 prisoners of war. Many Communist prisoners of war chose to defect.[39]

Although the armed services became racially integrated after the Korean war ended, they were still surrounded by segregated civilian communities. But federal insistence on integrated schooling and housing began to challenge the Jim Crow status quo in the towns and cities near military bases. Service members facilitated a growing, widespread awareness of the injustice of the racial caste system, helping spur the civil rights movement. Embarrassed by the Nuremberg trials (1945–1946), which prosecuted prominent members of the political, military, judicial, and economic leadership of Nazi Germany who planned, conducted, or otherwise participated in the Holocaust and other atrocities, coupled with the international implications of Jim Crow, the State Department and Department of Justice wrote letters of support to the Supreme Court for *Brown v. Board of Education*. Undeniably, there was much truth in Nazi and Communist propaganda, and there is no more effective propaganda than that which has the ring of truth. The fact that the majority of the world is not "white" didn't help America's cause either.

CONCLUSIONS

To the newly formed Air Force's credit, it embraced integration from the start, while the Navy, Marine Corps, and Army dragged their feet. Despite President Truman's executive order directing the integration of the armed forces in 1948, the Army did not begin desegregation in earnest until the intense pressure of combat in the Korean War forced the disbandment of the 24th Infantry Regiment and the distribution of its Black troops among three regiments of the 25th Infantry Division. Integration of the armed forces was difficult for commanders from the "old school" to accept. It took pressure from civilian leadership and the highest levels of the Defense Department to induce the military to integrate. The last army unit integrated in 1954, a six-year lag from Truman's directive. The success of integration in the arduous trial of combat finally overcame most military resistance; those who could not adjust were encouraged to find careers elsewhere.

As a result, the Department of Defense and each of the armed forces became progressively more integrated societies, sealed off in military bases at home and overseas from segregated American communities. With the services' roots in the civilian populace, it was inevitable that progress made in the armed forces would spill into society. The armed forces played a major factor in desegregation, with service members and eventually the Department of Defense applying increasing pressure for integration in the face of American society's "traditional" norms and customs.

CHAPTER 8

From Vietnam to the Present

> We are taking the young black men crippled by our society and sending them 8,000 miles away to guarantee liberties in Southeast Asia which they had not found in Southwest Georgia and East Harlem.
>
> Martin Luther King Jr.
> Riverside Church, New York, April 1967

The US Army resisted more than other services, integrating its last unit in 1954 and achieving full integration by the Vietnam War. Bigoted troops who resisted were gradually weeded out. As the advantages of integration became clear, talented, dedicated Black noncommissioned and commissioned officers rose in rank. General Colin Powell directed the Joint Chiefs of Staff during Desert Storm, during which General Calvin Walker was the deputy commander of forces in theater. Today, the Air Force chief of staff and the secretary of defense are African Americans, and the armed forces model the advantage of diversity for the rest of America. They also played a significant role in the civil rights movement.

BACKGROUND

On May 19, 1941, in a small village in northern Vietnam about a mile and a half from the Chinese border, Hô Chí Minh formed a national independence coalition, the "League for the Independence of Vietnam," or Viet Minh, a front for the Indochinese Communist Party. During

World War II, the Viet Minh was the only organized anti-French and anti-Japanese resistance group supported by the United States and Chiang Kai-shek's Republic of China. When the war ended, the Viet Minh rebelled against the French reoccupation of Vietnam, resulting in the first Indochina War (1946–1954). The United States supported France with $2.3 billion of funding and matériel for their operations in Vietnam.[1] After the French were evicted, the Viet Minh attempted to assimilate South Vietnam, supported by the United States, resulting in the second Vietnamese War (1955–1975).

In September 1953, President Eisenhower dispatched a 35-member military and economic mission to Saigon to review the situation on the ground. The chairman of the Joint Chiefs of Staff reported that Hô Chí Minh and the Viet Minh were certain to win, affirming assessments that had been made over the past two years.[2] The fall of the French stronghold at Điện Biên Phú on May 7, 1954, confirmed that assessment.

As a congressman, John Fitzgerald Kennedy, declared in 1951:

> We have allied ourselves to the desperate efforts of a French regime to hang on to the remnants of empire. To check the southern drive of communism makes sense but not only through reliance on the force of arms. The task is rather to build a strong native non-communist sentiment within those areas. . . . Without the support of the native population, there is no hope of success in any of the countries of Southeast Asia.[3]

After being elected to the Senate in 1954, John Kennedy declared:

> I am frankly of the belief that no amount of American assistance in Indochina can conquer. . . . For the United States to intervene unilaterally and to send troops into the most difficult terrain in the world, with the Chinese able to pour in unlimited manpower, would mean that we would face a situation which would be far more difficult than even we faced in Korea . . . a hopeless situation.[4]

However, Eisenhower's secretary of state, John Foster Dulles, declared neutrality to be "immoral,"[5] belying Eisenhower's later warning about the threat the nation faced from our "military-industrial complex."[6] Texas Senator Lyndon Baines Johnson was so disturbed by our conflicting Indochina policy that he declared in 1954, "we should turn our eyes from abroad and look homeward,"[7] reflecting awareness of the numerous US societal problems requiring attention. In 1957, Viet Cong (VC) indigenous insurgents began a low-level guerilla war against South Vietnam, at the time led by President Ngo Dinh Diem, the first of a series of South Vietnamese strongmen. By 1960, the number of VC grew to 10,000, and in 1963, the North Vietnamese sent 40,000 soldiers to fight in the south.[8]

After Vice President Lyndon Johnson visited Saigon in May 1961, he concluded, "We must decide whether to help these countries to the best of our ability or throw in the towel. . . . I recommend that we move forward promptly with a major effort to help these countries defend themselves. . . . American combat troop involvement is not only not required, it is not desirable.[9] But as the security situation continued to deteriorate, General Maxwell Taylor and presidential advisor Walter Rostow went to Vietnam

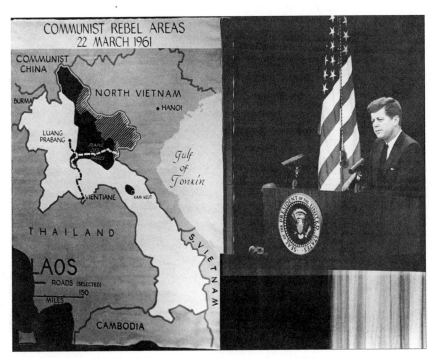

President Kennedy briefed on current situation from CIA map. SOURCE: NATIONAL PARK SERVICE AT JOHN F. KENNEDY PRESIDENTIAL LIBRARY.

that October and came back recommending covert troop deployment, which Kennedy refused to implement.[10] Through a series of contradictory decisions, the United States inched closer to war based on the "domino theory"—the spread of Communism had to be stopped at all costs because the fall of one country would lead to the loss of many more.

As US involvement escalated, a Military Assistance Advisory Group was established in January 1955, growing from just under a thousand military advisors at the end of 1959 to 23,000 in 1964. In 1959, the first two US advisors were killed (less than 500 were in the country at the time). In early August 1964, a US destroyer reportedly clashed with North Vietnamese fast attack craft in international waters in the Gulf of Tonkin. In reality, the incident occurred in North Vietnamese waters in an area where South Vietnamese commandoes had conducted covert operations the previous month.[11] In response, Congress passed the Gulf of Tonkin Resolution, giving President Lyndon B. Johnson broad authority to increase American military presence in Vietnam; Johnson responded by ordering the deployment of 184,000 American combat troops. On the domestic front, his War on Poverty was effectively dead. At its peak in April 1968,

1st Battalion, 7th Cavalry, 1st Cavalry Division at LZ X-Ray, Ia Drang Valley, November 1965. SOURCE: US ARMY PHOTOGRAPH, NATIONAL ARCHIVES & RECORDS ADMINISTRATION, COLLEGE PARK, MD.

roughly 543,000 troops were in the country. In all, about 2,710,000 US servicemen deployed by air or sea in the Republic of South Vietnam in South Vietnam during the 20 years of the United States' growing involvement before being ignominiously crushed by North Vietnam in May 1975.[12]

By April 1962, US Air Force pilots were flying combat missions, and American soldiers were fighting VC in rice paddies and jungles. Integration and equal treatment in the US Army were not achieved until 1963, when Secretary of Defense Robert McNamara issued an executive order that made it the responsibility of all commanding officers to ensure that no discriminatory actions were practiced in their units.

The first major confrontation of US forces with the North Vietnamese Army took place on November 15 and 16, 1965, in the Ia Drang Valley in the Central Highlands, when the 1st and 2nd Battalions of the 7th Cavalry, 1st Cavalry Division encountered two regiments of well-trained and -equipped North Vietnamese Army troops. The first phase of the battle was so intense that the battalion commander called in "Broken Arrow," the code for a unit about to be overrun. When the 1st Battalion, 7th Cavalry withdrew, they were reinforced by the 1st Battalion of the 5th Cavalry, which walked into a savage ambush. Black officers and noncommissioned officers were a large factor in both units' survival. Casualties on both sides were significant—nearly 500 US soldiers were killed, wounded, or missing, while the People's Army of North Vietnam lost up to 1,745 killed, an estimate derived by "body count," a problematic practice considered to be inflated by at least 30 percent.

Because active-duty Army and Marine forces proved insufficient, Johnson authorized an extensive draft to augment the regular army to avoid activating National Guard and Reserve component forces. Most draft boards were overwhelmingly white: of 17,123 board members, only 261, or 1.5 percent, were Black. Seven states had no Black members on their Selective Service Boards. Not surprisingly, in 1964, 30.2 percent of eligible Blacks were drafted compared to 18.8 of eligible whites, and as the war escalated, the percentage of Blacks drafted grew to 64 percent, in contrast to 32 percent of whites, due in large part to draft deferments.[13]

Mounting draft calls increased the war's unpopularity at home, especially among college students. The war's burden fell disproportionately on the poor, especially lower-class Blacks—upper- or middle-class males acquired deferments for college and graduate study until they were 26 years old. Malcolm X, the Black Panthers, Martin Luther King Jr., and others objected to placing the burden of fighting a war in distant jungles squarely on the backs of the least privileged in America. Dr. King declared,

> we have repeatedly been faced with the cruel irony of watching Negro and white boys on TV screens as they kill and die together for a nation that has been unable to seat them together in the same school. So we can watch them in brutal solidarity burning the huts of a poor village, but we realize that they could never live on the same block in Detroit.[14]

Most Blacks continued to respond to their induction notices or even volunteered for military service. But American heavyweight champion Cassius Marcellus Clay Jr., who changed his name to Muhammad Ali in March 1964, refused to comply with the draft, declaring, "I am not going ten thousand miles to help murder and kill and burn other people simply to help continue the domination of the white slave master over the dark people of the world."[15] Ali was sentenced to five years in prison (he was sentenced, but did not actually serve time) and fined $10,000. He was also stripped of his title, a move that was later rescinded.

INTEGRATION

President Kennedy's Committee on Equal Opportunity in the Armed Forces (the Gesell Committee) expanded and accelerated the process of integration in the military in 1962. In an unprecedented directive, Secretary of Defense Robert S. McNamara ordered military commanders at every level to oppose discriminatory practices *off* base as well as on. Openly racist attitudes evidenced by commanders and soldiers began to be non-career-enhancing, crippling chances of promotion. Black servicemen found widely expanding opportunities in service schools, promotions, and schooling and housing in communities adjoining military bases.[16] Even so, Captain Colin Powell, back from his first tour in Vietnam as an advisor, was refused service at a drive-in restaurant in Columbus, Georgia, in 1964. After passage of the Civil Rights Act later that year, he returned, got a hamburger, and settled into Fort Benning with his wife.[17]

Due to their predominance in the combat forces serving in the field, African Americans suffered a disproportionate level of casualties. Between 1965 and 1967, 20 percent of American battle casualties were Black, although they constituted only 13.5 percent of the military-age population.

But of 47,193 combat deaths in Vietnam, 12.1 percent were Black, proportionate to their share of the population.[18] Despite this, Blacks reenlisted at higher rates—45.7 percent of Blacks reenlisted in 1965, compared to only 17.1 percent of whites.[19]

Unfortunately, as pressures for manpower grew, the Department of Defense created Project 100,000, allowing acceptance of 100,000 individuals with lower test scores, couching this as an opportunity for the "subterranean poor" to end the "idleness, ignorance, and antipathy" of their lives and earn "their fair share of this nation's abundance."[20] Quotas were assigned to each service—the Army was required to accept a minimum of 25 percent, the Marines had to take 18 percent, and the Air Force and Navy each were required to accept 15 percent. Between October 1966 and June 1969, 246,000 previously unacceptable recruits were inducted. More than 80 percent had dropped out of high school, 15 percent functioned below fourth-grade level, and just over 40 percent were African American.[21] Both Black and white members of the Project 100,000 cohort experienced similar difficulties during and after training. Only 68 percent graduated basic training and went on to advanced training, and more than one-third were discharged before their enlistment was over due to unauthorized absences or other disciplinary causes. All told, 80,000 failed to receive honorable discharges. More than 37 percent, half of them African Americans, were sent to Vietnam as infantrymen. When the United States withdrew its major ground forces from Vietnam in 1972, 360,000 Project 100,000s had been inducted, of whom 145,000, nearly 46 percent, were Black.[22]

To break the stalemate on the battlefield, VC indigenous forces and the People's Army of Vietnam (PAVN) mounted a surprise large-scale offensive in January 1968, which provoked even more antiwar sentiment in the United States. The VC sustained heavy losses during the Tet Offensive and subsequent US–Army of the Republic of Vietnam (ARVN) operations over the rest of 1968, losing over 50,000 men. The CIA's Phoenix Program further degraded the VC, while the capabilities of the ARVN expanded, modeled after US forces. By the end of 1968, indigenous VC held little territory in South Vietnam, and their recruitment dropped by over 80 percent in 1969, requiring increased use of North Vietnamese Army forces. North Vietnam formed a Provisional Revolutionary Government in South Vietnam to give the diminished VC credible international stature. By 1970, over 70 percent of the Communist troops in the south were northerners, and few purely indigenous VC units existed. The war

US Soldiers wounded during the Tet Offensive, 1968. SOURCE: ARMY PHOTOGRAPH, NATIONAL ARCHIVES & RECORDS ADMINISTRATION, COLLEGE PARK, MD.

crossed national borders—North Vietnam invaded Laos using Cambodia as a supply route as early as 1967. The United States bombed the southern extension of the Hô Chí Minh Trail starting in 1969, while the Laotian route had been heavily bombed since 1964. The deposing of the monarch Norodom Sihanouk by the Cambodian National Assembly resulted in a North Vietnamese invasion of the country at the request of the Khmer Rouge, and the escalating Cambodian civil war resulted in a US–South Vietnamese Army counterinvasion in May 1970.

Time magazine observed in its May 25, 1967, issue:

> For the first time in the nation's military history, its Negro fighting men are fully integrated in combat, fruitfully employed in positions of leadership, and fiercely proud of their performance. More than anything else, the

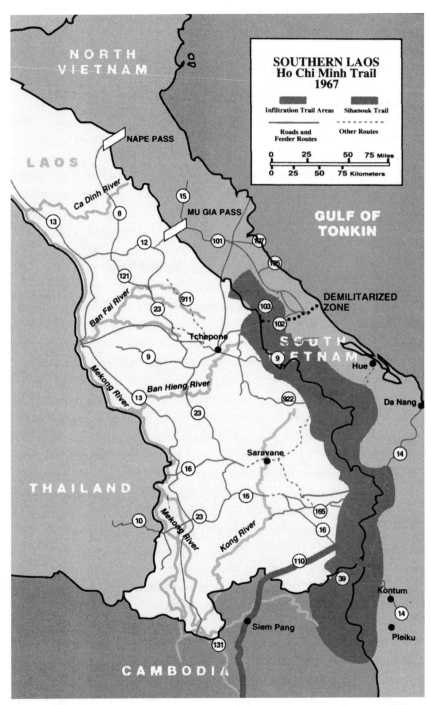

Hô Chí Minh Trail. Source: US Army Military Assistance Command Vietnam, Special Operations Group.

success of the Negro under fire reaffirms the success—and the diversity—of the American experiment.[23]

By 1973, the US Army had 12 Black generals, the Air Force had three, and the Navy had its first African American admiral.[24] But America's most integrated war was also its most unpopular, dividing the United States almost as much as the Civil War. The reluctance of upper- and middle-class whites to enlist or respond to draft calls greatly enhanced the possibilities of women to serve in the military. In 1967, the Department of Defense lifted the 2 percent ceiling on women in each service imposed shortly after the Korean War, opening more specialties and imposing no quotas on Black women. By 1971, there were 431 African American female officers, or 3.3 percent of all female officers in the armed forces. The total enlisted Black strength stood at 4,236, or 14.4 percent of the services' female strength.[25]

This time, the valor Blacks exhibited on the battlefield during the Vietnam War was not ignored. Among the first to be awarded the Medal of Honor was Chicago's Private First Class Milton Lee Olive III of the 503rd Infantry, 173rd Airborne Brigade, who fell on a grenade to save the lives of his comrades. New York's Specialist 6 Class Laurence Joel of the same unit earned the award for repeatedly exposing himself to enemy fire to treat wounded comrades despite being hit by small arms fire and shrapnel during a battle lasting more than 24 hours. Blacks won 21 Medals of Honor during the Vietnam War, 15 going to soldiers and 6 to Marines, one of whom received his award in 2018. Another Medal of Honor is still pending for Captain Paris Davis, among the first Black Special Forces officers, for heroic actions leading a 12-man Special Forces team and about 90 local South Vietnamese irregulars who attacked an enemy camp in Bình Định Province in June 1965. Initially successful, the team was counterattacked by a far superior force, and Davis and his men spent the next 10 hours holding off waves of attackers. Seriously wounded, Davis repeatedly rescued teammates and refused to leave the fight.[26]

President Richard Nixon began a policy of "Vietnamization" in 1969, transferring ground force combat to the South Vietnamese. Major Army and Marine units were withdrawn by early 1972, and US involvement was limited to air and artillery support, advisors, and equipment. The South Vietnamese Army, buttressed by US support, stopped a large mechanized North Vietnamese offensive during the 1972 Easter Offensive, resulting in heavy casualties on both sides, but South Vietnamese forces failed to recapture all lost territory. US forces began to be withdrawn after the Paris Peace Accord was signed in Paris on January 27, 1973. The Case–Church Amendment, passed by the US Congress on August 15, 1973, officially ended direct US military involvement. However, the Peace Accords were broken almost immediately, and fighting continued two more years, with US advisors providing continued support to ARVN forces and the Air Force continuing Operation Rolling Thunder, heavy aerial bombardment.

Operation Rolling Thunder. SOURCE: US AIR FORCE PHOTOGRAPH, NATIONAL ARCHIVES & RECORDS ADMINISTRATION, COLLEGE PARK, MD.

After a multiyear study headed by Thomas Gates Jr., a former secretary of defense during the Eisenhower administration, the draft, which caused such domestic turmoil during the Vietnam War movement, was abolished on January 27, 1973. The services embarked on another stage of integration, the challenge of recruiting an all-volunteer force. A significant concern was that relying on enlistment would create a racial imbalance, as Black youth with fewer options gravitated to the military. This did not happen.

Cambodia's capital, Phnom Penh fell to the Khmer Rouge in April 1975; the PAVN Spring Offensive resulted in the capture of Saigon on the last day of the month. North and South Vietnam were unified the following year. Officially, American losses during the war in Vietnam were 58,318 killed; 303,644 wounded; and 1,626 missing in action. Black deaths came to 7,115, approximately their proportion of the population.[27] The ARVN lost 254,256—313,000 killed; 1,170,000 wounded; and around 1 million captured. The PAVN suffered approximately 850,000 dead and more than 600,000 wounded, while at least 850,000 VC were killed. In addition, Chinese and North Korean advisors were killed in the field and in the air. Civilian losses in both North and South Vietnam were catastrophic and incalculable.[28]

FURTHER INTEGRATION OF THE ARMED SERVICES

Propelled by the civil rights movement of the 1960s and to counteract the former national policy of segregation and inequality, the Department of Defense mandated race relations training in 1971. Another impetus was the winding down of the Vietnam War, accompanied by a decay of military cohesion, as race riots broke out on several bases and aircraft carriers. This and the requirement to adjust to voluntary enlistments led military leaders to create the Defense Equal Opportunity Management Institute (DEOMI) at Patrick Air Force Base in Florida to address problems of race head-on. This institution evolved into one of the country's foremost training programs on matters of diversity, education, and training in human relations, equal opportunity, and equal employment opportunity. Specialized courses and seminars in addition to the core Equal Opportunity Advisor Course provide command and leadership personnel with human relations awareness training. DEOMI also advises the Department of Defense and other organizations on equal opportunity matters and conducts extensive research in progressive equal employment opportunity, diversity, and human relations, serving as a clearinghouse to monitor and disseminate research findings to interested agencies. So far, more than 50,000 individuals have graduated from DEOMI.

When nondiscrimination policies were reinforced by promotion outcomes, the climate in all branches of service underwent a sea change. Career military personnel now understood the impact of racism on their careers, although this hardly meant that all racists were eliminated. Some whites resent being forced to attend diversity workshops and insist that they have caused more friction than good. Conservatives sometimes criticize the training as mere "political correctness," or the most recent buzz word, "critical race theory." Facing the racism in our past does threaten the history many believed, which left out a lot of important facts. All of us must work through the difficult facts of our past to destroy racism.

Defense Equal Opportunity Management Institute. SOURCE: HTTPS://WWW.DEFENSECULTURE.MIL/.

OPERATION DESERT STORM

In response to Iraq's invasion and annexation of Kuwait, a coalition force of 35 nations led by the United States against Iraq invaded Iraq in a Gulf War codenamed Operation Desert Storm from January 17, 1991, to February 28, 1991. Deployment and buildup of coalition forces for the defense of Saudi Arabia was Desert Shield, from August 2, 1990, to January 17, 1991.

The Iraqi Army's occupation of Kuwait in August 1990 was met with international condemnation and immediate economic sanctions by members of the UN Security Council. UK Prime Minister Margaret Thatcher and US President George H. W. Bush deployed forces to Saudi Arabia and urged other countries to send troops. An array of nations formed the largest military alliance since World War II. Most of the coalition's forces were from the United States, Saudi Arabia, the United Kingdom, Egypt, and Kuwait. Saudi Arabia paid for more than half of military operations.

The effort to expel Iraqi troops from Kuwait began with an aerial and naval bombardment on January 17, 1991, and continued five weeks. Iraq launched Scud missiles against coalition targets in Saudi Arabia and Israel in an attempt to provoke a coalition-jeopardizing Israeli response, which failed to materialize. This was followed by a ground assault by coalition forces on February 24. This was a decisive victory for the coalition forces,

Lieutenant General Calvin A. H. Waller. SOURCE: GETARCHIVE, LLC, USED UNDER LICENSE.

which liberated Kuwait and advanced into Iraqi territory. The coalition ceased its advance and declared a ceasefire 100 hours after the ground campaign started. Aerial and ground combat was confined to Iraq, Kuwait, and areas on Saudi Arabia's border. Commanded by US General Norman Schwarzkopf, African American Lieutenant General Calvin A. H. Waller was deputy commander in chief for military operations. The Gulf War was notable for three of the largest tank battles in American history. General Colin Powell was chairman of the Joint Chiefs of Staff, supervising the overall conduct of these very successful operations. He developed the "Powell Doctrine": employ US forces only in overwhelming force with a definite exit plan.

New World Order. Copyright John W. Jones, permission from Gallery Chuma.

AFGHANISTAN

Most Taliban, who are students educated in traditional Islamic schools (*Talib*) from the Pashtun areas of eastern and southern Afghanistan, were veterans of the Soviet–Afghan War (1979–1989). They refer to themselves as the Islamic Emirate of Afghanistan (IEA) and are a Sunni Islamist movement, a military organization waging jihad, or "holy war," for control of Afghanistan. Emerging in 1994 as a prominent faction in the Afghan Civil War, Taliban forces held power over roughly three-quarters of Afghanistan from 1996 to 2001, enforcing a strict interpretation of Islamic law. In 1996, Northern Alliance leader Abdur Rasool Sayyaf invited Saudi dissident Osama bin Laden to Afghanistan. When the Taliban came to power, bin Laden forged an alliance between the Taliban and his Al-Qaeda terrorist organization. Al-Qaeda–trained fighters known as the 055 Brigade were integrated into the Taliban Army between 1997 and 2001. Most of the 19 terrorists who destroyed the Twin Towers in New York and damaged the Pentagon on September 11, 2011, were trained by Al-Qaeda.

Responding to the September 11 attacks, President George W. Bush announced airstrikes targeting Al-Qaeda and the Taliban. Operation Enduring Freedom, the US government's official name for the Global War on Terrorism, began on October 7, 2001. While Enduring Freedom primarily referred to the War in Afghanistan, it also described counterterrorism operations in other countries, such as the Philippines, Middle East, and Trans Sahara.

On December 28, 2014, 13 years after the war started, President Barack Obama announced the end of Operation Enduring Freedom in Afghanistan. Continued operations in Afghanistan by the US military forces, both noncombat and combat, were described as Operation Freedom's Sentinel. Although President Trump announced that all US combat troops would be withdrawn by May 2020, President Biden moved back the withdrawal date to the anniversary of 9/11 as the final deadline for withdrawal of American troops in August 2021, after 20 years of continuous combat.

IRAQ

On March 20, 2003, preceded by an intense "shock and awe" aerial campaign, the "Coalition of the Willing" invaded Iraq without declaring war. The US Central Command under General Tommy Franks led Operation

Iraqi Freedom. The coalition included roughly 40 nations, which provided troops, equipment, services, or security. The ground force included some 248,000 US soldiers and Marines; 45,000 British soldiers; 2,000 Australian soldiers; and 194 Polish special forces. US forces cooperated with roughly 70,000 Kurdish militia in the north along the Turkish border.

The invasion led to the rapid collapse of Iraqi defenses and the Ba'athist government. President George W. Bush gave an address on May 1 with a huge Mission Accomplished banner as a backdrop after landing on the aircraft carrier USS *Abraham Lincoln*. Saddam Hussein was captured in Operation Red Dawn that December and was executed three years later. Unfortunately, the United States grossly underestimated the troop level necessary to occupy a country and failed to secure Iraqi munition stockpiles. A power vacuum following Saddam's demise and mismanagement by the US-led Coalition Provisional Authority led to a civil war between Shias and Sunnis and a lengthy insurgency against coalition forces, during which unsecured munition dumps became sources for improvised explosive devices, wreaking havoc on the overstretched troops in the country. Many violent insurgent groups were supported by Iran or Al-Qaeda in Iraq.

The United States responded with a buildup of 170,000 troops in 2007, temporarily giving a respite to Iraq's government and military, but the next year, President Bush agreed to withdraw US combat troops from Iraq. The withdrawal was completed under President Barack Obama in December 2011, but the rise of the Islamic State in the Levant (ISIL or ISIS) led Obama to renew military actions in the region in June 2014. ISIS is a Wahabi (conservative Sunni) militant jihadist and terrorist group, which established a "state" in Libya, Nigeria, three provinces of Syria, and seven provinces of northern Iraq. ISIS was mostly driven out of Iraq, heavily attrited by Kurdish forces, whom President Trump abandoned by a tweet in September 2019 when he ordered US special forces serving as a buffer between US-aligned Kurdish militia and the Turkish Army to withdraw. At an extremely low cost, the United States achieved a fighting force in northern Syria capable of defeating the Islamic State, something larger regional powers such as Turkey, Iran, and Russia were unable to do. Unfortunate consequences ensued from that tweet.

Residual American troops remain in Iraq 17 years after the initial invasion and 9 years after the official end of the Iraq War. Over the past two decades, US units have rotated between Afghanistan and Iraq. Heavy reliance was also made of Reserve and National Guard forces. The pattern of deployment placed constant and heavy stress on individual service members and their families. Once again, the United States has expended tremendous sums, impacting the national debt, with little to show for it, but our integrated and highly effective armed forces have given their all.

RACIAL COMPOSITION OF THE ARMY'S FIGHTING FORCE TODAY

When the draft ended in 1973, there was a major concern that economic factors would heavily skew toward minority composition, a concern that continues to be unfounded. Several factors, including excellent training opportunities, leadership development, and competitive pay and benefits, especially medical coverage, ensured that the Army continued to attract recruits from a broad range of socioeconomic backgrounds.

The Department of the Army's Office of Army Demographics compiles statistical data regarding force composition. African American representation continues to be slightly higher than their corresponding share of the US population. For example, in Fiscal Year 2016, Black enlisted soldiers between 18 and 39 years of age comprised 21 percent of the Army, compared to 17 percent of the overall US population for that cohort.[29] Blacks represented 23 percent of total enlistments in 2016. Eleven percent of officers, 18 percent of warrant officers, and 24 percent of the Army's enlisted strength were African American. Counting active-duty army, National Guard, Reserve components, and civilian employees, 17.9 percent, roughly 243,000 out of 1,011,255 total army service members are Black. Presently, Blacks comprise 12.6 percent of the total national population.[30]

The Air Force's percentage of Black representation has held at a steady 15 percent for more than 20 years.[31] Over the same period, the Army's percentage of Black officers has far exceeded all other active-duty services, growing from almost 10 percent in Fiscal Year 1985 to 14 percent in Fiscal Year 2009. Naval Black officer growth went from 3 percent in Fiscal Year 1985 to 8 percent in Fiscal Year 2009.

Irrespective of race, it is a shocking fact that more than 70 percent of American youth cannot qualify for military service due to inability to meet minimum physical standards, having behavioral or criminal problems, or lacking a high school diploma. The national high school graduation rate is approximately 70 percent, but graduation rates from inner-city schools are only 50 percent. The national high school graduation rate for Blacks is about 58 percent.[32]

Nearly half (48 percent) of Black enlisted soldiers served in combat service support units in Fiscal Year 2009.[33] White, Hispanic, and Asian soldiers were more likely to serve in combat arms units. There was little differentiation of opportunities among enlisted soldiers serving in combat support units.

In recent years, the education achievement of Black females has exceeded that of Black males, resulting in an increased rate of Black female enlistments. Black females also have a higher reenlistment rate than any other racial or ethnic group.[34] As a result, Black females are now more highly represented in the active-duty army than Black males.[35]

By Fiscal Year 2009, almost half, or 48 percent, of Black enlisted soldiers served in combat service support or force sustainment/logistics jobs in the active-duty army. White, Hispanic, and Asian enlisted personnel were more likely to serve in combat arms. Black officers were more likely to serve in combat service support (27 percent) than in combat arms (22 percent). The ethnic distribution of officers was roughly equal in combat support units.[36]

Twenty-two percent of all Army Reserve soldiers are Black. This percentage has increased significantly over the years, growing from 7.6 percent of officers in 1985 to 17.1 percent in 2009 and from 4.3 percent of warrant officers in 1985 to 16.4 percent in 2006.[37] More than one-third of the females in Army Reserve forces are Black. Black males make up 20 percent of Reserves.[38]

However, the percentage of African Americans serving in the Army National Guard has been declining for decades, from 17 percent in Fiscal Year 1985 to 13 percent in Fiscal Year 2009.[39] There has been a resurgence to 15 percent as of 2016.[40] On the other hand, Black females in all ranks are more likely to serve in the Guard than Black males. In Fiscal Year 2009, Black females were 17 percent of all officers, 15 percent of female warrant officers, and 24 percent of enlisted personnel. The corresponding figures for Black males were 7, 4, and 12 percent, respectively.[41] In 2009, about 37 percent of Black enlisted soldiers were married, as were 56 percent of officers and 69 percent of warrant officers.[42]

MILITARY ACADEMIES

The United States Military Academy at West Point has made tremendous strides in the twenty-first century. As of September 2016, fully one-third of 4,469 cadets enrolled belonged to minorities and 20 percent were female. That is slightly more than the 16.9 percent female makeup of the "total" army.[43] West Point averaged less than four Black graduates per year from 1963 to 1967, but the following year, the Military Academy established an Equal Admissions Opportunity Program to increase minority numbers in the Corps of Cadets to coincide with the population. By 1969, there were 45 Black cadets: 12 graduated in 1972 and 36 in 1976. Major General Fred A. Gorden, an African American graduate of the West Point Class of 1962, served as commandant of cadets from 1987 to 1989. Gorden led the effort to accommodate the interests of younger plebes in technology, science, and mathematics while also maintaining subjects and majors traditionally associated with a West Point education. West Point graduated 148 African Americans in its Class of 2021. The Class of 2022 includes 400 minority cadets, among them 186 African Americans, 104 Hispanic Americans, 99 Asian Americans, and 11 Native Americans. The Class of 2023 has 443 minority cadets; the Class of 2025 will have 504, including 186 African Americans, 149 Hispanic Americans, 137 Asian Americans, 18 Native Americans, and 14 Native Hawaiian/Pacific Islanders.[44]

By 1971 the number of Black midshipmen at Annapolis had grown to 50. The Naval Academy Class of 2021 includes 327 women (27%) and a total of 451 minority midshipmen (37%). The Class of 2024 includes 364 women (30%) and 424 minority midshipmen (35%). Established only in 1954, the Air Force Academy in Colorado Springs, Colorado, graduated three Blacks in the Class of 1963. Thirty-one African Americans earned commissions with the Class of 1976, and the number continued to climb. New classes at the Colorado academy have since averaged 24 Black cadets each year.[45] As of 2021, there were 252 Black, 464 Hispanic, 251 Asian, 320 multiethnic, and 22 Hawaiian or Pacific Islander cadets at the Air Force Academy. While racial and gender diversification is improving, one concern remains: faculty diversification at the service academies lags well behind the student corps of cadets.

By 2020, the fruits of complete integration were manifest: the Air Force chief of staff was General Charles Q. Brown Jr., and retired general Lloyd James Austin III was President Biden's choice as secretary of defense, underscoring the fact that the US armed forces now recognize ability regardless of race. This is not to say that race no longer is an issue, but clearly racial difficulties are surmountable with talent and determination. The country is much better for this.

General Charles Q. Jones Jr., United States Air Force chief of staff. US Air Force. SOURCE: NATIONAL ARCHIVES & RECORDS ADMINISTRATION, COLLEGE PARK, MD.

Lloyd Austin III, secretary of defense. SOURCE: DEPARTMENT OF DEFENSE, NATIONAL ARCHIVES & RECORDS ADMINISTRATION, COLLEGE PARK, MD.

DOMESTIC TERRORISM

Timothy McVeigh, a Gulf War veteran, and his accomplice, Terry Nichols, who served a year in the Army before obtaining a hardship discharge, perpetrated America's most serious domestic terrorist act, detonating a truck loaded with high explosives in front of the Alfred P. Murrah Federal Building in Oklahoma City, Oklahoma, on April 19, 1995. Both were antigovernment extremists. The bombing killed at least 168 people, injured more than 680 others, and destroyed more than a third of the building. The blast also destroyed or damaged 324 other buildings. McVeigh was disgruntled over the Ruby Ridge incident in 1992 and the Waco siege in 1993, timing his attack to coincide with the second anniversary of the fire that ended the siege at the Branch Davidian compound in Waco, Texas. In December 1995, a racist white Army private and two sidekicks murdered a Black couple in North Carolina. An unending string of such incidents continues to occur—it is a challenge to unlearn hate and distrust of the "other" absorbed from our environment since birth. Although the services do background checks on enlistees, the effort to comb the ranks and eliminate extremists is a challenging, ongoing process.

This is reinforced by the recognition that domestic terrorism poses a greater threat than foreign extremists, heightened even more by the January 6 attack on the nation's capital to stop the formal presidential vote count. The military is a fertile source for militia, white supremacist, Nazi, and a wide range of other dangerous elements, including active-duty soldiers, who are capable of being influenced by persistent agitators, particularly in this age of false news and fake information.

CONCLUSIONS

In colonial times, the white power structure was ambivalent about arming Blacks, but the need to offset Native Americans often led to African Americans' acceptance in militia units. When the European military presence grew, Blacks were no longer needed, and after the slave revolt in Haiti, Blacks' access to arms was carefully curtailed out of fear of slave insurrections. While prejudice against Blacks was strongest in the South, it extended into the North. Both George Washington and Congress declined to accept enslaved persons in the Continental Army until the British began making use of them. When whites proved reluctant to enlist, Black manpower made up roughly 15 percent of the Continental Army, state militias, and the Continental Navy, state navies, and privateers. Two

Black battalions played a key role in the Battle of New Orleans at the end of the War of 1812, but legislation later restricted Blacks from serving in the Army or Navy.

Not until a year and a half of bloody confrontation during the Civil War had passed did Lincoln and his advisors decide to accept Blacks into the Army—sources of manpower were exhausted. Blacks' willingness to enlist and their demonstrated valor as soldiers turned the tide to the extent that the South, whose existence was predicated on the perpetuation of slavery, finally approved enlisting Blacks three weeks before Appomattox.

Due to US Colored Troops' effectiveness, Congress authorized six regular army African American regiments in 1866, reduced to four three years later due to budget cuts. As with US Colored Troops, these "Buffalo Soldiers" were led by white officers, a practice that predominated through the Korean war. A Black officers' candidate school was established during World War I, but there were few field grade Black officers—most were captains and lieutenants. Two African American infantry divisions and thousands of support troops served in both world wars. Even after Harry Truman's executive order in 1948, the senior command structure conducted "massive resistance" against integration, and the last segregated unit disbanded in 1954. By then, the services recognized that integration meant greater combat efficiency. The armed services also began to exert influence on communities surrounding military bases, playing an important if underappreciated role in the civil rights movement.

Once integration was achieved, promotion opportunities opened for qualified African American commissioned and noncommissioned officers. Colin Powell's selection as national security advisor, chairman of the Joint Chiefs of Staff during the Gulf War, and later secretary of state was only the first widely publicized evidence of this fact. As Appendix 3 documents, some 400 Blacks have achieved general officer or flag rank since Benjamin O. Davis was promoted to brigadier general in the fall of 1940. President Trump's selection of General Charles Q. Brown Jr. as chief of staff of the Air Force and President Biden's choice of retired general Lloyd James Austin III as secretary of defense underscore the fact that the US armed forces now recognize ability regardless of race.

APPENDIX A

AFRICAN AMERICAN MEDAL OF HONOR RECIPIENTS

The Medal of Honor is the highest military decoration presented by the United States government to a member of the armed forces. The Department of the Navy began awarding the Medal of Honor after Congress authorized the award on December 21, 1861. Congress authorized the award for the Army on July 12, 1862. On March 3, 1863, Congress made the Medal of Honor a permanently authorized decoration for sailors, soldiers, and Army officers. The secretary of war presented the first Medals of Honor to 6 of the 19 US Army volunteers who survived the Andrews Raid ("the Great Locomotive Chase") in his office on March 25, 1863. The first Navy medals were awarded on April 3.

Recipients must distinguish themselves beyond the call of duty in an action against an enemy of the United States, risking their own life. Because of the nature of this requirement, in recent years it has frequently been presented posthumously. However, in the past the medal was presented during peacetime for acts of valor such as rescuing shipmates at sea. For example, between 1891 and 1898, the Navy presented 101 medals, 83 for rescuing shipmates, and the Marine Corps presented two. Six of these sailors were Black.

Out of the 3,470 Medals of Honor awarded as of June 2015, 91 have been awarded to 90 different African American recipients. Sailor Robert

Augustus Sweeney is 1 of 19 men and the only African American to have been awarded the Medal of Honor twice for courage during peacetime.

AMERICAN CIVIL WAR

Eighteen US Colored Troops, 8 sailors, and 10 white officers who served with US Colored Troops earned the Medal of Honor during this fratricidal war.

Sergeant William Harvey Carney was the first African American who performed an action worthy of the Medal of Honor for his actions during the assault on Fort Wagner on July 18, 1863. However, he did not receive the medal until 1900.

Robert Blake, a contraband, recently escaped slave, serving aboard the USS *Marblehead*, earned his award on Christmas Day 1863 and was the first Black to receive the medal on April 16, 1864. Four of eight sailors earned their medals during the Battle of Mobile Bay.

Fourteen African American soldiers earned their medal for actions in the Battle of Chaffin's Farm, where a division of US Colored Troops was pivotal in that victory.

During the Civil War, more than a third of the Army medals awarded were for capturing a Confederate flag, saving a US flag from capture, planting the US flag on an objective, or recapturing a US flag from rebels. It was common for Medals of Honor for actions during Civil War to be awarded decades after the feat of valor. Andrew Jackson Smith's medal was not awarded until 2001, 137 years after the action for which he earned it. Smith's wait, caused by a missing battle report, is the second-longest delay of the award for any recipient and the longest delay for an African American.

President Obama awarded the Medal of Honor to West Point graduate First Lieutenant Alonzo Cushing in November 2014 for extreme heroism on July 3, 1863, during the Battle of Gettysburg, making this 151-year delay the longest gap between an action and an award of the medal.

Name		Rank	Unit	Place	Date	Action
Aaron Anderson	Navy	Landsman	USS *Wyandank*	Mattox Creek, VA	Mar 17, 1865	Continued rowing courageously despite devastating fire
Bruce Anderson	Army	Private	142nd NY Vol Inf Regt	2nd Battle of Fort Fisher, NC	Jan 15, 1865	Volunteered to lead assault column, removed palisades

Appendix A

Name	Rank		Unit	Place	Date	Action
William H. Barnes	Army	Private	38th USCI Regt	Chaffin's Farm, VA*	Sep 29, 1864	Despite wounds, among first to enter enemy works
Powhatan Beaty	Army	First Sergeant	5th USCI Regt	Battle of Chaffin's Farm, VA	Sep 29, 1864	Took command of company after officers killed or wounded
Robert Blake	Navy	Contraband	USS *Marblehead* (gunboat)	Stono River, Johns Island, SC	Dec 25, 1863	Served gun crew bravely throughout engagement
James H. Bronson	Army	First Sergeant	5th USCI Regt	Battle of Chaffin's Farm, VA	Sep 29, 1864	Took command of company after officers killed or wounded
William H. Brown	Navy	Landsman	USS *Brooklyn* (1858)	Battle of Mobile Bay, AL	Aug 5, 1864	As powder boy during action, helped in surrender of CSS *Tennessee*, crippling Ft. Morgan batteries
Wilson Brown	Navy	Landsman	USS *Hartford*	Battle of Mobile Bay, AL	Aug 5, 1864	Knocked unconscious, returned to gun crew and manned station
William Harvey Carney	Army	Sergeant	54th Mass Vol Inf Regt	Battle of Fort Wagner, Morris Island, SC	Jul 18, 1863	Carried colors to parapet, retreated under fierce fire despite being severely wounded twice
Decatur Dorsey	Army	Corporal	39th USCI Regt	Battle of the Crater, Petersburg, VA	Jul 30, 1864	Planted colors on Confederate works ahead of his regiment. When regiment driven back, carried flag, rallied troops
Thomas English	Navy	Signal Quartermaster	USS *New Ironsides*	1st and 2nd Battles of Fort Fisher, NC	Dec 1864– Jan 1865	Extraordinary heroism as ship's battery disabled nearly every gun on the fort facing the shore
Christian Fleetwood	Army	Sergeant Major	4th USCI Regt	Battle of Chaffin's Farm, VA	Sep 29, 1864	Seized colors after two color bearers were shot down and bore flag nobly through the fight

Name		Rank	Unit	Place	Date	Action
James Daniel Gardner	Army	Private	36th USCI Regt	Battle of Chaffin's Farm, VA	Sep 29, 1864	Ahead of his brigade, shot a rebel officer rallying his men and ran him through with his bayonet
James H. Harris	Army	Sergeant	38th USCI Regt	Battle of Chaffin's Farm, VA	Sep 29, 1864	Gallantry in the assault
Thomas R. Hawkins	Army	Private	6th USCI Regt	Battle of Deep Bottom, VA	Jul 21, 1864	Rescued regimental colors
Alfred B. Hilton	Army	Sergeant	4th USCI Regt	Battle of Chaffin's Farm, VA	Sep 29, 1864	Seized regimental colors, carried them and the national standard forward until disabled
Milton M. Holland	Army	Sergeant Major	5th USCI Regt	Battle of Chaffin's Farm, VA	Sep 29, 1864	Took command of company after all the officers were killed or wounded
Miles James	Army	Corporal	36th USCI Regt	Battle of Chaffin's Farm, VA	Sep 29, 1864	Loaded and fired his weapon with one hand and urged troops forward within 30 yards of the enemy's work
Alexander Kelly	Army	First Sergeant	6th USCI Regt	Battle of Chaffin's Farm, VA	Sep 29, 1864	Seized fallen colors near the enemy lines, rallied the men at a time of confusion and danger
John Henry Lawson	Navy	Landsman	USS *Hartford*	Mobile Bay, AL	Aug 5, 1864	Wounded and thrown violently against the side of the ship, continued to man his station
James Mifflin	Navy	Engineer's Cook	USS *Brooklyn*	Mobile Bay, AL	Aug 5, 1864	Powder division efforts resulted in surrender of CSS *Tennessee*, damaging batteries at Fort Morgan

Appendix A

Name		Rank	Unit	Place	Date	Action
Joachim Pease	Navy	Seaman	USS *Kearsarge*	Cherbourg, France	Jun 19, 1864	Exhibited marked coolness and gallantry under fire
Robert Pinn	Army	First Sergeant	5th USCI Regt	Battle of Chaffin's Farm, VA	Sep 29, 1864	Took command of his company after all the officers were killed or wounded and gallantly led them in battle
Edward Ratcliff	Army	First Sergeant	38th USCI Regt	Battle of Chaffin's Farm, VA	Sep 29, 1864	Led his company after commanding officer killed, was first enlisted man to enter the enemy works
Andrew Jackson Smith	Army	Corporal	55th Mass Vol Inf Regt	Battle of Honey Hill, SC	Nov 30, 1864	Saved regimental colors when color bearer killed
Charles Veale	Army	Private	4th USCI Regt	Battle of Chaffin's Farm, VA	Sep 29, 1864	Seized national colors after two color bearers were shot down

*Also known as the Battle of New Market Heights

Ten white officers won the Medal of Honor while leading US Colored Troops:

First Lieutenant William H. Appleton, Fourth USCI, New Market Heights/Chaffin's Farm, VA, Sep 29, 1964, led assault on rebel positions

First Lieutenant Charles L. Barrell, 102nd USCI, Camden, SC, Apr 1865, led march through enemy area to relieve command

First Lieutenant Orson W. Bennet, 102nd USCI, Honey Hill, SC, Nov 30, 1864, rescued troops on steamer despite heavy Confederate artillery fire

First Lieutenant Andrew Davidson, 30th USCI, Battle of the Crater, Petersburg, VA, July 30, 1864, helped save regiment after officers had been incapacitated

Lieutenant Nathan H. Edgerton, Sixth USCI, New Market Heights/Chaffin's Farm, Sep 29, 1964, seized flag after three color bearers killed, continued attack despite being wounded

Captain Ira H. Evans, 116th USCI, Hatchers Run, VA, Apr 2, 1865, went into enemy lines under heavy fire to obtain information

Lieutenant Colonel Henry C. Merriam, 73rd USCI, Fort Blakely, AL, Apr 9, 1865, voluntarily led assault on enemy works.

Captain Henry C. Nichols, 73rd USCI, Fort Blakely, AL, Apr 9, 1865, scouted enemy positions under heavy fire

Second Lieutenant Walter Thorn, 116th USCI, Dutch Gap Canal, VA, Jan 1, 1865, learning that the picket had not withdrawn, warned picket that the fuse to a mined bulkhead had been lit

Captain Albert D. Wright, 43rd USCI, Battle of the Crater, Petersburg, VA, Jul 30, 1864, advanced beyond enemy lines, captured colors and color guard while severely wounded

INDIAN WARS (1866–1890)

Eighteen African Americans earned the Medal of Honor during the Indian Wars. Fourteen were "Buffalo Soldiers," members of the army's Black regular regiments, the 9th and 10th Cavalry and 24th and 25th Infantry. The other four were Black Seminoles, Indian scouts.

Name	Service	Rank	Unit	Place	Date	Action
Thomas Boyne	Army	Sergeant	9th Cav Regt	Mimbres Mountains, Ojo Caliente, NM	May 29, 1879 and Sep 27, 1879	Bravery in action
Benjamin Brown	Army	Sergeant	24th Inf Regt	Arizona	May 11, 1889	Part of paymaster escort, resisted although shot in abdomen
John Denny	Army	Sergeant	9th Cav Regt	Las Animas Canyon, NM	Sep 18, 1879	Rescued comrade under heavy fire
Pompey Factor	Army	Private	Indian Scout	Pecos River, TX	Apr 25, 1875	With 3 other men, charged 25 hostiles while on scouting patrol
Clinton Greaves	Army	Corporal	9th Cav Regt	Florida Mountains, Luna County, NM	Jan 24, 1877	Helped small party surrounded by Apaches escape

Appendix A

Name	Service	Rank	Unit	Place	Date	Action
Henry Johnson	Army	Sergeant	9th Cav Regt	Milk River, CO	Oct 2, 1879–Oct 5, 1879	Left shelter to bring water to the wounded & help them escape
George Jordan	Army	Sergeant	9th Cav Regt	Ft. Tularosa & Carrizo Canyon, NM	May 14, 1880 & Aug 12, 1881	Twice repulsed larger force of Indians
Isaiah Mays	Army	Corporal	24th Inf Regt	Cedar Springs, AZ	May 11, 1889	Part of paymaster escort. Walked and crawled two miles for help
William McBryar	Army	Sergeant (later first lieutenant)	10th Cav Regt	Salt River, north of Globe, AZ	Mar 7, 1890	Coolness, bravery, and marksmanship pursuing Apaches
Adam Paine	Army	Private	Indian Scouts	Canyon Blanco, Staked Plains, TX (Red River War)	Sep 26, 1874–Sep 27, 1874	Assisted Colonel Mackenzie, 4th US Cav, in engagement
Isaac Payne	Army	Trumpeter	Indian Scouts	Pecos River, TX	Apr 25, 1875	With 3 other men, charged 25 hostiles on scouting patrol
Thomas Shaw	Army	Sergeant	9th Cavalry Regiment	Carrizo Canyon, Cuchillo Negra Mountains, NM	Aug 12, 1881	Held exposed position, kept superior numbers from surrounding his command
Emanuel Stance	Army	Sergeant	9th Cavalry Regiment	Kickapoo Springs, TX	May 20, 1870	Gallantry on Indian scout
Augustus Walley	Army	Private	9th Cavalry Regiment	Cuchillo Negro Mountains NM	Aug 16, 1881	Bravery in action against hostile Apaches
John Ward	Army	Sergeant	Indian Scouts, 24th Infantry Regiment	Pecos River, TX	Apr 25, 1875	With 3 other men, charged 25 hostiles on scouting patrol
Moses Williams	Army	First Sergeant	9th Cavalry Regiment	Cuchillo Negro Mountains, NM	Aug 16, 1881	Led detachment in running four-hour flight. Saved several lives
William Othello Wilson	Army	Corporal	9th Cavalry Regiment	Sioux Campaign	Dec 30, 1890	Bravery
Brent Woods	Army	Sergeant	9th Cavalry Regiment	Gavilan Canyon, NM	Aug 19, 1881	Saved lives of his detachment

Six white officers serving with Buffalo Soldier regiments during the Indian Wars were also awarded the Congressional Medal of Honor:

First Lieutenant George E. Albee, 41st Inf, Brazos River, TX, October 1868

Captain Louis Carpenter 10th Cav, Beecher Island & Beaver Creek, CO, Sep & Oct 1868

First Lieutenant Powhattan Clark, 10th Cav, pursuit of Geronimo, Sonora, Mexico, May 1886

Second Lieutenant Matthias W. Day, 9th Cav, Las Animas Canyon, NM, September 1879

Captain Francis S. Dodge, 9th Cav, White River Agency, CO, September 1879

Second Lieutenant Robert T. Emmet, 9th Cav, Las Animas, NM, September 1879

PEACETIME AWARD OF THE MEDAL OF HONOR

Before World War II, the Medal of Honor could be awarded for actions not involving direct combat with the enemy; eight African Americans earned the medal in this way, all of them sailors.

Robert Augustus Sweeney received two peacetime Medals of Honor, the only African American out of only 19 men to be awarded the medal twice. Most of the noncombat medals, including Sweeney's, were awarded for rescuing or attempting to rescue shipmates from drowning.

SPANISH–AMERICAN WAR (1898)

Six African Americans earned the Medal of Honor during the Spanish–American War, "a splendid little war" according to Secretary of State John Hay. Five were soldiers serving in the 10th Cavalry Regiment, and the other was a sailor. Four of the five soldiers received the medal for rescuing a stranded reconnaissance party at Tayacoba.

Many valorous actions were performed by soldiers in all four Buffalo Soldier regiments, but their commanders seem not to have been inclined to write recommendations, although many soldiers from all four regiments were awarded Certificates of Merit. A total of 112 Medals of Honor were awarded during the Spanish–American War—66 for the Navy, 31 for the Army, and 15 for the Marine Corps. Notably, the other three Buffalo Soldier regiments were shut out, while the Navy had a field day.

APPENDIX A

Name	Service	Rank	Unit	Place	Date	Action
Edward L. Baker Jr.	Army	Sergeant Major	10th Cav Regt	Santiago, Cuba	Jul 1, 1898	Rescued a wounded comrade from drowning under fire
Dennis Bell	Army	Private	10th Cav Regt	Battle of Tayacoba, Cuba	Jun 30, 1898	Went ashore to rescue wounded comrades after unsuccessful attempts
Fitz Lee	Army	Private	10th Cav Regt	Battle of Tayacoba, Cuba	Jun 30, 1898	Went ashore to rescue wounded comrades after unsuccessful attempts
Robert Penn	Navy	Fireman First Class	USS *Iowa* (BB-4)	Off Santiago de Cuba	Jul 20, 1898	At risk of scalding, banked fire while standing on a board a foot above boiling water
William H. Thompkins	Army	Private	10th Cav Regt	Battle of Tayacoba, Cuba	Jun 30, 1898	Went ashore to rescue wounded comrades after unsuccessful attempts
George H. Wanton	Army	Private	10th Cav Regt	Battle of Tayacoba, Cuba	Jun 30, 1898	Went ashore to rescue wounded comrades after unsuccessful attempts

WORLD WAR I (1917–1918)

With Woodrow Wilson as commander in chief, racism was virulent in the US armed forces during the "Great War." The Army awarded 90 Medals of Honor, 27 for posthumous action. Neither of the two eventual Black recipients received their award anywhere close to the performance of their actions, and numerous African American soldiers, noncommissioned officers, and officers performed valorous acts. Comparing the French recognition of the valor displayed by African American soldiers discloses a clear dichotomy.

Sailors garnered 21 Medals of Honor, and eight Marines received the medal. Five Marines received both Army and Navy medals because Marine units were attached to army divisions. The Medal of Honor was bestowed on two African Americans 73 and 95 years after their valorous action.

* **Corporal Freddie Stowers** was the first of two African American World War I soldiers to receive the Medal of Honor for leading an assault on German trenches atop Hill 188 on September 28, 1918, taking charge of his platoon when the platoon leader and noncommissioned officers were incapacitated and completing the mission. Stowers encouraged his men even after being seriously wounded twice, dying of his wounds on the objective. Shortly afterward, Stowers was recommended for the Medal of Honor, but the recommendation was never processed.

In 1990, the Department of the Army conducted a review and Stowers's recommendation was uncovered. Stowers's Medal of Honor was presented to his two sisters on April 24, 1991, by President George H. W. Bush—73 years after he was killed in action.

* Sergeant William Henry Johnson was manning a listening outpost in the Argonne Forest with Private Needham Roberts on May 14, 1918, when a platoon-size German unit assaulted their position. After expending his ammunition, he used his rifle as a club and with bayonet in hand-to-hand combat, killed multiple German soldiers and rescued Roberts despite suffering multiple wounds. This action was brought to the nation's attention by the *New York World* and *Saturday Evening Post*. The French government immediately awarded Johnson and Roberts the *Croix de Guerre* with star and bronze palm, the first US soldiers to receive that honor. Johnson paraded down Fifth Avenue in the 369th Regiment's triumphant march to Harlem.

Johnson died, poor and in obscurity, in 1929. US racism was so intense that Johnson was not awarded a Purple Heart for his 21 wounds until President Bill Clinton presented the award in June 1996. In 2002, the US military awarded him the Distinguished Service Cross.

On June 2, 2015, President Barack Obama presented the Medal of Honor posthumously to Johnson. In a ceremony in the White House, Command Sergeant Major Louis Wilson of the New York National Guard accepted the medal on Johnson's behalf—85 years after his death and 95 years after his act of valor.

Name	Unit	Place	Date	Action
*Corporal Freddie Stowers	371st Inf Reg, 93rd Inf Div	Hill 188, Champagne, Marne Sector	Sep 28, 1918	Led his platoon, destroying first trench, then to another trench despite being mortally wounded
*Private First Class (later Sergeant) William Henry Johnson	369th Inf Regt, 93d Inf Div	Argonne Forrest, Champagne, Marne Sector	May 14, 1918	Repelled 24-man German raiding party, rescued comrade

*Posthumous award

WORLD WAR II

No African American was awarded a Medal of Honor during World War II or in its immediate aftermath. The Army awarded 32 medals, the Navy 57, the Marines 82, and one Coast Guard member received the award during the war.

A study commissioned by the US Department of Defense and the US Army conducted by Shaw University in 1992 found that systematic racial discrimination existed in the criteria for awarding the medals during the war. After an exhaustive review of files, the study recommended that a number of Distinguished Service Cross awards received by African Americans be upgraded to the Medal of Honor.

On January 13, 1997, more than 50 years after World War II ended, President Bill Clinton awarded the Medal of Honor to seven African American World War II veterans. Vernon Baker was the only living recipient—the other six men had been killed in action or died in the intervening years. After the war, Baker became an Army parachutist in the 11th Airborne Division, served during the Korean War, and retired from the Army in 1968. He then worked for the Red Cross for 20 years. Baker collected handsomely on his unpaid tax-free Medal of Honor stipend, about $66,000 in back pay.

Name	Unit	Place	Date	Notes
First Lieutenant Vernon Baker	370th Inf Regt, 92nd Inf Div	Viareggio, Italy	Apr 5, 1945, & Apr 6, 1945	Voluntarily led battalion through heavy fire and mine field against entrenched enemy in mountainous terrain
Staff Sergeant Edward A. Carter Jr.	56th Arm Inf Bn, 12th Arm Div (Bastogne Volunteer)	Speyer, Germany	Mar 23, 1945	Led small patrol, wounded five times. Killed six of eight Germans who tried to capture him, capturing two. Recrossed field using them as shields, obtaining valuable information.
*First Lieutenant John R. Fox	Cannon Co, 366th Inf Regt, 92nd Inf Div; Arty Liaison w 598th Fld Arty Bn	Sommocolonia, Italy	Dec 26, 1944	Directed defensive artillery fire so unit could escape
*Private First Class Willy F. James Jr.	413th Inf Regt, 104th Inf Div (Bastogne Volunteer)	Lippoldsberg, Germany	Apr 7, 1945	Designated targets while leading assault until killed by enemy MG fire going to the aid of wounded platoon leader

Name	Unit	Place	Date	Notes
*Staff Sergeant Ruben Rivers	761st Tank Bn, attached to 26th Inf Div	Guebling, France	Nov 15, 1944– Nov 19, 1944	Refused medical evacuation, took command of another tank and advanced, directing tank's fire at enemy positions. Covered company's withdrawal
First Lieutenant Charles L. Thomas	614th Tk Destroyer Bn, attached to 411th Inf Regt, 103rd Inf Div, Task Force Bradshear	Climbach, France	Dec 14, 1944	Although suffering multiple gunshot wounds, directed his column to halt and helped crew of wrecked car dismount. Emplaced two antitank guns, oriented platoon commander on enemy gun dispositions
*Private George Watson	2nd Bn, 29th Quartermaster Regt	Porloch Harbor, New Guinea	Mar 8, 1943	Sacrificed self to save other crew members who could not swim when ship hit by enemy bombers, ship's suction pulled him under

*Posthumous award

KOREAN WAR

Two African Americans were among the 78 army soldiers who received the Medal of Honor for actions during the Korean War. Both were soldiers of the 24th Infantry Regiment, the last Buffalo Soldier regiment, which fought as a segregated unit until disbanded midway through the war, on October 1, 1951. No Black Marines received the award.

Both men were the last African Americans to receive the Medal of Honor for actions performed while serving in a segregated unit.

Name	Unit	Place of action	Date of action	Notes
*Private First Class William Henry Thompson	24th Inf Reg, 25th Inf Div	Near Haman	Jun 2, 1950	Manned his machine gun to allow rest of his unit to escape
*Sergeant Cornelius H. Charlton	24th Inf Reg, 25th Inf Div	Near Chipo-ri	Aug 6, 1950	Led platoon after leader was killed to repel swarm assault using grenades and machine-gun fire, until he was killed

*Posthumous award

VIETNAM

Twenty-two African Americans were awarded the Medal of Honor for actions in the Vietnam War, including Private First Class James Anderson Jr., the first African American Marine to receive the medal. In all, the Army awarded 159 medals, the Navy 16, the Marines 57, and the Air Force 13.

A Medal of Honor is still pending for Captain Paris Davis, one of the first Black special forces officers, for heroics while leading a 12-man special forces team and about 90 local South Vietnamese forces who were attacked in June 1965 by an overwhelming enemy force in remote Binh Dinh Province.

Name	Service	Unit	Place	Date	Actions
*Private First Class James Anderson Jr.	Marine Corps	3rd Marine Regt 3rd Marine Div	Cam Lo	Feb 28, 1967	Sacrificed life by smothering grenade with his body
Staff Sergeant Webster Anderson	Army	320th Fld Arty Regt 101st Abn Div (Airmobile)	Tam Kỳ	Oct 15, 1967	North Vietnamese forces attacked Anderson's unit near Tam Kỳ. Directed unit's defense, severely wounded twice, continued to lead.
*Sergeant First Class Eugene Ashley Jr.	Army	5th SF Gp (Abn), 1st Special Forces	Lang Vei	Feb 6, 1968– Feb 7, 1968	Led five assaults against the enemy, exposing self to enemy grenades, machine gun and automatic weapons fire until killed by mortar fire
*Private First Class Oscar P. Austin	Marine Corps	7th Marine Regt 1st Marine Div (Reinforced)	Da Nang	Feb 23, 1969	Sacrificed his life to save a wounded Marine
*Sergeant First Class William Maud Bryant	Army	5th SF Group 1st Special Forces	Long Khánh Province	Mar 24, 1969	Killed by an enemy rocket after leading his men on repeated attacks upon enemy bunkers
Gunnery Sergeant John Canley	Marine Corps	Co A, 1st Bn 1st Marine Div	Huế	Jan 31, 1968– Feb 6, 1968	Originally awarded the Navy Cross; upgraded to the Medal of Honor on Oct 17, 2018.
*Sergeant Rodney M. Davis	Marine Corps	5th Marine Regt 1st Marine Div	Quảng Nam Province, Vietnam	Sep 6, 1967	Sacrificed his life by smothering a grenade with his body
*Private First Class Robert H. Jenkins Jr.	Marine Corps	3rd Marine Div (Reinforced)	Fire Support Base Argonne, DMZ, Vietnam	Mar 5, 1969	Sacrificed his life to shield a wounded Marine from an exploding grenade

Name	Service	Unit	Place	Date	Actions
Specialist 6 Lawrence Joel	Army	503rd Inf Regt 173rd Abn Bde	Bien Hoa, War Zone D	Nov 8, 1965	After a long battle with enemy soldiers and despite his own wounds he continued to treat wounded until he was ordered to evacuate
Specialist 5 Dwight H. Johnson	Army	69th Armor Regt 4th Inf Div	Dak To, Kon Tum Province	Jan 15, 1968	Risked his life to repeatedly attack a group of enemy soldiers until all the enemy had been repulsed or killed
*Private First Class Ralph H. Johnson	Marine Corps	1st Marine Div (Reinforced)	Hill 146, Quan Duc Valley	Mar 5, 1968	Sacrificed his life by smothering a grenade with his body
*Private First Class Garfield M. Langhorn	Army	17th Cav Regt 1st Aviation Bde	Plei Djereng, Pleiku Province	Jan 15, 1969	Sacrificed his life by smothering a grenade with his body
*Sergeant First Class Matthew Leonard	Army	16th Inf Regt 1st Inf Div	Suoi Da	Feb 28, 1967	Although severely wounded he continued to fight the enemy until succumbing to his wounds
*Sergeant Donald Russell Long	Army	4th Cav Regt 1st Inf Div	Vietnam	Jun 30, 1966	Sacrificed his life by smothering a grenade with his body
Staff Sergeant Melvin Morris	Army	3rd Co, 3rd Bn, IV Mobile Strike Force	Chi Lăng	Sep 17, 1969	Shot three times while retrieving a wounded comrade
*Private First Class Milton L. Olive III	Army	503rd Inf Regt 173rd Abn Bde	Phu Cuong	Oct 22, 1965	Sacrificed his life by smothering a grenade with his body
*Captain Riley L. Pitts	Army	27th Inf Regt 25th Inf Div	Ap Dong	Oct 31, 1967	Led troops against numerous attacks against the enemy until they had been defeated
Lieutenant Colonel Charles Calvin Rogers	Army	5th Fld Arty Regt 1st Inf Div	Fishhook (Cambodian border)	Nov 1, 1968	Severely wounded, encouraged and directed troops to repel enemy attack
*First Lieutenant Ruppert L. Sargent	Army	9th Inf Regt 25th Inf Div	Hậu Nghĩa Province	Mar 15, 1967	Smothered two enemy grenades with his body
Private First Class Clarence Sasser	Army	60th Inf Reg, 9th Inf Div	Ding Tuong Province	Jan 10, 1968	Although wounded, gave first aid to others more than five hours until evacuated

Name	Service	Unit	Place	Date	Actions
*Staff Sergeant Clifford Chester Sims	Army	501st Abn Inf Regt 101st Abn Div	Huế	Feb 21, 1968	Sacrificed his life by smothering a grenade with his body
*First Lieutenant John E. Warren Jr.	Army	22nd Inf Regt, 25th Inf Div	Tây Ninh Province	Jan 14, 1969	Treated wounded and administered last rites to dead and dying until killed

*Posthumous award

AFGHANISTAN AND IRAQ

The services have been parsimonious in recognizing heroic action in the decades-long combat in Iraq and Afghanistan. As of the date of publication, only 21 Medals of Honor have been awarded for actions in Afghanistan and 8 in Iraq.

Only one has been African American:

Sergeant First Class Alwyn Crendall Cashe, Company A, 1st Battalion, 15th Infantry Regiment, 3rd Infantry Division, rescued six team members and their Iraqi interpreter from their Bradley fighting vehicle despite being covered with fuel and on fire near Daliaya, Iraq, on October 17, 2005. He suffered third-degree burns over three-quarters of his body and died of his injuries the following month. Cashe was posthumously awarded the Silver Star for gallantry.

A post office and Army reserve center were named in his honor and on May 20, 2021, and the 3rd Infantry Division, headquartered at Fort Stewart, Georgia, renamed its ceremonial grounds "Cashe Gardens." The area, used for battalion, brigade, and division changes of command and other significant ceremonies, adjoins the division headquarters.

On November 10, 2020, the US Congress voted to upgrade Cashe's initial award of the Silver Star to the Medal of Honor. On December 16, 2021, more than 16 years after his death at age 35, Cashe's widow, Tamara, accepted the Medal of Honor from President Joe Biden at a White House ceremony commemorating the bravery of Cashe and two other soldiers during the wars in Afghanistan and Iraq.

APPENDIX B

BUFFALO SOLDIER REGIMENTAL HISTORIES

Because US Colored Troops were unexpectedly effective during the Civil War, Congress authorized six Black regular army regiments in the Army Organization Act of July 16, 1867—two cavalry regiments (9th and 10th US Cavalry) and four infantry regiments (38th, 39th, 40th, and 41st US Infantry). This was the first time Black soldiers constituted a part of the regular army. Not all in Congress were enthusiastic—Delaware Senator Willard Saulsbury declared "Their presence would be a stench in the nostrils of the people from whom I come," a reflection that he was a Democrat representing a slave-owning border state. The Army's strength was fixed at 55,000, a drastic drop from the more than 1 million soldiers in the Union Army when the war ended. On March 3,1869, a budget cutback eliminated 20 infantry regiments. The four Black infantry regiments were consolidated into the 24th and 25th Infantry, and 18 white infantry regiments were disbanded.

The men who commanded the Black regiments were handpicked by Generals Sherman, Sheridan, and Thomas and were the cream of the army, young, vigorous officers. Historians Dobak and Phillips point out that of 106 former US Colored Troop officers who received commissions in the regular army, 51 served in the new Black regiments. Only 7 served in the cavalry, while 44 were assigned to the infantry.[1]

The Black regulars soon were nicknamed "Buffalo Soldiers" by their opponents, the Native American tribes of the Great Plains, although there is scant evidence that the Black soldiers used this term themselves. At Camp Supply in 1872, Frances Roe, the wife of an officer serving in the 3rd Infantry Regiment, noted that Plains Indians compared African American soldiers' "wooly heads" to the "matted cushion between the horns of the buffalo." The next year, a correspondent for *The Nation* wrote that the Comanches believed that the men of the 10th Cavalry and 25th Infantry had "woolly hair" like the buffalo. Frederic Remington, who used the term in a magazine article in 1889, gave the nickname wide circulation, and it seems to have been favored mainly by journalists.[2] According to historians Dobak and Phillips, soldiers describing army life to Black newspapers did not use the expression, which seems to have been used by them mainly as an insult.

About 3,000 veterans of the US Colored Troops and a like number of newly enlisted freed slaves enlisted in the new Black regiments. Stationed at isolated outposts, often as much as 600 miles from centers of habitation, these soldiers consistently had the lowest desertion, alcoholism, and court-martial rates in the Army. The regiments' strong backbone of US Colored Troop veterans who became sergeants serving well into the 1890s, over 20 or more years, doubtless influenced this. Secretary of War Elihu Root paid tribute to their extraordinary record in his annual report for 1889–1890, noting, "There are now two regiments of infantry and two regiments of cavalry of colored men, and their record for good service is excellent. They are neat, orderly, and obedient, are seldom brought before court-martial, and rarely desert."[3]

Their duties were identical to white units, battling Native American tribes, protecting railroad construction and lines against tribesmen and bandits, and guarding the border between the United States and Mexico. While doing all of this, they built the infrastructure needed for further development: good roads and telegraph and later, telephone lines connecting what was originally a vast area barren of Anglo presence. Other duties included providing guards at isolated stagecoach stations and railroad water tanks, riding "shotgun" on individual stagecoaches, and occasionally carrying the mail. They returned tribes and war parties to reservations and provided military escorts for cattle drives. Along with white regiments, they created infrastructure for settlers emigrating westward, protecting them from Native tribes. Near-constant cavalry and infantry

Guarding stagecoaches and Pony Express stations were among Black regulars' duties in the early years. SOURCES: ALEXANDER GARDINER, LIBRARY OF CONGRESS.

patrols mapped uncharted areas, facilitating future settlement. The men of these four regiments proved themselves equal if not superior to white army troops, exceeding the expectations of some of their own white officers, who often looked down on them. At the same time, they built a strong esprit de corps, causing commanders of the two cavalry regiments and some of their officers to develop such an affinity that they served extended tours with their regiments, turning down promotions in other units to the detriment of their careers.

In 1867, the Army was spread over 138 outposts, with a strength of 55,000. By the mid-1870s, with a mere 25,000 in the total force, the Army concentrated troops along rail lines for economy of movement and supply. Sheridan reported in 1880 that he had a single soldier per square mile in the Departments of Dakota, the Platte, and Missouri and one per 125 square miles in Texas, while hardly a year passed without Southern Democrats' attempts to cut the military budget.[4] In the early years, life at remote stations could sometimes be a waking nightmare. While their service was often appreciated, many Texas editors used the "N-word" and "coons" regularly when referring to soldiers of these regiments. The *Daily New Mexican* published an article, "Jokes on Sambo," and the *Helena Daily Herald* ran a "humorous" piece about "common traits . . . of the negro race" reflecting many Westerners' attitudes.[5] Mexicans, Chinese, and Native Americans, however, generally suffered worse treatment and were held in lower regard.

Service in the Indian Wars

Indian war posts and battles. SOURCE: AMERICAN MILITARY HISTORY, VOLUME 1, THE UNITED STATES ARMY AND THE FORGING OF A NATION, 1775-1917, US Government Printing Office, Washington, DC, 2005, 325.

9TH CAVALRY REGIMENT

Formed in New Orleans in September 1866 by order of Major General Philip H. Sheridan, commander of the Department of the Gulf, the 9th Cavalry Regiment's first commander was Edward Hatch, cavalry commander of the Army of Tennessee during the Civil War. Hatch commanded one of the regiments that was part of Colonel Grierson's legendary cavalry raid across Mississippi, a diversion for Grant's masterful operations against Vicksburg. Hatch commanded the 9th Cavalry Regiment until his death at Fort Robinson, Nebraska, in April 1889. In 1876, still commanding the 9th Cavalry, Hatch was appointed commander of the District of New Mexico (which included parts of Colorado and Texas), and he negotiated a treaty with Utes in 1880. When he first arrived in Santa Fe, Hatch remarked to the *Daily New Mexican* that "good and abundant food given to the Indians is much less costly than grape shot."[6] Colonel Grierson of the 10th Cavalry heartily agreed.

Appendix B

25th Infantry Regiment soldiers in formal dress uniforms worn between the 1860s and 1890s. Soldier on left with white braids across his chest is a musician.
SOURCE: LIBRARY OF CONGRESS.

In October 1866, Captain James S. Brisbin, recruiting officer for the 9th Cavalry, reported on the recent discharge of two US Colored Cavalry regiments that had been raised in Kentucky. According to historians Dobak and Phillips, he noted, "It would be greatly in the interest of the service if some of them could be re-enlisted as they are natural horsemen, and physically the finest Black men in the country."[7] Generally, recruiting parties made up of a white officer and two Black noncommissioned officers and several privates scoured the countryside enlisting candidates. Almost 40 percent of troops recruited for the 9th Cavalry Regiment came from the 116th US Colored Infantry, stationed at Ringgold Barracks in Texas.

By March 1867, the regiment had a total of 885 enlisted men, averaging over 70 men to a troop, the cavalry equivalent of a company. Shortly after its forming, the regiment was ordered to San Antonio, Texas, for three months of training. After completing initial training, the unit deployed to western and southwestern Texas to maintain law and order between the Rio Grande and Concho Rivers along a 630-mile sector dispersed among eight forts. The regiment's headquarters and four troops were stationed at Fort Stockton; Lieutenant Colonel Wesley Merritt, formerly the commander of Major General Sheridan's cavalry corps in the Shenandoah Valley, commanded six troops stationed at Fort Davis on the Trans-Pecos portion of the San Antonio–El Paso Road and the Chihuahua Trail.

The 9th Cavalry was regularly in the field for eight years, tracking and fighting hostiles, escorting mail, and rescuing civilians from hostile attacks. Men of the regiment also surveyed, constructed roads, strung telegraph wire, and otherwise built an infrastructure that would support civilization in miles of vast, trackless, uncharted territory, also policing the Mexican border. They also performed a range of additional but routine duties, including drill, inspections, parades, and care of their horses and equipment.

After a 53-day field campaign involving a 1,000-mile march, which ended with half of his command dismounted and walking barefoot, returning with tattered uniforms in the spring of 1870, Major Albert Morrow reported to the Army adjutant general:

> I cannot speak too highly of the officers and men under my command, always cheerful and steady, braving the severest hardships without a murmur. The negro troops are peculiarly adapted to hunting Indians, knowing no fear and capable of great endurance.[8]

The regiment participated in a large operation against hostile Comanches, Kiowas, Cheyennes, and Kawahdis from August to December 1874. Lieutenant Colonel George Buell of the 11th Infantry, commander of Fort Griffin, reported the 10th Cavalry troopers' performance to the adjutant general of the Department of Texas, "I cannot give them too much credit for manly endurance without complaint."[9] His observation echoed the comments made by General Christopher Columbus Augur, commander of the Department of Texas, in 1872:

> The labor and privations of troops in this Department are both severe. The cavalry particularly are constantly at work, and it is the kind of work that too often disheartens, as there is very little to show for it. Yet their zeal is untiring, and if they do not always achieve success they always deserve it. I have never seen troops more constantly employed.[10]

Appendix B

In late 1875, the 9th Cavalry Regiment was transferred to the New Mexico Military District to operate against Apaches. In 1877, a 9th Cavalry battalion assisted in suppressing a major political disturbance near El Paso in the "Salt War" over rights to dry saline lakes at the base of the Guadalupe Mountains. The struggle reached a climax after a mob of perhaps 500 Tejanos in the town of San Elizario, Texas, surrounded 20 Texas Rangers and forced them to surrender. The arrival of 9th Cavalry elements and a sheriff's posse of New Mexico mercenaries caused hundreds of Tejanos to flee to Mexico, some in permanent exile.

In September 1879, a company of the 9th Cavalry came to the rescue of three troops of the white 4th Cavalry and an infantry company guarding a wagon train surrounded by a band of Utes along the Milk River in northwest Colorado. Ute warriors taunted the "soldiers with Black faces":

> You ride behind the white soldiers,
> But you can't take off your Black faces,
> And the white soldiers make you ride behind them.[11]

The Utes' taunts had no impact. That night Sergeant Henry Johnson of D Troop, already a veteran of 12 years of service, which included the 10th Cavalry, made the round of rifle pits and encouraged the troopers. The surrounded soldiers were desperate for water, so on the fifth night, Johnson shot his way to the river, returning with a much-needed supply. Couriers reached Fort David A. Russell, and Colonel Wesley Merritt and five troops of the 5th Cavalry rescued the beleaguered band, driving off the Indigenous force, who were close to annihilating the encircled soldiers. Johnson was awarded the Medal of Honor at Fort Robinson on September 22, 1890, a lag of 15 years.

In September 1879, Victorio's Chiricahua Apaches left the reservation and caught the 9th Cavalry's Troops B and E from Fort Stanton in an ambush on the Las Animas River in southwestern New Mexico, firing down from steep and rocky canyon walls. Troops B and G rode to their rescue but were also pinned down by the Apaches firing down from high above them. The four troops finally withdrew under cover of darkness, leaving their baggage. The cavalry lost 27 horses and reported the death of six soldiers, two or three Navajo scouts, and one civilian, although there are 32 gravesites at the site. No Apache bodies were discovered. Three soldiers, Lieutenant Robert Temple Emmet, Lieutenant Mathias Day, and Sergeant John Denny received the Congressional Medal of Honor for acts of bravery during the battle.

A small element of the regiment led by Sergeant George Jordan participated in the battle of Fort Tularosa, New Mexico, in May 1880, saving the settlement's inhabitants and defeating another band of Victorio's Apaches. Sergeant Jordan received the Medal of Honor for his courage and resourcefulness throughout the action almost 10 years later, in May 1890. After the campaign against Victorio, General Pope commended Colonel Hatch and the soldiers of the 9th Cavalry:

> It is my duty, as it is my pleasure, to invite the special attention of the authorities to the meritorious and gallant conduct of Col. Edward Hatch, commanding the District of New Mexico, and to Major A. P. Morrow, 9th Cavalry, and the officers and soldiers under their command, in the difficult and trying campaign against the southern Apaches. Everything that men could do they did. . . . their services in the field were marked by unusual hardships and difficulties. Their duties were performed with zeal and intelligence and they are worthy of all considerations.[12]

The regiment lost 44 soldiers in combat with Native Americans, of whom 28 were inflicted by Apaches. In 1881, after 18 years of distinguished and arduous service in the Southwest, the 9th Cavalry Regiment was transferred to Fort Riley, Kansas, and to Fort Sill, Indian Territory, (Oklahoma after 1907), where in a new twist, the regiment joined with the 10th Cavalry in protecting Native Americans from settlers invading the future Sooner state, a disagreeable and thankless task. This ended in June 1885, when the regimental headquarters was transferred to Fort McKinney, Wyoming, with companies assigned to Forts Robinson and Niobrara in Nebraska and Fort Duchesne in Utah. In November 1887, one troop fought Crow Indians in Montana. The men of the regiment built or substantially rebuilt many of the posts where they were stationed while performing a range of housekeeping and peacekeeping duties.

The 9th Cavalry regiment participated in the last major campaign of the Indian Wars, the Ghost Dance War, with the Lakota in late December 1890, which ended with the Wounded Knee Massacre of more than 300 Native Americans, half of whom were women, children, and elders, by 7th Cavalry troopers on the Pine Ridge Lakota Reservation in South Dakota on December 29. Although not at Wounded Knee, elements of the 9th twice rescued 7th Cavalry units attacked by Indians, most significantly at Drexel Mission on December 30, 1890, the day after the Wounded Knee Massacre. The fight occurred on White Clay Creek, approximately 15 miles north of Pine Ridge, where Lakota were feared to have burned the Catholic mission. Eight troops of the 7th Cavalry and a platoon of artillery under the command of Colonel James W. Forsyth, engaged at Wounded Knee the previous day, were attacked by Brulé Lakota from the Rosebud Indian Reservation while reconnoitering the Catholic mission. These Indians were suspected to be the same Lakota under Chief Two Strike that attacked the 9th Cavalry's supply train earlier that morning. The 7th Cavalry was hotly engaged in a valley by the combined Lakota forces while trying to break contact and withdraw. A battalion of the 9th Cavalry commanded by Major Guy V. Henry responded to Forsyth's request for assistance. The combined cavalry forces drove the Lakota from commanding positions on the heights. Corporal William O. Wilson won a Medal of Honor for carrying a dispatch from the encircled wagon train through country occupied by hostile Lakota/Sioux. The regiment was the last unit to leave the area, spending the winter of 1890–1891 on the reservation in tents in near-arctic temperatures. A Black private, W. H. Prather, wrote a poem in which he observed, "The 9th were the first to come, will be the last to leave, and we poor devils and the Sioux are left to freeze."[13]

Troops from the 9th Cavalry intervened in violent political and economic disputes in Lincoln County, New Mexico, during the late 1870s and in Johnson County, Wyoming, in 1892.

CONGRESSIONAL MEDAL OF HONOR RECIPIENTS

Lieutenant Robert Temple Emmet, Troop G
Lieutenant Mathias Day, Apache scouts
Lieutenant George Burnett, Troop I
First Sergeant Moses Williams, Troop I

Sergeant Thomas Boyne, Troop C
Sergeant John Denny, Troop C
Sergeant George Jordan, Troop K
Sergeant Henry Johnson, Troop D
Sergeant Thomas Shaw, Troop K
Sergeant Emanuel Stance, Troop F
Sergeant Brent Woods, Troop B
Corporal William Wilson, Troop I
Corporal Clinton Greaves, Troop C

All four Black regiments fought alongside Theodore Roosevelt's Rough Riders in Cuba in the battles of Kettle Hill and San Juan Hill in 1898. Later, the 9th Cavalry served as Roosevelt's honor guard in San Francisco. In 1899, 1904, and again in 1905, the regiment patrolled Yosemite National Park, joining other cavalry and infantry units as the first park "rangers." National Park rangers' "Smokey the Bear" hat is modeled after the troopers' distinctive "Montana Pinch" campaign hat.

FIRST AFRICAN AMERICAN GENERAL OFFICER

On February 2, 1901, Benjamin O. Davis Sr. was commissioned a second lieutenant in the 9th Cavalry. Davis entered military service in July 1898 during the Spanish–American War as a first lieutenant in the 8th Volunteer Infantry. Mustered out in March 1899, Davis enlisted in June 1899 in Troop I, 9th Cavalry, rising through the ranks to squadron sergeant major. He served in the Philippines with the regiment on the Island of Samar. In August 1901, he transferred to the 2nd Squadron, 10th Cavalry, returning from the Philippines with the 10th for service as adjutant at Fort Washakie, Wyoming. In September 1905, he became professor of military science and tactics at Wilberforce University, Ohio, until September 1909, when he was detailed as military attaché to Monrovia, Liberia, until January 1912. Next assigned to the 9th Cavalry at Fort David A. Russell, Wyoming, and at Camp Douglas, Arizona, he remained on border duty until February 1915, when he returned to Wilberforce, remaining there until the summer of 1917, when he went to the Philippines with the 9th Cavalry. He returned to duty as professor of military science and tactics at Tuskegee Institute, Alabama, serving until July 1924, when he was assigned to the 372nd Infantry, Ohio National Guard, in Cleveland, Ohio. Davis was promoted to colonel in 1930 and assigned as instructor and commanding officer of the 369th Infantry, New York National Guard ("Harlem Hellfighters"), in 1938. Sadly, this renowned combat regiment was converted to the 369th Coast Artillery (Anti-aircraft) Regiment and deployed to Hawaii during World War II. On October 25, 1940, Davis was promoted to brigadier general, the first African American to achieve that rank. In January 1941, he was ordered to Fort Riley, Kansas, for duty as a brigade commander with the 2nd Cavalry Division. Retired in July 1941 due to age, he was recalled to active duty the following day and assigned as assistant to the inspector general in Washington, DC, serving as ombudsman for Africans throughout World War II. Davis's son, Benjamin O. Davis Jr., the fourth Black West Point graduate, led the Tuskegee Airmen and was one of two of the airmen who became Air Force four-star generals.

WORLD WAR I

A troop detached from the 9th Cavalry taught riding instruction, mounted drill, and cavalry tactics at West Point from 1905 to 1947. Their service was commemorated in August 2021 with the unveiling of a statue on the West Point plain of a Buffalo Soldier sergeant mounted on his steed.

As a result of racial incidents involving both infantry regiments in 1906 and 1917, the 9th Cavalry Regiment was transferred to the Philippines, where it served for the duration of the war.

WORLD WAR II

As World War II approached, Black regiments were understrength, often used for post maintenance and ancillary duties, with less emphasis on marksmanship and combat training. In March 1933, the regiment was assigned to the 3rd Cavalry Division. It became part of the 2nd Cavalry Division in October 1940 in a brigade commanded by Brigadier General Benjamin O. Davis Sr. Arriving in Oran, Algeria, in March 1944, the regiment was deactivated in May and converted to logistical units and stevedores who unloaded supply ships. White cavalry units became combat units. Many from the regiment later volunteered as replacements for combat units, principally the 92nd Infantry Division, which sustained heavy casualties fighting in Northern Italy.

10TH CAVALRY REGIMENT

The 10th US Cavalry was formed at Fort Leavenworth, Kansas, in 1866, commanded by Colonel Benjamin Grierson, leader of two legendary cavalry raids through Mississippi designed to divert attention before Grant's brilliant Vicksburg campaign. Because the Leavenworth post commander adamantly opposed African Americans serving in the regular army, Grierson requested the unit's transfer to Fort Riley, Kansas, in August 1867.

The regiment was tasked with protecting crews constructing the Kansas Pacific Railroad. One of its first battles with Native Americans was near Fort Hays, Kansas, in August 1867 after a railroad work party was wiped out. Patrols from the 38th Infantry Regiment (reorganized into the 24th Infantry Regiment in 1869), with a troop from the 10th Cavalry were sent out to locate the perpetrators. In 1867 and 1868, the regiment participated in General Sherman's winter campaigns against the Cheyenne, Arapahos, and Comanches. Units from the regiment prevented Indigenous tribes from withdrawing, allowing Custer's 7th Cavalry to defeat them near Fort Cobb in Indian Territory.

Troops H & I under the command of Captain Louis Carpenter, who had commanded a regiment of US Colored Troops during the Civil War, engaged in two notable actions in September and October 1868. The first was the rescue of Lieutenant Colonel George A. Forsyth and 48 white scouts pinned down by a large hostile force on a Colorado island. The second occurred two weeks later when about 500 Indians attacked Carpenter's troops. After a running fight, the "hostiles" retreated. With General Sheridan's recommendation, Carpenter received the Medal of Honor for these two actions. Sheridan also commended Carpenter's stalwart troopers.

Sheridan directed Colonel Grierson to establish Fort Sill in Indian Territory in 1869. Grierson was the first post commander, and his 10th Cavalry troopers constructed many of the stone buildings surrounding the post quadrangle. Sheridan was impressed with the fort, calling it one of the best he had seen, a fit facility for the "army of occupation" the regiment constituted on the reservation in Indian Territory. Other regimental elements were based farther to the west, at Camp Supply.

In early 1872, four companies of the 10th Cavalry were transferred to Fort Gibson in Indian Territory, where Grierson immediately faced a dispute among rival factions of the Creek Nation. With characteristic diplomacy, Grierson resolved the dispute peacefully. When Generals Sheridan and Augur, the Department of Texas commander, made a routine inspection tour, Augur, Grierson's immediate supervisor, reported, "Under his judicious management the removal [of intruders] has been effected [sic] without trouble, or a single complaint."[14] By June 1874, all troops of the regiment were re-equipped with new Model 1873 carbines and Colt revolvers. In 1879, one troop received Hotchkiss repeating carbines, the latest in military weaponry.

In April 1875, the regiment was transferred to Fort Concho, Texas, to protect mail and travel routes, control Indian movement, police Mexican revolutionaries and outlaws along the border, and gain knowledge of the area. The 10th Cavalry scouted 34,420 miles of uncharted terrain, built more than 300 miles of new roads, and laid over 200 miles of telegraph lines in harsh terrain, producing excellent maps detailing scarce water holes, mountain passes, and grazing areas that later facilitated combat action and settlement. In December 1877, Colonel William Shafter, commander of the 24th Infantry Regiment and operating on the southwest Texas border with a detachment of the 10th Cavalry Regiment, submitted a glowing report of their activities in the field:

> Officers and men were exposed to very severe weather and having only pack animals were necessarily restricted to the small allowance carried on the saddle. The country scouted in was exceedingly difficult, more so than any part of Texas, the officers and men deserving great credit for the patience, fortitude, and energy they exhibited on this scout.[15]

In 1879, the regiment protected Kiowa women and children from Texas Rangers. On other occasions, troopers protected Chickasaw and Cherokee farmers from deadly onslaughts by Kiowa and Comanche bands.

The regiment played an important role in the 1879–1880 campaign against Victorio's Mescalero band who left their reservation near Ruidoso, New Mexico, in August 1879 and for the next 11 months, struck terror in the hearts of ranchers and settlers in West Texas; New Mexico; and Chihuahua, Mexico. Colonel Grierson decided that the best way to intercept Victorio was to control the limited number of water holes and mountain passes. The regiment engaged in two significant confrontations, at Tinaja de las Palmas and Rattlesnake Springs, blocking Victorio's band, denying them water, and forcing their retreat to Mexico, where the exhausted and thirsty Apaches were annihilated by Mexican troops in October 1880. Colonel Grierson's tactics were a model of counterguerrilla operations, beating Victorio at his own game.

In 1885, the 10th Cavalry Regiment was transferred to the Department of Arizona, pursuing Apaches led by Geronimo and other chiefs. Colonel Grierson commanded the Department of Arizona in 1889 and found that nearly a quarter of the cavalry in the district were dismounted due to lack of serviceable horses—1,616 horses for 2,134 troopers.[16] A detachment of 10th Cavalry fought one of the last battles of the Apache Wars along the Salt River in March 1890, the same year that Colonel Grierson was finally rewarded for his 23 years of service with the regiment by promotion to brigadier general. Grierson would have been promoted much earlier but for his positive views toward both African and Native Americans. Grierson retired three months later. Apaches inflicted 9 of the regiment's 17 fatalities.

Despite widespread belief that African Americans could not cope with cold climates, after 20 years of service on posts in the Southwest, the regiment was transferred to the Department of Dakota in 1891, serving at various posts in Montana and the Dakotas until 1898. Lieutenant John J. Pershing, commanding a troop in north-central Montana, led an expedition that rounded up and deported a large number of Cree Indians to Canada. In 1894, elements of the regiment protected railroad property from striking workers.

10th Cavalry and 25th Infantry Regiment inspection at Fort Assiniboine, Montana. SOURCE: FORT ASSINIBOINE PRESERVATION SOCIETY.

Appendix B

General Ord recognized Grierson and the 10th Cavalry's "earnest and zealous efforts in the line of duty . . . long and severe service . . . in the field and at remote frontier stations." But Grierson was proudest of the correspondence he received from Ord's headquarters in late 1879:

> Thirty-four thousand four hundred and twenty miles of marches; three hundred miles of roads opened; two hundred miles of telegraph constructed,—all, except a portion of the telegraph, consummated on one year,—involve efforts that will lead to lasting results, of which, as tending greatly, to advance civilization, yourself and your command may be well proud.[17]

Congressional Medal of Honor Recipients

Captain Louis Carpenter, Troop H
Lieutenant Powhattan Clarke, Troop K
Sergeant Major Edward Baker
Sergeant William McBryar, Troop K
Private Dennis Bell, Troop H
Private Lee Fitz, Troop M
Private William Thompkins, Troop G
Private George Wanton, Troop M

The 10th Cavalry participated in the Spanish–American War with the other three Black regiments. The regiment's attack up San Juan Hill with regular cavalry regiments and the Rough Riders, Teddy Roosevelts's 1st Volunteer Cavalry Regiment, was the highlight of the campaign. Afterward, the 10th Cavalry was sent to the Philippines. When they returned in late 1902, the regiment served at various posts in the Southwestern United States. In 1909, the regiment was posted to Fort Ethan Allen, at Burlington, Vermont, where they enjoyed far greater comfort and displayed their horsemanship to appreciative civilians and dignitaries, including members of Congress, leaders of other countries, and President Woodrow Wilson. They also conducted a march to Winchester, Virginia, for training purposes.

Due to rising tension along the Mexican–American border, the 10th Cavalry was transferred to the Southwest in late 1913, headquartered at

Fort Huachuca, Arizona. The regiment, then commanded by the only Black regular officer in the Army, Major Charles Young, was an essential component of the expedition Pershing led against Pancho Villa in 1916. Because of Young's leadership and charisma, he was promoted to lieutenant colonel and commander of Fort Huachuca. Young was forcefully retired for medical causes the next year because of the "danger" that he might command white troops. Army headquarters had already received a complaint from a lieutenant serving in the regiment.

WORLD WAR I

The regiment spent World War I in the United States patrolling the Mexican border. In January 1918, the 10th Cavalry Regiment was involved in a firefight with Yaqui Indians just west of Nogales, Arizona. In August 1918, the regiment and elements of the 35th Infantry Regiment fought a border skirmish, the "battle of Ambos Nogales," involving German military advisors. This was the only battle fought against German soldiers in North America.

WORLD WAR II

As mentioned, as World War II approached, Black regiments were understrength and were often used for post maintenance and ancillary duties, with less emphasis placed on marksmanship and training for combat. Although war plans designated the 10th to serve in the Pacific in support of the Philippines from 1915 through 1942, they never deployed. In the summer of 1943, the regiment fought wildfires out west. Both cavalry regiments were assigned to the 2nd Cavalry Division, and in 1944, and the entire division shipped out to North Africa, where both Black cavalry regiments were deactivated that May. Although trained as combat soldiers, the 10th Cavalry Regiment was reorganized into the 1334th Engineer Construction Battalion (Colored) and built airfield facilities for the Tuskegee Airmen. Some troops volunteered for combat with the 92nd Infantry Division, which suffered heavy casualties fighting in Northern Italy.

24TH INFANTRY REGIMENT

The 38th Infantry Regiment was activated on October 1, 1866, at Jefferson Barracks, Missouri, under the command of Colonel William B. Hazen, XV Corps, Army of the Tennessee commander when the Civil War ended. The regiment soon got marching orders, stationed in New

Mexico Territory along the transcontinental railroads then under construction. During the summer of 1867, a detachment escorting supplies for the regiment assisted in the defense of Fort Wallace, Kansas. General Custer's wife reported, "When the skirmish line was reached, the colored men leaped out and began firing. No one had ordered them to leave their picket-station, but they were determined that no soldiering should be carried on in which their valor was not proved."[18] When consolidation orders came, the regiment marched from New Mexico across Texas to their new headquarters at Fort McKavett.

The 41st Infantry Regiment was organized at Baton Rouge, Louisiana, by order of Major General George H. Thomas. The regiment's first commander was Ranald S. Mackenzie, the young, dashing, and renowned Civil War and Indian Wars cavalry leader. Its companies were soon dispersed to numerous posts along the Rio Grande River and the Mexican border in southwest Texas.

The 24th Infantry Regiment was activated in November 1869 by combining the 38th and the 41st US Infantry Regiments (Colored). By then, both regiments had nearly three years of frontier experience. Mackenzie was the 24th Infantry Regiment's first commander, although his command of the 24th was brief. A year later, he was appointed colonel of the 4th Cavalry Regiment, which conducted a series of relentless campaigns against native tribes, winning him promotion to general and commander of the Department of Texas in 1882. The regiment's second commander was William Shafter, who commanded the 17th US Colored Infantry Regiment at the Battle of Nashville. Shafter later led V Corps, US Army forces operating in Cuba, during the Spanish–American War.

From its activation in 1869 until 1898, the 24th Infantry served in the Western United States, battling Native Americans, protecting roadways against tribesmen and bandits, and guarding the border between the United States and Mexico. Its headquarters was at Fort McKavett, with companies stationed at Forts Bliss, Clark, Davis, Duncan, Quitman, and Stockton. The regiment served longer in heat and humidity of the Texas frontier than any other infantry regiment of the Army, molding its soldiers into one of the Army's outstanding units. Although assigned to isolated posts and enduring rigorous duty, the 24th Infantry Regiment had the *lowest desertion rate in the army from 1880 to 1886*. White regiments sharing the same posts had rates of desertion 20 to 50 times that of the regiment. In 1877, the 3rd Cavalry, garrisoned with the 24th, had 104 desertions, while the 5th Cavalry racked up 99.[19] Desertion rates were even higher in other units. At the time, desertion was such a problem army-wide that Secretary of War Robert Lincoln noted in his 1882 annual report that one out of two soldiers who enlisted deserted.[20] The secretary of war's report for 1889 paid tribute to the record of the four Black regiments.[21] Army authorities seldom acknowledged the high state of morale, discipline, and esprit de corps that existed in all Black regiments despite their isolated and austere cantonments.

In May 1889, a detail of two noncommissioned officers and nine privates from the 24th Infantry and the 10th Cavalry was assigned to guard an Army payroll worth more than $28,000 under paymaster Major Joseph W. Wham. En route from Fort Grant to Fort Thomas in Arizona, 15 to 20 outlaws ambushed the party. The soldiers returned fire, but the bandits absconded with the payroll. Although wounded, Corporal Isaiah Mays managed to reach a nearby ranch and bring reinforcements. Major Wham recommended nine men for the Medal of Honor, which was approved for Sergeant Benjamin Brown and Corporal Isaiah Mays. Seven privates received certificates of merit, which at the time brought an additional $2 monthly in pay.[22] In his official report, Wham praised the valor of his escort: "I served in the infantry during the Civil War . . . in sixteen major battles, but I never witnessed better courage or better fighting than shown by these colored soldiers."[23]

The 24th Infantry was engaged in more civil disputes than any other Black regiment. In 1894, the second year of a four-year economic depression, the worst in United States history up to that time, they followed Coxey's army marching on Washington, DC. Elements were sent to a temporary camp in west Wyoming in the wake of anti-Chinese riots of 1885. Along with the 25th Infantry, elements from the regiment protected mining property in Idaho and Montana in labor disputes during the 1890s and guarded miners who were arrested at Coeur d'Alene during 1892 and at Wardner, Idaho, in 1899. As late as 1920, the 24th served in a coal mine dispute in New Mexico.

With the other Buffalo Soldier regiments, the 24th Infantry deployed to Cuba in 1898 for the Spanish–American War, where their former commander, William Shafter, was overall commander. The 24th distinguished itself in the gallant charge with the 3rd Brigade up San Juan Hill against heavy enemy fire on July 1, 1898, capturing the Spanish blockhouse and trenches guarding the approach to Santiago. The regiment suffered 17 killed and 82 wounded in the assault, with 16 members of the regiment cited for extraordinary valor. The regiment's extraordinary courage under fire was also noted in the regimental commander's after-action report. More than 50 members of the 24th Infantry volunteered as medical orderlies to nurse the many soldiers who contracted tropical fevers, and many of these volunteers were infected themselves. When they returned to the United States, some white hospitals refused to admit Black soldiers.

The regiment was deployed to garrisons at Fort Douglas, Utah, and Wyoming, Washington, and Montana when the 24th Infantry returned to the United States in September 1898. Company L was stationed in Alaska to "show the flag" in that sparsely occupied territory in the 1980s. In July 1899, elements of the 24th stationed at Fort Douglas, Utah, and in Wyoming arrived in the Philippine Islands to reinforce Army units under attack by Filipino insurgents fiercely resisting American administration. In one of the regiment's most noteworthy actions during the 10-year Philippine Insurrection, nine soldiers of the regiment routed 100 entrenched guerrillas in December 1899. The 24th Infantry served on the main island of Luzon until August 1902 and participated in the capture of the town of San Isidro in north-central Luzon in late 1899. The regiment conducted numerous small-unit actions on Luzon during 1900 to neutralize bands of insurgents and secure lines of communication. When the 24th Infantry returned to the United States, its headquarters was Fort Keogh, Montana.

In 1906, the regiment returned to Luzon for two years of garrison duty, after which it was stationed at Fort Ontario and Jefferson Barracks, New York, from 1908 to 1911, the first time Black soldiers were stationed in the East. The 24th returned to the Philippines in 1911, serving at Camp McGrath in Manila until 1915. The regiment then returned to the United States, stationed at the Presidio of San Francisco.

In 1916, the 24th Infantry Regiment, used mostly to secure supply bases and lines of communication, joined the 10th Cavalry Regiment and other white units in the Punitive Expedition of 10,000 troops, primarily composed of five cavalry regiments, four infantry regiments, and two field artillery battalions under General John J. "Black Jack" Pershing.

1917 RACIAL DISTURBANCES

In late May and early July 1917, outbreaks of race-related labor violence by white Americans in the riots in East St. Louis, Illinois, left roughly 40 whites and 250 African Americans dead and 6,000 Blacks homeless due to widespread vandalism, which cost around $400,000 in property damages ($8 million in 2021). In late July, two battalions of the 24th Infantry rioted at two locations in Texas in reaction to the white population's strong Jim Crow sentiments and vicious provocations. First Battalion soldiers guarding construction at Camp McArthur in Waco, Texas, aggravated by the town's Jim Crow laws, engaged in a shoot-out on city streets. Seven soldiers were court-martialed, sentenced to five years imprisonment, and given dishonorable discharges.

Racial animosity was intense in Houston, Texas, where 645 men of the 3rd Battalion were sent from Minnesota to guard airfield construction at Camp Logan in early July. The white populace and the Houston Police Department constantly harassed local Blacks as well as the newly arrived soldiers. In August 1917, a white policeman beat and arrested a Black private who intervened in the arrest of a Black woman. Both were jailed. A military police corporal sent to inquire after the private was arrested after being pistol-whipped and shot at by a particularly racist police officer. Rumors of the corporal's murder spread, causing about 150 soldiers to draw weapons and march toward Houston. Confronted by local policemen and a mob of armed Houston residents, the soldiers killed 15 armed whites, including four policemen and an Illinois National Guard officer mistaken for a local policeman. Twenty-four other whites were seriously wounded, and four Black soldiers were killed. The battalion was recalled to regimental headquarters in Columbus, New Mexico, while the Army convened a court-martial at Fort Sam Houston in San Antonio, Texas. Sixteen servicemen were hung without their sentences being reviewed as required by regulation. A subsequent court condemned 3 more soldiers to death and sentenced 47 others to life imprisonment.

WORLD WAR I

Both incidents convinced the War Department to revise its plans and avoid large concentrations of Black troops in the South. Some officials and many of the public became concerned about Blacks' loyalty. Congress considered disbanding all four regiments, and even though this was not done, regimental strengths diminished to about half of authorized levels. As a result of these incidents, the 24th Infantry served along the border during World War I, crossing the border to engage rebels and Mexican troops at Juárez, opposite El Paso, Texas, in 1919. Noncommissioned cadres from the regiment were used to train other Black units formed during the war.

WORLD WAR II

When World War II broke out, elements of the 24th Infantry were serving as school troops at the Infantry School at Fort Benning, Georgia. After participating in the fall maneuvers in Louisiana, the regiment deployed as a separate regiment to New Hebrides on April 4, 1942, used mostly for road building, off-loading ships, and installation maintenance. The regiment moved to Guadalcanal in August 1943 after the island had been seized by US forces. The 24th Infantry Regiment arrived on Saipan and Tinian in the Marianas in December 1944 for garrison duty and mopping up remaining Japanese forces. Their superior conduct in combat operations merited the attention of a War Department survey group. The regiment was deployed to the Kerama Islands off Okinawa in July 1945, accepting the surrender of Japanese forces on the island of Aka-shima, the first surrender of a Japanese Imperial Army garrison. When World War II ended, the 24th pulled occupation duty in Okinawa, assigned to the 25th Infantry Division on January 2, 1947, and relocated to Gifu, Japan, the next month. Despite Truman's Executive Order 9981 signed on July 26, 1948, directing desegregation of the US armed forces, the 24th Infantry was still all Black, except for senior officers. One of the three battalion commanders was Black, but he chose to remain in Gifu in charge of the barracks when the Korean War broke out.

KOREAN WAR

Among the first units to arrive on the Korean peninsula, the 24th Infantry compiled a mixed record and was subjected to much racial vilification until it was disbanded at Chipo-ri, Kangwon Province, North Korea, midway through the war. The regiment fought as a segregated unit for 17 months in temperature extremes ranging from over 100 degrees to minus 20 and participated in six campaigns, also receiving the Korean Presidential Unit Citation at Masan-Chinju for its heroism during the defense of the Pusan Perimeter early in the war. Soon after the regiment's arrival in August 1950, Private First Class William H. Thompson was the first American soldier to be awarded the Medal of Honor. Sergeant Cornelius H. Charlton also received the medal for remaining with his machine gun, permitting the bulk of his unit to extricate itself from a mass Chinese attack. Both received the award posthumously. Numerous officers and soldiers won an array of awards for valor. The regiment experienced a nearly 40 percent casualty rate, which was particularly damaging among noncommissioned and commissioned officers. Some companies went through five commanders in a month, and the regiment had to cope with inadequately trained replacements, some ignorant of basic infantry tactics. About 1,200 out of the 3,200 men assigned to the regiment were killed, wounded, or captured.[24]

The regiment had completed 85 years of continuous service when it was disbanded in September 1951. The regiment's experience in Korea is detailed in Chapter Seven.

THE MODERN ARMY

Under the Combat Arms Regimental System, the Army reactivated the 24th Infantry Regiment's 1st Battalion in August 1995, a component of the 25th Infantry Division at Fort Lewis, Washington. Awarded an Army Superior Unit Award in 1996, in the spring of 2002, it was reorganized and equipped as a Stryker (8 x 8-wheeled armored fighting vehicle) infantry battalion. In October 2004, the battalion deployed with the 1st Stryker Brigade, 25th Infantry Division to Mosul, Iraq, where the unit received a Valorous Unit Award and a Meritorious Unit Citation for distinguished service during Operation Iraqi Freedom during its 2008–2009 tour. Deactivated in June 2006, it was reactivated that December at Fort Wainwright, Fairbanks, Alaska. Since then, battalion elements served at Forward Observation Base Lagman, Zabul Province, Afghanistan, in 2011 and 2012. The battalion remains at Fort Wainwright today, now assigned to a part of a brigade combat team of the 11th Airborne Division, Alaskan Command.

Congressional Medal of Honor Recipients

Sergeant Benjamin Brown
Sergeant Cornelius H. Charlton
Sergeant John Ward, Seminole scout
Corporal Isaiah Mays
Private First Class William H. Thompson
Private Pompey Factor
Private Adam Paine
Trumpeter Isaac Payne

25TH INFANTRY REGIMENT

The 25th Infantry Regiment was formed from the 39th and 40th Infantry Regiments, which had been part of the military occupation forces in post–Civil War North Carolina and Louisiana. The 39th was activated at Jackson Barracks, Louisiana, in April 1866 under the command of Colonel Joseph A. Mower, Civil War commander of the Army of Georgia's 20th Corps.

Major General Nelson A. Miles directed the formation of the 40th Infantry Regiment from soldiers recruited in Virginia and the Carolinas. Miles soon became the regiment's first colonel, leading the regiment to several posts in North Carolina. Some idea of the low esteem many army personnel had for Black troops can be inferred by the transfer of the 40th Regiment in cattle and freight cars from Goldsboro, South Carolina, to New Orleans, a trip requiring 10 days. When the regimental commander complained to the quartermaster general, that officer replied that the officer in charge, Miles, was at fault for accepting substandard transportation.[25]

The 25th Infantry Regiment was formed by an act of Congress of March 3, 1869, consolidating the 39th and 40th Regiments in April at Jackson Barracks, Louisiana, under the command of Colonel Mower. The regiment was hardly a day old when Louisiana Governor H. C. Warmoth requested help putting down civil unrest by the white populace in Opelousas. In May 1870, the regiment, with a strength of 1,045 men, was ordered to San Antonio, Texas. The regiment marched to San Antonio, was given 10 days to rest and refit, and then resumed the march, with companies distributed across five small west Texas posts covering a 1,300-mile sector, with 400 miles on the Rio Grande. The regiment was posted on the Mexican border in Texas and New Mexico for the next 10 years, building roads and telegraph lines, providing two- to three-man details to guard stagecoach stations, and occasionally participating in operations against Indians. They were also charged with housekeeping duties such as wood chopping, construction, and maintenance chores and care of their mounts and equipment.

Between 1875 and 1880, the regiment worked with the 10th Cavalry in an unsuccessful effort to clear Native Americans from the *Llano Estacado*, the Staked Plains, a semi-arid high tableland and grassland traversing west Texas and eastern New Mexico. Companies and detachments of the regiment made brief, illegal raids across the Mexican border in pursuit of warriors or Mexican or American outlaws. Detachments of five or so men were stationed at stagecoach remount stations, not just to guard horses, but to ride shotgun on stagecoaches. In 1878, a detachment from the regiment entered Mexico on a punitive expedition.

In 1880, the regiment was transferred to Dakota Territory, which included Montana and Minnesota. Quartermaster General Montgomery Meigs observed that the transfer would likely be the death knell for any Black regiment, yet men of the 25th were soon skating happily on the frozen Missouri River near Fort Randall and were also stationed at Forts Meade and Hale. The soldiers adapted to the cold with buffalo hide greatcoats, but otherwise survived, dispersed at three posts in the northern Great Plains. Some companies guarded Northern Pacific Railroad crews. Company F provided disaster relief for nearly 800 hungry and homeless settlers along the Keya Paha River after extreme flooding in the spring of 1881.

After a Black soldier was lynched in Sturgis City, Dakota Territory, in August 1885, several troopers stationed at nearby Fort Meade went into town and shot up several houses of ill repute with the precision of a military firing squad. Local citizens complained to President Grover Cleveland, and the matter was referred to General Alfred H. Terry, commander of the Department of Dakota. Terry responded that Black soldiers were far less trouble than white soldiers and that in allowing brothels to operate in town, the townspeople were as much to blame as the soldiers. That was the end of the matter.[26]

The 25th Infantry served in Montana between 1888 and 1898, headquartered at Fort Missoula, with companies at Forts Shaw, Assiniboine, Harrison, and Custer. In 1889, regimental units helped prevent violence on the Flathead Indian Reservation near Ravalli, Montana, after an illegal incursion onto reservation lands by a sheriff's posse.

In December 1890, elements of the 25th Infantry joined the 9th Cavalry and 7th Cavalry in the last major Indian campaign against starving and destitute Lakota near Pine Ridge, South Dakota, at Wounded Knee Creek. Up to 300 Indians, nearly half of whom were women, children, and old men, were killed by artillery and 7th Cavalry troops under Colonel George A. Forsythe. Most of the band was disarmed, and half of those killed were women, children, and elders. Colonel Philip Harvey, the 25th Regiment's commander, noted, "there can be little doubt that the condition of destitution . . . brought about by reduced rations and the dishonesty and mismanagement of minor government officials had a far-reaching effect."[27] The government consistently reneged on its promises to honor its treaties with Native Americans, especially feeding and caring for the tribes. Rampant corruption among the Indian agents who were employed to provide the essential commodities agreed to by treaties to the tribes was a large part of the problem.

While some white officers assigned to the four regiments retained pre-existing prejudices, others learned to appreciate the sterling qualities of the troops they led. An example of racial bias was provided by the 25th Infantry's Lieutenant G. P. Ahern, who wrote a local newspaper while bivouacking with the regiment near Fort Keough, Montana, during the Pine Ridge campaign:

> Our "cullud" battalion here is under canvas and in fine shape for a winter campaign, and when Jack Frost freezes the mercury out of sight the gay and festive coon will be found ready to dance the "Virginia essence" and be ready to sing as joyfully as ever.[28]

In 1896, the War Department decided to explore the possibility of using bicycles instead of horses. In 1896, seven soldiers from the 25th Infantry under the command of Lieutenant James A. Moss took a 700-mile round trip from Fort Missoula, Montana, to Yellowstone National Park. The following year, 20 soldiers from the regiment rode 1,900 miles from Montana to Saint Louis, Missouri. When hostilities in Cuba ended, a 100-man-strong bicycle company from the 25th Infantry performed riot duty in Havana. Lieutenant Moss commanded the 367th Infantry Regiment, 92nd Infantry Division during World War I.

25th Infantry Regiment experimental bicycle contingent led by Lieutenant James Moss. SOURCE: LIBRARY OF CONGRESS.

A battalion of the 25th was deployed to Anaconda, Montana, to protect Northern Pacific Railroad property and break the strike in 1894. The editor of the local paper opined, "If soldiers had to be called out there could have been none better than the companies of the 25th Infantry who were encamped here. The prejudice against the colored soldiers seems to be without foundation, for if the 25th Infantry is an example of the colored regiments . . . there are no better troops in the service."[29]

The 25th Infantry was the first regiment to receive orders for Cuba, deploying in March 1898, a month before the declaration of war. By early May, all eight companies had arrived in Tampa, Florida, where they experienced Jim Crow "because they insist upon being treated as white men." Within a month of arriving in Cuba, nearly half the regiment came down with malaria. On July 1, the regiment was part of a 660-man assault force on the Spanish fort and 500 defenders at El Caney. Four companies participated in assaulting the fort and its trenches. Two privates from the regiment insisted they were first to enter the fort, seizing the Spanish flag. An officer of the 12th Infantry demanded the flag, leaving in doubt the question of who had conquered the position. The regiment lost one officer and six men in the attack. This was the regiment's only engagement of any import. The regiment landed on Long Island, New York, on August 22, and was assigned to posts in the southern Rockies, with headquarters and four companies at Fort Logan, Colorado, and companies in Arizona and New Mexico.

Late in 1889, the regiment was sent to the Philippines, the advance guard of 70,000 American troops who participated in the conflict against the nationalist movement of General Emilio Aguinaldo. The regiment lost one officer and nine enlisted men in this tour, more than its casualties in Cuba. The 25th had been officered exclusively by white officers until Corporal John E. Green passed the Army's officer examinations in July 1901 and was appointed to the rank of second lieutenant in the regiment. When the regiment returned from the Philippines in 1902, its 1st and 3rd Battalions were stationed at Fort Niobrara, Nebraska, with its 2nd Battalion at Fort Reno, Oklahoma. Three companies were deployed for the Coeur D'Alene mining strike in Idaho after President Benjamin Harrison declared martial law. The regiment was dispatched to assist in a labor dispute between the Northern Pacific Railroad and striking workers, tasked with "preventing disorder and guarding the trains and mail." Troopers were stationed from Fort Missoula to Billings to protect railroad property. Their conduct prompted high praise from the local press.

In May 1906, the War Department transferred the 25th Infantry to Texas. Headquarters and 2nd Battalion were located at Fort Bliss, near El Paso; the 3rd Battalion was at Fort McIntosh; and the 1st Battalion was at Fort Brown, near Brownsville, the center of the lower Rio Grande valley cattle range.

BROWNSVILLE, TEXAS, DISTURBANCE, 1906
When a battalion of the 25th Infantry Regiment was sent to Brownsville in the summer of 1906 to train with Texas National Guard units, the Army's commanding general in Texas warned, "The Citizens of Brownsville entertain race hatred to an extreme degree." The regiment's chaplain, Theophilus G. Steward, wrote, "Texas, I fear, means a quasi-battleground for the 25th."[30] Gunfire erupted in Brownsville in August 1906, killing a white bartender and wounding two others, including a Hispanic police officer. The local Cameron County grand jury thought that the Army's case was so flimsy that they refused to return any indictments against the soldiers. Soldiers of the 25th were *suspected* and without evidence, a hearing, or trial, President Theodore Roosevelt issued dishonorable discharges to 167 soldiers from three companies on no other basis than they *might* be guilty—including three soldiers who were on leave when the incident occurred. Some were veteran soldiers who had charged up San Juan Hill alongside Roosevelt and the Rough Riders, but all were denied pensions or benefits. After Roosevelt left office, 14 of the soldiers were reinstated by the War Department.

Boston lawyer A. E. Pillsbury declared, "they were not punished for not telling who the offenders were, but for not knowing who they were."[31] The *New York Word* editorialized, "The logic of the verdict is as clear as day. As the report reads, nobody is guilty; therefore, everyone is guilty; and everybody being guilty, nobody is innocent."[32] After Brownsville, a bill calling for the elimination of African Americans from the Army nearly passed in Congress, and Blacks began to abandon the Republican Party. President Nixon granted the men honorable discharges, with no compensation in 1972. The sole survivor, 87-year-old Dorsie W. Willis, stated, "It was a frame-up straight through. They checked our rifles, and they hadn't been fired."[33] Congress finally passed a bill granting Willis $25,000 and authorizing his treatment at Veterans Administration hospitals.[34]

In the summer of 1910, the 25th Infantry assisted the newly created Forest Service in fighting hundreds of fires across northern Idaho, western Montana, and eastern Washington. One company of the 25th Infantry was sent to Avery, Idaho, to suppress a fire threatening the town. After the fire, they assisted with cleanup and the search and recovery of the numerous dead. A 2015 PBS documentary, "The Big Burn," credited the men of the 25th Infantry with saving the town by building a backfire that extinguished the fire.

WORLD WAR I

Because of the Brownsville disturbance and two others involving the 24th Infantry in 1917, the 25th Infantry Regiment performed garrison duty at Schofield Barracks, Hawaii, during the First World War.

WORLD WAR II

The 25th Infantry Regiment was assigned to the 93rd Division, activated in California in May 1942 and trained at Fort Huachuca, Arizona. Advance elements deployed to Guadalcanal in the Pacific theater in January 1944. Along with the 93rd Division's 368th and 369th Infantry Regiments, the 25th Infantry campaigned in New Guinea, Northern Solomons (Bougainville), and the Bismarck Archipelago (Admiralty Islands), mostly conducting mop-up operations, unloading ships, and clearing battlefield damage. Due to General MacArthur's distrust of African American troops, in the main, the division was used as a rear echelon force, reflected in its combat losses: 12 men killed and 121 wounded. When the war ended, the regiment was demobilized at Camp Stoneman, California, in February 1946 with the rest of the 93rd division, leaving the 24th Infantry as the sole Buffalo Soldier regiment on active duty.

BUFFALO SOLDIERS' LEGACY

Historian Rayford Logan, in his *The Betrayal of the Negro from Rutherford B. Hayes to Woodrow Wilson*, observed that African Americans "had little, at the turn of the century to help sustain our faith in ourselves except the pride we took in the 9th and 10th Cavalry, the 24th and 25th Infantry. They were our Ralph Bunche, Marian Anderson, Joe Louis and Jackie Robinson."[35]

For many years, the record of Buffalo Soldiers' stalwart service to the nation, participating in over 200 confrontations and battles with Native

Americans, was lost to memory. Massive changes had taken place before Colin Powell, chairman of the Joint Chiefs of Staff, dedicated a monument to their achievements at Fort Leavenworth, Kansas, on July 25, 1992. General Powell remarked:

> Look at him, Soldier of the Nation—courageous, iron-willed, every bit the soldier that his white brother was. African Americans had answered the country's every call but had never before received the fame and fortune they deserve. The Buffalo Soldier believed that hatred and bigotry and prejudice could not defeat him, that . . . someday, through his efforts and the efforts of others to follow, future generations would know different.[36]

CONCLUSIONS

The Black regiments Congress authorized in 1866 demonstrated tremendous pride and professionalism, lasting for 85 years for the 24th Infantry Regiment. The other three were aborted earlier for various reasons. In a

Buffalo Soldier monument at Fort Riley, Kansas, dedicated by General Colin Powell. SOURCE: US ARMY PHOTOGRAPH, NATIONAL ARCHIVES & RECORDS ADMINISTRATION, COLLEGE PARK, MD.

time when African Americans were almost universally persecuted, these regular army units were the one institution in which Blacks took great pride. All four regiments consistently had the lowest desertion, alcoholism, and court-martial rates in the Army. Despite this, Black soldiers continued to be victims of racism and experienced a massive failure of American jurisprudence on more than one occasion.

Strangely, the soldiers themselves appear to have rarely used the nickname "Buffalo Soldiers." It appears to have been popularized by artist Frederic Remington and other journalists at the end of the 19th century and then appropriated by the 92nd Infantry Division in World War I.

While few Black soldiers rose through the ranks to become commissioned officers, three West Point graduates survived four years of intense racism and demonstrated leadership skills as good or better than fellow white cadets serving in the two cavalry regiments. Brigadier General Benjamin Oliver Davis Sr. served as an enlisted man in the Black cavalry before the turn of the last century and became the first African American to wear a star in 1940, paving the way for many others who followed. Integration has finally demonstrated the full capabilities of the African American soldier, which for those not blinded by racism had already been made clear during the War for Independence and the Civil War, as well as repeatedly during the four regiments' decades-long service in the West, Cuba, the Philippines, and the Mexican Punitive Expedition.

APPENDIX C

BLACK GENERAL OR FLAG-RANK OFFICERS

Although not complete, this list provides a good indication of the major contribution African Americans have made and continue to make to our national security leadership since Benjamin O. Davis Sr. was promoted to brigadier general in the US Army by President Franklin D. Roosevelt on October 25, 1940, on the eve of the 1940 presidential election. He was the first African American general in the history of the United States military, although West Point graduate Charles Young had been medically retired against his will in 1918 to avoid his promotion and his commanding white troops.

Since 1940, roughly 400 African American women and men have been appointed to flag rank. In addition to General Colin Powell serving as the Army's Chief of Staff during the Gulf Wars, the Trump administration appointed General Charles Q. Brown Jr. as the Air Force's chief of staff, and President Biden appointed retired general Lloyd James Austin III, secretary of defense.

While general officers are as sure sign of achievement and contribution, the number of Blacks promoted to field grade and company grade officers has changed markedly. Furthermore, it would be remiss not to mention that Black noncommissioned officers have become the backbone of most services. Integration has proven to be beneficial for the nation.

FOUR-STAR ARMY GENERALS, YEAR OF APPOINTMENT
Roscoe C. Robinson Jr., 1982
Colin Powell, 1989
Johnnie E. Wilson, 1996
Larry R. Ellis, 2001
William Ward, 2006
Lloyd J. Austin, 2010—first Black secretary of defense, 2021
Dennis L. Via, 2012
Vincent K. Brooks, 2013

OTHER ARMY GENERALS
Lieutenant General Arthur J. Gregg
Lieutenant General Henry Doctor Jr.,
    Inspector General of the U.S. Army
Lieutenant General Calvin Augustine Hoffman Waller
Lieutenant General Julius W. Becton, Jr.
Lieutenant General Edward Honor Sr.
Lieutenant General Marvin Delano Brailsford
Lieutenant General Andrew Phillip Chambers Jr.
Lieutenant General James Reginald Hall Jr.
Lieutenant General Robert Earl Gray
Lieutenant General Joe Nathan Ballard
Lieutenant General Samuel Emanuel Ebbesen
Lieutenant General Billy King Solomon
Lieutenant General Larry R. Jordan Jr.
Lieutenant General Russel L. Honoré After retiring, commanded
    Joint Task Force Katrina and led investigation into January 6, 2012,
    attack on the Capitol
Lieutenant General Alonzo Earl Short Jr.
Lieutenant General Michael D. Rochelle
Major General Fred A. Gordon
Major General Frederic E. Davison, first African American to become a
    division commander and attain the rank of major general.
Major General John Q. Taylor King
Brigadier General Dallas Brown, Russian Foreign Area Officer

FOUR-STAR NAVY ADMIRALS, YEAR OF APPOINTMENT
Joseph Paul Reason, 1997

Cecil Eugene Diggs Haney, 2012
Michelle Janine Howard, 2020

OTHER NAVY ADMIRALS
Vice Admiral Samuel Lee Gravely, first Black admiral in 1971
Vice Admiral David L. Brewer, III
Rear Admiral Barry C. Black, Chaplain, U.S. Senate chaplain 27 years after retirement
Rear Admiral Lawrence Chambers
Rear Admiral Lillian Elaine Fishburne
Rear Admiral John W. Smith Jr.
Rear Admiral Gerald Eustis Thomas
Rear Admiral Annie Belle Andrews
Rear Admiral Victor G. Guillory

FOUR-STAR AIR FORCE GENERALS, YEAR OF APPOINTMENT
Daniel "Chappie" James, 1975
Bernard P. Randolph, 1987
Lloyd W. Newton, 1997
Benjamin Oliver Davis Jr., 1998*
Lester Lyles, 1999
Edward A. Rice Jr., 2010
Larry O. Spencer, 2014
Edward A. Rice Jr.
Charles Q. Brown Jr.

* President Clinton reactivated Benjamin Oliver Davis Jr. (1918–2002) in 1998 to award him a fourth star. Davis was the son of the first Black general officer and the fourth Black graduate of West Point (Class of 1936). In 1941, Davis was among the first Tuskegee Airmen. He commanded the 99th Pursuit Squadron, flying tactical missions in the Mediterranean and European theater. Davis also commanded the 332nd Fighter Group, which escorted bombers in the European theater and as the war was ending, the 477th Bombardment Group (M) (Colored). By war's end, Davis's airmen flew more than 15,000 sorties, shot down 112 enemy planes, and destroyed or damaged 273 more on the ground at a cost of 66 of their own. He retired from active military service in 1970.

OTHER AIR FORCE GENERALS
Lieutenant General Darren W. McDew, 2014
Lieutenant General Richard M. Clark, first Black superintendent of the
    Air Force Academy, June 2020
Brigadier General Francis Xavier Taylor

COAST GUARD ADMIRALS
Vice Admiral Manson K. Brown
Rear Admiral Erroll Mingo Brown
Rear Admiral Stephen W. Rochon

OTHER UNIFORMED SERVICES
Rear Admiral Evelyn J. Fields, National Oceanic and
    Atmospheric Administration
Vice Admiral Regina Marcia Benjamin, Public Health Service
Vice Admiral Joycelyn M. Elders, Public Health Service
Vice Admiral Audrey F. Manley, Public Health Service
Vice Admiral David Sacher, Public Health Service

US MARINE CORPS
Marine generals are listed last to emphasize the long path the Corps has traveled since January 1942, when Marine Corps Commandant General Thomas Holcomb bluntly declared:

> The Negro race has every opportunity now to satisfy its aspirations for combat in the Army . . . and their desire to enter the naval service is, I think, to break into a club that doesn't want them.

Fortunately for America, despite rampant racism, African Americans wanted to serve their country regardless of how badly the Corps treated them. Blacks began their long, distinguished service record in the Marine Corps during World War II in the face of considerable opposition.

General Michael Langley, United States Africa Command
General Walter E. Gaskin: Graduate of Naval Reserve Officer Training
    Corps program at Savannah State University; retired in 2013, after

serving 39 years in the Corps. Gaskin was the fourth African American in Marine Corps history to achieve three stars.

Lieutenant General Frank E. Petersen Jr.: First African American Marine Corps aviator and the first African American Marine Corps general, retiring from the Corps after 38 years of service. In 2010, President Obama appointed Petersen to the Board of Visitors of the United States Naval Academy.

Lieutenant General Willie J. Williams: When he retired with more than 40 years of service, he had been director of the Marine Corps staff for over five years, advising two commandants and working with senior military leaders.

Lieutenant General Vincent R. Stewart: 20th director of the Defense Intelligence Agency and former commander, Joint Functional Component Command for Intelligence, Surveillance and Reconnaissance. He also served as the commander of Marine Forces Cyber Command.

Lieutenant General Ronald L. Bailey: Deputy commandant for Plans, Policies and Operations; first Black commander of the First Marine Division.

Major General Charles F. Bolden: Fighter pilot, astronaut, and former NASA administrator.

Major General Craig Crenshaw: Commanding general, Marine Corps Logistics Command.

Major General Arnold Fields: Deputy commander of Marine Corps Forces in Europe, Stuttgart, Germany; retired from the Marine Corps in January 2004 after 34-plus years of active military service.

Major General Anthony L. Jackson: Commanded Marine Corps Installations West; retired after more than 36 years of service.

Major General Clifford L. Stanley: First African American to command a regiment; served 33 years in uniform, retiring as the deputy commanding general, Marine Corps Combat Development Command, Quantico, Virginia.

Major General Craig Q. Timberlake: Enlisted in the Marine Corps in 1977 and was promoted to staff sergeant in January 1982. Two years later, he was commissioned through the Enlisted Commissioning Program, and he commanded the 3rd Marine Division.

Major General Leo V. Williams III: Retired after 33.5 years of service, deputy commanding general, Marine Corps Combat Development Command, Quantico, Virginia.

Major General Cornell Wilson Jr.: Deputy J-3 for Central Command in Tampa, Florida, from September to December 2002 in support of Operation Enduring Freedom; deputy commander, Marine Corps Forces Command on retiring.

Brigadier General Lorna M. Mahlock: First Black female Marine Corps brigadier general in March 2019; born in Kingston, Jamaica, immigrated to Brooklyn, and enlisted. Director, Command, Control, Communications and Computers (C4) and the Department of the Navy deputy chief information officer, Marine Corps.

Brigadier General Terry Van Williams: Became the first African American to command Parris Island boot camp and the Eastern Recruiting Region in June 2014.

Brigadier General Anthony Henderson

Brigadier General Ahmed T. Williamson: Military assistant to the Marine Corps assistant commandant.

STATE ADJUTANTS GENERAL

State adjutant generals command state military forces, including Army National Guard, Air Force National Guard, naval and other reserve components, and state defense forces in peacetime. Appointed by the state governor (respective state and date of appointment):

Major General Errol R. Schwartz (District of Columbia 2008)
Major General Michael A. Calhoun (Florida 2005)
Brigadier General Joseph C. Carter (Massachusetts 2007)

ARMY NATIONAL GUARD

Brigadier General Walter W. Whitfield, Illinois National Guard
Brigadier General Julia Jeter Cleckley, National Guard Bureau Military Personnel Branch
Brigadier General Rufus Smith, Ohio National Guard
Brigadier General Owen Monconduit, Commander, 225th Engineer Brigade, Louisiana National Guard
David Fleming, Delaware National Guard
Brigadier General Wayne L. Black, Indiana National Guard

AIR NATIONAL GUARD

Lieutenant General Russell C. Davis
Major General James T. Whitehead, Jr.

Major General Garry C. Dean
Major General James T. Whitehead, Jr.

GRADUATES OF HISTORICALLY BLACK COLLEGES AND UNIVERSITIES (HBCUS)

Reserve Officer Training Corps (ROTC) programs exist at 1,700 colleges and universities across the country. ROTC programs at 25 of the country's 102 HBCUs have produced thousands of officers, as well as enlisted men, with a record of distinguished service to our national security.

Retired Army General Carter Ham, president and CEO of the Association of the United States Army, the Army's nonprofit advocacy arm, observed recently, "HBCUs as a group value service, perhaps more so than other groupings of colleges and universities, perhaps with the sole exception of the service academies. The ethos of service instilled in HBCU students seems to be a natural fit for ROTC." By any measure, the number of general officers produced by HBCUs is remarkable.

ROCKS, Inc., provided the information detailed in the remainder of this appendix. The organization was founded on October 9, 1974, under the leadership of Brigadier Roscoe C. Cartwright, the Army's third Black general officer, and 65 other Army officers in Washington, D.C., to foster promising officers' careers. Founded on October 9, 1974, by 65 Army officers in Washington, DC, under the leadership of Brigadier General Roscoe C. Cartwright, the Army's third Black general officer. ROCKS' mission is to foster promising officers' careers. With over 1,100 members, it is the largest professional military officers' organization with majority African American membership. Its headquarters are in Forestville, Maryland. Some of the graduates which HCBUs have produced are listed below.

Alabama A&M University
General Patrick Burden

Bowie State University
Major General Robert Harding

Central State University
Major General Fredric Leigh
Major General Fred C. Sheffey

Florida A&M University
Major General Eugene Cormartie
Major General William Russ

Fort Valley State University
Major General Jerome Johnson

Hampton University
Lieutenant General Robert Ferrell
Major General Wallace Arnold
Major General Rudolph Francis
Major General Arthur Holmes
Major General Charles Hood
Major General Darrell K. Williams

Howard University
General John Hawkins
Major General Cunningham Bryant
Brigadier General Melvin Byrd
Brigadier General Nowell V. Coots
Major General Frederick Davison
Major General Robert Gaskill, Sr.
Major General Michael Harrison, Sr.
Brigadier General David Hamlar
Brigadier General Guthrie Turner

Jackson State University
Brigadier General Eddie Cain
Brigadier General Robert Crear
Major General Reuben Jones
Brigadier General Donna Williams

Lincoln University
Brigadier General Donald L. Scott
Brigadier General Julius F. Johnson

Mississippi Valley State University
Major General Everett H. Thomas

Morgan State University
General Larry R. Ellis
Lieutenant General Allen E. Chandler
Lieutenant General William "Kip" Ward
Lieutenant General Raymond Scott Dingle
Major General Arthur Dean
Major General Thomas Levi Prather
Major General Jackson Rozier
Major General Bennie Williams
Brigadier General Avon C. James
Brigadier General Talmadge J. Jacob
Brigadier General George M. Brooks

Norfolk State University
Rear Admiral Evelyn Fields
Major General LaWarren Patterson
Lieutenant General Michael Rochelle

North Carolina A&T State University
Major General Hawthorne Proctor
Major General Charles D. Bussey
Major General Reginal G. Clemmons
Brigadier General Voneree Deloatch
Brigadier General Clara Adams-Ender

Prairie View A&M University
Lieutenant General Marvin D. Brailsford
Lieutenant General Julius W. Becton Jr.
Lieutenant General Billy K. Solomon
Lieutenant General Calvin Augustine Hoffman Waller
Vice Admiral Dave Brewer
Major General Julius Parker Jr.
Brigadier General James Cheatham
Brigadier General Johnnie Forte Jr.

Savannah State University
Rear Admiral Willie Metts
Lieutenant General Walter E. Gaskin

South Carolina State
Lieutenant General Henry Doctor
Major General George Bowman
RADM John Smith
Major General Stephen Twitty
Major General Arnold Fields
Major General Clifford Stanley
Major General Abraham Turner
Major General James Klugh
Major General Larry Knightner
Major General Harold Mitchel
Brigadier General Nolen Bivens
Brigadier General Bruce Crawford
Brigadier General Richard Dix
Brigadier General Amos M. Gailliard
Brigadier General Norman Green
Brigadier General Kenneth Hubbard
Brigadier General Frederick Johnson
Brigadier General Julius Lawton
Brigadier General Ervin Pearson
Brigadier General George Price

Southern University and A&M College
Lieutenant General Joe Ballard
Lieutenant General Edward Honor
Lieutenant General Russel Honoré
Major General Charles Honoré
Major General Gregory Rountree
Major General Isaac D. Smith
Brigadier General Sherian Grace Cadoria, first Black female general
Brigadier General Don Delandro
Brigadier General Jude Patin

Texas A&M University-Corpus Christi
Lieutenant General Larry Wyche

Tuskegee University
General Daniel "Chappie" James Jr. (1920–1978): Was the first Black Air Force African American general.
General Mark A. Brown
Major General Oliver Dillard
Major General Ernest Harrell
Major General Charles Williams

Virginia State University
General Dennis L. Via
Lieutenant General Alonzo E. Short Jr.
Major General Ernest R. Morgan
Major General W. Montague Winfield
Brigadier General Alfred F. Abramson III
Brigadier General Shelia Baxter
Brigadier General Leo Brooks
Brigadier General Alfred J. Cade
Brigadier General Charles R. Hamilton
Brigadier General Bert Holmes

West Virginia State College
Major General Kenneth Gray
Major General Edward Greer
Major General James Monroe
Major General Charles C. Rogers, Medal of Honor recipient
Major General Harvey Williams
Major General Joseph Turner
Brigadier General Frank Bacon Jr.
Brigadier General Dallas Brown, Russian foreign area officer
Brigadier General Walter Johnson III
Brigadier General Earl Simms
Brigadier General Robert Stephens Jr.

Xavier University
Lieutenant General Michael X. Garrett

APPENDIX D

Phantoms of the Alaskan Highway

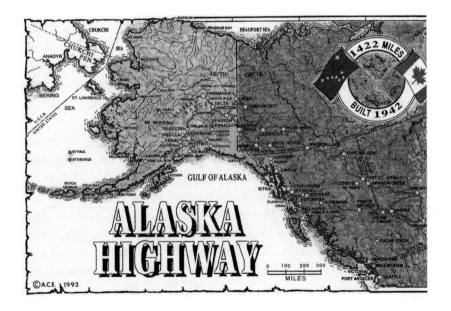

Map of Alaska.

Although a road connecting Alaska to the "lower forty-eight" had been discussed since the 1920s, the Japanese attack on Pearl Harbor put the project on overdrive. President Roosevelt approved construction of this

1600-mile road through virgin forest crossed by hundreds or rivers and streams through the Canadian Rockies on March 9, 1942. No one knew how long it would take to construct the "Alcan Highway," the project's initial name. Some predicted that a survey would take a year. The International Highway Commission disapproved of the route the US Army Corps of Engineers selected but said construction would take five to six years. Brigadier General William M. Hoge, the engineer entrusted with overseeing construction, originally estimated that a survey alone would take a year, but subsequently agreed to a shorter target. The "rough cut" pioneer road to the east of the Rockies was completed in eight months and 21 days.

The Alaska Highway has been compared to the construction of the Panama Canal. This miracle was accomplished by eight US Army Engineer Construction Regiments, half of them Black. Approximately 20,000 civilian workers did the finish work—15,900 white American Public Roads Agency contractors and 3,700 Canadian workers whose pay dwarfed that of Army enlisted men. A reporter noted that carpenters made $500 to $800 a month, welders and mechanics $800 to $900, plumbers $1,000 to $1,200, and cooks $600. Even camp waiters and dishwashers received $250 to $300 a month, while enlisted men made less than $100 each month. Although civilian workers made more money in one or two days than the soldiers did each month, civilian workers left in droves before their contract was up due to the harsh working conditions. Soldiers didn't have that option.

Three Black Engineer General Service Regiment (Separate) were created early in 1941: the 93rd at Camp Livingston, Louisiana, February 10; the 97th at Eglin Field, Florida on February 22; and the 95th at Fort Belvoir, Virginia, on February 28 and transported north with their heavy equipment on troop trains. Moving every three days, they worked 7 days a week, 16 hours a day. They endured mosquitoes, black flies, heat, treacherous peat bogs, melting permafrost, and mud in summer, then glacial ice, snow, and sub-zero temperatures in winter. In addition, the Black 388th Engineer Construction Regiment, formed at Camp Claiborne, Louisiana, worked in every capacity including as stevedores on the Canol Pipeline from Norman Wells, Northwest Territory to a refinery at Whitehorse, Yukon, helping bring in nearly sixty producing wells. This project was ultimately connected to the Alaska Highway.

Each regiment was allocated twenty D-8 diesel, 10 feet tall Caterpillar bulldozers with 21-foot blades, 24 four D-4 gas bulldozers and R-4 tractors, two half-yard power shovels, 50 to 90 dump trucks, 12 pickup trucks, 6 tractor-drawn graders, 3 patrol graders, 6 rooter plows and six 12-yard-carrying scrapers. Each regiment was also equipped with one portable sawmill, concrete mixers, one truck crane, six 12-cubic-yard carryalls, and two pile drivers, a variety of other vehicles, plus an allocation of construction tools, shovels and axes. Typically, the larger equipment worked 20 to 22 hours daily, stopping only two hours for maintenance; their appetite for fuel was prodigious, and the task of keeping them supplied was a constant challenge. The regiments gouged a 60– to 90-foot slash through virgin woodland with these monsters, to be paved later by the Public Roads Agency and other contractors.

Because travel by airplane was intermittent, as were radio-telephone transmissions, the Army installed 2,000 miles of telephone line from Edmonton to Fairbanks. General Hoge supervised the toughest section of the road, from Watson Lake, just north of the Yukon-British Columbia border, to Big Delta, just south of Fairbanks, Alaska. Brigadier General James A. ("Patsy") O'Connor commanded the 800-mile Southern Sector, served by the Black 95th Engineer Regiment and the white 35th and 341st Regiments. Although the 95th was the best trained of the three Black regiments, it was directed to give up its equipment to the white 341st Regiment, formed three months previously. The 95th followed behind the 341st, grading, building bridges, and installing culverts, often eight or ten per mile.

Two Black regiments (the 93rd and 97th) and two white (the 18th and 340th) constructed the 800 miles through the northern sector's more difficult terrain. General Simon Bolivar Buckner, whose father surrendered to General Grant at Vicksburg, didn't welcome Black soldiers to Alaska, nor did he want to equip them. He was most concerned with contact with natives and "miscegenation." Two feet of snow was on the ground when the 97th disembarked from a troopship in April 1942 in the tiny fishing village of Valdez. The 97th's commander rejected the fleet of used trucks assigned and requisitioned new ones, which never arrived. Although the Army abolished segregated latrines in October 1942, the 97th used latrines with separate entrances marked for white officers, white enlisted men, and Black troops.

On September 24, crews from the Black 35th and the white 340th regiments met on the bank of Contact Creek. Days earlier, the deputy chief engineer combined the northern and southern segments, sacking General Hoge and tasking the engineers with cutting a road to Haines,

Alaska, building a road from Johnson's Crossing to the oilfields at Norman Wells and improving the rough cut through the forest and across rivers. That meant 8,000 engineers would remain for the arctic winter, the coldest winter ever recorded in northwest Canada and Alaska starting in October. Soldiers slept with their down-filled parkas in their "double mummy" sleeping bags with two blankets and a comforter, plus artic underwear, gloves, a sweater, and multiple layers of socks with oversize boots to keep them pliable. Black troops also had to contend with relentless racism and inferior supplies, sleeping in canvas tents in weather 40 to 60 degrees below zero while white soldiers had Quonset huts—or barracks built for them by Black engineers. At forty below, skin froze in seconds. The record cold increased the likelihood of a vehicle breakdown, and in such a case,, it was a life-threatening situation. Snow and ice made travel treacherous on many of the rough-hewn grades, and ice welled up and had to be removed to pass safely. In one case, a white officer ordered ten Blacks into the back of an open truck for a 130-mile drive. Knowing the ride would kill or maim them, all refused and were court-martialed and sentenced to twenty years at hard labor. The arctic cold was a killer.

The 93rd's commander had nothing but praise when he left the regiment: "The record of the 93rd Engineers speaks for itself—240 miles of Alcan Highway constructed from June 5, 1942, to October 1, 1942 . . . through muskeg,* mountains, and deep canyons." He noted that the Army's assistant chief of engineers had declared that 93rd 's section of the road was "The best section of road on the Alcan Highway," recommending his regiment for a Meritorious Unit Citation. The 95th's commander reported to General O'Connor:

> The commendable performance of the 95th Engineer General Service Regiment while stationed at Dawson Creek Railhead and Depot should not pass unrecognized. For a period of four months this Regiment provided the bulk of the labor necessary to the establishment and operation of this section of the roadway.

* North American swamp or bog consisting of a mixture of water and partly dead vegetation, frequently covered by a layer of sphagnum or other mosses, generally acting like quicksand.

News of Blacks' participation was largely suppressed until the *Chicago Defender* sent a reporter north to describe "the world's greatest monument to Negro labor . . . with the sweat of 4,000 Black brows." FBI Director J. Edgar Hoover saw the Black press as enemies of the state, a threat to national security, and the maintenance of the "Jim Crow" status quo. Hoover orchestrated a hearing before a select congressional committee on this danger and demanded that Attorney General Francis Biddle indict the African American press for treason. Fortunately, *Chicago Defender* editor John Sengstacke conferred with Biddle and reached an agreement that if the Black press agreed not to "escalate the campaign for equality" during the war, they would not be prosecuted under the Espionage Act. This agreement certainly constituted a serious infringement on African Americans' First Amendment rights.

The Black units' performance changed General Buchner's opinion: he ordered the removal of Confederate flags and directed the 93rd to complete construction projects in the Aleutians. Once their efforts were completed, all four Black regiments departed for other theaters. Two deployed to the Pacific and two to Europe, where some soldiers volunteered for combat roles during the Battle of the Bulge. All four got excellent reviews—but continued to be exposed to racism.

General Hoge went on to a distinguished career, commanding the Provisional Engineer Special Brigade Group during the assault on Omaha Beach. He later commanded Combat Command B of the 9th Armored Division in its heroic actions in the Ardennes during the Battle of the Bulge, stopping the German offensive at St. Vith and capturing the Ludendorff Bridge over the Rhine River at Remagen. By war's end, Hoge commanded the 4th Armored Division and, at the request of General Matthew Ridgway, Eighth Army commander, Hoge commanded IX Corps during the Korean War. Promoted to full general in October 1953, Hoge retired as Commander-in-Chief of United States Army Europe in January 1955.

Blacks' participation in this grand project remained undiscovered until April, 1993, when Colin Powell declared, "I had no idea black men had done anything like this." Powell ensured that the essential role Black troops played in the construction of the Alaska Highway was recognized on June 14, 1993, when ALCAN veterans were honored at the Pentagon. Congress finally passed a joint resolution recognizing Blacks' major contribution in January 2005 and their participation in the construction of the Alaska Highway was finally recognized by the Alaska legislature in 2017.

Sources: Christine and Dennis McClure, *We Fought the Road*. Epicenter Press, 2017.

Heath Twitchell, *Northwest Epic: The Building of the Alaska Highway*. St. Martin's Press, 1992.

John Virtue, *The Black Soldiers who Built the Alaska Highway: A History of Four U.S. Army Regiments in the North, 1942-1943*. McFarland, 2013.

APPENDIX E

The Highest and Purest Democracy

Eulogy by Rabbi Roland B. Gittlesohn at the Dedication of the 5th Marine Division cemetery on Iwo Jima, 21 March 1945

5th Marine Division cemetery. SOURCE: HTTPS://WWW.NATIONALWW2MUSEUM.ORG/WAR/ARTICLES/GITTELSOHN-IWO-JIMA-EULOGY.

This is perhaps the grimmest, and surely the holiest task we have faced since D-Day. Here before us lie the bodies of comrades and friends. Men who until yesterday or last week laughed with us, joked with us, trained with us. Men who were on the same ships with us, and went over the sides with us, as we prepared to hit the beaches of this island. Men who fought with us and feared with us. Somewhere in this plot of ground there may lie the individual who could have discovered the cure for cancer. Under one of these Christian crosses, or beneath a Jewish Star of David, there may rest now an individual who was destined to be a great prophet to find the way, perhaps, for all to live in plenty, with poverty and hardship for none. Now they lie here silently in this sacred soil, and we gather to consecrate this earth in their memory.

It is not easy to do so. Some of us have buried our closest friends here. We saw these men killed before our very eyes. Any one of us might have died in their places. Indeed, some of us are alive and breathing at this very moment only because men who lie here beneath us, had the courage and strength to give their lives for ours. To speak in memory of such men as these is not easy. Of them, too, can it be said with utter truth: "The world will little note nor long remember what we say here. It can never forget what they did here."

No, our poor power of speech can add nothing to what these men and the other dead of our division who are not here have already done. All that we can even hope to do is follow their example. To show the same selfless courage in peace that they did in war. To swear that, by the grace of God and the stubborn strength and power of human will, their sons and ours shall never suffer these pains again. These men have done their job well. They have paid the ghastly price of freedom. If that freedom be once again lost, as it was after the last war, the unforgivable blame will be ours, not theirs. So it be the living who are here to be dedicated and consecrated.

We dedicate ourselves, first, to live together in peace the way they fought and are buried in war. Here lie men who loved America because their ancestors, generations ago helped in her founding, and other men who loved her with equal passion because they themselves or their own fathers escaped from oppression to her blessed shores. Here lie officers and [privates], [Blacks] and whites, rich and poor . . . together. Here are Protestants, Catholics, and Jews . . . together. Here no man prefers another because of his faith or despises him because of his color. Here there are no quotas of how many from each group are admitted or allowed. Among these men there is no discrimination. No prejudice. No hatred. Theirs is the highest and purest democracy.

Anyone among us the living who fails to understand that, will thereby betray those who lie here. Whoever of us lifts his hand in hate against another or thinks himself superior to those who happen to be in the minority, makes of this ceremony and of the bloody sacrifice it commemorates, an empty, hollow mockery. To this, them, as our solemn, sacred duty, do we the living now dedicate ourselves: to the right of Protestants, Catholics, and Jews, of all races alike, to enjoy the democracy for which all of them have here paid the price.

To one thing more do we consecrate ourselves in memory of those who sleep beneath these crosses and stars. We shall not foolishly suppose, as did the last generation of America's fighting, that victory on the battlefield will automatically guarantee the triumph of democracy at home. This war, with all its frightful heartache and suffering, is but the beginning of our generation's struggle for democracy. When the last battle has been won, there will be those at home, as there were last time, who will want us to turn our backs in selfish isolation on the rest of organized humanity, and thus to sabotage the very peace for which we fight. We promise you who lie here; we will not do that. We will join hands with Britain, China, Russia—in peace, even as we have in war, to build the kind of world for which you died.

When the last shot has been fired, there will still be those eyes that are turned backward not forward, who will be satisfied with those wide extremes of poverty and wealth in which the seeds of another war can breed. We promise you, our departed comrades: this, too, we will not permit. This war has been fought by the common man; its fruits of peace must be enjoyed by the common man. We promise, by all that is sacred and holy, that your sons, the sons of miners and millers, the sons of farmers and workers—will inherit from your death the right to a living that is decent and secure.

When the final cross has been placed in the last cemetery, once again there will be those to whom profit is more important than peace, who will insist with the voice of sweet reasonableness and appeasement that it is better to trade with the enemies of mankind than, by crushing them, to lose their profit. To you who sleep here silently, we give our promise: we will not listen: We will not forget that some of you were burnt with oil that came from American wells, that many of you were killed by shells fashioned from American steel. We promise that when once again people seek profit at your expense, we shall remember how you looked when we placed you reverently, lovingly, in the ground.

Thus do we memorialize those who, having ceased living with us, now live within us. Thus do we consecrate ourselves, the living, to carry on the struggle they began. Too much blood has gone into this soil for us to let it lie barren. Too much pain and heartache have fertilized the earth on which we stand. We here solemnly swear: this shall not be in vain. Out of this, and from the suffering and sorrow of those who mourn this, will come—we promise—the birth of a new freedom for all humanity everywhere. And let us say . . . Amen.

—Rabbi Roland Gittelsohn

Museum of World War II's Comments:

The United States Marine Corps abounds in heroes and leaders: Puller, Vandegrift, Basilone, LeJeune, Cates, Shepherd, Shoup, Krulak, DelValle, . . . the list goes on. The battle history of the Marine Corps is similarly filled with places that stand out in American military history, like Tripoli, Belleau Wood, Wake, Guadalcanal, Tarawa, Peleliu, Chosin, Khe Sahn, Hue, Fallujah, and others.

Iwo Jima stands out above all of the rest because of the sheer heroism behind every rock and in every foxhole and in every pair of filthy, bloodstained dungarees, heroism that stood out so often that Admiral Chester Nimitz said before the battle was over, "uncommon valor was a common virtue." This battle stands out for the sheer amount of American blood spilt in the 36 days on that one sulfur island in the vast Pacific Ocean. It was a name that none of those who fought on the island had heard of before, but a name that none of the survivors could ever forget. Over 26,000 Americans were casualties on Iwo Jima, more casualties than the defending Japanese, the only time that imbalance occurred in the Pacific War.

After the battle was over, three cemeteries were established on the island, one for each division that fought there. The 5th Marine Division's Protestant Chaplain, Warren Cuthriel, asked his colleague, Jewish Rabbi Roland Gittelsohn, to prepare and deliver a sermon at the dedication ceremony for the 5th Marine Division's cemetery. Rabbi Gittelsohn worked through the night, but the prejudice of the day reigned as the other Protestant and Catholic chaplains objected that a Jewish Rabbi would deliver the sermon in a mostly Christian cemetery. Gittelsohn spared his friend embarrassment and did not deliver his sermon during the dedication but did deliver it to his Jewish congregation at their own ceremony. Chaplain Cuthriel obtained Gittelsohn's sermon and, deeply moved at what he read, forwarded a copy of the Rabbi's sermon up the chain of command.

When Gittelsohn's sermon reached more receptive eyes, the power and depth of his words quickly spread. Newspapers from coast to coast printed the sermon in its entirety. Radio announcers across the breadth of the country read it as the rabbi's poetic, forward-thinking prose fell on astonished and deeply touched American ears.

It was after the fighting on Iwo Jima was over that Gittelsohn truly made his mark on history. The sermon he wrote for the fallen has become Marine Corps legend, and holds a hallowed place in the archives of the Corps. His thoughts were nearly revolutionary in the mid-1940s. Today, the words that Rabbi Gittelsohn spoke over his deceased warrior comrades are no less true and even more important to the ideals of democracy.

Source: https://www.nationalww2museum.org/war/articles/gittelsohn-iwo-jima-eulogy

NOTES

CHAPTER 1
1. Bernard C. Nalty, *Strength for the Fight: A History of Black Americans in the Military* (New York: Free Press, 1986), 6.
2. Ibid.
3. Sidney Kaplan and Emma Nogrady Kaplan, *The Black Presence in the Era of the American Revolution* (Amherst: University of Massachusetts Press, 1989), 8.
4. John U. Rees, *"They Were Good Soldiers": African Americans Serving in the Continental Army* (Warwick, UK: Helion & Company, 2019), 25.
5. Nalty, *Strength for the Fight*, 10; Rees, "They Were Good Soldiers," 29.
6. Michael Lee Lanning, *Defenders of Liberty: African Americans in the Revolutionary War* (New York: Citadel Press, 2000), 45.
7. Ibid., 67.
8. Nalty, *Strength for the Fight*, 11.
9. Thomas Fleming, *A Disease of the Public Mind: A New Understanding of Why We Fought the Civil War* (New York: Da Capo Press, 2013), 40; Gail Buckley, *American Patriots: The Story of Blacks in the Military from the Revolution to Desert Storm* (New York: Random House, 2002), 27; Lanning, *Defenders of Liberty*, 68, Appendix G, 203.
10. Lou Potter, William Miles, and Nina Rosenblum, *Liberators: Fighting on Two Fronts in World War II* (Orlando, FL: Harcourt, Brace Jovanovich, 1992), 5.

11. Lanning, *Defenders of Liberty*, 67.
12. Ibid., 69.
13. Ibid., 71.
14. Ibid.
15. Ibid., 72.
16. Rees, "They Were Good Soldiers," 27.
17. Lanning, *Defenders of Liberty*, 75. Lanning notes that the 1st Rhode Island continued to serve for nearly two years after Yorktown. In February 1783, the unit participated in the arduous winter campaign to capture the British trading post at Oswego on Lake Ontario. They remained in New York until discharged at Saratoga, more than five years after the first enlistees had volunteered to serve in exchange for their freedom. Colonel Olney, their commander, praised his soldiers for "faithfully persevering in the best of causes . . . with unexampled fortitude and patience through all the dangers and toils of a long and severe war." He also conceded that they had never received the bounties promised by the Rhode Island General Assembly, nor had their pay been equal to white soldiers'. There was no welcome-home parade; most Rhode Islanders apparently believed freedom alone was ample recompense for faithful service. Some even had to fight efforts of former masters to re-enslave them.
18. Ibid., 78; Buckley, *American Patriots*, 25. During the Revolutionary War, "battalion" and "regiment" were often used interchangeably.
19. Lanning, *Defenders of Liberty*, 79.
20. Nalty, *Strength for the Fight*, 15.
21. Potter et al., *Liberators: Fighting on Two Fronts in World War II*, 6.
22. Rees, "They Were Good Soldiers," 36, fn; Potter et al., *Liberators: Fighting on Two Fronts in World War II*, 6; Lanning, *Defenders of Liberty*, 177.
23. Lanning, *Defenders of Liberty*, 177.
24. Bonnie Watson Coleman, "Let's Honor the Black and Indigenous Soldiers Who Helped Win Our Independence," *Washington Post*, July 6, 2021, A19.
25. Buckley, *American Patriots*, 5.
26. Ibid., xvii.
27. Potter et al., *Liberators: Fighting on Two Fronts in World War II*, 5.
28. Rees, "They Were Good Soldiers," 30.
29. Ibid.

30. Benjamin Quarles, *The Negro in the American Revolution* (Chapel Hill: University of North Carolina Press, 1961), 78; Rees, "They Were Good Soldiers," 30; Kaplan and Kaplan, *The Black Presence in the Era of the American Revolution*, 34.
31. Burke Davis, *Black Heroes of the American Revolution* (San Diego, CA: Odyssey Books, 1976), 3–4.
32. Lanning, *Defenders of Liberty*, 15.
33. Davis, *Black Heroes of the American Revolution*, 21–22; David Barton, "Black Patriots of the American Revolution," The Massachusetts Society Sons of the American Revolution (blog) accessed June 1, 2021, https://www.massar.org/2011/05/07/black-patriots-of-the-american-revolution.
34. Davis, *Black Heroes of the American Revolution*, 9–10.
35. Lanning, *Defenders of Liberty*, 90.
36. Ibid., 178.
37. Ibid., 92.
38. Ibid., 89.
39. Ibid., 20, 95–96.
40. Ibid., 130; Quarles, *The Negro in the American Revolution*, 95.
41. Davis, *Black Heroes of the American Revolution*, 58.
42. Ibid.; Lanning, *Defenders of Liberty*, 129.
43. Lanning, *Defenders of Liberty*, 132.
44. Rees, "They Were Good Soldiers," 17.
45. Potter et al., *Liberators: Fighting on Two Fronts in World War II*, 5.
46. Buckley, *American Patriots*, 34.
47. Ibid., 28.
48. Lanning, *Defenders of Liberty*, 151.
49. Ibid.
50. Ibid., 160–61.
51. Buckley, *American Patriots*, 44.
52. Ibid., 46.
53. Ibid.
54. Ibid., 49.
55. Potter et al., *Liberators: Fighting on Two Fronts in World War II*, 7; Michael Lee Lanning, *The African American Soldier: From Crispus Attucks to Colin Powell* (Secaucus, NJ: Citadel Press, 1999), 25.
56. Buckley, *American Patriots*, 49.
57. Quarles, *The Negro in the American Revolution*, 74.

58. Buckley, *American Patriots*, 72; Davis, *Black Heroes of the American Revolution*, 2.
59. Buckley, *American Patriots*, xviii.
60. Lanning, *The African American Soldier*, 28.

CHAPTER 2

1. Dudley T. Cornish, *The Sable Arm: Black Troops in the Union Army, 1861-1865* (Lawrence: University Press of Kansas, 1987), vii and xii. A fuller text of the *New York Times* article provides additional insight:

> There has been no more striking manifestation of the marvelous times that are upon us than the scene in our streets at the departure of our first colored regiments. Had any man predicted it last year he would have been thought a fool, even by the wisest and most discerning. . . . never, in this land at least, has it presented a transition so extreme and yet so speedily as what our eyes have just beheld.
>
> Nor was it solely the raging horde in the streets that visited upon the black man the nefarious wrong. Thousands and *tens of thousands of higher social grade*, of better education, cherished precisely the same spirit. It found expression in contumelious speech rather than in the violent act, but it was persecution none the less for that. In fact, the mob would never enter upon that career of outrage but for the fact that *it was fired and maddened by the prejudice which had been generated by the ruling influences*, civil and social, here in New York, till it had enveloped the City like some infernal atmosphere.
>
> It is only by such occasions that we can all realize the **prodigious revolution which the public mind** everywhere is experiencing. Such developments are infallible tokens of a new epoch. (emphasis added)

The phrases in italics continue to be valid, as political demagogues continue to demonstrate.

The second paragraph alluded to the four-day antidraft and race riot in Copperhead-controlled New York City that began on July 13,

1863, after newspapers complained that citizens were being called upon to fight the battles for "niggers and abolitionists." The governor and mayor simply asked the mob to wait for the response to their request that Lincoln suspend the draft. The riot was suppressed with the aid of four combat regiments fresh from the Battle of Gettysburg.

2. Richard R. Duncan, *Beleaguered Winchester: A Virginia Community at War, 1861-1865* (Baton Rouge: Louisiana State University Press, 2007), 4.
3. Ibram X. Kendi, "History's Emancipator: Did Abraham Lincoln Have 'a Drop of Anti-Slavery Blood in His Veins'?," Truthout, published November 23, 2017, accessed July 15, 2021, https://truthout.org/articles/history-s-emancipator-did-abraham-lincoln-have-a-drop-of-anti-slavery-blood-in-his-veins/.
4. W.E.B. Du Bois, *Black Reconstruction in America, 1860-1880* (New York, NY: Athenaeum, 1992), 63.
5. Connection to Your Community, "Freedman's Village: A Lost Chapter of Arlington's Black History," published September 30, 2004, accessed May 21, 2020, http://www.connectionnewspapers.com/news/2004/sep/30/freedmans-village-a-lost-chapter-of-arlingtons/.
6. National Archives Pieces of History, "Lincoln to Slaves: Go Somewhere Else," published December 1, 2010, accessed September 12, 2021, https://prologue.blogs.archives.gov/2010/12/01/lincoln-to-slaves-go-somewhere-else/.
7. Du Bois, *Black Reconstruction in America, 1860-1880*, 85.
8. Ibid.
9. James M. McPherson, *Drawn with the Sword: Reflections on the American Civil War* (New York: Oxford University Press, 1996), 203.
10. Frederick Douglass, *Frederick Douglass on Slavery and the Civil War: Selections from His Writings*, ed. Philip S. Foner (Mineola, NY: Dover Publications, 2003), 44; Cornish, *The Sable Arm*, 4.
11. Cornish, *The Sable Arm*, 51.
12. Bob O'Connor, *The U.S. Colored Troops at Andersonville Prison* (West Conshohocken, PA: Infinity Publishing, 2009), 9; Carroll "C. R." Gibbs, *Black, Copper and Bright: The District of Columbia's Civil War Regiment* (Silver Spring, MD: Three Dimensional Publishing, 2002), 46; Du Bois, *Black Reconstruction in America, 1860-1880*, 102; Douglass, *Frederick Douglass on Slavery and the Civil War*, 50.
13. Douglass, *Frederick Douglass on Slavery and the Civil War*, 43.

14. Ibid., 51.
15. O'Connor, *The U.S. Colored Troops at Andersonville Prison*, 3–4.
16. Joseph T. Glatthaar, *The Civil War's Black Soldiers* (Salem, MA: Eastern National Park and Monument Association, 1996), 14.
17. Ibid., 18.
18. Gail Buckley, *American Patriots: The Story of Blacks in the Military from the Revolution to Desert Storm* (New York: Random House, 2002), 103.
19. Ron Chernow, *Grant* (New York: Penguin Press, 2017), 298.
20. Ibid., 136.
21. O'Connor, *The U.S. Colored Troops at Andersonville Prison*, 14.
22. Joseph T. Glatthaar, *Forged in Battle: The Civil War Alliance of Black Soldiers and White Officers* (New York: The Free Press, 1990), 10; and M. A. Shaffner, *How Many Served? Clues from the Records of the Second Regiment, United States Colored Infantry, July 2019*.

    Shaffner describes the effort conducted by the Church of Latter-Day Saints at the behest of the African American Civil War Memorial. While the LDS team arrived at 230,000 names, the AACWM reduced the number to 209,145 by eliminating duplicate names. Most slaves—and even some freemen—were illiterate, and many used pseudonyms. Hundreds of slaves had the same name. Many units merely put new men acquired in the field in the place of combat loses.

    Moreover, combat strengths are derived from hundreds of morning reports prepared by clerks in the field, summarized by others at various echelons before the final total was prepared in the adjutant general's office. One can see that this is an exercise not calculated to result in any kind of precision.
23. Glatthaar, *The Civil War's Black Soldiers*, 34.
24. Cornish, *The Sable Arm*, 191.
25. Our Own Correspondent, "H," "Affairs in the West: A Negro Regiment in Action—The Battle of Mound Island—Desperate Bravery of the Negroes—Defeat of the Guerrillas," *New York Times*, November 18, 1862.
26. Ibid.
27. Cornish, *The Sable Arm*, 147.
28. Ibid., 126.
29. Ibid., 147.
30. Cornish, *The Sable Arm*, 161–62; Operations Report (OR) 14:599; House Divided: The Civil War Research Engine at Dickenson Col-

lege, "The Retaliatory Act, Confederate Congress, May 1, 1863," http://hd.housedivided.dickinson.edu/node/39620.

∞ Joint Resolution on the Subject of Retaliation, May 1, 1863

Resolved by the Congress of the Confederate States of America, in response to a message of the President, transmitted to Congress at the commencement of the present session, that, in the opinion of Congress, the commissioned officers of the enemy ought **not** to be delivered to the authorities of the respective States as suggested in the said message, but all captives taken by Confederate forces ought to be dealt with and disposed of by the Confederate Government.

Sec. 2. That, in the judgment of Congress, the proclamations of the President of the United States dated respectively September twenty-second, eighteen hundred and sixty-two, and January first, eighteen hundred and sixty-three, and other measures of the Government of the United States and of its authorities, commanders and forces, designed or intending to emancipate **slaves** in the Confederate States, or to abduct such slaves, or to incite them to insurrection, or to employ negroes in war against the Confederate States, or to overthrow the institution of African slavery, and bring on a servile war in these States, would, if successful, produce *atrocious consequences*, and they are inconsistent with the spirit of those usages which in modern warfare prevail among civilized nations; they may, therefore, be properly and lawfully repressed by retaliation.

Sec. 3. That in every case, wherein, during the present war, any violation of the laws or usages of war among civilized nations shall be, or has been, done and perpetrated by those acting under the authority of the Government of the United States, on the persons or property of citizens of the Confederate States, or of those under the protection or in the land or naval service of the

Confederate States, or of any State of the Confederacy, the President of the Confederate States is hereby authorized to cause full and ample retaliation to be made for every such violation, in such manner and to such extent as he may think proper.

Sec. 4. That *every white person, being a commissioned officer, or acting as such*, who, during the present war, shall command negroes or mulattoes in arms against the Confederate States, or who shall arm, train, organize or prepare negroes or mulattoes for military service against the Confederate States, or who shall voluntarily aid negroes or mulattoes in any military enterprise, attack or conflict in such service, shall be deemed as inciting servile insurrection, and *shall, if captured, be put to death*, or be otherwise punished at the discretion of the court.

Sec. 5. Every person, being a commissioned officer, or acting as such in the service of the enemy, who shall, during the present war, excite, attempt to excite, or cause to be excited, a servile insurrection, or who shall incite, or cause to be incited, a slave to rebel, shall, if captured, *be put to death*, or be otherwise punished at the discretion of the court.

Sec. 6. Every person charged with an office punishable under the preceding resolutions shall, during the present war, be tried before the military court attached to the Army or corps by the troops of which he shall have been captured, or by such other military court as the President may direct, and in such manner and under such regulations as the President shall prescribe, and, after conviction, the President may commute the punishment in such manner and on such terms as he may deem proper.

Sec. 7. All negroes and mulattoes who shall be engaged in war, or be taken in arms against the Confederate States, or shall give aid or comfort to the enemies of the Confederate States, shall, when captured in the Confederate States, *be delivered to the authorities of the State or States* in which they shall be captured, and dealt with according to the present or future laws of such State or States. (Emphasis added)

This resolution was not consistently followed, despite Southern racial animosity and fear of "servile insurrection." Moreover, the legislation had a "boomerang effect," causing USCT units to fight more resolutely, knowing that slavery or death was the consequence of surrender.

Major General David Hunter wielded his sarcastic pen again upon hearing of Jeff Davis's general order proclaiming him, Phelps, and Major General John H. Milroy subject to the death penalty, mincing no words in his missive to the Confederate president:

> You say you are fighting for liberty. Yes you are fighting for liberty: liberty to keep four millions of your fellow-beings in ignorance and degradation;—liberty to separate parents and children, husband and wife, brother and sister;—liberty to steal the products of their labor, exacted with many a cruel lash and bitter tear;—liberty to seduce their wives and daughters, and to sell your own children into bondage ;—liberty to kill these children with impunity, when the murder cannot be proven by one of pure white blood. This is the kind of liberty—the liberty to do wrong—which Satan, Chief of the Fallen Angels, was contending for when he was cast into Hell.

Quoted in Gordon C. Rhea, *Stephen A. Swails: Black Freedom Fighter in the Civil War and Reconstruction* (Baton Rouge: Louisiana State University Press, 2022), 21–22.

31. Noah Andre Trudeau, *Like Men of War: Black Troops in the Civil War, 1862-1865* (Edison, NJ: Castle Books, 2002), 61.
32. Glatthaar, *The Civil War's Black Soldiers*, 23.
33. O'Connor, *The U.S. Colored Troops at Andersonville Prison*, 9.
34. Trudeau, *Like Men of War*, 44–45.
35. O'Connor, *The U.S. Colored Troops at Andersonville Prison*, 9.
36. William H. Leckie and Shirley A. Leckie, *Unlikely Warriors: General Benjamin Grierson and His Family* (Norman: University of Oklahoma Press, 1984), 101.

37. William A. Dobak, *Freedom by the Sword: The US Colored Troops, 1862-1867* (New York: Skyhorse Publishing, 2013), 107.

Beginning on page 106, a more extensive excerpt from Banks's after-action report provides additional praise:

> The position occupied by these troops (Native Guards) was one of importance and called for the utmost steadfastness and bravery. It gives me great pleasure to report that they answered every expectation. In many respects their conduct was heroic. No troops could be more determined or more daring. They made three charges upon the batteries of the enemy, suffering very heavy losses.... Whatever doubt may have existed heretofore as to the efficiency of organizations of this character, the history of this day proves conclusively ... that the Government will find this class of troops effective supporters and defenders.... They require only good officers ... and careful discipline to make them good soldiers.

38. Chernow, *Grant*, 298.
39. O'Connor, *The U.S. Colored Troops at Andersonville Prison*, 12; Chernow, *Grant*, 129.
40. Glatthaar, *Forged in Battle*, 134.
41. Ibid.
42. Trudeau, *Like Men of War*, 59.
43. Buckley, *American Patriots*, 95.
44. Trudeau, *Like Men of War*, 59.
45. Glatthaar, *Forged in Battle*, 137; Rhea, *Stephen A. Swails*, 37.
46. Glatthaar, *Forged in Battle*, 140; Glatthaar, *The Civil War's Black Soldiers*, 31.
47. Glatthaar, *The Civil War's Black Soldiers*, 31; Glatthaar, *Forged in Battle*, 141.
48. Buckley, *American Patriots*, 103.
49. Melvin Claxton and Mark Puls, *Uncommon Valor: A Story of Race, Patriotism and Glory in the Final Battles of the Civil War* (Hoboken, NJ: John Wiley and Sons, 2006), 114–16; Cornish, *The Sable Arm*, 173–75; Glatthaar, *Forged in Battle*, 156.
50. Cornish, *The Sable Arm*, 173 and 175.

51. Dobak, *Freedom by the Sword*, 387.
52. Glatthaar, *Forged in Battle*, 165.
53. Ibid.
54. John David Smith, *Black Soldiers in Blue: African American Troops in the Civil War Era* (Chapel Hill: University of North Carolina Press, 2002), 239.
55. Bernard C. Nalty, *Strength for the Fight: A History of Black Americans in the Military* (New York: The Free Press, 1986), 43.
56. Bruce Levine, *Confederate Emancipation: Southern Plans to Free and Arm Slaves during the Civil War* (New York: Oxford University Press, 2006), 80.
57. Ibid.
58. Cornish, *The Sable Arm*, 289.
59. Robert R. Jefferson, Jr., *Brothers in Valor: Battlefield Stories of the 89 African Americans Awarded the Medal of Honor* (Guilford, CN: LP, 2019), 19 and 190. See also Congressional Medal of Honor Society, "African American Medal of Honor Recipients," accessed November 11, 2021, https://www.cmohs.org/recipients/lists/black-african-ameri can-recipients/page/3.

    Sergeant Major Christian Fleetwood, an 1860 graduate of the Ashmun Institute (later Lincoln University) in Pennsylvania, who worked for the Maryland Colonization Society, traveled to Liberia and Sierra Leone in Africa and later published the *Lyceum Observer*, among the first African American newspapers in the border slave states.

    Fleetwood was the first Black to receive the Medal of Honor, one of 14 African Americans who received that honor for action at Chaffin's Farm on September 29, 1864. He attempted to obtain an officer's commission and remain in the Army at war's end even though he had been offered a position as rector of an Episcopal parish.

    Rejected by his chain of command, Fleetwood wrote an angry letter from the front:

    > Upon all our record here is not a single blot, and yet no member of this regiment is considered deserving of a commission, or if so, cannot receive one. I trust you will understand that I speak not of and for myself individually, or that the lack of pay or honor of a commission induces me to quit the service. Not by any means.

> But I see no good that will result to our people by continuing to serve; on the contrary, it seems to me that our continuing to act in a subordinate capacity, with no hope advancement or promotion, is an absolute injury to our cause. It is a tacit but telling acknowledgement on our part that we are not fit for promotion, and that we are satisfied to remain in a state of marked and acknowledged subservience.

Nonetheless, Fleetwood continued to serve, commanding the District of Columbia's National Guard battalion as a major. Disillusioned when his offer to serve during the Spanish–American War was dismissed by the War Department, Fleetwood wrote describing the military legacy of Black soldiers who fought in America's wars for the 1895 Cotton States and International Exposition:

> After each war—The War of Independence and the War of 1812, the Civil War, the Indian Wars, Spanish American War, Philippine Insurrection, history repeats itself in the absolute amnesia of the gallant deeds done for the country by brave black soldiers and sailors; their deeds are relegated to oblivion.

Fleetwood clearly kept the faith in the face of massive ignorance and bias.

60. Du Bois, *Black Reconstruction*, 118–19; Levine, *Confederate Emancipation*, 85.
61. Levine, *Confederate Emancipation*, 85.
62. Joseph P. Reidy, "Black Men in Navy Blue During the Civil War," *Prologue Magazine* 33, no. 3 (2001), accessed February 4, 2020, https://www.archives.gov/publications/prologue/2001/fall/black-sailors-1.html.
63. Smith, *Black Soldiers in Blue*, 145.
64. "Report from Brig. Gen. Jno. P. Hatch Commanding Officer, U.S. Forces, District of Florida, on the engagement at Olustee, Florida, concerning Union wounded and dead," accessed November 16, 2021, http://battleofolustee.org/reports/hatch.htm.

65. Trudeau, *Like Men of War*, 465; McPherson, *Drawn with the Sword*, xv. A major propaganda film produced by the War Department during World War II, "The Negro Soldier," failed to mention the vital part African Americans played in winning the Civil War.

CHAPTER 3

1. Sam Smith, "Black Confederates: Truth and Legend," National Battlefield Trust, accessed May 23, 2020, https://www.battlefields.org/learn/articles/black-confederates.
2. Edward H. Bonekemper III, *The Myth of the Lost Cause: Why the South Fought the Civil War and Why the North Won* (Washington, DC: Regnery Press, 2015), 80.
3. Ibid., 71.
4. Ervin L. Jordan Jr., *Black Confederates and Afro-Yankees in Civil War Virginia* (Charlottesville: University Press of Virginia, 1999), 234–35.
5. Ibid., 235.
6. Ibid.
7. Bonekemper, *The Myth of the Lost Cause*, 80–81.
8. Ibid., 81–83; Jordan, *Black Confederates and Afro-Yankees in Civil War Virginia*, 233–34.

    The existence of Cleburne's proposal remained a secret for 30 years until it was published in the US War Department's Official Records.

    Cleburne's impassioned and well thought out plea continued:

    > We can do this more efficiently than the North can now do, for we can give the negro not only his freedom, but that of his wife and child, and can secure to him his home. To do this, we must immediately make his marriage and parental relations sacred in the eyes of the law and forbid their sale.

    > [W]e propose . . . that we immediately commence training a large reserve of the most courageous of our slaves, and further that we *guarantee freedom within a reasonable amount of time to every slave in the South who shall remain true to the Confederacy* in this war. As between the loss of independence and the loss of slavery, we assume that the patriot will freely give up the latter—give up the negro slave rather than be a slave himself. (Emphasis added)

As noted, many of Cleburne's fellow division commanders expressed outright horror at his proposal, declaring his proposal was an "abomination." Lieutenant General Braxton Bragg, Davis's military advisor, regarded the document as "treasonous."

Small wonder that despite official acknowledgment by the Confederate Congress of Cleburne's heroic performance at Ringgold Gap, where his stalwart division saved the remnants of the Army of the Tennessee after the battle of Nashville, Cleburne was not promoted to corps command even though he was highly esteemed as the "Stonewall Jackson of the West."

9. Bonekemper, *The Myth of the Lost Cause*, 85.
10. Ibid., 86.
11. Jordan, *Black Confederates and Afro-Yankees in Civil War Virginia*, 234.
12. Ibid.
13. Ibid., 232–33.
14. Ibid., 234.
15. Ibid.
16. Ibid., 239; James M. McPherson, *Marching toward Freedom: Blacks in the Civil War, 1861-1865* (New York: Facts on File, 1994), 38.
17. Jordan, *Black Confederates and Afro-Yankees in Civil War Virginia*, 239. Lee's intelligence sources obviously slightly overestimated US Colored Troop strength.
18. Ibid., 243.
19. Ibid., 235.
20. Ibid., 239.
21. James McPherson, *Battle Cry of Freedom: The Civil War Era* (New York: Oxford University Press, 1988), 816.
22. Ibid.
23. Ron Chernow, *Grant* (New York: Penguin Press, 2017), 469.
24. Eric A. Foner, *A Short History of Reconstruction, 1863-1877* (New York: Harper & Row, Perennial Library, 1990), 7; Chernow, *Grant*, 469; Jean Edward Smith, *Grant* (New York: Simon & Schuster, 2001), 390.
25. Chernow, *Grant*, 469.
26. Jordan, *Black Confederates and Afro-Yankees in Civil War Virginia*, 232 and 245.
27. Chernow, *Grant*, 470.
28. Ibid.

29. Ibid.
30. Ibid., 241.
31. Ibid.
32. Ibid., 241–42.
33. Ibid., 241.
34. Ibid., 232 and 245.
35. McPherson, *Battle Cry of Freedom*, 834.
36. Ibid.; Bruce Levine, *Confederate Emancipation: Southern Plans to Free and Arm Slaves during the Civil War* (New York: Oxford University Press, 2006), 57.
37. Bonekemper, *The Myth of the Lost Cause*, 88.
38. Bonekemper, *The Myth of the Lost Cause*, 88 and 89; and McPherson, *Battle Cry of Freedom*, 834.
39. Levine, *Confederate Emancipation*, 57.
40. Bonekemper, *The Myth of the Lost Cause*, 89.
41. Ibid.
42. Jordan, *Black Confederates and Afro-Yankees in Civil War Virginia*, 237.
43. Ibid., 238.
44. Ibid.
45. Ibid.
46. Ibid., 237.
47. Ibid., 243.
48. Chernow, *Grant*, 470.
49. Jordan, *Black Confederates and Afro-Yankees in Civil War Virginia*, 243.
50. Ibid., 236–37.
51. Ibid., 227.
52. McPherson, *Battle Cry of Freedom*, 835.
53. Ben Alpers, "The Myth of Black Confederates and Fake Racial Tolerance," *US Intellectual History Blog*, January 12, 2018, accessed June 16, 2020, https://s-usih.org/2018/01/the-myth-of-black-confederates-and-fake-racial-tolerance/.
54. Bonekemper, *The Myth of the Lost Cause*, 89; Jordan, *Black Confederates and Afro-Yankees in Civil War Virginia*, 242; McPherson, *Battle Cry of Freedom*, 837; James M. McPherson, *The Negro's Civil War: How American Blacks Felt and Acted during the War for the Union* (New York: Ballentine Books, 1991), 248.
55. Jordan, *Black Confederates and Afro-Yankees in Civil War Virginia*, 248.
56. Ibid.

57. McPherson, *Battle Cry of Freedom*, 837.
58. Levine, *Confederate Emancipation*, 141.
59. Jordan, *Black Confederates and Afro-Yankees in Civil War Virginia*, 243.
60. Ibid., 245.
61. Ibid., 246.

    The Union hardly needed the Confederate supplies, and the warehouse fires spread and caused serious damage to Richmond. It was fortunate indeed that elements of Major General Weitzel's XXV Corps, 33 African American regiments, including the 5th Massachusetts Cavalry Regiment, entered Richmond and were able to extinguish the flames.

62. Ibid., 247.
63. Ibid.
64. Ibid.
65. Ibid.
66. Ibid., 249–50.

    Jordan's Appendix E, 322–23, contains the roster of officers Lee recommended to command Black troops.

67. Ibid., 250–51.
68. Ibid., 251.
69. Bonekemper, *The Myth of the Lost Cause*, 90–91.
70. Ibid., 91.

CHAPTER 4

1. Charles River Editors, *Buffalo Soldiers: The History and Legacy of the Black Soldiers Who Fought in the U.S. Army during the Indian Wars* (Middletown, DE: Charles River Publishers, 2021), 9, 23–24.

   Subsequently, the enlistment term was five years for both branches.

2. Gail Buckley, *American Patriots: The Story of Blacks in the Military from the Revolution to Desert Storm* (New York: Random House, 2002), 111.

   They were from the Lakota tribe. The Ojibwa, their enemies, called them Sioux, meaning "little snakes."

3. Ibid.
4. Formed in New Orleans in September 1866, the 9th Cavalry Regiment's commander was Edward Hatch, cavalry commander of the Army of Tennessee during the Civil War.

   Commissioned at Fort Leavenworth, Kansas, in 1866, the 10th US Cavalry Regiment was commanded by Colonel Benjamin Grierson, leader of two legendary cavalry raids through Mississippi designed to divert attention from Grant's brilliant Vicksburg campaign. Lieutenant Colonel J. W. Davidson and Majors J. W. Forsyth and M. H. Kidd were also assigned. Colonel Grierson commanded the regiment until 1890, when he was promoted to brigadier general, retiring three months later.

The 24th Infantry Regiment was formed in November 1869 when the 38th and the 41st US Infantry Regiments (Colored) were merged at Fort McKavett, Texas. Both regiments already had nearly three years of frontier service. The regiment's first commander was renowned Civil War and Indian Wars cavalry leader Colonel Ranald Slidell Mackenzie. He was succeeded by William Shafter, commander of V Corps, US Army forces in Cuba in 1998.

The 38th Infantry was commanded by Colonel William B. Hazen, with Lieutenant Colonel Cuvier Grover as second in command, and Major Henry C. Merriam.

The 41st Infantry was commanded by Colonel Ranald Slidell Mackenzie, with Lieutenant Colonel William Shafter as second in command, and included Major George W. Schofield.

The 25th Infantry Regiment combined the 39th and 40th Infantry Regiments at Jackson Barracks, Louisiana, in April 1869 under the command of Colonel Joseph A. Mower, commander of the 20th Corps, Army of Georgia, during the Civil War. Its lieutenant colonel was Edward W. Hinks; Major Zenas R. Bliss, who would become a frontier legend, was also assigned.

5. Arlen L. Fowler, *The Black Infantry in the West, 1869-1891* (Norman: University of Oklahoma Press, 1971), 16. (Reprinted in 1996).
6. Frank N. Schubert, *Voices of the Buffalo Soldier: Records, Reports, and Recollections of Military Life and Service in the West* (Albuquerque: University of New Mexico Press, 2003), 1.
7. Ibid., 48–49; Charles River Editors, *Buffalo Soldiers: History and Legacy*, 6, notes that historian Dr. Walter B. Hill Jr. observed that Colonel Grierson of the 10th Cavalry related that his regiment got this name during their 1871 campaign against the Comanches in Indian Territory because braves of the tribe respected the Black soldiers' tireless marching and dogged trailing skills. The 10th later used the buffalo on its coat of arms.

The book also suggests that this nickname might also have originated from the buffalo coats troopers wore while campaigning in

winter, but other US soldiers wore them as well. In any case, the name eventually was applied to all four regiments of Black regulars.
8. Schubert, *Voices of the Buffalo Soldier*, 1.
9. Fowler, *The Black Infantry in the West*, 4.
10. Ibid., 5.
11. Ibid. See also William H. Leckie, *The Buffalo Soldiers: A Narrative of Negro Cavalry in the West* (Norman: University of Oklahoma Press, 1967), 164.

    Army records show that in 1877, the desertion rates of the 9th and 10th Cavalry were far below any other army unit. The 9th Cavalry experienced a total of 6 desertions, while the 10th Cavalry had 18 desertions, compared, for instance, to 184 deserters from Colonel Mackenzie's hard-hitting 4th Cavalry, and Custer's 7th Cavalry with 179 desertions.
12. Buckley, *American Patriots*, 112; "List of Medal of Honor Recipients," Wikipedia, accessed July 20, 2020, https://en.wikipedia.org/wiki/List_of_Medal_of_Honor_recipients#Spanish %E2%80%93American_War.
13. Leckie, *The Buffalo Soldiers*, 158.
14. Buckley, *American Patriots*, 133.

    Pine Ridge seems to have been a "grudge match" between the 7th Cavalry and Native Americans to settle the score for their Little Big Horn fiasco 14 years earlier. The Lakota were surrounded, and most braves were disarmed. Of the roughly 300 Indians killed in the Wounded Knee Massacre, 84 were old men, 44 women, and 18 children. Army casualties were 25 dead and 39 wounded, some caused by "friendly fire" from four Hotchkiss guns, each having five 37mm barrels, capable of firing 68 high-explosive shrapnel rounds per minute out to a range of 2,000 yards.

    Fifty-one survivors (4 men and 47 women and children) were loaded onto wagons and taken to the Pine Ridge Reservation, where they were placed in the Episcopal mission church, which still had a banner hanging across its chancel reading, "Peace on Earth, good will to men." When civilians hired to bury the dead reached the snow-covered and frozen battlefield, they found four infants still alive, wrapped in their dead mothers' shawls.

The Army awarded 20 Congressional Medals of Honor to massacre participants, 4 to artillerymen, 16 to members of the 7th Cavalry.

Colonel Philip Harvey, commander of the 25th Infantry Regiment, observed, "many causes are ascribed to the outbreak among the various Indian tribes throughout Montana and the Dakotas in the winter of 1890-'91, but *there can be little doubt that the condition of destitution . . . brought about by reduced rations and the dishonesty and mismanagement of minor government officials had a far-reaching effect.*" (Emphasis added)

Major General Nelson A. Miles, commander of the Military Division of the Missouri, observed in a dispatch to Army Commanding General John Schofield in Washington, D.C., on December 19, 1890:

> The difficult Indian problem cannot be solved permanently at this end of the line. It requires the fulfillment of Congress of the treaty obligations that the Indians were entreated and coerced into signing. They signed away a valuable portion of their reservation, and it is now occupied by white people, for which they have received nothing.
>
> They understood that ample provision would be made for their support; instead, their supplies have been reduced, and much of the time they have been living on half and two-thirds rations. Their crops, as well as the crops of the white people, for two years have been almost total failures.
>
> The dissatisfaction is widespread, especially among the Sioux, while the Cheyennes have been on the verge of starvation and were forced to commit depredations to sustain life. These facts are beyond question, and the evidence is positive and sustained by thousands of witnesses.

In a letter to his wife, Miles, destined to be the last commanding general of the US Army, described the action as "*the most abominable criminal military blunder and a horrible massacre of women and children*" (emphasis added). Miles fought for compensation for survivors of the massacre and relieved Colonel Forsyth, the 7th Cavalry commander,

who although court-martialed, was exonerated. Forsyth retired a major general.
15. Schubert, *Voices of the Buffalo Soldier*, 117–30.
16. Darlene Clark Hine, William C. Hine, and Stanley Harrold, *African-American History* (Upper Saddle River, NJ: Pearson/Prentice Hall, 2006), 513.
17. Buckley, *American Patriots*, 150.
18. Fowler, *The Black Infantry in the West*, 107.
19. Buckley, *American Patriots*, 141.
20. Ibid., 150.
21. Hine, Hine, and Harrold, *African-American History*, 516.
The Indianapolis Freeman observed,

> The government of the United States will allow some of its most loyal and true citizens to be burned and butchered and shot to pieces like dogs, without protection, and go right on ignoring their rights and claims as if all were peace and happiness in the family; and yet, when a foreign war is threatened, these same ill-treated citizens are wont to be rushed to the front in the name of protecting the nation's honor. . . . If the government wants our support and services, let us demand and get a guarantee for our safety and protection at home. We want to put a stop to Lynch law, the butchering of our people like hogs, burning our houses, shooting our wives and children and raping our daughters and mothers.

22. Buckley, *American Patriots*, 144.
23. Ibid., 145.
24. Ibid.
    Many soldiers of the four regiments were recommended for the Medal of Honor for actions during the Spanish–American War, but only five members of the 10th Cavalry Regiment received the Medal:

    - Sergeant Major (later captain) Edward L. Baker Jr. left cover under fire to rescue a soldier from drowning at Santiago.
    - Corporal Dennis Bell, Troop H, rescue at Tayacoba.*
    - Private Fitz Lee, Troop M, rescue at Tayacoba.*

- Private William H. Thompkins, Troop G, rescue at Tayacoba.*
- Private (later master sergeant) George H. Wanton, Troop M, rescue at Tayacoba.*

* These four men were among 49 members of the 10th Cavalry selected for special operations and reconnaissance missions. When one team, which included Spanish resistance fighters, was discovered, enemy artillery fire sunk their boat. Survivors were left stranded on the beach. After four attempts, these four men and an officer launched a successful night operation that found and rescued the survivors. For some reason, the officer did not receive the Medal of Honor.

In addition, Seaman Robert Penn was the only Black sailor to receive the Medal of Honor for his bravery and quick thinking while serving aboard the USS *Iowa*, extinguishing a coal fire that could have destroyed the ship.

All five soldiers of the 10th Cavalry received medals for rescuing comrades. A total of 112 Medals of Honor were awarded during the Spanish–American War—66 for the Navy, 31 for the Army, and 15 for the Marine Corps. Notably, the other three Buffalo Soldier regiments were shut out, while the Navy had a field day. 94

25. Ibid.
26. Ibid., 145–46.
27. Lou Potter, William Miles, and Nina Rosenblum, *Liberators: Fighting on Two Fronts in World War II* (Orlando, FL: Harcourt, Brace Jovanovich, 1992), 17.
28. Buckley, *American Patriots*, 141–42.
29. Ibid., 146.
30. Ibid., 147.
31. Ibid.

The Cuban guerrilla leader, General Calixto Garcia Iniguez, was prophetic: Benjamin Oliver Davis Sr. was the first African American to receive a star in 1940, and General Colin Powell became chairman of the Joint Chiefs of Staff in 1989, overseeing the Gulf War (August 1990–February 1991). General Norman Schwarzkopf's deputy for that operation, Desert Storm, was African American Lieutenant General Calvin Waller.

Since the Vietnam War, there have been approximately 400 Black general and flag-rank officers. Currently, the Air Force chief of

staff and the secretary of defense are African Americans. See Appendix C.
32. Ibid., 146.
33. Ibid., 152; Michael Lee Lanning, *The African American Soldier: From Crispus Attucks to Colin Powell* (Citadel Press, 1999), 91.
34. Buckley, *American Patriots*, 152; Lanning, *The African American Soldier*, 94.
35. Buckley, *American Patriots*, 146.
36. Ibid., 147.
37. John Hope Franklin, *From Slavery to Freedom*, third ed. (New York: Alfred A. Knopf, 1967), 423.
38. Buckley, *American Patriots*, 148.
39. Digital History, "The Philippines," accessed April 27, 2020, https://www.digitalhistory.uh.edu/disp_textbook.cfm?smtID=2&psid=3161&msclkid=84dfe59fc6fd11ecb612ea980152901e.
40. Maria Teresa Trinidad Pineda Tinio, *The Triumph of Tagalog and the Dominance of the Discourse on English: Language Politics in the Philippines during the American Colonial Period*, ScholarBank@NUS, 2009, accessed April 27, 2020, http://scholarbank.nus.edu.sg/handle/10635/16861.
41. Hine, Hine, and Harrold, *African-American History*, 517; Lanning, *The African American Soldier*, 85 and 87. See also Charles River Editors, *Buffalo Soldiers: The History and Legacy*, 74; Black History Museum & Cultural Center of Virginia, "1898—'No Officers, No Fight,'" accessed June 13, 2020, https://www.blackhistorymuseum.org/announcement/1898-no-officers-no-fight/.
42. Buckley, *American Patriots*, 142. See the description of Charles Young's career in the "West Point" section of this chapter.
43. Charles River Editors, *Buffalo Soldiers: The History and Legacy*, 79–80.
44. Ibid., 157.
45. Ibid., 155.
46. Bernard C. Nalty, *Strength for the Fight: A History of Black Americans in the Military* (New York: Free Press, 1986), 64 and 73.
47. Jeffrey T. Sammons and John H. Morrow Jr., *Harlem's Rattlers and the Great War: The Undaunted 369th Regiment and the African American Quest for Equality* (Lawrence: University of Kansas Press, 2014), 79.
48. Charles River Editors, *Buffalo Soldiers: The History and Legacy of the Black Soldiers*, 87.

49. Buckley, *American Patriots*, xvi. Pershing's nickname, "Black Jack," was a sanitization of "Nigger Jack," an epithet he acquired while serving as a tactical officer at West Point after his service with the 10th Cavalry.
50. Ibid., 160.
51. Ibid., 186.
52. David P. Kilroy, "Alone at West Point: The Military Education of Charles Young, 1884-1889," *Historian* 64, no. 3-4 (Spring and Summer, 2002), 596–97.
53. Buckley, *American Patriots*, 121.
54. Ibid., 125.
55. Ibid., 129.
56. The US Army Center of Military History published a comprehensive and more objective reexamination of the 24th Infantry's record in 1996, *Black Soldier, White Army: The 24th Infantry Regiment in Korea*. That book was commissioned and published to correct the initial racially biased and unfair conclusions Roy E. Applebee drew regarding the regiment in the Army's account of the Korean War published in 1961, *South to the Naktong, North to the Yalu*.

CHAPTER 5

1. C. Vann Woodward, *The Strange Career of Jim Crow* (New York: Oxford University Press, 1974), 93–94.

    Colonel Anderson's views typified the attitude of most white men. Elsewhere, Anderson wrote:

    > There remains a large percentage of colored men of the ignorant illiterate day laborer class. These men have not, in a large percentage of cases, the physical stamina to withstand the hardships and exposure of hard field service, especially the damp and cold winters of France. The poorer class of backwoods negro has not the mental stamina and moral sturdiness to put him in the line against opposing German troops who consist of men of high average education and thoroughly trained. The enemy is constantly looking for a weak place in the line held by troops composed of the culls of the colored race, and all he has to do is concentrate on that.

Even after the record of the 92nd and 93rd Divisions' eight regiments during the war, army leaders persisted in this biased thought, all the while ignoring the fact that many Blacks were illiterate due to the grossly inferior education provided. There was also widespread ignorance and illiteracy among poor whites, up to and including during World War II.

Ultimately, education is a national security issue.

2. Ibid.; Nicholas Lemann, *Redemption: The Last Battle of the Civil War* (New York: Farrar, Straus and Giroux, 2006), 187.
3. Lemann, *Redemption*, 188.
4. Ibid., 190.
5. Ibid., 189.

Wilson's stereotypical Southern views led him to write, "Unscrupulous adventurers appeared, to act as the leaders of the inexperienced Blacks in taking possession, first of the conventions, and afterwards of the state governments. . . . [Blacks] submitted to the unrestrained authority of small and masterful groups of white men whom the instincts of plunder had drawn from the North." See A. Scott Berg, *Wilson* (New York: G. P. Putnam's Sons, 2013), 44.

6. Professor Buzzkill, "Woodrow Wilson: 'It is like writing history with lightning.' Quote or No Quote?," August 30, 2017, https://www.professorbuzzkill.com/qnq-29/.
7. Ibid.
8. Jerrold M. Packard, *American Nightmare: The History of Jim Crow* (New York: St. Martin's Griffin, 2002), 127–28.
9. Ibid., 127.
10. Ibid., 125.
11. When Pershing served as tactical officer at West Point in 1897, the cadets called him "Nigger Jack" due to his strictness and rigidity as well as his assignments with the 10th Cavalry Regiment. The epithet was subsequently "softened" to "Black Jack" when he attained national prominence.
12. Packard, *American Nightmare*, 123.
13. Chad L. Williams, *Torchbearers of Liberty: African American Soldiers in the World War I Era* (Chapel Hill: University of North Carolina Press, 2010), 32.
14. Isabel Wilkerson, *The Warmth of Other Suns: The Epic Story of America's Great Migration* (New York: Random House, 2010), 39.

15. Robert H. Ferrell, *Unjustly Dishonored: An African American Division in World War I* (Columbia: University of Missouri Press, 2011), 5.
16. Emmett Jay Scott, *Scott's Official History of the American Negro in the World War* (Chicago: Homewood Press, 2018), 69.
17. Michael Lee Lanning, *The African American Soldier: From Crispus Attucks to Colin Powell* (Citadel Press, 1999), 132.
18. Arthur E. Barbeau and Florette Henri, *Unknown Soldiers: African American Troops in World War I* (Boston: Da Capo Press, 1996), 86.
19. Ibid., 137.
20. Williams, *Torchbearers of Liberty*, 140.
21. Byron Farwell, *Over There: The United States in the Great War, 1917-1918* (New York: W. W. Norton & Company, 1999), 17.
22. Ibid., 38.
23. Ibid., 17.
24. Ibid., 16 and 40.
25. Ibid., 68.
26. Ibid., 75.
27. Williams, *Torchbearers of Liberty*, 143; Barbeau and Henri, *Unknown Soldiers*, 158.
28. Peter N. Nelson, *The Harlem Hellfighters Struggle for Freedom in WWI and Equality at Home* (New York: Basic Civitas, 2009), 5; Nelson, 36.
29. Ibid.
30. Ferrell, *Unjustly Dishonored*, 70 and 90.
31. Scott, *Scott's Official History of the American Negro in the World War*, 167.
32. Barbeau and Henri, *Unknown Soldiers*, 111.
33. Williams, *Torchbearers of Liberty*, 124–27.

For some reason, there was a long struggle to achieve awards for Johnson and Roberts from the US military. Although President Theodore Roosevelt called Johnson "one of the five bravest men who fought in World War I," Johnson received no US award until President Bill Clinton awarded him the Purple Heart in June 1996. In February 2003, the Distinguished Service Cross, the Army's second-highest award, was presented to his son Herman A. Johnson, a Tuskegee Airman. On June 2, 2015, President Barack Obama presented the Medal of Honor to Command Sergeant Major Louis Wilson of the New York Army National Guard who accepted on Johnson's behalf.

Johnson's 21 wounds left him permanently disabled, unable to resume his former position as baggage handler. At first, Johnson was paid to participate in a series of lecture tours, but one evening in St. Louis, instead of delivering the expected tale of racial harmony in the trenches, Johnson revealed the abuse that Black soldiers suffered. Soon afterward, a warrant was issued for Johnson's arrest for wearing his uniform beyond the prescribed date, and the lecturing engagements stopped. Without a veteran's pension and penniless, Johnson died a destitute alcoholic suffering from tuberculosis in 1929 at the age of 32.

Needham Robert's fate was no better. He and his wife committed suicide due to the hopelessness of their poverty. This a disgraceful commentary of the nation's bigotry, lack of gratitude, and respect for Blacks.

34. Scott, *Scott's Official History of the American Negro in the World War*, 211–12.
35. Barbeau and Henri, *Unknown Soldiers*, 121.
36. Jeffrey T. Sammons and John H. Morrow Jr., *Harlem's Rattlers and the Great War: The Undaunted 369th Regiment and the African American Quest for Equality* (Lawrence: University of Kansas Press, 2014), 376.
37. Williams, *Torchbearers of Liberty*, 130.
38. Scott, *Scott's Official History of the American Negro in the World War*, 259.
39. Barbeau and Henri, *Unknown Soldiers*, 132.

   Colonel Perry L. Miles, commander of the 371st Regiment, is reported to have declared, "This is the first information I have had that I am to obey any French Army officer I happen to find at a railway station or anywhere else." Apparently, staff work was not what it ought to have been at AEF headquarters—or disdain for Black troops was absolute.

40. Williams, *Torchbearers of Liberty*, 128.
41. Barbeau and Henri, *Unknown Soldiers*, 129.
42. Ibid., 128.
43. Ibid., 129.
44. Scott, *Scott's Official History of the American Negro in the World War*, 246.
45. Ibid., 250.
46. Barbeau and Henri, *Unknown Soldiers*, 114–15.

47. Ibid., 115.
48. Ibid., 194.
49. Williams, *Torchbearers of Liberty*, 168.
50. Ibid., 172.
51. Barbeau and Henri, *Unknown Soldiers*, 157, 172.

    After the war, Osceola McKain, a Black lieutenant who served in the 92nd Division, complained to the War Department about Greer's libelous charges, which impugned the entire division over the poor performance of a single battalion. Although Greer amazingly admitted having made all of them, no further action was taken by the War Department, whose postwar policy continued to severely limit the number of Black officers. See Barbeau and Henri, *Unknown Soldiers*, 172–73.

52. Ibid., 133.
53. Sammons and Morrow, *Harlem's Rattlers and the Great War*, 371–72.
54. Ibid., 373.
55. Ibid., 284 and 319.
56. Arthur W. Little, *From Harlem to the Rhine: The Story of New York's Colored Volunteers* (New York: Covici Friede Publishers, 1936), 305; Stephen L. Harris, *Harlem's Hell Fighters: The African-American 369th Infantry in World War I* (Washington, DC: Potomac Publishers, 2003), 258.
57. Scott, *Scott's Official History of the American Negro in the World War*, 164.
58. Barbeau and Henri, *Unknown Soldiers*, 131.
59. Ibid., 127 and 131.
60. Nelson, *The Harlem Hellfighters Struggle for Freedom in WWI and Equality at Home*, 209.
61. Ibid., 136.
62. Scott, *Scott's Official History of the American Negro in the World War*, 174 and 189.
63. Barbeau and Henri, *Unknown Soldiers*, 166–67.
64. Ibid., 165.
65. Williams, *Torchbearers of Liberty*, 24.
66. Ibid.
67. Barbeau and Henri, *Unknown Soldiers*, 184–85.
68. *The Crisis*, May 1919; Williams, *Torchbearers of Liberty*, 206–07.
69. Williams, *Torchbearers of Liberty*, 207.

70. Ibid., 189 and 185.
71. Ibid., 245.
72. Ibid., 256.
73. Ibid., 235.
74. Ibid., 245.
75. Barbeau and Henri, *Unknown Soldiers*, 175; Lanning, *The African American Soldier*, 150–51.
76. Williams, *Torchbearers of Liberty*, 254–56; Barbeau and Henri, *Unknown Soldiers*, 175.
77. Packard, *American Nightmare*, 149–50; The Black Wall Street Times, "On the 1921 Greenwood Massacre," published March 31, 2017, updated January 3, 2021, accessed October 5, 2021, https://theblackwallsttimes.com/2017/03/31/on-the-1921-greenwood-massacre-dont-call-it-a-riot/.
78. Franklin, John Hope, *From Slavery to Freedom: A History of African Americans*, 6th ed. (New York: McGraw-Hill, 1988), 316.
79. Ibid., 317.
80. Ibid.

CHAPTER 6

1. Michael Lee Lanning, *The African American Soldier: From Crispus Attucks to Colin Powell* (Citadel Press, 1999), 109; Jerrold M. Packard, *American Nightmare: The History of Jim Crow* (New York: St. Martin's Griffin, 2002), 154–55.
2. Gail Buckley, *American Patriots: The Story of Blacks in the Military from the Revolution to Desert Storm* (New York: Random House, 2002), 262.
3. Bernard C. Nalty, *Strength for the Fight: A History of Black Americans in the Military* (New York: Free Press, 1986), 187.
4. Buckley, *American Patriots*, 235–36 and 262.
5. Graham Smith, *When Jim Crow Met John Bull: Black American Soldiers in World War II Britain* (New York: St. Martin's Press, 1987), 142–44, 150; Nalty, *Strength for the Fight*, 154–55.
6. Buckley, *American Patriots*, 257.
7. Ibid.

   Starr was drafted in 1943, but this request to enlist in a Black unit managed to keep him out of Officer Candidate School and followed him wherever he was assigned. He eventually dropped into China by

the Office of Secret Services, the clandestine forerunner of the Central Intelligence Agency.
8. Buckley, 258.
9. Ibid., 258; Robert R. Jefferson Jr., *Brothers in Valor: Battlefield Stories of the 89 African Americans Awarded the Medal of Honor* (Guilford, CT: LP, 2019), 67.
10. Buckley, *American Patriots*, 259.

    Obviously, the record of Henry Johnson, Freddie Stowers, and other heroic Black service members, as well as the record of the 369th Infantry and the three other regiments of the 93rd Infantry Division, had been totally forgotten in little more than six years, suggesting that the problem was more bigotry and denial than faulty memory.
11. Ibid.
12. Lanning, *The African American Soldier*, 164.
13. Buckley, *American Patriots*, 259.
14. Ibid., 260–61.
15. Ibid., 273–74.
16. Ibid., 268.
17. Ibid., 280.
18. Lanning, *The African American Soldier*, 173–74; Nalty, *Strength for the Fight*, 179.
19. Nalty, *Strength for the Fight*, 167–68.
20. Lanning, *The African American Soldier*, 177.
21. Lou Potter, William Miles, and Nina Rosenblum, *Liberators: Fighting on Two Fronts in World War II* (Orlando, FL: Harcourt, Brace Jovanovich, 1992), 161; Jefferson, *Brothers in Valor*, 100; and Buckley, *American Patriots*, 327.
22. Jefferson, *Brothers in Valor*, 100.
23. Buckley, *American Patriots*, x, 328.
24. Ibid., 329; Lanning, *The African American Soldier*, 181.
25. Buckley, *American Patriots*, 331; Potter, Miles, and Rosenblum, *Liberators*, 164; George S. Patton, *War as I Knew It* (Boston: Houghton Mifflin, 1947), 160.

    Patton called on the men of this battalion in a dark hour to relieve beleaguered forces around Bastogne, and they, as always, came through. "Skedaddling" white infantrymen running away from the communications center asked, "Where the hell are you niggers going with those tanks? You've got no business in them."

When the movie *Patton* was released in 1970, the 761st Tank Battalion, which constantly fulfilled its unit motto, "Come Out Fighting," was not even mentioned, a galling omission that reflects America's utter lack of appreciation for Black heroism and military excellence.

Despite their record of remaining on the front line longer than any other armored battalion, serving as the spearhead that penetrated through Germany into Austria, only one Black was portrayed in this movie: his orderly, Sergeant William C. Meeks.

Nor was his African American driver throughout most of the war, Master Sergeant John L. Mimms, portrayed, although Patton acknowledged

> You have been the driver of my official car since 1940. During that time you have safely driven me in many parts of the world under all conditions of dust and snow and ice and mud, of enemy fire and attack by enemy aircraft. At no time during these years of danger and difficulty have you so much as damaged a bumper.

Another driver, Private First Class Horace Woodring, drove during Patton's fatal accident in Germany near Mannheim, Germany, in early December 1945.

26. Tanya Lee Stone, *Courage Has No Color: The True Story of the Triple Nickels, America's First Black Paratroopers* (Sommerville, MA: Candlewick Press, 2013), 96–97; Buckley, *American Patriots*, 279–80; Lanning, *The African American Soldier*, 181.

    General Gavin, who served in the 25th Infantry Regiment along the Mexican border for three years after being commissioned from West Point in 1929, took the battalion under his wing when they were assigned to the 13th Airborne Division in October 1945. Gavin described the unit's billeting area as a "mud pond" and was angry that they were housed in "old tar-paper-covered shacks." He was the youngest general in the Army and could not abide injustice. Gavin had to go to Washington for permission to integrate the 555th into the 82nd Airborne Division.

27. Denise George and Robert Child, *The Lost Eleven: The Forgotten Story of Black American Soldiers Brutally Massacred in World War II* (New York: Dutton Caliber, 2017), 299–310.

The same day, 86 white GIs of the 285th Field Artillery Observation Battalion taken prisoner by the main spearhead of the offensive, Task Force Pfeifer, were gunned down at a crossroads in the small town of Baugnetz in what became known as the Malmedy massacre. Some men escaped to tell the story, fostering a steely resolve in American units. A team sent to investigate Malmedy examined the murders at Wereth, but they went unreported. Although the war crime at Malmedy was prosecuted at the Nuremburg Trials, Wereth was ignored until 1949, when a Senate Armed Services subcommittee reviewed Nazi war crimes. Even the Army's official account of African American participation in the war, *The Employment of Negro Troops*, fails to address the incident. Congress did not officially recognize the incident until 2017.

The son of the Belgian family that sheltered the 11 erected a modest monument on the site in September 2004. In 2004, the monument was expanded, dedicated to these 11 men as well as all African Americans who fought in the European theater. The tragedy is commemorated with a ceremony each year, with US Army representation, and occasionally attended by the victims' descendants.

28. Buckley, *American Patriots*, 323.

    Senator Byrd apologized for his comments years later and proved by his actions that his contrition was sincere.

29. Ibid., 322.

    Bruce M. Wright, a Black medic, and many others were insulted by Supreme Allied Headquarters' message announcing, "To Our Negro Troops": "You may now fight at the side of your white brothers who have borne the brunt of combat." Assigned to a 1st Infantry Division regiment, which supported the war crimes trial at Nuremburg at war's end, he was angered when Black volunteers were sent to Paris to dig trenches with German POWs. On some details, Germans or other Axis POWs even supervised Black Americans!

30. Lanning, *The African American Soldier*, 182.
31. Ibid.; Lee, 697.
32. Lee, 696.
33. Lanning, *The African American Soldier*, 183; Buckley, *American Patriots*, 323, 326, 327.
34. https://en.wikipedia.ork/wiki/Blue_discharge#:=A%20blue%20discharge%20%28also%20known%20asdischarge%20%20%28,to%20remove

%20service%20members%20from%20rgw%20thw%20ranks, accessed July 20, 2021.
35. Lanning, *The African American Soldier*, 185.

   Among the Department of Defense's observations, "Segregated units by race complicated and slowed training, exacerbated relations between officers and enlisted men and between commanders and their units and undermined the morale of these units in both subtle and obvious ways."

   The study included remarks by Lieutenant General (retired) William McCaffrey, who served as a white officer in the ranks of captain through colonel in the 92nd Infantry Division under General Almond: "Almond came out of Luray, Virginia, and he had the attitudes of that time and place. Hell, everybody in the army then was a racist."
36. Ibid.
37. See Jefferson, *Brothers in Valor*, 97–115, for details on each recipient.
38. Lanning, *The African American Soldier*, 190–91.
39. Buckley, *American Patriots*, 291; Lanning, *The African American Soldier*, 195.
40. Lanning, *The African American Soldier*, 195.
41. Buckley, *American Patriots*, 293.
42. Nalty, *Strength for the Fight*, 158–61.
43. Lanning, *The African American Soldier*, 201.
44. Buckley, *American Patriots*, 263.
45. Lanning, *The African American Soldier*, 201.
46. Nalty, *Strength for the Fight*, 293; Lanning, *The African American Soldier*, 207.
47. Lanning, *The African American Soldier*, 208–09; Nalty, *Strength for the Fight*, 193.

   The *Mason*'s crew was recognized 50 years later for braving 90-mile-an-hour winds and 40-foot waves while escorting a convoy safely to England in 1944. The recommendation the convoy commander submitted had simply been "lost" in official channels.
48. Buckley, *American Patriots*, 308.
49. Ibid., 311.
50. Ibid., 312.
51. Ibid., 310.
52. Ibid.

53. Buckley, *American Patriots*, 311; Lanning, *The African American Soldier*, 210.
54. Buckley, *American Patriots*, 312.
55. Ibid., 315.
56. Ibid., 319–20. Woodward initially received the Bronze Star, which was subsequently upgraded to a Silver Star.
57. Ibid., 321.
58. Buckley, *American Patriots*, 319; Lanning, *The African American Soldier*, 212.
59. Lanning, *The African American Soldier*, 213.
60. Buckley, *American Patriots*, 322.
61. Isabel Wilkerson, *The Warmth of Other Suns: The Epic Story of America's Great Migration* (New York: Random House, 2010), 9.
62. Ibid.
63. Buckley, *American Patriots*, 336; Nalty, *Strength for the Fight*, 214–15.
64. Lanning, *The African American Soldier*, 219.
65. Buckley, *American Patriots*, 337.
66. Ibid.
67. Nalty, *Strength for the Fight*, 204–06; Buckley, *American Patriots*, 338. See also Richard Gergel, *Unexampled Courage: The Blinding of Sgt. Isaac Woodard and the Awakening of President Harry S. Truman and Judge J. Waties Waring* (New York: Sarah Crichton Books, 2019).
68. Buckley, *American Patriots*, 337. President Truman sent a civil rights message to Congress on February 2, 1948, presenting a comprehensive program, including statehood for Alaska and Hawaii, home rule and suffrage for the District of Columbia, settlement of claims by Japanese Americans for their wartime internment, a federal antilynching law, a permanent Fair Employment Practices Commission on Civil Rights, and a civil rights division in the Department of Justice. It also guaranteed every American citizen's right to vote. Many of these recommendations have since come to pass, except perhaps the last item, the bedrock of democracy.

CHAPTER 7

1. Wikipedia, "Korean War," accessed May 6, 2021, https://en.wikipedia.org/wiki/Korean_War#Comparison_of_forces.
2. Bernard C. Nalty, *Strength for the Fight: A History of Black Americans in the Military* (New York: Free Press, 1986), 256.

3. Ibid., 257.
4. William T. Bowers, William T. Hammond, and George L. MacGarrigle, *Black Soldier, White Army: The 24th Infantry Regiment in Korea* (Washington, DC: United States Army Center of Military History, 1996), Foreword.
5. Michael Lee Lanning, *The African American Soldier: From Crispus Attucks to Colin Powell* (Secaucus, NJ: Citadel Press, 1999), 230.
6. Gail Buckley, *American Patriots: The Story of Blacks in the Military from the Revolution to Desert Storm* (New York: Random House, 2002), 351; Bowers, Hammond, and MacGarrigle, *Black Soldier, White Army*, 77–78, 84.
7. Bowers, Hammond, and MacGarrigle, *Black Soldier, White Army*, 272–73.
8. Lanning, *The African American Soldier*, 230.
9. Ibid., 231.
10. Bowers, Hammond, and MacGarrigle, *Black Soldier, White Army*, 81–82.
11. Ibid., 69, 82–83, 93.
12. Buckley, *American Patriots*, 352.
13. Charles M. Bussey, *Firefight at Yechon: Courage and Racism in the Korean War* (Washington, DC: Brassey's, 1991), 107.

    Bussey flew 70 missions, had two kills and two "probables," and seriously damaged two more enemy aircraft as a Tuskegee Airman in the 333rd Fighter Group, a unit intensely proud of its record low of strategic bombers it lost to German aircraft. He joined in the California National Guard in 1946 as "an opportunity to make some money" and happened to transfer into the engineers because that was the local unit.
14. Bowers, Hammond, and MacGarrigle, *Black Soldier, White Army*, 105.
15. Buckley, *American Patriots*, 357.
16. David K. Carlisle [West Point graduate, member of 77th Engineer Combat Company], "The Last Black Combat Unit of the US Army Fights Alongside the Last Black 24th Infantry Regiment," American War Library, accessed August 16, 2021, http://www.americanwarlibrary.com/personnel/dkc1.htm.
17. Lanning, *The African American Soldier*, 233; Buckley, *American Patriots*, 362–63.

According to Buckley, David Hackworth, who began his storied military career as a 19-year-old soldier in Korea, reported another variant: "When the Chinese yell 'banzai,' the Deuce-Four says 'goodbye' and heads south." But Hackworth noted that the deuce-four "had been responsible for the first significant ground victory of the war." He decried the loss of "fine" Black noncommissioned officers replaced by whites who were "unwilling or unable to bond with the troops . . . and vice versa." Hackworth's final assessment was that the regiment's "leadership was too thin and its combat scars too many."

A unit's performance in combat depends on many factors, some of which are intangible. The US Army Center of Military History's reassessment of the regiment's performance in Korea published in 1996 found that most soldiers of the 24th displayed commendable fortitude and performed acts of heroism even if the unit, like other US units, exhibited multiple problems in the crucible of a desperate struggle against overwhelming forces.

18. Bowers, Hammond, and MacGarrigle, *Black Soldier, White Army*, 258.
19. Buckley, *American Patriots*, 357.
20. Bussey, *Firefight at Yechon*, 263–64.
21. Ibid., 203.
22. Bowers, Hammond, and MacGarrigle, *Black Soldier, White Army*, 159.
23. Ibid., 175, fn. 89.
24. Nalty, *Strength for the Fight*, 257.
25. Bowers, Hammond, and MacGarrigle, *Black Soldier, White Army*, 186.
26. Ibid.
27. Lanning, *The African American Soldier*, 234.
28. Ibid., 233.
29. Bowers, Hammond, and MacGarrigle, *Black Soldier, White Army*, 187.
30. Lanning, *The African American Soldier*, 23.
31. Ibid., 235.
32. Buckley, *American Patriots*, 358.
33. Lanning, *The African American Soldier*, 238.
34. Nalty, *Strength for the Fight*, 262.
35. Ibid., 263.
36. Lanning, *The African American Soldier*, 241.
37. Ibid., 232.
38. Nalty, *Strength for the Fight*, 261–62.
39. Bruce Cummings, *The Korean War: A History*. Modern Library, 35.

CHAPTER 8

1. Gail Buckley, *American Patriots: The Story of Blacks in the Military from the Revolution to Desert Storm* (New York: Random House, 2002), 368–74.
2. Ibid., 369.
3. Ibid.
4. Ibid.
5. Ibid., 370.
6. *The Military–Industrial Complex: The Farewell Address of President Eisenhower* (Basementia Publications, 2006), accessed July 13, 2021, https://books.google.com/books?id=v7Mj0qYxjFgC&printsec=frontcover&source=gbs_ge_summary_r&cad=0#v=onepage&q&f=false.
7. Buckley, *American Patriots*, 370. These problems still exist; in fact, they have gotten much worse because of the intransigence of the two political parties and the United States' resistance to "socialism."
8. Wikipedia, "Vietnam War," accessed June 20, 2021, https://en.wikipedia.org/wiki/Vietnam_War.
9. Buckley, *American Patriots*, 379.
10. Ibid.
11. Michael Lee Lanning, *The African American Soldier: From Crispus Attucks to Colin Powell*. (Secaucus, NJ: Citadel Press, 1999), 251.
12. Wikipedia, "Vietnam War."
13. Lanning, *The African American Soldier*, 259; Bernard C. Nalty, *Strength for the Fight: A History of Black Americans in the Military* (New York: Free Press, 1986), 298–99.
14. Ibid., 256.
15. Ibid.
16. Ibid., 259.
17. Buckley, *American Patriots*, 384–85.
18. Ibid., 398.
19. Lanning, *The African American Soldier*, 259.
20. Ibid., 260–61. Obviously, the announcement reflected little cultural sensitivity. It also brought the services many problems.
21. Ibid., 260.
22. Ibid., 261.
23. Ibid., 252.
24. Ibid., 268.

25. Ibid., 269.
26. Ibid., 253 and 253; New York Times, "A Black Soldier's Heroism, Overlooked in 1965, May Finally Be Lauded in 2021," accessed September 10, 2021, https://www.nytimes.com/2021/02/15/us/paris-davis-medal-of-honor.html.
27. Wikipedia, "Vietnam War."
28. Ibid.
29. Headquarters, Department of the Army, Deputy Chief of Staff, Army G-1, Office of Demographics, Army Demographics, FY 16.
30. Headquarters, Department of the Army, Deputy Chief of Staff, Army G-1, Office of Demographics, "Blacks in the U.S. Army: Then and Now," 1.

    Over the past 20 years, the percentage of Black soldiers has ranged from a high of 30 percent in Fiscal Year 1985 to about 20 percent in Fiscal Year 2009. The number of Black sailors has increased significantly, from 12 percent in Fiscal Year 1985 to almost 17 percent in Fiscal Year 2009. However, the percentage of Blacks in the Marine Corps declined from nearly 19 percent in Fiscal Year 1985 to only 10 percent in Fiscal Year 2009.
31. "Blacks in the U.S. Army: Then and Now," 4, 5.
32. Ibid., 11.
33. Ibid.
34. Ibid., 14.
35. Ibid.
36. Ibid., 2.
37. Ibid., 22.
38. Ibid., 18.
39. Army Demographics FY 16, Army Profile, 2.
40. "Blacks in the U.S. Army: Then and Now," 20.
41. Ibid., 26.
42. Army Demographics FY 16, Army Profile, 1.
43. Ibid.
44. Mark Palmer, "Class of 2025 to Enter West Point," West Point Society of Washington, posted June 20, 2021, accessed July 2, 2021, https://wpswps.org/?p=3362.
45. Lanning, *The African American Soldier*, 268–69.

APPENDIX B

1. William A. Dobak and Thomas D. Phillips, *The Black Regulars, 1866-1899* (Norman: University of Oklahoma Press, 2001), 31.
2. Ibid., 231.
3. Arlen L. Fowler, *The Black Infantry in the West, 1869-1891* (Norman: University of Oklahoma Press, 1971), 87. (Reprinted in 1996).
4. Dobak and Phillips, *The Black Regulars*, 101.
5. Ibid., 225.
6. Ibid., 233.
7. Ibid., 5.
8. William H. Leckie and Shirley A. Leckie, *The Buffalo Soldiers: A Narrative of the Black Cavalry in the West* (Norman: University of Oklahoma Press, 2003), 96.
9. Ibid., 131.
10. Ibid., 106.
11. Ibid., 210. Another band of Ute warriors attacked Indian agent Nathan Meeker and killed all the white employees at his agency on the reservation in what became known as the "Meeker Massacre."
12. Leckie and Leckie, *Buffalo Soldiers*, 278–79. After 30 years of impeccable service, Jordan retired in 1896 at Crawford, Nebraska. He became seriously ill in October 1904 but was twice denied care in the Fort Robinson hospital, dying from lack of care later that month.
13. Darlene Clark Hine, William C. Hine, and Stanley Harrold, *African-American History* (Upper Saddle River, NJ: Pearson/Prentice Hall, 2006), 513. Enemies of the Lakota termed the Sioux tribe "little snakes."
14. William H. Leckie and Shirley A. Leckie, *Unlikely Warriors: General Benjamin Grierson and His Family* (Norman: University of Oklahoma Press, 1984), 208.
15. Leckie and Leckie, *Buffalo Soldiers*, 158.
16. Dobak and Phillips, *The Black Regulars*, 110–11.
17. Leckie and Leckie, *Buffalo Soldiers*, 232.
18. Fowler, *The Black Infantry in the West*, 17.
19. Ibid., 79.
20. Ibid.
21. Ibid.

22. Leckie and Leckie, *Buffalo Soldiers*, 236; Frank N. Schubert, *Buffalo Soldiers and the Medal of Honor, 1870-1898* (Wilmington, DE: Rowman & Littlefield, 1997), 7.
23. Fowler, *The Black Infantry in the West*, 86.
24. Gail Buckley, *American Patriots: The Story of Blacks in the Military from the Revolution to Desert Storm* (New York: Random House, 2002), 133.
25. Fowler, *The Black Infantry in the West*, 16.
26. Dobak and Phillips, *The Black Regulars*, 241.
27. Buckley, *American Patriots*, 133.
28. Fowler, *The Black Infantry in the West*, 134.
29. Dobak and Phillips, *The Black Regulars*, 231.
30. Buckley, *American Patriots*, 160.
31. Ibid., 161.
32. Ibid.
33. Ibid.
34. Ibid., 161–62.
35. Rayford Logan, *The Betrayal of the Negro from Rutherford B. Hayes to Woodrow Wilson* (London: Collier Books, 1965), 335, quoted in John H. Nankivell, *Buffalo Soldier Regiment: History of the Twenty-Fifth United States Infantry, 1869-1826* (Lincoln: University of Nebraska Press, 2001), xxi.
36. Brynn Baker, *Heroes of the American West* (North Mankato, MN: Capstone Press, 2015), 22–23.

BIBLIOGRAPHY

CHAPTER 1: COLONIAL WARS TO THE WAR OF 1812

Buckley, Gail. *American Patriots: The Story of Blacks in the Military from the Revolution to Desert Storm.* New York: Random House, 2002.

Coleman, Bonnie Watson. "Let's Honor the Black and Indigenous Soldiers Who Helped Win Our Independence," *Washington Post*, July 6, 2021, A19.

Davis, Burke. *Black Heroes of the American Revolution.* San Diego, CA: Odyssey Books, 1976.

Fleming, Thomas, *A Disease of the Public Mind: A New Understanding of Why We Fought the Civil War.* New York: Da Capo Press, 2013.

Fleetwood, Christian A. *The Negro as a Soldier.* Washington, DC: Howard University Print, 1895. Monograph prepared for the National Negro Congress at the Cotton States and International Exposition, Atlanta, GA.

Gilbert, Alan. *Black Patriots and Loyalists: Fighting for Emancipation in the War for Independence.* Chicago: University of Chicago Press, 2012.

Green, Jack P., and J. R. Pole. *Colonial America: Essays in the New History of the Early Modern Era.* Baltimore, MD: Johns Hopkins University Press, 1984, 1991.

Kaplan, Sidney, and Emma Nogrady Kaplan. *The Black Presence in the Era of the American Revolution.* Amherst, MA: University of Massachusetts Press, 1989.

Lanning, Michael Lee. *The African American Soldier: From Crispus Attucks to Colin Powell.* Secaucus, NJ: Citadel Press, 1999.

Lanning, Michael Lee. *Defenders of Liberty: African Americans in the Revolutionary War.* New York: Citadel Press, 2000.

Nalty, Bernard C. *Strength for the Fight: A History of Black Americans in the Military.* New York: Free Press, 1986.

Nash, Gary B. *The Forgotten Fifth: African Americans in the Age of Revolution.* Cambridge, MA: Harvard University Press, 2006.

Nell, William Cooper. *The Colored Patriots of the Revolution.* Boston, MA: Robert F. Wallcut, 1855. Reprinted in Middletown, DE, 2020.

Potter, Lou, William Miles, and Nina Rosenblum. *Liberators: Fighting on Two Fronts in World War II.* Orlando, FL: Harcourt, Brace Jovanovich, 1992.

Quarles, Benjamin. *The Negro in the American Revolution.* Chapel Hill: University of North Carolina Press, 1961.

Rees, John U. *"They Were Good Soldiers": African Americans Serving in the Continental Army.* Warwick, UK: Helion & Company, 2019.

CHAPTER 2: US COLORED TROOPS

Ashby, Thomas A. *The Valley Campaign, Being the Reminiscences of a Non-Combatant between the Lines in the Shenandoah Valley during the War of the States.* New York: The Neale Publishing Company, 1914. (Kessinger Legacy Reprint).

Ayers, Edward L. *In the Presence of Mine Enemies: War in the Heart of America, 1859-1863.* New York: W. W. Norton & Company, 2003.

Ayers, Edward L. *The Thin Light of Freedom: The Civil War and Emancipation in the Heart of America.* New York: W. W. Norton & Company, 2017.

Berlin, Ira, Joseph P. Reidy, and Leslie, S. Rowland, editors. *Freedom's Soldiers: The Black Military Experience in the Civil War.* Cambridge, UK: Cambridge University Press, 1996.

Bernstein, Iver. *The New York City Draft Riots: Their Significance for American Society and Politics in the Age of the Civil War.* New York: Oxford University Press, 1990.

Blight, David W. *Race and Reunion: The Civil War in American Memory.* Cambridge, MA: Belknap Press, 2001.

Bonekemper, Edward H. III. *The Myth of the Lost Cause: Why the South Fought the Civil War and Why the North Won*. Washington, DC: Regnery Press, 2015.

Buckley, Gail. *American Patriots: The Story of Blacks in the Military from the Revolution to Desert Storm*. New York: Random House, 2002.

Butts, Heather. *African American Medicine in Washington D.C.: Healing during the Civil War Era*. Charleston, SC: The History Press, 2014.

Chernow, Ron. *Grant*. Penguin Press, 2017.

Claxton, Melvin, and Mark Puls. *Uncommon Valor: A Story of Race, Patriotism and Glory in the Final Battles of the Civil War*. Hoboken, NJ: John Wiley and Sons, 2006.

Connection to Your Community. "Freedman's Village: A Lost Chapter of Arlington's Black History." Published September 30, 2004. Accessed May 21, 2020. http://www.connectionnewspapers.com/news/2004/sep/30/freedmans-village-a-lost-chapter-of-arlingtons/.

Cornish, Dudley T. *The Sable Arm: Black Troops in the Union Army, 1861-1865*. Lawrence: University Press of Kansas, 1987.

Dobak, William A. *Freedom by the Sword: The US Colored Troops, 1862-1867*. New York: Skyhorse Publishing, 2013.

Douglass, Frederick. *Frederick Douglass on Slavery and the Civil War: Selections from His Writings*. Edited by Philip S. Foner. Mineola, NY: Dover Publications, 2003.

Du Bois, W.E.B. *Black Reconstruction in America, 1860-1880*. New York: Athenaeum, 1992.

Duncan, Richard R. *Beleaguered Winchester: A Virginia Community at War, 1861-1865*. Baton Rouge: Louisiana State University Press, 2007.

Egerton, Douglas R. *Thunder at the Gates: The Black Civil War Regiments That Redeemed America*. New York: Basic Books, 2016.

Emilio, Luis F. *A Brave Black Regiment: The History of the 54th Massachusetts, 1863-1865*. New York: Da Capo Press, 1995. (Original edition 1884).

Faust, Drew Gilpin. *This Republic of Suffering: Death and the American Civil War*. New York: Random House, 2008.

Flood, Charles Bracelen. *Grant and Sherman: The Friendship That Won the Civil War*. New York: Harper Perennial, 2006.

Gibbs, Carroll "C. R." *Black, Copper and Bright: The District of Columbia's Civil War Regiment*. Silver Spring, MD: Three Dimensional Publishing, 2002.

Gladstone, William A. *United States Colored Troops 1863-1867*. Gettysburg, PA: Thomas Publications, 1990.

Glatthaar, Joseph T. *The Civil War's Black Soldiers*. Salem, MA: Eastern National Park and Monument Association, 1996.

Glatthaar, Joseph T. *Forged in Battle: The Civil War Alliance of Black Soldiers and White Officers*. New York: The Free Press, 1990.

Higginson, Thomas Wentworth. *Army Life in a Black Regiment*. Mineola, NY: Dover Publications, 2002. (Originally published by Fields, Osgood, Co., Boston 1870).

Hollandsworth, James G., Jr. *The Louisiana Native Guards: The Black Military Experience in the Civil War*. Baton Rouge: Louisiana State University Press, 1995.

Holmes, Clay W. *The Elmira Prison Camp*. London: Forgotten Books, 2013. (Originally published in 1912).

Holsworth, Jerry W. *Civil War Winchester*. Charleston, SC: The History Press, 2011.

Kendi, Ibram X., "History's Emancipator: Did Abraham Lincoln Have 'a Drop of Anti-Slavery Blood in His Veins'?" Truthout. Published November 23, 2017. Accessed July 15, 2021. https://truthout.org/articles/history-s-emancipator-did-abraham-lincoln-have-a-drop-of-anti-slavery-blood-in-his-veins/.

Lanning, Michael Lee. *The African American Soldier: From Crispus Attucks to Colin Powell*. Secaucus, NJ: Citadel Press, 1999.

Leckie, William H., and Shirley A. Leckie, *Unlikely Warriors: General Benjamin Grierson and His Family*. Norman: University of Oklahoma Press, 1984.

Levine, Bruce. *Confederate Emancipation: Southern Plans to Free and Arm Slaves during the Civil War*. New York: Oxford University Press, 2006.

Lockwood, John, and Charles Lockwood. *The Siege of Washington: The Untold Story of the Twelve Days That Shook the Nation*. New York: Oxford University Press, 2011.

McPherson, James M. *Battle Cry of Freedom: The Civil War Era*. New York: Oxford University Press, 1988.

McPherson, James M. *Drawn with the Sword: Reflections on the American Civil War*. New York: Oxford University Press, 1996.

McPherson, James M. *The War That Forged a Nation: Why the Civil War Still Matters*. New York: Oxford University Press, 2015.

Nalty, Bernard C. *Strength for the Fight: A History of Black Americans in the Military*. New York: The Free Press, 1986.

National Archives Pieces of History. "Lincoln to Slaves: Go Somewhere Else." Published December 1, 2010. Accessed September 12, 2021. https://prologue.blogs.archives.gov/2010/12/01/lincoln-to-slaves-go-somewhere-else/.

Nevins, Allan. *The War for the Union: The Organized War to Victory, 1864-1865*. New York: Charles Scribner's Sons, 1971.

Noyalas, Jonathan A. *"My Will Is Absolute Law": A Biography of Union General Robert H. Milroy*. Jefferson, NC: MacFarland & Company, 2006.

Noyalas, Jonathan A. *Plagued by War: Winchester, Virginia during the Civil War*. Leesburg, VA: Gauley Mount Press, 2003.

Noyalas, Jonathan A. *Two Peoples, One Community: The African American Experience in Newtown (Stephens City), Virginia, 1850-1860*. Stephens City, VA: Stone House Foundation, 2007.

O'Connor, Bob. *The U.S. Colored Troops at Andersonville Prison*. West Conshohocken, PA: Infinity Publishing, 2009.

Paradis, James M. *Strike the Blow for Freedom: The 6th United States Colored Infantry in the Civil War*. Shippensburg, PA: White Mane Books, 1998.

Quarles, Garland R. *Occupied Winchester, 1861-1865*. Winchester-Frederick County Historical Society, 1976.

Rhea, Gordon C. *Stephen A. Swails: Black Freedom Fighter in the Civil War and Reconstruction*. Baton Rouge: Louisiana State University Press, 2022.

Rudisel, Christine, and Bob Blaisdell, editors. *Slave Narratives of the Underground Railroad*. Mineola, NY: Dover Publications, 2014.

Salter, Krewasky A. *The Story of Black Military Officers, 1861-1948*. New York: Routledge, 2014.

Shaffer, Donald R. *After the Glory: The Struggles of Black Civil War Veterans*. Lawrence: University of Kansas Press, 2004.

Sharpe, Hal F. *Shenandoah County in the Civil War: Four Dark Years*. Charleston, SC: The History Press, 2012.

Shepard, Ray Anthony. *Now or Never: 54th Massachusetts Infantry's War to End Slavery*. Honesdale, PA: Calkins Creek, 2017.

Sherwood, G. L., and Jeffrey C. Weaver. *The 20th and 39th Virginia Infantry Regiments*. Lynchburg, VA: H. E. Howard Company, 1985.

Smith, Andrew F. *Starving the South: How the North Won the Civil War.* New York: Martin's Press, 2011.

Smith, John David. *Black Soldiers in Blue: African American Troops in the Civil War Era.* Chapel Hill: University of North Carolina Press, 2002.

Snell, Mark A. *West Virginia and the Civil War: Mountaineers Are Always Free.* Charleston, SC: The History Press, 2011.

Stout, Harry S. *Upon the Altar of the Nation: A Moral History of the Civil War.* London: Penguin Books, 2006.

Trudeau, Noah Andre. *Like Men of War: Black Troops in the Civil War, 1862-1865.* Edison, NJ: Castle Books, 2002.

Urwin, Gregory J. W., editor. *Black Flag over Dixie: Racial Atrocities and Reprisals during the Civil War.* Carbondale: Southern Illinois University Press, 2004.

Wallenstein, Peter, and Bertram Wyatt-Brown, editors. *Virginia's Civil War.* Charlottesville: University of Virginia Press, 2005.

Wiley, Bell Irvin. *Southern Negroes, 1861-1865.* Baton Rouge: Louisiana State University Press, 1938.

Williams, George Washington. *A History of the Negro Troops in the War of the Rebellion.* Middletown, DE: 2017. (Originally published 1888).

Wilson, Joseph T. *The Black Phalanx: African American Soldiers in the War of Independence, the War of 1812, & the Civil War.* New York: Da Capo Press. 1994. (Originally published 1890).

CHAPTER 3: BLACK SOLDIERS IN GRAY AND BUTTERNUT

Alpers, Ben. "The Myth of Black Confederates and Fake Racial Tolerance." *US Intellectual History Blog*, January 12, 2018, https://s-usih.org/2018/01/the-myth-of-black-confederates-and-fake-racial-tolerance/.

Bonekemper, Edward H. III. *The Myth of the Lost Cause: Why the South Fought the Civil War and Why the North Won.* Washington, DC: Regnery Press, 2015.

Chernow, Ron. *Grant.* New York: Penguin Press, 2017.

Foner, Eric A. *A Short History of Reconstruction, 1863-1877.* New York: Harper & Row, Perennial Library, 1990.

Hollandsworth, James G. *The Louisiana Native Guard: The Black Military Experience during the Civil War.* Baton Rouge: Louisiana University Press, 1995.

Jordan, Ervin L. Jr. *Black Confederates and Afro-Yankees in Civil War Virginia.* Charlottesville: University Press of Virginia, 1995.

Levin, Kevin M. *Searching for Black Confederates: The Civil War's Most Persistent Myth*. Chapel Hill: University of Carolina Press, 2019.

Levine, Bruce. *Confederate Emancipation: Southern Plans to Free and Arm Slaves during the Civil War*. New York: Oxford University Press, 2006.

McPherson, James, *Battle Cry of Freedom: The Civil War Era*. New York: Oxford University Press, 1988.

McPherson, James M. *Marching toward Freedom: Blacks in the Civil War, 1861-1865*. New York: Facts on File, 1994.

McPherson, James M. *The Negro's Civil War: How American Blacks Felt and Acted during the War for the Union*. New York, Ballentine Books, 1991.

Rollins, Richard, ed. *Black Southerners in Gray: Essays on African Americans in Confederate Armies. Journal of Contemporary History Series, Volume XI*. Murfreesboro, TN: Southern Heritage Press, 1994.

Smith, Jean Edward. *Grant*. New York: Simon & Schuster, 2001.

Smith, Sam. "Black Confederates: Truth and Legend." National Battlefield Trust, accessed May 23, 2020, https://www.battlefields.org/learn/articles/black-confederates.

CHAPTER 4: BUFFALO SOLDIERS

Black History Museum & Cultural Center of Virginia. "1898—'No Officers, No Fight.'" Accessed June 13, 2020. https://www.blackhistorymuseum.org/ announcement/1898-no-officers-no-fight/.

Buckley, Gail. *American Patriots: The Story of Blacks in the Military from the Revolution to Desert Storm*. New York: Random House Trade Paperbacks, 2002.

Cashin, Hershel V. *Under Fire with the Tenth Cavalry*. Niwot: University Press of Colorado, 1993. (Originally published in 1889).

Charles River Editors. *Buffalo Soldiers: The History and Legacy of the Black Soldiers Who Fought in the U.S. Army during the Indian Wars*. Middletown, DE: Charles River Publishers, 2021.

Digital History. "The Philippines." Accessed April 27, 2020. https://www.digitalhistory.uh.edu/disp_textbook.cfm?smtID=2&psid=3161&msclkid=84dfe59fc6fd11ecb612ea980152901e.

Field, Ron. *Buffalo Soldiers 1889-1918*. Great Britain: Oxford: Osprey Publishing, 2005.

Fowler, Arlen L. *The Black Infantry in the West, 1869-1891*. Norman: University of Oklahoma Press, 1971. (Reprinted in 1996).

Franklin, John Hope. *From Slavery to Freedom*. Third edition. New York: Alfred A. Knopf, 1967.

Hine, Darlene Clark, William C. Hine, and Stanley Harrold. *African-American History*. Upper Saddle River, NJ: Pearson/Prentice Hall, 2006.

Jefferson, Robert R. Jr. *Brothers in Valor: Battlefield Stories of the 89 African Americans Awarded the Medal of Honor*. Guilford, CT: LP, 2019.

Kilroy, David P. "Alone at West Point: The Military Education of Charles Young, 1884-1889." *Historian* 64, no. 3-4 (Spring and Summer, 2002).

Lanning, Michael Lee. *The African American Soldier: From Crispus Attucks to Colin Powell*. Secaucus, NJ: Citadel Press, 1999.

Leckie, William H. *The Buffalo Soldiers: A Narrative of Negro Cavalry in the West*. Norman: University of Oklahoma Press, 1967.

Leckie, William H. *The Military Conquest of the Western Plains*. Norman: University of Oklahoma Press, 1963.

Leckie, William H., and Shirley A. Leckie. *Unlikely Warriors: General Benjamin Grierson and His Family*. Norman: University of Oklahoma Press, 1984.

Nalty, Bernard. C. *Strength for the Fight: A History of Black Americans in the Military*. New York: Free Press, 1986.

Potter, Lou, William Miles, and Nina Rosenblum. *Liberators: Fighting on Two Fronts in World War II*. Orlando, FL: Harcourt, Brace Jovanovich, 1992.

Rodenbough, Theophilus F., and William L. Haskin. *The Army of the US Historical Sketches of Staff and Line with Portraits of Generals-in-Chief*. New York: Maynard, Merrill, and Company, 1896. Accessed through US Army Center Military History, September 3, 2021.

Salter, Krewasky A. *The Story of Black Military Officers, 1861-1948*. New York: Routledge, 2014.

Sammons, Jeffrey T., and John H. Morrow Jr. *Harlem's Rattlers and the Great War: The Undaunted 369th Regiment and the African American Quest for Equality*. Lawrence: University of Kansas Press, 2014.

Schubert, Frank N. *Black Valor: Buffalo Soldiers and the Medal of Honor, 1870-1898*. Wilmington, DE: Scholarly Resources, 1997.

Schubert, Frank N. *Voices of the Buffalo Soldier: Reports, Records, and Recollections of Military Life and Service in the West*. Albuquerque: University of New Mexico Press, 2003.

Shellum, Brian G. *Black Officer in a Buffalo Soldier Regiment: The Military Career of Charles Young.* Lincoln: University of Nebraska Press, 2010.

Steward, T. G. *Buffalo Soldiers: The Colored Regulars in the United States Army.* Mineola, NY: Dover Publications, 2014. (Originally published in 1904 by A.M.E. Book Concern, Philadelphia, Pennsylvania).

Tinio, Maria Teresa Trinidad Pineda. *The Triumph of Tagalog and the Dominance of the Discourse on English: Language Politics in the Philippines during the American Colonial Period.* ScholarBank@NUS, 2009. Accessed April 27, 2020. http://scholarbank.nus.edu.sg/handle/10635/16861.

CHAPTER 5: AFRICAN AMERICANS IN WORLD WAR I

Barbeau, Arthur E., and Florette Henri. *Unknown Soldiers: African American Troops in World War I.* Boston, MA: Da Capo Press, 1996.

Buckley, Gail. *American Patriots: The Story of Blacks in the Military from the Revolution to Desert Storm.* New York: Random House, 2002.

Conwill, Kinshash Holman. *We Return Fighting: World War I and the Shaping of Modern Black Identity.* Washington, DC: Smithsonian Books in association with the National Museum of African American History and Culture, 2019.

Farwell, Byron. *Over There: The United States in the Great War, 1917-1918.* New York: W. W. Norton Company, 1999.

Ferrell, Robert H. *Unjustly Dishonored: An African American Division in World War I.* Columbia: University of Missouri Press, 2011.

Franklin, John Hope. *From Slavery to Freedom: A History of African Americans.* 6th ed. New York: McGraw-Hill, 1988.

Harris, Stephen L. *Harlem's Hell Fighters: The African-American 369th Infantry in World War I.* Washington, DC: Potomac Publishers, 2003.

Hogan, E. B. *The Last Buffalo: Walter E. Potts and the 92nd "Buffalo" Division in World War I.* Fort Worth, TX: Eakin Press, 2000.

Horn, James Francis. *World War I and Jefferson County, West Virginia.* Charleston, SC: History Press, 2017.

Jefferson, Robert R. Jr. *Brothers in Valor: Battlefield Stories of the 89 African Americans Awarded the Medal of Honor.* Guilford, CT: LP, 2019.

Lanning, Michael Lee. *The African American Soldier: From Crispus Attucks to Colin Powell.* Secaucus, NJ: Citadel Press, 1999.

Lemann, Nicholas. *Redemption: The Last Battle of the Civil War.* New York: Farrar, Straus and Giroux, 2006.

Little, Arthur W. *From Harlem to the Rhine: The Story of New York's Colored Volunteers.* New York: Covici Friede Publishers, 1936.

Madigan, Tim. *The Burning: Massacre, Destruction, and the Tulsa Race Riot of 1921.* New York: St. Martin's Griffin, 2001.

McWhirter, Cameron. *Red Summer: The Summer of 1919 and the Wakening of Black America.* New York: St. Martin's Griffin, 2011.

Nalty, Bernard C. *Strength for the Fight: A History of Black Americans in the Military.* New York: Free Press, 1986.

Nelson, Peter N. *The Harlem Hellfighters Struggle for Freedom in WWI and Equality at Home.* New York: Basic Civitas, 2009.

Packard, Jerrold M. *American Nightmare: The History of Jim Crow.* New York: St. Martin's Griffin, 2002.

Salter, Krewasky A. *The Story of Black Military Officers, 1861-1948.* New York: Routledge, 2014.

Sammons, Jeffrey T., and John H. Morrow, Jr. *Harlem's Rattlers and the Great War: The Undaunted 369th Regiment and the African American Quest for Equality.* Lawrence: University of Kansas Press, 2014.

Scott, Emmett Jay. *Scott's Official History of the American Negro in the World War.* Chicago: Homewood Press, 2018. (Originally published in 1919).

Scott, Emmett J. *The True Story of the Harlem Hellfighters in World War I.* First published in *The American Negro in the World War*, 1919. Republished as a pamphlet, Bayside, New York: A. J. Cornell Publications, 2016.

Shellum, Brian G. *Black Officer in a Buffalo Soldier Regiment: The Military Career of Charles Young.* Lincoln: University of Nebraska Press, 2010.

Wells-Barnett, Ida. *The Arkansas Race Riot.* Chicago: Ida Wells-Barnett, 1920. (Aquila reprint, 2017).

Williams, Chad L. *Torchbearers of Liberty: African American Soldiers in the World War I Era.* Chapel Hill: University of North Carolina Press, 2010.

Wilkerson, Isabel. *The Warmth of Other Suns: The Epic Story of America's Great Migration.* New York: Random House, 2010.

Woodward, C. Vann. *The Strange Career of Jim Crow.* New York: Oxford University Press, 1974.

CHAPTER 6: AFRICAN AMERICANS IN WORLD WAR II

Abdul-Jabbar, Kareem, and Anthony Walton. *Brothers in Arms: The Epic Story of the 761st Tank Battalion, WW II's Forgotten Heroes*. New York: Harlem Moon Broadway Books, 2004.

Bowers, William T., William M. Hammond, and George L. MacGarrigle. *Black Soldier White Army: The 24th Infantry Regiment in Korea*. Washington, DC: US Army Center of Military History, 1996.

Brown, Harold H., and Marsha S. Bordner. *Keep Up Your Airspeed: The Story of the Tuskegee Airmen*. Tuscaloosa: University of Alabama Press, 2017.

Buckley, Gail. *American Patriots: The Story of Blacks in the Military from the Revolution to Desert Storm*. New York: Random House, 2002.

Charles River Editors. *The Tuskegee Airmen: The History and Legacy of America's First Black Fighter Pilots in World War II*. Middletown, DE: Charles River Editors, 2020.

Davis, Benjamin O. Jr. *American*. Washington, DC: Smithsonian Institution Press, 1991.

Dryden, Charles W. *A-Train: Memoirs of a Tuskegee Airman*. Tuscaloosa: University of Alabama Press, 1997.

Farrell, Mary Cronk. *Standing Against Hate: How Black Women in the Army Helped Change the Course of WW II*. New York: Abrams Book for Young Children, 2019.

George, Denise, and Robert Child. *The Lost Eleven: The Forgotten Story of Black Soldiers Brutally Massacred during World War II*. New York: Dutton Caliber, 2017.

Gergel, Richard. *Unexampled Courage: The Blinding of Sgt. Isaac Woodard and the Awakening of President Harry S. Truman and Judge J. Waties Waring*. New York: Sarah Crichton Books, 2019.

Hargrove, Hondon B. *Buffalo Soldiers in Italy: Black Americans in World War II*. Jefferson, NC: McFarland Publishers, 1985.

Hervieux, Linda. *Forgotten: The Untold Story of D-Day's Black Heroes, at Home and at War*. New York: HarperCollins, 2015.

Houston, Ivan J. *Black Warriors: The Buffalo Soldiers in World War II*. Bloomington, IN: iUniverse, 2009.

Jefferson, Robert R. Jr. *Brothers in Valor: Battlefield Stories of the 89 African Americans Awarded the Medal of Honor*. Guilford, CT: LP, 2019.

Lanning, Michael Lee. *The African American Soldier: From Crispus Attucks to Colin Powell*. Secaucus, NJ: Citadel Press, 1999.

Lanning, Michael Lee. *The Court-Martial of Jackie Robinson*. New York: Stackpole, 2020.

Latty, Yvonne. *We Were There: Voices of African American Veterans from World War II to the War in Iraq*. New York: HarperCollins, 2004.

Lee, Ulysses. *US Army in World War II: The Employment of Negro Troops*. Washington, DC: Center of Military History, US Army (US Government Printing Office), 1994. (First edition, 1963).

McLaurin, Melton A. *The Marines of Montford Point: America's First Black Marines*. Chapel Hill: University of North Carolina Press, 2007.

Motley, Mary Penick. *The Invisible Warrior: The Experience of the Black Soldier, World War II*. Detroit, MI: Wayne State University Press, 1975.

Nalty, Bernard C. *Strength for the Fight: A History of Black Americans in the Military*. New York: Free Press, 1986.

Patton, George S. *War as I Knew It*. Boston: Houghton Mifflin, 1947.

Potter, Lou, William Miles, and Nina Rosenblum. *Liberators: Fighting on Two Fronts in World War II*. Orlando, FL: Harcourt, Brace Jovanovich, 1992.

Salter, Krewasky A. *The Story of Black Military Officers, 1861-1948*. New York: Routledge, 2014.

Sasser, Charles W. *Patton's Panthers: The African American 761st Tank Battalion in World War II*. New York: Pocket Books, 2004.

Seranno, Richard A. *Summoned at Midnight: A Story of Race and the Last Military Executions at Fort Leavenworth*. Boston, MA: Beacon Press, 2019.

Smith, Charlene E. McGee. *The Biography of Charles E. McGee Air Force Fighter Combat Record Holder*. Fifth Edition. Wellesley, MA: Branden Books, 2015. (First edition, 1999).

Smith, Graham. *Jim Crow and John Bull*. New York: St. Martin's Press.

Stone, Tanya Lee. *Courage Has No Color: The True Story of the Triple Nickels, America's First Black Paratroopers*. Sommerville, MA: Candlewick Press, 2013.

Wilkerson, Isabel. *The Warmth of Other Suns: The Epic Story of America's Great Migration*. New York: Random House, 2010.

CHAPTER 7: AFRICAN AMERICAN SERVICE IN KOREA

Bowers, William T., William M. Hammond, and George L. MacGarrigle. *Black Soldier, White Army: The 24th Infantry Regiment in Korea*. Washington, DC: US Army Center of Military History, 1996.

Buckley, Gail. *American Patriots: The Story of Blacks in the Military from the Revolution to Desert Storm.* New York: Random House, 2002.

Bussey, Charles M. *Firefight at Yechon: Courage and Racism in the Korean War.* Washington, DC: Brassey's, 1991.

Jefferson, Robert R. Jr. *Brothers in Valor: Battlefield Stories of the 89 African Americans Awarded the Medal of Honor.* Guilford, CT: LP, 2019.

Lanning, Michael Lee. *The African American Soldier: From Crispus Attucks to Colin Powell.* Secaucus, NJ: Citadel Press, 1999.

Latty, Yvonne. *We Were There: Voices of African American Veterans from World War II to the War in Iraq.* New York: HarperCollins, 2004.

Nalty, Bernard C. *Strength for the Fight: A History of Black Americans in the Military.* New York: Free Press, 1986.

Salter, Krewasky A. *The Story of Black Military Officers, 1861-1948.* New York: Routledge, 2014.

Smith, Charlene E. McGee. *The Biography of Charles E. McGee Air Force Fighter Combat Record Holder.* Fifth Edition. Wellesley, MA: Branden Books, 2015 (First edition, 1999).

CHAPTER 8: FROM FROM VIETNAM TO TODAY

Buckley, Gail. *American Patriots: The Story of Blacks in the Military from the Revolution to Desert Storm.* New York: Random House, 2002.

Jefferson, Robert R. Jr. *Brothers in Valor: Battlefield Stories of the 89 African Americans Awarded the Medal of Honor.* Guilford, CT: LP, 2019.

Lanning, Michael Lee. *The African American Soldier: From Crispus Attucks to Colin Powell.* Secaucus, NJ: Citadel Press, 1999.

Latty, Yvonne. *We Were There: Voices of African American Veterans from World War II to the War in Iraq.* New York: HarperCollins, 2004.

Nalty, Bernard C. *Strength for the Fight: A History of Black Americans in the Military.* New York: Free Press, 1986.

Salter, Krewasky A. *The Story of Black Military Officers, 1861-1948.* New York: Routledge, 2014.

DOCUMENTS AND PERIODICALS

"African-Americans in The United States Navy—A Short History." Video 4:29. Posted by LionHeart FilmWorks. https://www.youtube.com/watch?v=se_cW8--whE.

Chapter 2: US Colored Troops and Black Confederates

Berlin, Ira. "Documentary History of Emancipation, 1861-1867." In *Reconstruction Almanac*. New York: Cambridge University Press, 1982.

Besch, Edwin W. "Action at Wilson's Warf, 24 May 1864 & Fort Pocahontas," http://www.fortpocahontas.org/battle/.

Joseph P. Reidy, "Black Men in Navy Blue during the Civil War," *Prologue Magazine*, Fall 2001, Vol. 33, No. 3. (https://www.archives.gov/publications/prologue/2001/fall/black-sailors-1.html, accessed 5 February 2020).

Young, Patrick, Esq. "German General Weitzel and His African Canadians at Petersburg.," Blog Post, February 24, 2015. https://longislandwins.com/columns/immigrants-civil-war/german-general-weitzel-and-his-african-canadians-at-petersburg/?fbclid=IwAR2cnC9qTBhFNABtRRXphx0pkqStEgZt1YttcXyrv1dSswh3i2SXnzYc18w, accessed February 6, 2020.

Young, Patrick, Esq. "Richmond Burning: The German Immigrant and Black Troops Who Saved the City." Blog Post, March 19, 2015. https://longislandwins.com/columns/immigrants-civil-war/richmond-burning-the-german-immigrant-and-black-troops-who-saved-the-city/?fbclid=IwAR3rXv7FzuQ0Mi-vowThW6-Iwvm1b1zuoHuvOWNgAxG-86Bke75HD-qyZMs, accessed February 5, 2020.

Chapter 4: Buffalo Soldiers

24th Infantry Regiment (Deuce Four), 25th Infantry Division Association "Tropic Lighting," https://www.25thida.org/units/infantry/24th-infantry-regiment/, accessed September 1, 2021.

24th Infantry Regiment, Wiki Military, accessed August 31, 2021.

24th Infantry Regiment, Buffalo Soldiers Online Museum, accessed July 15, 2021.

25th Infantry Regiment, Wiki Military, accessed August 31, 2021.

"Buffalo Soldier Statue Installed at US Military Academy at West Point," *Washington Post*, August 31, 2021, accessed September 1, 2021.

Chapter 5 African Americans in World War I

Du Bois, W. E. Burghardt. "The Negro Soldier in Service Abroad during the First World War." Journal of Negro Education 12 Summer 1943), 324-334.

Du Bois, W. E. Burghardt. "Returning Soldiers" in Crisis, May 1919.

Chapter 6: African Americans in World War II

Black History Museum and Cultural Center of Virginia, "1898—"No Officers, No Fight," https://www.blackhistorymuseum.org/announcement/1898-no-officers-no-fight/.

Jefferson, Robert. "93rd Infantry Division (1942-1946). Black Past, https://www.blackpast.org/ african-american-history/u-s-ninety-third-infantry-division-1942-1946/, accessed December 28, 2021.

Lutz, Stephen D. "The 93rd Infantry Division: African-American Soldiers in the Pacific." Warfare History Network, https://warfarehistorynetwork.com/2019/01/19/the-93rd-infantry-division-the-african-american-soldiers-in-the-pacific/, accessed September 12, 2021.

Secretary of the Navy Carlos Del Toro's 2022 Black History Month Message. https://www.youtube.com/watch?v=HQ_1n80PqZ4

The Story Behind an American Hero, Ship's Mess Attendant Doris Miller https://www.youtube.com/watch?v=qaLhoCViEmY.

INDEX

2nd Cavalry Division (WW II), 103, 156

9th Cavalry Regiment, 78, 82, 83, 84, 87, 89, 93, 95, 97, 102, 103, 107, 113, 156

10th Cavalry Regiment, xviii, 79, 80, 82, 88, 89, 90, 91, 93, 95, 97, 98, 101, 102, 104, 107, 113, 114, 156, 244

24th Infantry Regiment, xix, 85, 88, 89, 92, 93, 94, 96, 97, 104, 105, 106, 107, 116, 142, 158, 188, 189, 190, 192, 195, 197 198

25th Infantry Regiment, 80, 82, 83, 84, 85, 86, 88, 93, 94, 95, 96, 97, 105, 106, 107

25th US Army Corps (Civil War), 52

38th, 39th, 40th and 41st US Infantry Regiments (1866–1869), 78

92nd Infantry Division (WW I), xix, xviii, xix, 108, 116, 117, 118, 131, 133, 134, 136, 137, 147, 201; 365th Infantry Regiment, 116; 366th Infantry Regiment, 116; 367th Infantry Regiment, 116, 136; 368th Infantry Regiment, 116, 117; 183rd Brigade (365th and 366th Regts), 136; 167 Artillery Brigade, 118; 317 Engineer Regiment, 118, 119

93rd Infantry Division (WW I), xix, xviii, 108, 120–136, 137, 147; 369th Infantry Regiment, xix, 120–128, 137, 144, 159; ("Harlem Hell Fighters"), 370th Infantry Regiment, 120, 128, 129, 133, 144, 145; 371st Infantry Regiment, 120, 130, 131, 134, 136; 372nd Infantry Regiment, 120, 124, 130, 131, 136

92nd Infantry Division (WW II); xix, xx, 104, 116, 160, 149, 156, 157, 158, 160, 189, 201; 365th

Infantry Regiment, 160, 161; 370th Infantry Regiment, 160, 161, 162, 170; 371st Infantry Regiment, 160, 161; (366th Attached in November 1944), 161, 162, 170; 758th Tank Battalion (attached), 160; 679th Tank Destroyer Battalion (attached), 160; 442nd Regimental Combat Team (Nisei) 161, 195; 473rd Infantry Regiment (white), 161

93rd Infantry Division (WW II), xix, 105, 149, 157, 158; 25th Infantry Regiment, xix, xx, 105, 106, 158, 159; 368th Infantry Regiment, 105, 158, 159; 369th Infantry Regiment, 105, 158, 159

Other Black WWII units: 24th Infantry Regiment, xix, xx, 104, 105, 158, 189, 190, 192, 195, 198; 25th Infantry Division, xx, 106, 158, 189, 195, 198; 57th Ordnance Ammunition Company, 157; 93rd Engineer General Service, 296, 297, 298; Regiment (Separate) 95th Engineer General Service Regiment (Separate), 296, 297; 97th Engineer General Service Regiment (Separate), 296, 297; 388th Engineer General Service Regiment (Separate), 296; 320th Very Low Altitude

Adams, John, 4
AEF (American Expeditionary Force, WW I), xviii

Afghanistan, 228–230, 251
Air Force, xx, 206, 211, 213, 222, 230, 232, 233, 235
Air Force Academy, 232
Alaskan Highway (Appendix D), 149, 295–298
Alexander, John Hanks, 101
Almond, Lieutenant General Edward M., 160, 161, 162, 193
American Revolution, 1–22
Angelou, Maya, xvii
Annapolis (U.S. Naval Academy), 176, 209, 232
Appomattox, 73
Army Organization Act of 1866, 78

Bacon Rebellion, 3
Baker, Newton, xix, 124, 134
Baker, First Lieutenant Vernon, 247
Ballou, Major General Charles, 116, 118, 132
Banks, General Robert, 45
Barrage Balloon Battalion (D-Day), 157; 333rd Field Artillery Battalion, 165, 166; 442nd Regimental Combat Team (Nisei), xx, 161; 452nd Anti-Aircraft Battalion, 165; 490th Port Battalion (D-Day), 157; 555th Airborne Battalion, 163, 199; 614th Tank Destroyer Battalion, 165, 170; 679th Tank Destroyer Battalion, 160; 758th Tank Battalion; 761st Tank Battalion, 162–164, 166, 170; 969th Field Artillery Battalion,

Index

165; 6888 Central Postal Directory Battalion (WAC), 164
Bastogne, 165–168
Battle Mountain (Korea), 198
Battle of New Orleans, 27
bicycles, 86, 277
Biden, President Joseph, 164, 228, 232, 235, 251
Birth of a Nation, 110, 111
Black generals, 283–293
Black nurses, 134
Black officers, 93, 95, 98, 115, 116, 117, 133, 168, 210, 230. 235
Black units serving in the Korean War, 193
Blue discharge, 168
body count, 217
Boston Massacre, 4
Bronze Star, 160, 162, 163
Brown, John, 29, 30
Brown, Westley A., 176
Brownsville, Texas, Disturbance, 96, 279
Buffalo Soldiers,, 78, 81, 97, 107, 151, 186, 235, 242, 253–282; 9th Cavalry Regiment, 78, 82, 83, 84, 87, 89, 93, 95, 97, 102, 103, 107, 113, 156; 10th Cavalry Regiment, xviii, 79, 80, 82, 88, 89, 90, 91, 93, 95, 97, 98, 101, 102, 104, 107, 113, 114, 156, 244; 24th Infantry Regiment, xix, 85, 88, 89, 92, 93, 94, 96, 97, 104, 105, 106, 107, 116, 142, 158, 188, 189, 190, 192, 195, 197 198; 25th Infantry Regiment, 80, 82, 83, 84, 85, 86, 88, 93, 94, 95, 96, 97, 105, 106, 107; 38th, 39th, 40th and 41st Infantry Regiments, 78
"Bugouts," 197, 198, 199, 203
Bulge, Battle of, 183
Bullard, General Robert Lee, 117, 118, 119
Bunker Hill, 6
Bureau of Colored Troops, 40, 41
Bush, President George W., 246
Bush, President George H. W., 228, 229
Bussey, Lieutenant Colonel Charles M., 197, 200
Butler, Major General Benjamin, 31, 36, 44, 45
Butler, Sergeant William, 123
Byrd, Senator Robert, 166

Calhoun, Senator John C., 26
Camp Logan/Houston "Riot," 96, 97, 272
Carrizal, Battle of, 95, 96
Carter, Staff Sergeant Edward A., 247
casualties, 200, 205, 206, 210, 211, 218, 224
Charlton, Sergeant Cornelius H., 248
chattel slavery, 36
chemical warfare, 119
China, Chinese People's Republic of, 193, 202, 203, 210
Chinese Peoples Volunteer Army (PVA), 202, 203, 211
Civil Rights Movement, xx, 213, 224, 235

Civil War, 28–77, 222, 235
Cleburne, General Patrick, 62, 63, 77
Clinton, President Bill, 247
Clinton, Sir Henry, 21
combat service support units, xix
communist propaganda, 189
Confederacy, xviii, 47, 59; Black troops, 59, 60, 68, 69, 71–77; Confederate Congress, 73; Resolution on treatment of USCT, 46
Committee of Safety, 7
Concord (skirmish), 4
Congress (U.S.), 31, 33, 234, 235, 237, 298
Congressional Medal of Honor, 53, 71, 105, 107, 129, 130, 162, 163, 168, 169, 170, 205, 237–251
contrabands of war, 32, 35, 36
Continental Army, xvii, 1, 7, 12, 27, 234
Continental Congress, 7, 10
Continental Navy, 1, 17
Corps d'Afrique (Louisiana Black militia), 44, 46
court-martial, 97, 131, 203
criminal justice system (U.S.), 106, 137, 142, 143
Crisis, The (NAACP magazine), 139, 140, 204
Crispus Attucks, 4
critical race theory, 225
Croix de Guerre, 123, 126, 128, 129, 130, 134, 135, 136, 147, 157
Cuba, 86–95

Daejon (24th Infantry Division disaster), 196
Daiquiri, 88
Davis, Benjamin O., Jr., 168, 170, 174
Davis, Benjamin O., Sr., 86, 151, 158, 166, 235
Davis, Jefferson, 60, 64, 65, 66, 67, 73
Declaration of Independence, xiv, 185
Defense Equal Opportunity Management Institute, 224, 225
Delany, Major Martin R., 45
Demilitarized Zone (DMZ), 210
democracy, 299
Department of the Army, 169, 230
Department of Defense, 169, 211, 212
deportation of African Americans, 36
Desert Storm, xx, 213, 226, 227
desertion, 68
Des Moines, Iowa (WW I Black officer training), 115
discrimination, 130; *see* racial bias
disenfranchisement, xiv, 141, 183
Distinguished Service Cross, 129, 130, 135, 136, 160, 162, 168, 204
Distinguished Service Medal, 160, 162
Distinguished Unit Citation, 166
diversity training, 224
Dixon, Thomas F. Jr., 109
domestic terrorism, 234
Double "V," 168
Douglas, William O., 110, 111, 142

Douglass, Frederick, v, 27, 37, 37, 38, 42, 72
draft, 217, 222
Du Bois, Walter Edward Burghardt, 101, 139, 140, 147
Duncan, LTC Otis, 128
Dunmore, Lord, 10, 20

Easter Offensive (Vietnam, 1972), 222
Eisenhower, President Dwight David, 210, 214
El Caney, 88
emancipation, xiii, 92, 167
Emancipation Proclamation, 35, 39
enlisted men, 169
Europe, First Lieutenant James Reese, 123
Executive Orders: 8802, Fair Employment Practices, 1941, 156, 174; 9981, Desegregation of Armed Forces, 1948, 105, 107, 186, 189; McNamara's EO making nondiscrimination the responsibility of commanders, 217

Fifteenth Amendment, xiv
Fleetwood, Christian, Command Sergeant Major, v
Flipper, Henry Ossian (West Point graduate), 98–100
Foreign Military Units: 157th "Red Hand" Division (French), 130, 131, 136
Forrest, Lieutenant General Nathan Bedford, 50
Forrestal, James, 177, 183

Fort Davis, Texas, 99
Fort Duchesne, Utah, 101
Fort Huachuca, Arizona, 103
Fort Pillow, 50
Fort Sill (Indian Territory), 80, 98
Fort Wagner (54th Massachusetts Infantry), 42, 47, 49, 50
Fourteenth Amendment, xiv
Fox, First Lieutenant John R. (WW II MOH awardee), 247
Free Men of Color, 24, 25, 26, 27
French and Indian War, 4
French National Assembly, 132

General Grant National Park, 101
GI Bill, 168
Gittlesohn, Rabbi Roland B., 299, 303
Gordon, General John B., 68, 69
Gothic Line, xx, 160
Grant, Lieutenant General Ulysses S., 39, 47, 56, 57, 67, 77, 79, 98
Great Britain, 17
Greenwood, Tulsa, Oklahoma "Black Wall Street," 145
Greer, Colonel Allen T., 117, 133
Grierson, Brigadier General Benjamin, 47, 80, 82, 99
Gulf of Tonkin Resolution, 216
Gulf War, 226

Haiti, xvii, 15, 234
Hamilton, Alexander, 9
Harpers Ferry, West Virginia, 29–31
Hayward, William Leland, Sr., 120, 121, 122, 127

HBCUs (Historically Black Colleges and Universities), 289–293
Higginson, Colonel Thomas Wentworth, 33
Hitler, 149
Ho Chi Minh Trail, 220, 221
Hoge, General William M., 296, 298
Hoover, J. Edgar, 298
Houston/Camp Logan Riot, 96, 97
Howard, Major General Oliver Otis, 100
Howard University, 100
Hussain, Saddam, 229

Ia Drang Valley, Battle of (Vietnam), 217
illiteracy, 85, 185, 328
Immunes (Spanish-American War), 84, 86
Indian Territory (Oklahoma), 80
Indian Wars, 79–84, 242
integration, 201, 209, 211, 212, 217, 218, 220, 224
Iraq, 228–230
Iraqi Army, 226, 227
Island Mound (first Black troops' battle), 44
ISIS (Islamic State in the Levant), 229
Iwo Jima, 299

Jackson, President Andrew, 24, 26, 27, 44
James, General Daniel "Chappie," 208
James, Private First Class Willy F., 247
Jefferson, President Thomas, 21
jihad, 228
Jim Crow, 113, 116, 118, 119, 126, 134, 155, 185, 211, 298
Johnson, James Weldon, 141
Johnson, Sergeant Henry Lincoln, 123, 121, 125, 134, 246, 247
Johnson, President Lyndon Baines, 215, 216
Johnston, General Joseph, 62

KATUSA, 195, 197, 199
Kennedy, President John Fitzgerald, 214
King, Rev. Martin Luther, Jr., 213, 217, 218
Knox, Frank, 90, 91, 154, 177
Korea, 187, 188, 193
Korean War, 185, 186–212, 188, 189, 192–208, 222, 248; U.S. Eighth Army, 204, 207: 24th Infantry Division, 195; 25th Infantry Division, 195, 198, 201, 202, 204, 207, 211; 24th Infantry Regiment, 189, 195, 196, 198, 201, 202, 204, 206, 207, 211; 77th Combat, 158, 195, 196, 199, 200, 207. Engineer Company: 159th Field Artillery Battalion, 158, 195, 207; Military Police, 195; 9th Infantry Regiment, 193
Ku Klux Klan, 109, 111, 142, 159
Kumch'on, 195
Kurdish forces, 229
Kuwait (Gulf War), 226, 227

Index

labor forces (slaves or ex-slaves), 55, 56, 60
Lafayette, Marquise de, 1
Las Guasimas, Battle of, 88
Laurence, John, 9
Lee, General Robert E., 29, 60, 61, 65, 67, 73, 74, 76
Ledo Road (Burma to China), 150
Legion of Honor (French award), 135, 136
Legion of Merit (U.S. award), 160, 162
Legree, Simon, 109
Lexington (skirmish), 4
Lanard, Colonel Louis Albert, 131, 132
Lincoln, President Abraham, 36, 65, 72, 235
Logan, Rayford W., 150
Longstreet, General James "Pete," 74
Lost Cause, 58, 59
lynching, xix, 113, 133, 141, 142, 144, 146, 153, 159, 183, 185

McKellar, Senator Kenneth, Tennessee, 133
Maine, USS, 86
MacArthur, General Douglas, 193, 202, 203, 207
Marines, U.S., 17, 150, 179, 207, 208, 211
Marshall, George C., 150, 153, 155
Marshall, Thurgood, 179, 203
mass deportation, 36
McNamara, Robert, 217
Médaille Millitaire (French Award for gallantry), 130, 135

Medal of Honor, 53, 81, 82, 105, 107, 123, 129, 130, 134, 162, 163, 168, 169, 170, 198, 205, 222
Meritorious Unit Citation, 164, 298
Messenger, 139
Migration, The Great, 181, 182
Military Police (MPs), 126, 132, 137, 142, 150, 152, 195
Miller, Doris "Dorie," 176
Milliken's Bend, Mississippi, 47
Montford Point (USMC WW II), 180

NAACP (National Association for the Advancement of Colored People), 101, 139, 147, 150, 153, 155, 174, 203
National Urban League, 177
Native Americans, 2, 79, 81, 82, 83, 84, 97
Native Guards (Louisiana Black militia), 44, 45, 46
Naval Unit Citation, 181
Navy, xviii, 1, 2, 17, 149, 174, 209, 211, 222, 235
Navy Cross, 181, 208
Navy Presidential Unit Citation, 207
Nazis, 185
New Orleans, Battle of (War of 1812), 2, 24–25, 235
Nixon, President Richard Millhouse, 222
noncommissioned officers, 41, 201
nondiscrimination, 225
Northern Italy, 160–162

370 INDEX

North Korea, 202
North Korean Army, 192, 193, 201, 211
North Vietnam, 213, 214, 217
North Vietnamese Army, 214, 217, 219

Obama, President Barack H., 228, 229, 245
officers, xx, 115, 168, 169, 200, 210, 235
Osama bin Laden, 228
Osan (Battle of), 195

Pancho Villa, 106
Patton, Lieutenant General George, 162, 164, 167
People's Republic of China, 193
Pershing, John J., "Nigger Jack" or "Black Jack," xviii, 84, 89, 91, 95, 113, 119, 122, 132
Philadelphia Free Military School, 41
Philippine Insurrection, xviii, 92–95, 101, 107
Pine Ridge, 81
political correctness, 225
Pollard, Edward A., 72, 76
Port Chicago, California (munitions disaster), 178, 179
Powell, General Colin, v, xx, 213, 218, 227, 235, 281 283, 298
Powell Doctrine, 227
prejudice, xxi, 29
Presidential Unit Citation, 264, 181
privateer, 1
Project 100, 219

propaganda, 126, 211
Punitive Expedition (Mexico), 106, 107
Purple Heart, 163
Pusan Perimeter, 195, 198

Quarles, Benjamin, 21 25, 76

race, xiii, 123, 133, 153
race relations training, 224
race riots, 96, 141, 144, 145, 151, 158, 173, 224
racial bias, 131, 133, 136, 137, 138, 153, 154, 155, 160, 168, 174, 175, 180, 181, 183, 185, 186, 195, 199
racial incidents, xviii, 96, 120, 150, 155
racism, viii, xix, xviii, xxi, 36, 106, 113, 116, 133, 136, 137, 147, 153, 166, 168, 185, 195, 206, 225
Randolph, A. Phillip, 139
rape, 132, 133, 134, 137, 140, 147
Reconstruction, 98, 109, 111
Red Ball Express, 149
Red Cross, 156, 182
"Red Summer," xix, 141, 143
Regular army Black regiments (Buffalo Soldiers), xviii, 81, 156, 186, 235, 281: 9th Cavalry Regiment, 78, 82, 83, 84, 87, 89, 93, 95, 97, 102, 103, 107, 113, 156; 10th Cavalry Regiment, xviii, 79, 80, 82, 88, 89, 90, 91, 93, 95, 97, 98, 101, 102, 104, 107, 113, 114, 156, 244; 24th Infantry Regiment, xix, 85, 88,

89, 92, 93, 94, 96, 97, 104, 105, 106, 107, 116, 142, 158, 188, 189, 190, 192, 195, 197 198; 25th Infantry Regiment, 80, 82, 83, 84, 85, 86, 88, 93, 94, 95, 96, 97, 105, 106, 107; 38th, 39th, 40th, and 41st Infantry Regiments, 78

Republic of Korea Presidential Unit Citation, 201

Revolutionary War, 4

Ridgeway, General Matthew, 207

Rivers, Staff Sergeant Ruben, 248

Roberts, Corporal Needham, 123, 125, 134

Robinson, Lieutenant Jackie, 155

Rolling Thunder (B-52 bombardment in Vietnam), 223

Roosevelt, President Franklin Delano, 150, 154

Roosevelt, Eleanor, 154, 155, 179

Roosevelt, President Theodore, 78, 91, 96, 113

Rough Riders, 89, 91, 113

Saltville, 51

San Juan Hill, 78, 89, 91, 106,

Saxton, Brigadier General Rufus, 33

Schofield, Major General John, 98

Scott, Emmett, 115, 119, 129

Second Army (WW I), xix, 108, 136

Second Confiscation Act, 1862, 33

Secretary of the Army, 189

Secretary of Defense, 213, 217, 232, 233, 235

Secretary of the Navy, 175, 177, 183

Secretary of War, 32, 61, 65, 94, 99, 153, 154, 183

segregation, 150, 155, 157, 159, 183, 186, 206, 211, 212

Seoul, South Korea, 202

servile insurrection, 59

Sequoia National Park, 101

Services of Supply troops, 122, 134, 137, 138, 166

Seward, William, 35

Shafter, Major General William, "Pecos Bill," 82, 87, 99

Shaw, Colonel Robert Gould, 49

Shaw University study, 169, 247

Sheridan, General Philip, 79, 80, 81

Sherman, General William Tecumseh, 65, 79, 98

Silver Star, 135, 160, 162, 163, 181

Sioux (victims at Wounded Knee), 93

slave patrols, 30

slavery, 36, 37, 62, 63, 70, 71, 72, 77

Soldier's Medal, 160, 162

South Korean Army, 192, 195, 197, 199, 202

Soviet Union, 193, 203, 210

Spanish-American War, 78, 86–92, 106, 107, 244

spies, guides, and scouts, 19, 20, 22, 65

Spingarn, Joel, 115

Stanton, Erwin, 39

Stowers, Corporal Freddie, 130, 246

Taliban, 228
Taylor, General Maxwell, 215
Tet Offensive, 219, 220
Thomas, First Lieutenant Charles L., 248
Thomas, General George, 52
Thomas, General Lorenzo, 39, 40
Thompson, Private First-Class William Henry, 248
Truman, President Harry, xx, 105, 107, 183, 185, 186, 189, 203, 207, 211, 212, 235
Trump, President Donald J., 210, 228
Tubman, Harriett, 49
Tulsa, Oklahoma, massacre, 145, 146
Tuskegee Airmen, 149, 170–175, 171, 197; 99th Pursuit Squadron, 170; 332nd Fighter Group "Red Tails:" 100th Fighter Squadron, 171; 301st Fighter Squadron, 171; 302nd Fighter Squadron, 171. 477th Bombardment Group (M) (colored): 317th Bombardment Squadron, 172; 616th Bombardment Squadron, 172; 618th Bombardment Squadron, 172; 619th Bombardment Squadron, 172

Uncle Tom's Cabin, 109
Uniform Code of Military Justice, 133
Union League, 120
U.S. Army, 2, 211, 213, 222, 230, 235

U.S. Marines, 149, 174, 183; 51st Defense Battalion, 180, 181; 52nd Defense Battalion, 180, 181; Ammunition and Depot Companies, 180, 181
USO (United Services Organization), 182
United Nations Command, 193, 201, 202, 207, 211
United Nations Security Council, 193
United States Colored Troops, xviii, 34, 35, 40, 47, 107, 235; casualties, 56, 57; evaluation, 42, 51–54, 58, 59, 63; numbers, 41; officers, 41; pay, 41, 42
U.S. Constitution, 185
U.S. Naval Academy (Annapolis), 176, 209

Victorio, 82, 989
Viet Cong, 215, 219
Vietnam, 248, 249
Vietnam War, xx, 213
Vietnamese Army, 222
Vietnamization, 222

Waller, Lieutenant General Calvin, 213
War of 1812, 22–27
War Department, 168, 170
Washington, Booker T., 115
Washington, President George, 7, 9, 11, 14, 20, 234
Watson, Private George, 248
Wereth massacre, 165
West Point, 98–101, 103, 170, 175, 209, 232

Wheeler, General "Fighting Joe," 87, 89
White, Edward Douglas, 110, 111, 142
white vigilantes, mobs, 145, 146
white supremacy, xiv, xvii, 25, 36, 58, 76, 77, 78, 94, 95, 109, 112, 113, 118, 120, 126, 137, 147, 187
Whittaker, Johnson Chestnut, 100, 101
Wilberforce University, 101, 103
Wilson, President Woodrow, 107, 108, 110, 111, 113, 154, 245
Wounded Knee, 83

Yech'on, 196
Yellowstone National Park, 86
YMCA, 134
Young, Colonel Charles, 93, 95, 101–103, 107, 283

ABOUT THE AUTHOR

Eugene DeFriest Bétit served twenty years in the U.S. Army as a military intelligence analyst and linguist and received a doctorate from Georgetown University. Since then, he has written books about the Civil War and African American history, served as docent at Belle Grove Plantation, and volunteered at Cedar Creek National Battlefield Park. He lives in Winchester, Virginia.